OXFORD
Past Times

CHRIS KOENIG

Signal Books

Signal Books, *Oxford*

First published in 2013 by
Signal Books Limited
36 Minster Road
Oxford
OX4 1LY
www.signalbooks.co.uk

A catalogue record for this book is available from the British Library

ISBN 978-1-908493-65-1

Design & Production: Baseline Arts
Cover Design: Baseline Arts
Cover Images: Duncan Walker/istockphoto; courtesy *The Oxford Times*; Wikipedia Commons
Illustrations/photos: courtesy *The Oxford Times*; Wikipedia Commons pp.1, 12, 31, 53, 75, 80, 84, 91, 93, 96, 115, 129, 171, 195, 197, 203, 207, 248, 253; courtesy Oxfam p.47; Steve Wynn/istockphoto p.77; Christie's handout/PA pp.208/9
Printed by Short Run Press Ltd., Exeter, UK

Contents

FOREWORD BY BRIAN ALDISS   XI

PREFACE   XIII

1 Around Oxford City: *Centre and Suburbs*   **1**
What's in a Name?   2
Folly Bridge   4
Oxford Castle   5
Osney Abbey   6
Gloucester Green   7
St Clements   8
Grandpont House   10
Botley Road   11
Cowley   13
Blackbird Leys   14
North Oxford   16
Summertown   18
Port Meadow   19
Oxford Airport   21

2 Oxford in History: *Landmarks and Events*   **23**
Anglo-Saxon Oxford   25
The Jewish Quarter   26
The Mad Parliament of 1258   28
St Scholastica's Day Riot, 1355   29
John Wycliffe   31
The Catholic Martyrs of 1589   32
Anthony Wood, Historian   34
John Aubrey, Biographer   35
Royalists and Parliamentarians   37
Abolitionists and Quakers   38
The Rise and Fall of Duelling   40
Suffragettes and Pacifists   41
Oxford 1939-45   42

The Floods of 1947   44
Alice and Adenauer   46
Oxfam   47

3 **The Changing City:** *Everyday Life Through the Centuries*   **49**
Poor Relief   50
Public Health   52
Washing and Water Supply   54
Carriers   56
The Oxford Canal   57
The Coming of the Railways   58
Rewley Road Station   59
Trams and Buses   61
The Postal Service   63
The Fire Service   64
Oxford's Weather Station   66
Oxford's Breweries   68
Victorian Photography   69
John Radcliffe Hospital   71
Woolworth's: End of an Era   72
Palm's Delicatessen   73
Oxford United Football Club   75

4 **The University:** *From Medieval to Modern*   **77**
Sir Thomas Bodley   79
The Royal Society   81
Gargoyles and Grotesques   82
Academic Gowns   84
Sir William Blackstone   86
Real Tennis   87
Barges and Boathouses   88
Victorian Architecture   90
T. G. Jackson   92
The Pitt Rivers Museum   94
Women Students   95
Refugee Academics   96
The Discovery of Penicillin   98
Restoring the Emperors' Heads   99
Sir Isaiah Berlin   100
Modern Architecture in Oxford   101

5 **The Colleges:** *Academics and Eccentrics*   **103**

Queen's College   105

Magdalen College   106

Magdalen College's *Last Supper*   108

Brasenose College   109

Corpus Christi College   111

Christ Church's Old Tom   113

Christ Church Riots   114

Green College and the Radcliffe Observatory   117

Ruskin College   118

6 **Around Oxfordshire:** *Towns and Villages*   **121**

Old Marston   123

Hampton Gay   124

Great Tew   126

Chipping Norton   128

Witney   130

Taynton   132

Burford   133

Filkins   134

Uffington   136

Abingdon   137

Wallingford   139

The Thames Towpath   141

7 **County History:** *The Rich and the Poor*   **143**

King Alfred   145

Radcot Bridge, 1387   146

Reformation in Abingdon, 1538   148

The Burford Levellers, 1649   149

The Duke of Marlborough, 1712   151

The Marquesses of Blandford   152

Jethro Tull   154

Mutiny of the Oxfordshire Militiamen, 1795   156

The Rural Poor, 1891   158

RAF Benson   159

8 Houses and Parks: *The Architectural Heritage*   **161**
Vanbrugh House   163
Shotover Country Park   164
Garsington Manor   166
Nuffield Place   167
Mapledurham House   168
Ditchley Park   169
Blenheim Palace   171
Capability Brown at Blenheim and Nuneham Courtenay   172
Cotswold Wildlife Park   173
Rousham and Enstone Water Features   175
Sulgrave Manor   176
Faringdon Folly   178
Kelmscott Manor   179
Wychwood Forest   181

9 Churches and Religion: *Centuries of Faith*   **183**
St Cross Church   185
St Frideswide   187
Black Bourton   188
South Leigh   189
St Lawrence, Combe   191
Churchill   192
St Peter, Daylesford   194
Swinbrook   195
Cote Baptist Chapel   197
Charles Wesley   199

10 The Arts: *Writers, Painters, Composers*   **201**
Oxfordshire Writers   203
Shakespeare in Oxfordshire   204
Handel in Oxford   206
Haydn in Oxford   207
Shelley in Oxford   208
Matthew Arnold   210
Kenneth Grahame   211
Gustav Holst and the Cotswolds   213
T. E. Lawrence   214
Flora Thompson   215
Paul Nash   216
John Piper   218

J.R.R. Tolkien   220
C. S. Lewis   221
John Betjeman   223
Barbara Pym   225

11 Customs and Legends: *Rural Traditions*   **227**
Michaelmas   229
All Souls Day   230
Christmas   232
May Day   233
Oak Apple Day   234
Harvest   236
Otter Hunting   238
Smoked Eels   239
Sundials   240
Ghosts   242
Dialect   243

12 Names from History: *Personalities of City and County* **245**
Amy Robsart   247
Nell Gwyn   248
William Buckland   249
Thomas Beecham   250
Charles Darwin   252
Alice Liddell   254
Sir Arthur Evans   256
Prime Minister H.H. Asquith   257
Unity Mitford   259
Blue Plaques   261

INDEX   263

Past Times, the History Man and The Oxford Times

The local history column of *The Oxford Times* has been growing ever-more popular with readers over the years. Now, with the re-launch of the paper in 2012 to celebrate our 150th anniversary, we have expanded it to fill a whole page and changed its name from *Past Times* to *History Man*. We are also running a series of 150 memorable pictures from the archives of *The Oxford Times*.

Oxford and Oxfordshire have particularly interesting histories (Oxford was the nation's capital during the civil war in the 17th century) and more and more people are realising just how important the past is to the present. Reading Chris Koenig every week you begin to understand, to some degree at least, why things are the way they are now. More extraordinary people, including politicians, writers, artists and sportsmen, have lived in Oxford than probably anywhere else in Britain, with the exception of London. But it still comes as a surprise each week to learn of some of their exploits.

Local history in newspapers is about much more than a few old pictures on a page. It should remind us of great people and events from the past and do so in a style that is both entertaining and informative. Chris Koenig's *History Man* articles do just that and more. I enjoy the fact that he can fascinate me with topics I previously considered rather dull, challenge my perception of past events and provide an endless stream of what I call 'well I never' moments.

I hope you enjoy this book and that, if you are not doing so already, you catch up with the *History Man* in *The Oxford Times* every week. You will not be disappointed.

Simon O'Neill
Editor, *The Oxford Times*

Foreword by Brian Aldiss, OBE

Here is a most enjoyable book about Oxford, our lovable city, and some of its surroundings. The author, Chris Koenig, has an easy style, and its publishers have been generous in scattering illustrations throughout the text.

Although we may move more in the heart of the city, the fringe benefits of nearby villages and recreation places are also taken care of. I was glad to see that Koenig mentions skating on Port Meadow, and if you wish to know on what dates the Meadow flooded or froze, here they are. Many such items are included: pre-industrial Morris dancing, where to find mushrooms and nuts, and so on... Another instance: when two more blocks were built on Blackbird Leys in 1961, Alderman Lionel Harrison described them as 'the best of modern living'.

Writers of forewords may point out omissions, both the regrettable and the preferable. Perhaps it is just as well that Oxford's Osney Mead industrial estate is only fleetingly mentioned, though it is but a stone's throw away from the rail station. But in a book subtitled 'The Changing Face' we should expand on two noteworthy changes in both stone and mind. Apart from Oxford's colleges, our city has two great bastions, the much-revived Ashmolean Museum, and the majestic Bodleian Library. The Ashmolean in its first year of reopening enjoyed an extraordinary 1.2 million visitors, and now serves 850,000 visitors per year. While anyone taking a stroll just now along the Broad will see a splendid hoarding composed of 26 panels, endowed with portraits and devices relating to each letter of the alphabet (pray that this masterpiece will be saved!). The hoarding protects work being done on the New Bodleian, which will soon be open in its grandeur to all—again, as with the Ashmolean, inviting not only scholars but ordinary people. These two bastions will signify a more open Oxford, in accord with the many foreign residents and scholars who work and gain from residence here.

Koenig pays tribute to a wide range of Oxfordshire writers and artists, such as Percy Bysshe Shelley, Tolkien and Barbara Pym—oh, and Holst, composer of the lovely carol, ''Twas in the Bleak Midwinter'—though it seems that Holst never came near Oxford. But you can buy his music at HMV in the Cornmarket.

The book has an enjoyable section on nearby towns and villages. Now, I have the good fortune to live in Old Headington on the hill (here before Oxford was there) and I regret to find no section on Headington in these pages. Headington was once the place you drove through to get to Oxford. That has changed. We have all the great hospitals up here—including the elegant and fairly recent Manor Hospital. Also, we have Brookes: once a polytechnic, it is now a startlingly successful college; so where once you saw only old people on the streets, pushing zimmer frames, now you see the young and the foreign, smiling, dropping litter as they move from coffee shop to coffee shop. And of course Headington has the beautiful Bury Knowle Park close by, for adults and children. Whether you are well or ill—try Headington!

So do try Chris Koenig's book! Everyone will have their own personal preferences for inclusions and omissions, and despite my grunts of dispute it is amazingly enjoyable simply as a read. You may think you know well our wonderful unique city: Koenig will put you right...

(And note, it's from a local publisher too!)

Preface

My working life stumbled into existence when I became a tour guide for well-heeled Americans. I persuaded a great aunt, who had just inherited money from a proverbial rich American uncle, to buy me a second-hand Humber Imperial car, and together with two friends set up in business as a company called True England Guides. There was one American, so famous that I had better not mention names here, who rang me up one day: 'Will you show me England, please? Let's start at the top; and show me some dukes.' So important was the owner of that voice that when I cold-called a couple of dukes—out of the blue, of course—they were happy to come on parade and show themselves off in their stately homes.

Then journalism set in. I wrote a few travel pieces for various papers, including *The Times*, the *Observer* and the *Guardian*, which duly appeared; and there I was, hooked. So much easier to be the one to whom others are paid to be kind, than to be the one having to tend the livestock. Thereafter I lived the precarious life of a freelance journalist in Combe, near Woodstock, first in a borrowed cottage and then in a semi-converted barn, before being lucky enough to land a part-time staff job with the free newspaper the *Oxford Star*. From there I progressed to *The Oxford Times*.

The 'Past Times' pieces began appearing in 2001, initially as little more than a few paragraphs. Gradually they grew in length as it became clear that they were well read and that local history was something that increasingly interested people. Now renamed 'The History Man', as part of a make-over to mark the 150th anniversary of *The Oxford Times*, they occupy most of a page each week. In producing the articles, the questions constantly lurking in the back of my mind have been: How did things get to be the way they are? What was there before? Who changed things? And why? These angles challenged me especially because, when it comes to reporting news stories for a newspaper (which of course deals with news rather than history), those are questions seldom answered. Yet I wanted to show that however different were the circumstances in which people in past times lived in this place we now call Oxfordshire, their actions, beliefs and attitudes are still relevant to the way we live today.

I have now written more than 500 articles for the series. Over the years the articles have frequently led me into lively correspondence with readers; sometimes the most seemingly innocuous comments cause concern, like for instance the question of whether it is right to uncover church paintings that were whitewashed during the Reformation, or whether the reasons they were obliterated in the first place are still valid.

For this book a representative selection from that total has been chosen. It does not aim to be comprehensive or provide all the chronological links; it is more an arrangement of beads on a string, rather than the continuous string itself. The various chapter headings under which the pieces have been grouped cover both city and county, through historical and geographical exploration. We hope that the book will bring them to a broader audience, and demonstrate the extraordinary impact that both Oxford and Oxfordshire have had on the development of the nation—not least thanks to the amazing gallery of people who have lived here.

I. Around Oxford City
Centre and Suburbs

Way back in the misty days known as the Dark Ages, after the Romans had left Britain but before William of Normandy had conquered it, a place called Oxford came into being, its geographic location determined by its highly defendable position: surrounded to west, south and east by rivers.

It grew up during the early 8th century around the Priory of St Frideswide, the patron saint of both the city and the university, which stood where Christ Church and the cathedral stand today: next to the oxen ford across the Thames that gave the place its name. It was built on a spit of gravel at the point where the Thames and the Cherwell meet: damp, marshy and foggy, but close to the very heart of England.

Those rivers, in particular the Thames, are key to Oxford's foundation and growth; for from earliest times they were important means of communication and transport. Recent research has shown that the Thames, which in later centuries was hard to navigate much above Henley, thanks to silting up, was in Anglo-Saxon and indeed medieval times navigable to a point much closer to Oxford.

After the Norman Conquest in 1066, William's henchman Robert d'Oilly built his Grandpont causeway across the Thames. He also built Oxford Castle in order to guard the crossing point around which Oxford was by that time establishing itself. As for overland communication, at the centre of the Norman city lay a road junction of national importance and on a precise north-south, east-west axis. It was called Carrefour—a name more familiar to most of us as that of a French supermarket chain, but in fact meaning Cross Roads—from which we derive the modern word Carfax. And Carfax is still the name of the road junction at the heart of Oxford. Here trading routes from the four points of the compass met in the middle of a walled city.

Ironically enough, the geographical advantages that led to Oxford establishing itself at the centre of English trade in earlier times are now seen by some as a constraint on further development, with the rivers causing traffic bottlenecks at bridges in a city that is now home to about 155,000 people (as opposed to about 4,500 at the time of the Domesday survey of 1086).

The gates in the city walls were demolished in the 18th century. In the 19th century the Victorian suburbs of North Oxford grew up along the roads to Banbury and Woodstock; and in the 20th century the country to the south and east became a centre for industry, notably the manufacture of cars in Cowley. Interestingly, once again, as happened when Oxford University established itself in the 12th century, brawn is giving way to brain: much of the Cowley area is now a science park, and the BMW Mini factory is sleek, clean and high tech compared to its predecessors, the Morris and Pressed Steel factories.

What's in a Name?

The name of 'Oxford' is associated with many items, from the mundane to the unusual. Many everyday items and names have the prefix Oxford attached to them: bags, shoes, frames, shirting, oolite, and the *English Dictionary*, to name a few.

Oxford bags were flannel trousers with very wide bottoms fashionable with effete undergraduates in the 1920s. An Oxford shoe is a style of footwear with a toecap. It is laced over the instep. Oxford shirting is a good quality material in which two yarns are woven as one to achieve fancy effects including stripes. An Oxford frame is a picture frame in which the horizontals and verticals overlap each other at the corners to form a cross. Similar crosses, in printing terms, are known as Oxford Corners. These occur when the text on a page is enclosed by lines which cross at the corners. As for Oxford oolite, it is a stratum of jurassic rock found largely beneath Oxfordshire and containing a series of marine deposits left over from when our familiar county was covered by water. Beneath it may be found Oxford clay, a deposit of stiff blue clay.

The *Oxford English Dictionary* is more obviously derived from Oxford: the first time the name was used was for the1933 reprint of what had originally been known as *A New English Dictionary on Historical Principles*. The historical principle is the process of tracking words down to their earliest appearance anywhere. Work began on the dictionary in 1858.

But a more surprising association for Oxford is that the earliest surviving national newspaper in England was produced in Oxford. It appeared on Tuesday 14 November 1665, and was called the *Oxford Gazette*. It came out as a result of the Great Plague, which had caused Charles II and his entire Court to flee from London to Oxford (where Parliament sat that year in the Divinity School). Journalist Henry Muddiman realised that courtiers needed a newspaper to let them know what was going on. He produced the *Oxford Gazette* by authority of the King. When the Court moved back to London the paper changed its name to the *London Gazette*—still published by Her Majesty's Stationery Office twice a week by authority—which came out for the first time under its new name in February 1666. The *London Gazette*, the official organ of the government, still lists official news items such as honours, changes of names or coats of arms, officers' promotions (or demotions!) within the armed services, and bankruptcies. Now the verb 'to be gazetted' as an officer, or mentioned in dispatches to the *London Gazette*, or as someone featuring in the bankruptcy courts, has made it into the *Oxford English Dictionary*.

But Oxford had already featured in journalistic activities even before the advent of the *Oxford Gazette*. During the Civil War, when Oxford became the nation's capital in the England of Charles I, a fellow of All Souls, Sir John Berkenhead, began producing Royalist news sheets to counter the propaganda emanating from Cromwell's side. Distribution of the Oxford Gazette was interesting. Muddiman was granted permission to send the gazette by post anywhere in the kingdom without paying. And contributors could also send items of news to him free of charge too. Running anything like a modern newspaper was a tricky and dangerous business until the Glorious Revolution of 1688 when censorship was relaxed—although it was not officially abandoned until 1693.

Folly Bridge

Oxford at the time of the Norman Conquest was damp, foggy and marshy. Just right for scholars seeking somewhere cheap in which to puzzle out the mysteries of the human condition. Oxford owes its very existence to its main artery, the Thames.

However, until the Conquest the river was little more than a series of rivulets and wet patches. This was particularly the case around Grandpont, the district west of Folly Bridge, which the city's Norman overlord, Robert d'Oilly, took in hand. He built a causeway consisting of a series of bridges, including Folly Bridge, which served as the main entrance to the city, replacing the original ford. It was crowned by an old tower or 'folly', which for centuries was also known as Friar Bacon's Study, Bachelor s Tower or New Gate. Roger Bacon (1214-94) is reputed to have used the old tower as a lookout for star gazing while studying astronomy.

In 1530, President of Corpus Christi, John Claymond, made the mistake of paying to have the bridge repaired. Consequently, the college was cited as being responsible for the bridge's upkeep in the following century. Legal disputes about who should pay continued for the next two centuries between the county of Berkshire, Oxford City, the university, and Corpus Christi. Like Magdalen Bridge, Folly Bridge was for most of its life financed by charity, with people called bridge-hermits collecting alms (not tolls) at wayside chapels. Navigation along the river, which had a habit of diminishing to a series of trickles in dry summers, and flooding in wet winters, was a haphazard business until 1790 when Osney Lock was cut. It frequently meant paying a miller to open his sluice gate and flush a boat through a flash lock at alarming speed. The irony is that the river—and the Oxford Canal too—had only recently become a serious conduit for commercial transport when it was eclipsed by the railway.

Not until 1824 was d'Oilly's old Folly Bridge largely rebuilt by Ebenezer Perry. In the true spirit of public-private partnership, a group of trustees advanced the money for the project: a new arch for barges, but the old tower was finally demolished. The toll house (now a sweet shop) was built in 1844 by James Gardner. By 1850 tolls levied had recouped the money advanced by the trustees and crossing the bridge became free.

Oxford Castle

The redevelopment of the Oxford Castle site marks an important moment in the city's history. For more than a thousand years, inhabitants have shuffled and shuddered past the grim, grey castle. Just as the city's St George's Tower, constructed by the Norman governor Robert d'Oilly, and the even older Saxon Castle Mound, the castle was forbidden for anyone to enter except as a prisoner. Now we can all go in and out at will. We pass through the front door, beneath that dreaded arch above which many a felon was publicly hanged, and look around at hotel rooms and restaurants which, a mere decade ago, were still prison cells.

Between 1700 and 1742 four successive members of the Etty family (including a woman, Elizabeth) were gaolers. Then came three successive members of the inappropriately named Wisdom family. The Wisdom dynasty lasted until 1786 when Solomon Wisdom was peremptorily sacked and replaced by the energetic and enlightened young Daniel Harris, formerly the city's clerk of works. He supervised the much-needed rebuilding and repairs at the festering old gaol, in which inmates fell into two camps—debtors and felons.

Until the rebuilding, a particularly gruesome aspect of public executions in Oxford was the unseemly tussle for the body that often took place between relatives of the victim and anatomists from Oxford University, who wanted it for dissection. After 1787 the hangings happened above the crowd, out of reach. Before that date, felons were sometimes hanged at Green Ditch, that part of St Margaret's Road running between Woodstock Road and Banbury Road, and sometimes at the castle.

To mark the redevelopment, Mark Davies, who runs the Oxford Towpath Press from his narrow boat on the Oxford Canal, wrote and published *Stories of Oxford Castle*, tracking the prison's history from Norman times to 1809, paying particular attention to the 18th century. He describes desperate degradation at the castle. Now it has evolved into something useful for our times, though the condemned cell remains.

Osney Abbey

Of course I know that most landscapes, whether natural or man-made, are constantly evolving, changing, or even (with any luck) improving. But I suspect that many of us, deep down, are incurable romantics who, like me, enjoy nothing more than the sight of a bit of old-fashioned, falling-to-pieces Romantic Decay. The case in point I have in mind here is the old Osney Mill building, next door to the only remaining fragment of Oxford's Osney Abbey.

Osney Abbey was originally an Augustinian priory founded by Robert d'Oilly in 1129, according to legend after d'Oilly's wife Edith was persuaded into believing that a flock of magpies flying over the meadow were in reality restless souls from Purgatory. It was raised to the rank of Abbey in about 1154. Then in 1222 the Synod of Oxford was convened at the Abbey, during which meeting the assembled divines not only adopted St George as England's patron saint but also decided to take a harder line towards non-Christians. Interestingly the remaining Abbey gatehouse bears a plaque to someone called Robert of Reading who, poor man, was executed near there on 17 April 1222 simply for having a Jewish girlfriend and himself taking up Judaism.

By 1542, when Henry VIII made the last Abbot, Robert King, Bishop of the new diocese of Oxford, the church was 332 feet long. It then became Oxford Cathedral until 1546, when that status was transferred to St Frideswide's at Christ Church.

After that, the long ruination of the abbey began: first the bells and lead were taken away—with the main bell, ironically enough, finding its way eventually to Christ Church; then, after the place was leased to a clothier, the stained-glass windows, along with iron and woodwork, were removed. And, as if this was not bad enough, an explosion in a powder house in 1643 destroyed much of what remained. All the same, a surprising amount of the building survived late into the 17th century.

Of the old mills in Oxford, Osney was one of the last to cease grinding flour. Castle Mill, which had been in existence since the 11th century, was demolished for a road-widening scheme in 1930; Iffley Mill burned down in 1908; and Sandford Mill made way for a housing development as late as 1985.

Now the Osney Mill building, which was gutted by fire in 1946, is covered in scaffolding and is being turned into ten riverside apartments which, I am sure, will be wonderful in every way; and which of course, when I stop being sentimental and start thinking sensibly, I applaud; particularly as the new homes will largely be powered by a mini hydro-electric plant, based on an Archimedean screw, and using the fast-flowing water of the Osney Mill Cut, the old mill race, to generate energy and at the same time reduce the risk of flooding.

The site being developed belongs to the Munsey family, four generations of whom have worked in Oxfordshire as millers, and who still own a mill at Wantage. The mill site includes an old gatehouse of the Abbey, which has now been dated to 1410.

For the past couple of decades, whenever I walked to or from *The Oxford Times* offices in Osney Mead (built on what was once a meadow belonging to the monks), I have enjoyed the view across the Thames of the rotting, red brick remains of the old mill—with a sizable sycamore growing on its inside and poking its branches through the vaguely classical windows. 'Lovely', I have always thought to myself (guiltily and secretly). *Tout ça change*, as they say. No point being sentimental.

Gloucester Green

Gloucester Green has long been known as the place to wait for buses in the rain, penned in rudimentary shelters that have the look of a livestock market. Curiously, that could be an indicator of the site's rich history... The origin of the name comes from the Benedictine monastic Gloucester College, which stood where Worcester College now stands, across the street from Beaumont Palace where Richard I was born. The original college was founded in 1283, then refounded in 1560 as Gloucester Hall following the Reformation. Worcester College came into existence in 1714. The medieval cottages on the south side of the main Worcester College quad are survivors of the old college.

As for the Green part of the name, the place was always surrounded by trees. In the Civil War, when Oxford was the Royalist capital, the Green was used for military parades. In Puritan times, executions were carried out on a tree. Then it was used as a bowling green until 1789. A charter granted to Oxford in 1601 allowed a fair to be held on 3 May at Gloucester Green, but Oxford University opposed it and the fair did not come into being until 1783. The last one was held in 1903.

In 1789 the city gaol was, incongruously enough, built in the middle of the Green, where it remained until 1878 when it was demolished. It was an elegant, low building with a dome. It gained notoriety in 1839 when the gaoler was himself gaoled there for debt. Prisoners sentenced to hard labour walked the treadwheel there.

Its next phase of use was as a cattle market for nearly a century, 1835-1932. Then the cattle market was moved to Oxpens, and the Green became the county bus station, with buses leaving from the western end of the so-called green. The Settling Room, where cattle bargains were settled, became a cafe. Some of us remember the interestingly shaped waiting room at the bus station, which has been cleverly incorporated into the site we know today. It was once part of the Oxford Boys Central School, with classrooms leading off a round hall.

Gloucester Green seems to have been the site of continuous change over the centuries. Of the many pubs that used to surround it, *The Blue Pig* was demolished in the 1930s to make way for a scheme that never happened; only one other of the original pubs is still standing.

St Clements

Poor old St Clements. Over the centuries its inhabitants have had more than their fair share of bad luck, being all too often poverty-stricken and disease-ridden. In the 17th century, during the Civil War, the parish was all but demolished by the Royalist army. So how did it rise again after the Civil War? Answer: until the Municipal Reform Act of 1835, only tradespeople deemed by the university to be Privileged Persons were allowed to trade in Oxford; as a result many unprivileged persons found it expedient to trade just outside its boundary. By 1675, there were more houses in St Clements than there had been at the start of the war some 35 years before.

The Black Horse Inn, at 102 St Clements, was one of the very few buildings to survive the Civil War. It remained a centre of village activity for many hundreds of years, with parish meetings being held outside the half-timbered building until 1914.

In 1771, there were rowdy but ultimately useless demonstrations against the building of Iffley Road. It cut right through St Clements and its building involved the demolition of several houses.

St Clements did not become part of Oxford until 1835. Until then it suffered from the misfortune of lying on the busy road to London. The parishioners were expected to pay for the road's upkeep: an expensive business, particularly since stone (from Headington) and wood (from Shotover), both needed for constructing university buildings, had to be hauled along it.

Ironically, St Clements became poorer as Oxford University became richer; for when houses were pulled down to make way for college buildings, the families displaced tended to move across Magdalen Bridge to St Clements—where poverty became acute during university vacations when there was little work about for college servants, washer women and so forth.

St Clements was known as the location for bull and bear baiting until the 1820s, with members of the university's bear baiting club—which, amazingly, only closed in 1826—making up much of the audience. There were also stocks on the cobbles until

Penson's Gardens, St Clements

about the same time. During the 18th and 19th centuries a fair, selling mainly toys, was also held in St Clements on the Thursday before Michaelmas (29 September). It later developed into a full-blown funfair which continued as an annual event until the 1930s.

Interestingly, the Victoria Fountain on the Plain, constructed in 1899, stands on the site of the medieval St Edmund's Well, once a sort of unofficial holy place which local people supposed had miraculous powers. The Bishop of Lincoln twice forbade the well's veneration, in 1290 and 1304, perhaps because it was beginning to represent competition for Oxford's official holy well at Binsey.

Sadly, good water was something St Clements lacked for centuries. Its drinking water came from the Cherwell, into which also flowed its sewage. It therefore suffered severely from outbreaks of cholera, notably in1832 when a third of all deaths in Oxford and St Clements occurred there.

The medieval parish church of St Clements, described by historian Thomas Hearne as 'a very pretty little church', stood on the Plain until 1829 when it was demolished. The present, larger church, built in a curious Georgian-Norman style, contains Oxford's oldest bell, cast in the 13th century and taken from the old St Clements church. The last traces of the old churchyard on the Plain disappeared in the 1950s when the present roundabout was constructed.

Grandpont House

It is fitting somehow that one of Oxford's two centres of Opus Dei, the Catholic organisation suddenly thrown into unwelcome limelight by the film *The Da Vinci Code* that revives the theory that Christ was married to Mary Magdalene and has progeny walking the earth today, should be at the beautiful Grandpont House.

It is near Folly Bridge (formerly Grandpont, as opposed to Pettypont, now Magdalen Bridge) and just across the river from Christ Church where St Frideswide founded her nunnery.

Grandpont is at the very root of Oxford, on the site of the original oxen ford across the Thames and debate—and conflict—about the precise nature of Christianity has sustained Oxford University since time immemorial. Founder of Opus Dei, the Portuguese prelate Jose Maria Escriva visited Oxford in 1958 and acquired the 18th-century house from Brasenose College. Since then it has acted as a hostel for male students and also as a debating centre. A building called Winton in Canterbury Road fulfils a similar purpose for women. Oxford was also a leading European centre for that other keeper of the dread secret promulgated in author Dan Brown's *The Da Vinci Code*: the order of the Knights Templar.

This military order, formed in 1128, owned huge estates in what is now Temple Cowley and Sandford. Their vow was to protect pilgrims visiting the Holy Land.

Sadly, many knights, pilgrims, and crusaders returning from the Middle East brought with them leprosy. King Henry I, a fan of the Templars, founded the hospital of St Bartholomew in Temple Cowley in 1128 on what was then an isolated spot. Only the chapel remains. It was granted to Oriel College in 1327, shortly after the Templars were suppressed and their lands throughout Europe confiscated. In Oxford, some of the Templars were imprisoned in the castle.

And how would conspiracy theorists such as Dan Brown have been treated in earlier times in Oxford? Doubtless they would have been either burned at the stake or hanged, drawn and quartered. They would have infuriated both Catholic Mary I and Protestant Elizabeth I by undermining Christianity itself. As for Opus Dei, Oxford members will probably be pleased to hear that an audience at the Phoenix laughed in the wrong places at a recent showing. The UK branch of the organisation this week described the use of the celice for self-mortification in the film as 'grotesque'. Nevertheless, it added: 'Some of the celibate members of Opus Dei use the celice. It is a small, light metal chain with little prongs worn around the thigh. The celice is uncomfortable but it does not in any way hinder one's normal activities and there is absolutely no Da Vinci Code gore.'

Botley Road

Succeeding generations move into each other's buildings, much as the guests at the March Hare's Tea Party moved round the table—with all except the Mad Hatter inheriting the used crockery of his predecessor.

The site in Botley Road where the nondescript Halfords premises now stands once housed Oxford's original ice rink. It was a wondrous Art Deco construction, built in 1930, in a sort of Regal Cinema style which until recently people loved to hate—but which has since come back into fashion.

In its early days the ice rink staged figure skating displays with top performers, and ice hockey matches too. Indeed, in 1930 Oxford University beat Germany there 3-1 in a much-talked-about contest. As early as 1933, however, the place was feeling the financial pinch.

That summer it opened its space as a cinema, with Mae West playing *I'm No Angel*. It re-opened as an ice rink in the winter of 1933-4. Then it became the Majestic Picture Palace until 1947, when the manufacturers of Frank Cooper's famous Oxford Marmalade moved in.

The grocer Frank Cooper had begun selling marmalade in earthenware pots at his shop at 84 High Street, Oxford in 1874, after his wife, Sarah Jane, had made too much of the stuff (76lb to be precise) for the family's own use. Modern marmalade makers might be interested to learn that she made her chunky variety according to a recipe she had learned from her mother. Undergraduates and dons (probably including the creator of the Mad Hatter, Lewis Carroll) took to it immediately. Indeed, it soon became the preserve of the Victorian breakfast table all over the British Empire.

Such was its success that in 1900 Frank Cooper moved his cauldrons into that funny old edifice called Victoria Building, then a purpose-built marmalade works, which still stands in what is now called Frideswide Square (opposite the Said Business School), and houses, among other things, a restaurant called The Jam Factory.

Not that any self-respecting Victorian would have called marmalade jam! Nor would he or she ever have considered having any other preserve than marmalade for breakfast—though few probably realised that even applying the word to something made of oranges was a misnomer. The word marmalade is derived from the Portuguese for quince: *marmelada*. Perhaps quince marmalade came to Britain with the Portuguese wife of Charles II, Catherine of Braganza, or earlier?

However that may have been, Frank Coopers went on making marmalade on the Botley Road site from 1947 until 1967, when the company was taken over by the Midlands firm Brown & Polson. Marmalade production moved first to Wantage in

1967 and then to Manchester, where it is still made. Premier Foods acquired the brand recently and now there is talk—wait for it—of moving production to Cambridgeshire!

Ice skating in Oxford came to a halt (except in such places as Port Meadow, which frequently flooded and froze over in those days) from 1947 until 1985 when the Oxpens rink opened. As for the original rink, it was demolished, as tends to happen when a certain style goes out of fashion.

Sometimes, it seems, a guest at the tea party moves into his predecessor's place and throws away the crockery, replacing it with something more modern. But would anyone ever suggest preserving (or listing) the present unlovely occupant of the site? Perhaps they will.

Cowley

That prolific writer, Anon, once said: 'Oxford is the Latin quarter of Cowley.' But the part of Oxford which for nearly 100 years has manufactured cars—which the other part of Oxford now bans from its historic streets for fear of congestion—grew up without the city walls comparatively recently. Only in 1928 was it finally incorporated as part of the County Borough of Oxford, though its population had been rising steadily throughout the 19th century, long before William Morris began building cars there in 1912.

Originally known by its Saxon name of Covelea, meaning a clearing between forest and river, in this case between Shotover Royal Forest and the Thames, the early settlements of Church Cowley (Chirchecovele) and Temple Cowley developed around the Preceptory of the Knights Templars. This chivalrous band of knights had been given their Cowley estates in 1139 by Queen Maud, wife of Stephen. Their fishponds were discovered during excavations some 30 years ago. However, despite having given

their name to a part of modern Oxford, they only stayed there until 1240 when they decamped to Sandford. Middle Cowley, beween Temple Cowley and Church Cowley, was established in about 1300 by the mighty Osney Abbey. The monks built St James's Church there in the late 12th century.

But from Oxford's earliest days Cowley Road was a major thoroughfare to the city. Evidence of a pottery industry dating from Roman times has been found near what is now Roman Way but was once part of the Roman road from Dorchester to Alcester. The road from London, known in medieval times as London Road, crossed the marsh, which was common pasture, by way of a causeway, passing St Bartholomew's Hospital before reaching Magdalen Bridge. The hospital with its simple chapel, known from earliest times as the Bartlemas, was founded by Henry I in 1127 as a lepers' home, with a staff of 12 brethren and one chaplain. In 1327, it was given to Oriel College as a 'rural retreat' for scholars, enabling them to breathe 'the wholesome air in times of pestilential sickness'.

The population of Cowley began to rise dramatically from the mid 1800s. The Oxfordshire and Buckinghamshire Light Infantry Barracks were built on Bullingdon Green (where, interestingly enough, Charles I had reviewed his troops during the Civil War) and the area's first major industry arrived in the shape of the agricultural machinery firm, the Steam Plough Company. As for the 'wholesome air' of Cowley, once known as champagne compared to Oxford's beer, it became somewhat polluted in the 1980s when some 12,000 people worked at Rover and the paintshop sprayed the area with small particles of paint.

Blackbird Leys

Lady Ottoline Morrell, the eccentric inhabitant of Garsington Manor during the First World War who provided sanctuary for talented conscientious objectors, including D. H. Lawrence, and Bertrand Russell, would be astonished were she to see what has happened to the sewage works down the road. The land at Sawpit Farm, now part of Blackbird Leys, had belonged to the family of her husband Philip, Liberal MP for South Oxfordshire from 1857 until 1895. Then it had been sold off to the City of Oxford, although the western part had already been bought and turned into a sewage works as early as 1877.

In her day, Oxford was regarded as a university city and market town, rather than an industrial centre. With a population of 57,399 in 1901 (up from just 12,690 a century before), the arguments which still rage today about Oxford expanding into the surrounding countryside had not really begun. By the end of the Second World War,

the city's population had topped the 100,000 mark (in reality it was much more since unplanned development had occurred immediately outside the city limits) and by 2001 it had hit 134,248.

Just over 50 years ago, planners realised that a major council estate was needed near the burgeoning Cowley car factory. The availability of jobs was attracting ever more people to the area. A plan for 2,800 houses was given outline planning permission for land used by the sewage works and at Sawpit Farm. In 1958 ten families moved into the first houses built on the estate: 23-33 Sandy Lane. In 1961, the two 150 ft high blocks of flats—Evenlode and Windrush Towers—went up. They were described at their opening by Alderman Lionel Harrison as 'the best of modern living'. As they were being built—on the site of former sewage workers' homes—*The Oxford Times* commented: 'When the nationwide planning schemes were made as far back as 1945, the present rapid increase in population was not anticipated.'

Originally, Blackbird Leys was intended to provide homes for about 10,000 people, but such was the unrelenting demand that it ended up with a far higher density. Some 13,400 people live there now, making it bigger than some Oxfordshire market towns. In the 1980s the estate was further extended with the building of Greater Leys. The old sewage works formed most of what is now the estate, but it was named Blackbird Leys after a nearby farm, sometimes called Blacford Leys, because it sounded more attractive.

The sewage works were famous for attracting wild birds, and many of the roads on the estate are named after the different species. Carole Newbigging, author of *The Changing Faces of Blackbird Leys* (Robert Boyd, 2000) quotes George Bampton of Littlemore, reminiscing on the sewage works: 'Other parts of the sewage farm were dug by hand into grid-iron shapes known locally as the beds, and on these, that is the raised or banked portion, was grown such crops as marigolds, cabbages and Brussels sprouts.'

Lady Ottoline would have known those beds of flowers and vegetables. Britain's population in her day was 42 million. Little would she have guessed that it would reach 60 million during the next 100 years and change the landscape forever. The villages of Cowley, Iffley and Headington became incorporated into Oxford in 1929, the year after she moved out of Garsington.

North Oxford

Funny old thing is fashion; and sometimes dangerous too. Take North Oxford, for instance, that area of mainly Victorian buildings north of St Giles, so beloved of Sir John Betjeman, where houses these days change hands for millions.

In the early days of its existence it was almost too fashionable. No less a figure than John Ruskin, writing in the late 1870s, wondered why visitors should want to see Magdalen walks rather than 'stroll under the rapturous sanctities of Keble'—that apogee of high Victoriana, designed by William Butterfield (1814-1900). Then he asked: 'In

the name of all that's human and progressive, why not walk up and down the elongated suburb of the married fellows on the cock-horse road to Banbury?' (By which he meant Banbury Road, of course.)

Interesting that he already thought of these extraordinary edifices as being the abodes of married dons. For centuries the myth has persisted that North Oxford grew up after college fellows were allowed to marry, and that they and their families were the first inhabitants. But cold fact spoils the myth: the celibacy rule for fellows only came to an end in 1877 as part of the University Reform Act which, after a hard battle, finally implemented at least some of the recommendations of a Royal Commission set up in 1871. Oxford's expansion northward was well under way by then.

True, according to the *Encyclopaedia of Oxford* (edited by Christopher Hibbert and published by Macmillan in 1988) some married university coaches lived there before 1877, but it was not until after that date that university fellows arrived. And there was much snobbery between town and gown, with incoming academics often looking down their noses at tradesmen next door who had got there first.

As early as 1826, T. Little wrote in his *Confessions of an Oxonian*: 'Pastry cooks who had made fortunes out of cheating members of the University' should 'not be allowed to pollute the magnificent entrances to the most beautiful of cities in the kingdom', and the *Encyclopaedia* says that sentiment was flourishing into the 1870s.

But far from being too popular, by 1900 the popometer had already veered violently the other way. In that year the Reverrend W. Tuckwell, in his *Oxford Reminiscences*, wrote of 'the interminable streets of Villadom, converging insatiably protuberant upon distant Wolvercote and Summertown'. He was the first of the 20th-century commentators who almost universally ridiculed North Oxford architecture for the next 70 years or more.

This fashion of loving to hate the place could well have resulted in the destruction of much of it, particularly in the 1960s when many of the original 99-year leases were running out. Indeed, in March 1962 St John's College, the owner of much of the southern part of North Oxford, announced that it was preparing a development plan that would involve the demolition of several notable houses. The architect of the plan, Lionel Brett, remarked: 'My personal view of North Oxford is that it is one of the most beautiful sites it is possible to imagine for modern buildings.'

One of the splendid Victorian houses, at 31 Banbury Road, was pulled down to make way for St Anne's College. It had originally been built for a local tradesman called George Ward in 1866 by William Wilkinson, who used its picture in his book of recently erected English Country Houses.

Councillor Anne Spokes emerged as a champion of high Victoriana, even at a time when it was unloved and laughed at by many. She turned to John Betjeman for help, and by 1964, several of the threatened houses had been listed. Among the houses saved was Wykeham House, at 56 Banbury Road. It had been built in 1866 for Henry Hatch, the owner of a clothes shop in Magdalen Street. Mr Hatch never lived there himself but let it to distinguished tenants including Prince Leopold, youngest son of Queen Victoria, who lived there when he was an undergraduate at Christ Church.

Summertown

Diamond Place in Summertown is so called, I am told, because a highwayman's booty was found there more than a century after he had helped himself to it from people travelling along what was then the wild and woolly way from Oxford to Banbury.

Until well into the 19th century, Summertown was a farm settlement consisting of just a few cottages connected to Oxford by a muddy road. Over the course of that century it became the source of much money-making, through house building and property speculation, for many of the shrewder tradesmen of Oxford.

Already in 1821 a farm was divided into 117 building plots, with houses varying in style from little more than huts to grand Regency-style villas springing up. The heart of the community, Middle Way, had long existed as a farm track, but by the 1850s Rogers Street, Hobson Road and Grove Street had been built. By 1881 there were 282 houses. By 1889 Oxford's boundary was extended northwards as far as a line marked by what is now Hernes Road, thereby embracing Summertown. In 1895 a successful grocer, resident of Summertown and one-time mayor of Oxford, Francis Twining, bought 50 acres of land further out of town, enough to build 350 more houses and the parish church.

It seems that Summertown developed separately to that ill-defined place, so beloved by Betjeman, called North Oxford, stretching originally from St Giles to a rough line marked by Marston Ferry, Staverton Road and Frenchay Road. St John's College owned much of this area, which goes some way to explain why it is now Oxford's richest college, having bought Norham Manor—where Norham Gardens now stands—in the 16th century, when the whole area was called Walton Field.

All this development was well under way in 1850, but it received a boost in 1877 when a Royal Commission abolished the dons' celibacy rule and they were allowed to marry.

As for the diamonds and other treasure found in Diamond Place during building there, I am told that descendants of the unfortunates robbed were tracked down wherever possible and the plundered property restored to them. I am also led to believe that the highwayman in question was the notorious gentleman robber Claude Duval, still supposed to haunt the Hopcrofts Holt Hotel, which is further up the Banbury Road. Anyone with information on this outlaw, executed despite pleas to Charles II for clemency from many of his female victims, please let me know.

Port Meadow

The fun of laughing at some mythical and impossibly thick American sightseer in Oxford seems to have gone out of fashion. But I well remember the tale of how he once asked the way to the University and was told it was 'everywhere'. Then there was the time he wanted to know how to achieve a perfect lawn—and was told that the trick was to lay it carefully and roll it daily for 300 years. And then there was the one about his request to be shown Oxford's oldest historical sight. He found himself wandering around Port Meadow along with the cattle and horses.

Had he done so in summer, he might have hit lucky and witnessed a sort of tamer version of cowboy activity, a little reminiscent of his own Wild West, that must indeed be one of Oxford's oldest ceremonies. For on a surprise date every summer the Sheriff of Oxford organises a dawn round-up of all animals grazing on the common, sometimes impounding them in the ruins of Godstow Nunnery or, less romantically, in a pound built in 1981, and imposing fines on the owners of any animals found grazing there without authorisation.

The flat expanse of water meadow on the north-west of Oxford is described in the Domesday Book of 1086 as the place where 'all the burgesses (or Freemen) of Oxford have a pasture outside the city wall in common, which pays 6s. 8d' (or 33p a year in modern money).

It was originally called Portmaneit (though the name Port Meadow was in use by 1285) and may have been as much as 500 acres in extent, including what is now Wolvercote Common, Wolvercote Green and Binsey Green—though when it was registered as common land in 1970 it comprised about 342 acres. Since at least 1562, inter-commoning rights have been shared with the Wolvercote Commoners, i.e. Wolvercote residents.

Sheep were never allowed on the meadow but geese were kept there and led to the river daily by goose boys and goose girls. Some of these geese interbred with wild geese, and over the centuries a recognised hybrid goose evolved called the Port Meadow Special.

Horse racing was an important feature of Port Meadow from the 17th to 19th centuries. Zacharias Conrad von Uffenbach (1683-1734), a German traveller and collector of books and manuscripts, visited the races on 17 September 1710 and described them thus: 'There were many booths set up, where beer was sold, and each one had its sign, a hat, or glove or some such matter. Nearly everyone from the City was there and many visitors, some on horseback, some in coaches, some in boats. The horses that had to run were six in number. They had to run twice round the meadow, five English miles, which was done within ten minutes.'

The next day he wrote—more controversially—that he did not want to go again because: 'When you have seen it twice you get no more enjoyment out of it unless you are an Englishman, fond of torturing horses and take pleasure in overdoing the poor animals.' However, more revealingly he added : 'Still we would have gone out again, if there had been this time, as is usual on the third day a Smoake-race (Smock-race) where the women folk run for a prize in petticoats and low necked shifts, and the men folk in breeches without shirts. This time however it did not take place...' (I wonder which he would have preferred if it had!).

During the Civil War the meadow was the scene of one of the most skillfully conducted Royalist moves, when King Charles I escaped from Oxford for the first time. By June 1644 the Parliamentarians had decided that the time had come to capture Oxford and indeed the king himself. But on the night of 3 June at about 9 p.m. the king and about 2,500 musketeers managed to march out of the city to Port Meadow, where 3,000 horses were already drawn up. Then the whole lot silently marched out of town along a track to Yarnton used by drovers and farmers, without the Parliamentarians even seeing them.

In the First World War, and indeed in the years just preceding it, the meadow was used as an aerodrome. In 1911 it was a matter of national marvel that a Mr Latham succeeded in flying from Brooklands to Royal Flying Corps (RFC) Port Meadow and back again. Sadly, though, the next year saw one of the country's first aviation accidents when Lieutenants Bettington and Hotchkiss, flying a Bristol Coanda, were killed at Wolvercote—an event recorded by a memorial plaque on the bridge between Wolvercote and Godstow.

Nowadays the Meadow belongs to the Freemen of Oxford, who are the only people allowed to graze animals there. Freemen, sometimes called *hanasters*, are the successors of tradesmen who in former times were allowed to trade in Oxford 'freely'. Until 1835 only Freemen could be elected to the council. Now the 'freedom' is granted as an honour to people whom the city reckons deserve it, and to sons and (since 2008) daughters of existing Freemen.

Oxford Airport

Laugh at the name if you will, but 'London Oxford Airport' is probably now fulfilling a commercial role closer to that intended by its original founders than at any time in its 75-year history.

Oxford City Council bought the now-familiar airfield lying between the Woodstock and Banbury Roads in 1935 in order to establish something then called the Oxford Municipal Aerodrome. The council paid £19,671 for three tracts of land, with Campsfield Farm at their centre, from the Duke of Marlborough and farmers Frank Henman and G. J. E. Bulford.

Negotiations to buy the 580 acres of flat land had been conducted in secret ever since *The Oxford Times* had urged the council to establish a commercial airfield back in 1932. The newspaper had argued then that, as civil aviation was developing with internal airlines and mail flights, the city would be left behind without its own airport, in much the same way as Abingdon had been left behind in the previous century—losing its county town of Berkshire status in 1867—after turning its back on the railway.

But although originally bought with commercial purposes in mind, with war on the horizon the impetus for early developments at Kidlington came from the Royal Air Force, which planned to establish a fast-track training school for pilots there. In 1938 a machine-gun emplacement was established near the old farm buildings at what was then referred to by the City Engineer as Campsfield Aerodrome.

During the war, the airfield—which to confuse matters further was sometimes called Kidlington, or Oxford, or even Thrupp Aerodrome, in official documents—was twice attacked by German Junkers. The first incident was in November 1940, when a lone Ju88 flying at just 50 ft dropped five bombs, killing one airman and, setting on fire two Harvard aircraft; a bomb that failed to explode closed the road (now the A44) for a while.

The second incident was in August 1941, when a night-flying Ju88 attacked an Oxford aircraft with tracer fire and then overflew Kidlington, dropping bombs on the plane, but luckily missing it. Minutes before, the German pilot had destroyed another Oxford craft over *Sturdy's Castle*, killing its pilot, and he went on to shoot down yet another near Weston-on-the-Green, killing its pilot too.

Sadly, though, it seems that most wartime casualties at Kidlington resulted from accidents. In the afternoon of 4 March 1943 alone, three Spitfire pilots lost their lives: two were killed in a collision ten miles north of Oxford and one crashed at Kidlington.

Amy Johnson, the first woman to fly solo from Britain to Australia, lost her life on 5 January 1941 while delivering an Airspeed Oxford aircraft to Kidlington. She bailed out in the Thames estuary but her body was never recovered. Some aspects of the incident are still secret.

Talking of secrets, the wreckage of the Messerschmitt Bf110 in which German Deputy Führer Rudolph Hess flew to Scotland, apparently to negotiate peace terms in 1941, was flown to Kidlington and temporarily went on display—until whisked away as Top Secret. Hess had arrived at the Duke of Hamilton's estate in Scotland, and the Duke was flown to Kidlington to meet Sir Winston Churchill who often stayed at nearby Ditchley Park.

Not until 1959 did the Air Ministry finally cease to operate from Kidlington, returning the field to full civil use. In that year Lord Kildare moved from Dublin and established Vigors Aviation at Kidlington as the main UK Piper distributor. In 1962 the company CSE was founded as a commercial pilot-training enterprise. It was owned mainly by members of the Guinness family, though Lord Kildare was its managing director. In 1967 it rented the airport on a 21-year lease from Oxford City Council at £7,000 a year. By 1968 the training school was so successful that the airport was Britain's second busiest in terms of aircraft movements after Heathrow.

In 1981 CSE bought the 577-acre airport from the council for £1.4 m—not much compared to the £55.4 m which present owners Reuben Brothers Holdings paid for the airport in 2000, even though its area had by then been depleted to 375 acres. Only very recently, though, with the expansion of scheduled services, has the airport begun to resemble the civil airport which the city council originally envisaged.

2. Oxford in History
Landmarks and Events

Oxford's early development into a university city of national and international importance closely mirrors the development of England as a nation. Both evolved from established French entities: Oxford from the university of Paris, and England, some might argue, as a result of its conquest by Duke William of Normandy—who paid feudal homage to the King of France for his Norman lands (though not of course for England).

But it sometimes comes as a surprise to learn that Oxford, despite its fame, beauty and general importance, is not really a place of very great antiquity. There are no Roman remains to speak of, and indeed the earliest mention of pre-Conquest Oxford is in the *Anglo-Saxon Chronicle* for 912.

Sad to say, its earlier 'history'—for instance of the 8th-century St Frideswide restoring the sight of a lascivious Danish invader with the healing waters of Binsey's holy well, and then sailing down the river to found her nunnery where the cathedral now stands—rightly belongs in the land of legend. All the same a nunnery did certainly exist here; it was burned down in 1002.

By 1015 Oxford had developed into a place of sufficient size and importance for a Great Council of the kingdom to be held here—and King Canute of Denmark and England called more Great Councils to Oxford in succeeding years. St Michael's church at the Northgate, Oxford's oldest building, dates from about this time. It is typical of the early 11th century, with its twin bell-openings.

After the Conquest, the Domesday Book of 1086 was able to describe Oxford as a *civitas*, with houses 'within and without its wall'—and of course sections of that wall still exist today, notably in the gardens of New College. Much of the Norman castle, built by Duke William's henchman Robert d'Oilly in 1071, survives too, in the shape of the late 11th-century crypt and tower of the church of St George (himself later adopted as the patron saint of England at the Synod of Oxford in 1222).

These buildings pre-date the university, the roots of which stretch back to the early 12th century—but were reinforced when Henry II's quarrels with the Archbishop of Canterbury, Thomas à Becket, and with Louis VII of France, led to a temporary ban on English scholars going to Paris University and the repatriation of those already there. First came the monks and nuns to Oxford, then came the university proper. The church of St Frideswide's Priory was re-founded in 1122; then came Osney Priory (later Abbey, and later still Cathedral) in 1129, of which only one very small building survives; then Godstow Abbey for Benedictine nuns in 1133; and finally Rewley Abbey in 1281, of which only one archway survives near the Said Business School.

By then the friars had already arrived. First the Blackfriars established the first Dominican house in England in 1222, and then the Franciscan Greyfriars three years later. But why were there so many monks, nuns and friars in Oxford? Answer: because the city already contained a rudimentary university, or *universitas*—which, put simply, translates as a place containing a group of people trained and licensed to teach; with the degree conferred (still sometimes called a 'licentiate' at some ancient continental universities) being no more or less than a licence to teach.

As for the parallel development of England itself, it seems that the early Plantagenet Kings, few of whom spent much time here—or even spoke English—originally treated the nation as a source of revenue for fighting their continental battles. Only as those continental lands were lost did England emerge as a vibrant independent entity; and Oxford with it.

Anglo-Saxon Oxford

The first written evidence of the existence of Oxford appears in *The Anglo-Saxon Chronicle*, kept in the Bodleian Library under the year 911-912. The date is surprisingly late: this is some 250 years after the time of the fabled foundress of Oxford, the Saxon princess and patron saint of the city, Frideswide.

The name of course means Oxenford (a ford over the Thames for oxen), which is directly comparable with other place names nearby such as Shifford (sheep-ford) or Swinford (swine-ford). Most recent research and archaeology, particularly work based on deep tunnelling near Grandpont by British Telecom, has shown that the ford in Saxon times was not one but a series of fords allowing travellers and their flocks to 'island-hop' across the flood plain. New research reaffirms the traditional view that the ford was indeed on the north–south route through the city, at the end of the present St Aldates. This view was challenged by some academics not long ago, when they produced convincing evidence that the ford lay on the line of the footpath from Osney Mead to Hinksey. The fact is that there was probably a crossing point across the plain there too.

Tunnelling for BT has also produced evidence of a wooden bridge south of Oxford that existed more than 100 years before the Norman Conquest. Six timber supports suggest a trestle bridge from one island to another south of Oxford which was about 3.3 metres wide. As for Oxford in the time of St Frideswide (born about AD 650) archaeological evidence now includes the skeleton of a middle-aged woman who may have been buried at the abbey founded on the site of the present cathedral during the requisite period.

However, Oxford began to emerge as something approaching a permanent settlement some 200 years later, when the kings of Wessex chose the site as a defensive position against the attacks of Vikings. The town was built on a grid pattern with present-day Carfax the main crossroads at its centre. The whole settlement was surrounded by an earth rampart long before the city walls (remains of which may be seen in New College gardens) were built.

Only in the 11th century did Oxford rise to prominence over the other 'fords' nearby. By that time its streets were lined with buildings and it had become a shopping centre of sorts. In addition to the original Minster of St Frideswide, the city would, by this time, have contained several new churches including St Michael at the Northgate, Oxford's oldest building, dating from 1010-60.

Indeed, the period just before the Conquest seems to have been something of a high point. Just after 1066 Oxford went into decline after William I's protégé, Robert d'Oilly, built his castle on top of the west end of the Saxon city, thereby obliterating dozens of houses. To counter that sin he did at least undertake the construction of the stone causeway (Grandpont) across the Thames, which recent work has shown still survives beneath the present St Aldates and the Abingdon Road.

The Jewish Quarter

Next time you drink a cup of coffee, particularly if you do so in a coffee bar near St Aldates, Oxford, you might like to reflect that you are close to the place where coffee first made its appearance to the English consumer. The history of coffee, that exotic beverage from the East to which so many of us are now so hopelessly addicted, is closely bound up with the history of the Jews in Oxford.

The Jews were here even before the university, and they lived for the most part in Old Jewry, now St Aldates, which stretched from Carfax southwards to the South Gate of the city, demolished in 1613. Some say the name St Aldates—probably Oxford's oldest street—is derived from the 'Old Gate' which barred the road between present-day Christ Church and Brewer Street.

The earliest mention of Jews in Oxford is dated 1141, and refers to a levy forced from them during the Civil War between Stephen and Matilda. As the university expanded, many Jews in Oxford became extremely prosperous through lending money and letting lodgings to students and academics. Many were also scholarly, though as non-Christians they were not allowed officially to become members of the university.

Jewish property investment became an important element of the early university since they rebuilt in stone rather than lath and plaster, and some of their accommodation blocks for students became parts of colleges—notably Merton College, as 13th-century documents between Walter de Merton and Jacob of Oxford show.

The path along the outside of the city wall between Merton College and Merton Field, leading from St Aldates to the Botanic Garden, is called Deadman's Walk to this day; it is the route that Jewish funerals used to take. The Botanic Garden, founded in 1621 by the Earl of Danby and known as the Physic Garden until 1840, was formerly the Jewish Cemetery. The cemetery closed on 1 November 1290, when an edict of Edward I expelled all Jews from England. In the years leading up to that fateful day, Jews suffered increasing persecution, though thankfully in Oxford, unlike in many other towns and cities, there were no massacres.

However, on 17 May 1268, Ascension Day, the Oxford Jews were imprisoned for desecrating the processional cross. They were forced to pay for a marble and gold crucifix which was inscribed with their alleged misdeed and erected opposite the synagogue—which stood on the east side of Old Jewry near what is now the north corner tower of Christ Church.

Until their expulsion, Queen Eleanor had also been taxing the Jews to the brink of poverty, helping herself to their property by means of 'death duties'. Mystery still surrounds the question of where the prosperous medieval Jewish community had their *mikveh*, or ceremonial bath house. Some say that a remarkable spring-fed culvert unearthed at Magdalen College in 1987 may have been it, particularly as it was found across the road from the Botanic Garden on land that would have been part of the cemetery in the 12th and early 13th centuries; others maintain that the find is relevant to the Hospital of St John the Baptist which superseded the cemetery, or Jewish Garden, but preceded Magdalen College (founded in 1458).

Interestingly, baptism into Christianity was the way some former Jews obtained permission to stay in England, some remaining in Oxford to teach Hebrew at the university. Jews returned to England (and Oxford) when their banishment was lifted in the 17th century after negotiations between Oliver Cromwell and the Dutch rabbi Manasseh ben Israel. Many came from the Levant, where they had acquired a taste for coffee; and one, a gentleman known as Jacob the Jew, in 1650 set up England's first coffee house at the Angel Inn—which stood until 1866 on a site now partly occupied by the Examination Schools in the High Street.

The Mad Parliament of 1258

Famously, Charles II summoned Parliament to Oxford in 1681, and addressed both houses—Lords and Commons—in Convocation House at the Bodleian. Less well known is another Oxford Parliament, held in 1258, and sometimes known as the Mad Parliament, or the First English Parliament.

Here it was more a question of Parliament summoning the King, Henry III, to Oxford, than the other way round. For the King was forced to accept the Provisions of Oxford—a set of rules limiting Henry's power which some say amounted to nothing short of a written constitution.

The Parliament was presided over by a commoner, namely Sir Peter de Montfort (1215-65), who is now credited as being the forerunner of the modern-day Speaker of the House of Commons, though in his day he was known as the *parlour* or *prolocutor*. The fact that the name of his office changed to English from Norman French (*parler*, to speak) or Latin is significant too, because a major bone of contention between ruler and ruled was that too many foreigners were getting too many favours. The Provisions were the first Government documents since the Conquest to be produced in English (as well as French and Latin), probably as a protest against the rampant Frenchification of England and things English.

Specifically the Provisions demanded that the King keep to the Magna Carta agreement signed by King John at Runnymede in 1215, as well as demanding yet more. Henry was forced to hand over power to a caucus of 24 men, twelve selected by the King and twelve by the disgruntled earls and barons, headed by Peter de Montfort's more famous relative Simon, 6th Earl of Leicester. Each twelve of the 24 then elected two from the other twelve, and this committee of four in turn appointed a King's

Council of 15 to appoint senior officers of state. Parliament would also meet three times a year and summon commissioners from all over the realm to air their grievances.

One of the reasons why the King had been forced to eat humble pie was his foolish acceptance, on behalf of his son Edmund, of Pope Innocent IV's offer of the throne of Sicily. This involved paying out huge sums of money (which he did not possess) for troops—because the Sicilian throne was already occupied by the powerful Hohenstaufen kings.

Sadly, these tentative and enlightened steps towards something like democracy—far ahead of their time, worked out in Oxford, and strengthened the following year in Westminster—came to nothing because, firstly, the Pope absolved Henry of his oath to uphold the Provisions, and secondly, because when the matter was brought before Louis IX, acting as arbitrator at the Mise of Amiens, he also found in favour of the King and his Royal Prerogative. In the end the dispute erupted into war between Simon de Montfort and Henry—a war which Henry won. Both Simon and Peter de Montfort were killed at the Battle of Evesham of 1265 and the Provisions of Oxford were finally annulled by the Dictum of Kenilworth in 1266.

Some say that the Mad Parliament, so-called by Royalists, was remarkably sane compared to many; but the question remains, where was it held? If at St Frideswide's Priory, which stood where Christ Church stands now, it would indeed have set a precedent: Charles I summoned a Parliament at Christ Church in 1644, during the Civil War, and most peers and about a third of MPs turned up. Then again Charles II addressed Parliament there in 1665 when it was thought that the Plague had rendered Westminster too dangerous a place in which to meet. Only the 1681 Parliament was convened at the Bodleian.

Certainly Speaker Peter de Montfort's granddaughter Elizabeth Montagu was a great benefactor of St Frideswide. Indeed her tomb may still be seen in the Latin Chapel in Christ Church Cathedral.

The St Scholastica's Day Riot, 1355

Once upon a time a comparatively small town of about 5,000 inhabitants was the scene of riots that saw 90 people killed. That town was Oxford and the occasion was the famous fracas known as the St Scholastica's Day riot of 1355.

For many centuries, rioting—including bloodshed, looting and burning—was so frequent that it seems that violence was perpetually simmering away just beneath the surface of Oxford's schizophrenic Town and Gown personality. As early as 1209, for instance, two clerics of the university were hanged after a student had killed a woman, either intentionally or accidentally; and several of their colleagues—the begowned hoodies of their day—fled to Cambridge where another university may or may not have already been founded, in order to escape further revenge from townsmen.

In 1238, the papal legate was forced to flee to Wallingford from Osney, and his brother was killed in a riot there; and more trouble erupted in 1248, 1263 and 1272, with death on both sides. But the Crown usually sided with Gown after each outbreak of violence, and gradually the authority of the university's Chancellor became stronger and that of the town's mayor proportionately weaker.

In 1290, the Mayor complained to Edward I of the Chancellor's autocratic rule, but the king reaffirmed the university's right to try all crimes in which students or academics were involved, except murder and mayhem.

In 1335, scholars again felt that Oxford was too hot for them, and many again fled away, this time to Stamford in Lincolnshire. But Edward III ordered them back and gave them further rights and privileges in the town. Among the things left behind in Stamford was the door knocker of Brasenose College. It was not returned to Oxford until 1890, when the college bought the house in which it had hung for 550 years. Now the bronze knocker, with a grotesque face in its design, is kept safely in the great hall of the college. The knocker was important in the context of riots, since any suspected wrongdoer being chased during a 'hue and cry' could claim sanctuary by holding on to the knocker—the face of which acquired the brazen nose after which the college is now named.

On the Gown side, resentment bubbled away about rents and the perceived high prices that tradesmen charged for food and (in particular) drink. Huge amounts of wine were at that time brought from Bordeaux, then an English possession, and in addition there were dozens of breweries in Oxford. Drink sparked off the St Scholastica's Day riot that began on Tuesday, 10 February 1355, and continued for three days. Some students complained about the quality of the wine served at the Swindlestock Tavern, on the corner of Queen Street and St Aldates, and 'snappish words' passed between them and the innkeeper—which ended with the students throwing the wine at the innkeeper's head. In the scuffle that ensued, the townsmen rang the bell of the town church of St Martin's (at Carfax; now only the tower remains) to summon help, and the students rang the bell of the university church of St Mary to summon help on their side; and battle commenced. About 30 townsmen were killed and 63 gownsmen.

The mayor rode to Woodstock, where the king was residing, to seek his support, but to no avail. Indeed, the university's privileges were extended. It was given powers to regulate the drink trade. Most humiliating of all, though, the mayor and corporation were required to attend a mass at the university church every St Scholastica's Day thereafter, and to swear an oath to recognise the privileges of the university forever. They also had to pay the university 63 pence (5s 3d) each year, one penny for every scholar slain. The ritual continued until 1826, when the then mayor simply refused to comply.

But that was by no means the end of town and gown riots in Oxford, which continued even into the 20th century, particularly on Guy Fawkes Night. In Cuthbert Bede's 19th-century novel *The Adventures of Verdant Green*, students regarded St Scholastica's Day as a splendid opportunity for a punch-up.

John Wycliffe

Although students have always been notoriously anti-establishment, Oxford has not been a good place to try to exercise that prerogative.

For instance, just thinking that the communion bread and wine was not really the body and blood of Christ was enough to get you into serious trouble during the reign of Mary I, as poor Archbishop Cranmer found out — burned at the stake on a spot now marked with a cross in Broad Street, Oxford, 450 years ago. Whereas thinking the opposite (transsubstantiation) could get you into equally serious trouble during the reign of her sister, Elizabeth I. Nor was simply not going to church a choice. Turning up for communion was compulsory.

Interestingly, much of this business of seeing any deviation from the official line as being somehow subversive has its roots in Oxford. Back in the 14th century, a young student called John Wycliffe, working away at Merton College, decided that the Bible should be translated from Latin into English so that all could understand it, not just the ruling classes. He also contended that anything which was not in the Bible, but merely based on Papal rulings, was invalid.

Dynamite that, particularly as the Church had something to say on almost every aspect of life — its authority being all important to the established status quo. He endeared himself even less to the priestly hierarchy by suggesting that because Christ was poor, the Church should follow in his footsteps and give away all its riches! The point is that, in the absence of course of a Book of Common Prayer or an English Bible, the priests relied on mystery for their power: conducting services behind screens in Latin but letting it be known that the power of God was revealed to them and existed on Earth, plain as a pikestaff.

In the 1380s, Oxford became a hotbed of subversion, leading the fight against the greatest single source of authority in the Western world. Wycliffe was helped by Nicholas Hereford, of The Queen's College, and others to translate and distribute his Bible from 1384, which duly became a bestseller. Amazingly, 160 copies still survive. Needless to say, a synod in London condemned Wycliffe's efforts, complaining that 'the gospel is scattered abroad and trodden underfoot by swine'. Luckily, perhaps, Wycliffe died of a stroke when Latin was restored to the churches.

The Catholic Martyrs of 1589

Two hundred years after John Wycliffe's Bible, religious issues were still rife with the sometimes forgotten deaths of four Catholic martyrs, in 1589. Just recently, a couple of hundred people gathered in the drizzle near the junction of Cornmarket and Broad Street, to commemorate the martyrs. The group included Dorrien Belson, an inconspicuous figure in the crowd but a significant one for whom this was a poignant occasion. The small crowd was shuffling about near the site of the Catherine Wheel pub, where Thomas Belson and three others were arrested in 1589 (and where, coincidentally, some Gunpowder Plot conspirators held meetings some fifteen years later).

Mr Belson, aged 91, a descendant of Thomas's cousin, said: 'We've waited more than 420 years for this recognition and it's on its way at last.' They were a surprisingly cheery bunch, too, considering their mission—which was to process to 100 Holywell Street and watch Bishop Kelly unveil a plaque to the Catholic martyrs George Nichols and Richard Yaxley, both priests, Thomas Belson, a member of a prominent Oxfordshire recusant family, and serving man Humphrey Prichard, who were hanged, drawn and quartered near there that year.

After a short and sheeplike muddle, during which the flock tried to assemble itself correctly, with the bishop and his singers from Blackfriars 'leading' from behind in true Lord-is-my-Shepherd style, they were off, with some chanting responses as they went.

Almost immediately upon entering Broad Street a slightly surreal moment occurred as the Catholic friars and bishop, resplendent in their surplices, shuffled over the cross in the street surface which marks the spot where the Protestant martyrs—Cranmer,

Holywell Street, scene of martyrdom

Ridley and Latimer—had been burned some 30 years before the Catholic executions. Back then Broad Street would have been the city ditch, just outside the North Gate; and the horrible Boccardo Prison, in which the condemned were held, stood near to it, alongside the Church of St Michael at the North Gate—which, of course, still stands, probably Oxford's oldest building.

But some of the architecture in Holywell Street (in medieval times a street of pilgrimage along the way to the Holy Well at Binsey) may have been familiar to the Catholic martyrs. For example, I saw an undergraduate staring at the procession from New College, framed in a window with gargoyles and grotesques above it; her forbear in that room may well have been similarly framed as he (of course he) watched the martyrs shuffle by on their last journey on that dismal summer day of July 5, 1589.

The big difference, though, between the deaths of the Protestants (in the reign of the Catholic Mary I) and the Catholics (in the reign of her Church of England sister, Elizabeth) was that the former were condemned for heresy and the latter for treason. Elizabeth indeed was reasonably accommodating towards Catholics within the realm—until, that is, Pope Pius V issued his Bull Regnans in Excelsis excommunicating Elizabeth and urging all good Catholics to overthrow her.

It all amounted to something similar to a fatwa, after which the Crown felt itself forced to treat Catholics as enemies of the state. Oxford, and indeed Oxfordshire, unlike Cambridge, was a particularly strong Catholic centre, the strongest indeed in the country, according to the then Archbishop of Canterbury, Edmund Grindal. As for the modern Catholic Bishop William Kenny on the day he guided his flock to the new plaque, on 25 October: he simply urged all to remember the glorious triumph of the martyrs and to 'remember their example of what it means to be a Christian'.

Anthony Wood, Historian

Grumpiness in Oxford through the ages has usually stemmed from people wanting to change things. The historian Anthony Wood (1632-95), the grumpiest of grumpy old men, saw more than his fair share of change. Born in a house opposite Merton College, he saw as a boy the siege of Oxford and the arrival of the court of Charles I and Henrietta Maria; then the installation of Puritans as masters of colleges and the chancellorship of the University of Oliver Cromwell; then the restoration of the King.

Anthony Wood—or Anthony à Wood as he liked to style himself, presumably in order to sound grander—was the archetypal crotchety old scholar. He went to war, not without provocation, with the translator into Latin of his famous magnum opus, *History and Antiquities of the University of Oxford*: one Dick Peers. At first Mr Peers came off worse in these unfortunate encounters, receiving a bloody nose and experiencing the thrill of having his ears boxed in various pubs and at the Oxford University printing house, then occupying, incongruously, the upper part of the Sheldonian Theatre.

A contemporary of Wood, Humphrey Prideaux, wrote: 'They had a skirmish at Sol Hardeing [keeper of a tavern in All Saints parish], another at the printing house, and several other places.' He added: 'As Peers always cometh off with a bloody nose or a black eye, he was for a long time afraid to goe anywhere where he might chance to meet his too powerful adversary, for fear of another drubbing.'

Then the tide of battle turned in favour of Mr Peers. He was made a university pro-proctor. Mr Prideaux wrote: 'Now Wood is as much afraid to meet him, least he should exercise his authority upon him. And although he had been a good bowzeing blad [boozer], yet it hath been observed that never since his adversary hath been in office hath he dared to be out after nine, least he should meet him and exact the rigor of the statute upon him.'

The statute required all scholars to be in their rooms before Great Tom, the bell housed in the tower of Christ Church, stopped peeling out its nightly curfew. And the cause of all this belligerence? The pusillanimous Mr Peers was taking orders from the autocratic Dean of Christ Church, Dr Fell, instead of from Wood: the whole business was a sub-plot of a much larger academic dispute between Dr Fell and no less a person then the 'Philosopher of Malmesbury' himself, Thomas Hobbes.

Poor Mr Wood had eyes to see the greatness of Hobbes, but the mighty Dr Fell considered him a pipsqueak; he therefore calmly altered all that Mr Wood had written about Hobbes. Obviously, Dr Fell thought that ordinary disciplines that applied to other mortals did not affect him! The dispute even reached royal ears when the old man Hobbes met King Charles II in Pall Mall and begged leave to defend himself. He attacked Dr Fell with cold reason, eliciting the famous (in some circles at any rate) riposte referring to him as the 'Malmesbury animal'.

In old age we read of Anthony Wood rising at 4 o'clock every morning to write his waspish accounts of other academics' lives. He died in 1695 and was buried in Merton College Chapel, where a plaque was later placed in his memory.

John Aubrey, Biographer

What an adorable old dilettante was John Aubrey (1626-97); and how wonderful that he has managed to achieve lasting fame despite having only published one short (bad) book in his whole lifetime.

He was what you might call a successful failure: born into a prosperous Wiltshire family with every advantage, as a boy he led a peaceful but lonely sort of life, poking around hill forts and suchlike. This was the end of one of England's longest periods of peace it had ever known, for he had the bad luck to come up to Trinity College, Oxford, as a gentleman commoner in the very year that the world as he knew it convulsed itself into Civil War.

The Puritans then busily destroyed not only the ideas and precepts with which he had grown up, but also, physically, many of the 'antiquities' (churches, wall paintings, statues: what I suppose we might nowadays call 'Heritage') that were the very things that most interested him as an antiquarian. He wrote, 'the first brush occurred between the Earl of Northampton and Lord Brooke, near Banbury, which was the latter end of July 1642. But now Bellona thundered, and as a clear sky is sometimes suddenly overstretched with a dismal cloud and thunder, so was this serene peace by the civil wars through the factions of those times.'

Typically, on arrival at Oxford aged 18, one of his first acts was to explore the ruins of Osney Abbey which, until the dissolution a century before, had been one of the largest monasteries in Europe. He wrote of it later: 'I got Mr Hesketh, Mr Dobson's man, to draw the ruins of Osney two or three ways before it was pulled down. Now the very foundation is digged up [*sic*].' Part of that destruction was caused by the Royalists using the place as a powder storehouse which, sadly, blew up, killing one man in 1643; but trust Mr Aubrey to get someone else to do the drawing, even though he was a very competent artist himself. The fact is that, despite being an original thinker, genius even, he was lazy and disorganised.

Thanks to the war he had to leave Oxford after only a few months, called back by his father to his ancestral home at Easton Piers, Wiltshire, for safety's sake. But he was back in 1643. He wrote: 'with much ado I got my father to let me to beloved Oxon again, then a garrison *pro Rege*', i.e. a very different place than the one he had left. According to historian Anthony Wood, indeed, the courtiers were 'very nasty and beastly, leaving at their departure their excrements in every corner, in chimneys, studies, coal-houses, cellars. Rude, rough, whoremongers; vain, empty, careless.'

As the war drew to its close, Mr Aubrey went home again in order to look after his father in his final illness. When he eventually took over the family estates he earnestly asked himself what on earth to do with his life. He answered: 'truly nothing: only Umbrages' [*sic*]. But all the same, he 'began to enter into pocket books, philosophical antiquarian remarks'—which was all very well but cost money rather than earned it. In time, therefore, he discovered that he had mismanaged his property to such an extent that he had lost it all.

Thenceforth he existed as a sort of long-term guest in various houses belonging to well-heeled friends (including Lord Abingdon at Boarstall); and in these houses he used to get up early, as often as not with a hangover, and write up prose portraits of contemporaries and near-contemporaries, thereby sowing the seeds of what eventually metamorphosed into his famous *Brief Lives*. The breakthrough in his life (if there ever was such a thing) came when he offered his services as a biographer to Anthony Wood, then writing his *Athenae Oxoniensis*, commissioned by Oxford University to record all the writers and bishops educated there 1500-1690, a project that gave Aubrey's *Brief Lives* purpose and focus.

Pity he didn't have a computer though, for his approach to work was simultaneously scatter-brained and scientific. At Oxford he was a member of the Experimental Philosophy Club, which later developed into the Royal Society (of which he became a fellow); but his notes—ultimately given to Elias Ashmole for his new museum—were totally chaotic. The element of finishing anything was alien to his nature and only a work called *Miscellanies*—all about supernatural phenomena—was published during his life.

Aubrey died suddenly while passing through his beloved Oxford, and is buried in the churchyard of St Mary Magdalene. Various editions of *Brief Lives*, based on the 426 biographies now in the Bodleian, have appeared since his death, with more still in the pipeline.

Royalists and Parliamentarians

Both sides in the run-up to the English Civil War labelled William Lenthall a time-server, but history has been kinder to him. He was born in a beautiful half-timbered merchant's house in Hart Street, Henley-on-Thames (which still stands), and died in Burford, where he was buried in an unostentatious grave, now lost. In between he played a leading role in one of the great set-pieces in the making of the English constitution as we know it.

As Speaker of the House of Commons and MP for Woodstock during the Long Parliament, he famously told King Charles I on 4 January 1642: 'I have neither eyes to

see nor tongue to speak in this place but as the House is pleased to direct me, whose servant I am here; and humbly beg your Majesty's pardon that I cannot give any other answer than this to what your Majesty is pleased to demand of me.'

The King and a posse of retainers had of course barged into the House to arrest five members whom His Majesty reckoned were showing too independent a spirit in denying him money; posing, indeed, a challenge to his doctrine of the Divine Right of Kings. The five included John Hampden, who lived across the border in Buckinghamshire but was educated at Thame Grammar School. The others were John Pym, David Holles, Sir Arthur Haselrig and William Strode.

'I see the birds have flown,' declared the King. Ever since, at the opening of Parliament, a Royal official named Black Rod has suffered the indignity of having the door slammed in his face whenever he arrives at the Commons to call members to the Lords to hear the speech from the throne. The gesture is designed as a perpetual reminder of the Commons' independence from the crown.

But what sort of a man was William Lenthall? A moderate Parliamentarian who nevertheless conducted affairs from the Speaker's chair with a bias towards the King, might sum up his career. He found the expenses of his job burdensome and was exhausted by the sheer weight of work in keeping order in the long and unruly parliamentary sittings. As a reward for defying the King in person he was given a huge grant (£6,000) and bought Burford Priory from that other romantic Oxfordshire 17th-century luminary, Lucius Cary, Viscount Falkland.

It is ironic, perhaps, that he is buried in Burford churchyard where some Leveller soldiers were executed. The Levellers objected to Parliamentarians such as Lenthall living in comfort while the army fought. He was not imprisoned when Charles II was restored to the throne but was evidently ashamed of himself for denouncing the regicide Thomas Scot for words spoken in Parliament. His tombstone epitaph (now lost) read simply: 'I am a worm.'

Abolitionists and Quakers

A full 18 years before the eventual Abolition of the Slave Trade Act was passed in 1807, the MP for Oxford University, William Dolben, managed to push through a parliamentary bill that at least attempted to tackle overcrowding in the ghastly slave ships.

Part of the problem for Abolitionists was that, without means of recording the evidence, most of the British population either did not know about or found it easy to ignore the cruelty. But Mr Dolben had been aboard a slave ship, called the *Brookes*, and seen the conditions for himself. He described the 'crying evil of the middle passage' and slaves 'packed as closely as books upon a shelf' at the mercy of drunken crews. The middle passage, of course, was the leg of a slavers' journey from Africa to North America, taken by more than 3 million slaves transported on British ships during the second half of the 18th century alone, when Britain was by far the largest slaving nation. The first leg was the journey from Britain to Africa when the cargo would be manufactured goods with which to pay for the slaves, and the third would be raw materials brought back from North America, such as cotton.

The Dolben Act of 1789 attempted to limit the number of slaves on a ship in relation to its overall size. Of course it was flouted and, as Abolitionist Thomas Clarkson was able to show, even if the act had been obeyed, conditions on board would have been appalling. But the fact that the Dolben Act was passed at all shows that some years before the 1807 act people in high places were concerned about the trade. As another instance, on 3 February 1788 a fellow of Magdalen called William Agutter preached a sermon at St Martin's Church before the Corporation of the City of Oxford, opposing the slave trade.

Oxford is indeed an excellent place to study the slave trade: Rhodes House bought the papers of the Anti-Slavery Society during the 1950s and the Bodleian Library houses the Wilberforce papers. William Wilberforce, who became an MP at the age of 21, embarked on his life's work of abolishing the trade as a result of effective lobbying by Quakers. He, together with Granville Sharp, Thomas Clarkson and nine Quakers, formed the Committee for Effecting the Abolition of the Slave Trade in 1787. He must have known Oxford since his maternal grandfather, Thomas Bird, lived in Barton. His son, Samuel Wilberforce, became Bishop of Oxford. His book about his father and the slave trade became the standard text on the subject, though it should be said that there are some scholars who still maintain that poor old Clarkson was not given a fair share of praise.

Quakers, some of whom came from America to join the committee, were themselves forbidden from becoming MPs as they were non-conformists. What they needed was a powerful, popular MP such as Wilberforce to act for them. Quakers were active in Oxford already in the 17th century, even though they were persecuted. Famously, the founder of Pennsylvania, William Penn, was thrown out of Christ Church for non-conformity in 1662. He was a friend of the first Quaker, George Fox, who, like him, was uneasy about slavery. Originally, the Quakers only advocated the humane treatment of slaves. Only slowly did they emerge as out and out Abolitionists.

The Rise and Fall of Duelling

Few undergraduate careers at Oxford University can have been shorter than that of the fiery future translator of *The Arabian Nights* and *The Karma Sutra*, Sir Richard Burton. He came up to Oxford, aged 19, in 1840 and was sent down the same year for challenging a fellow student at Trinity to a duel for insulting the budding military moustache he was assiduously cultivating. Had the duel taken place it would have been among the last in Britain, an event that indeed took place at Englefield, Buckinghamshire, 12 years later when two Frenchmen named Bartholmy and Cournet fought to the death. The victor, Bartholmy, was eventually tried and hanged, a process which showed that the law was finally determined to stamp out the practice. Earlier, though illegal, it was the height of dishonour to ignore a challenge and army officers could be thrown out of the force for the offence.

Duelling became popular in Britain with the restoration of Charles II, who brought many habits from France, where duelling was already more prevalent. Duelling then grew in popularity after the accession of the Hanoverian kings. Indeed, George II is said to have challenged the King of Prussia to a duel. By the turn of the 18th century, the practice was rampant, with the Duke of Wellington himself fighting a notorious duel.

The ostensible cause of a political duel between James, Duke of Hamilton, and Charles Lord Mohun, fought in November 1712, had its roots in Oxfordshire. Then (as now, as it happens) a tedious and expensive lawsuit surrounded the estates of the Earl of Macclesfield of Shirburn Castle near Watlington. Both protagonists were married to nieces of the first earl and were claiming his property. In fact, the duel was probably arranged as a Whig way of getting rid of the Tory duke who was suspected of favouring the Pretender to the British throne. In the event, both fighters managed to stab each other through the body at the same time, though Mohun's second was later accused of stabbing the duke again. That duel became a popular cause and led to riots in Hyde Park with crowds shouting 'No Hanover' and 'No foreign king'.

But most duels, certainly by the 19th century, had less provocative causes. One was even fought over *Don Giovanni*—not Mozart's version—between two characters who argued over the production. No death occurred: only a shattered collar bone restored honour.

Suffragettes and Pacifists

Civilisation came to an end in 1914, or so I remember elderly school teachers, both male and female, wryly remarking to each other as they surveyed the post-war world they had inherited in the 1950s. They had lived through two world wars and were perhaps the unluckiest of generations.

The Great War changed the entire social order, not least for women and not least in Oxford and Oxfordshire. Emily Davison (1872-1913), for example, the Suffragette who died by throwing herself in front of the King's horse at the Epsom Derby in June 1913, had earned a first-class English degree from St Hugh's College, Oxford, but was never awarded it. Not until after the war—in 1920—did Oxford University finally agree to award degrees to women.

Ms Davison had earned the fees to put herself through Oxford by working as a teacher. She was a militant member of the Women's Social and Political Union (WSPU) led by mother and daughter team Emmeline and Christobel Pankhurst. On the night of 2 April 1911, in order to claim the House of Commons as her address on the census of that year, she hid herself in a cupboard in the Palace of Westminster.

Not until 1918 did women over 30 get the vote, and not until 1928 did they get it on the same terms as men. Not until 1919 did the American Christian Scientist Nancy Astor become the first woman to take her seat as an MP. Famously, she is reputed to have told Winston Churchill at Blenheim: 'If you were my husband I would poison you.' He replied: 'If you were my wife I would take it.'

The 1914 declaration of war led immediately to a sort of armistice in the conflict between the Suffragist movement and the government. The Pankhursts suspended their civil disturbances and in return the government freed all Suffragette prisoners. 'This was national militancy. As Suffragettes we could not be pacifists at any price,' wrote Christobel (1880-1958).

Plenty of women felt that Pacificism was perfectly compatible with Suffragism. Virginia Woolf, for one, detached herself from the war. She recorded seeing 'the faces of our rulers in the light of the shellfire. So ugly they looked—German, English, French—so stupid.' She was a frequent visitor to Garsington Manor, the home from 1915 to 1927 of Lady Ottoline Morrell and her husband Philip.

Lady Ottoline (1873-1928), half-sister of the Duke of Portland, was an ardent pacifist feminist. In 1915 she was one of 156 women anxious to travel to The Hague to attend a peace conference organised by the Women's International Congress in order to raise a voice 'above the present hatred and bloodshed' and 'to demand that international disputes shall in future be settled by some other means than war'. In the

event, only three British women attended
the conference—attended by women from
Germany and Austria—and Lady Ottoline
was not one of them. This was because
Winston Churchill, then at the Admiralty,
had 'closed' the North Sea to British
shipping in order to prevent the women,
called by some 'unpatriots', from going to
the unpopular conference. According to
Frances Stonor Saunders' excellent book
The Woman Who Shot Mussolini (Faber and
Faber, 2010), Lady Ottoline comforted
herself with a trip to the spa in Buxton
instead!

Lady Ottoline Morrell

But Garsington became a hotbed of
pacifism all the same, playing host to such
literary conscientious objectors as D. H.
Lawrence and Aldous Huxley (as well as
war poet Siegfried Sassoon on leave in
1916). And when the quantity of 'conscies'
became too great for the manor, they
overflowed into the bailiff's house opposite. Amazingly, it seems that they were tolerated
with benign amusement by locals despite the foundation in 1914 of the Order of the
White Feather—which encouraged women to follow the official line and urge their men
to don khaki.

Oxford 1939-45

Why were Oxford and Oxfordshire bombed so little in the Second World War? Rumour
had it that a squadron of Heinkel III bombers on their way to obliterate the Morris
Radiators factory in Woodstock Road, Oxford, and probably the Cowley works, too,
was on 30 August 1940 itself attacked and turned back over Surrey.

But despite the presence of such obvious targets, Air Raid Precautions throughout
the county were in much the same state as those reported in Benson. Namely, in
'constant preparation against air attack, which mercifully never came'. Dr Malcolm
Graham, Head of Oxfordshire Studies at Westgate Library, in his invaluable book

Oxfordshire At War, remarks: 'No further raids seem to have been launched against these important targets and the city's escape from 'Baedecker' raids has never been satisfactorily explained...'

Received wisdom among Oxfordshire people in the years following the war was that Hitler had in mind turning Blenheim Palace into the HQ of a Nazi Government in Britain. Mr Graham goes on: 'More plausibly perhaps, Oxford was spared because it would have been a vital centre of communication in the event of an invasion.' In any case, early in the war Blenheim became home to boys evacuated from the public school Malvern College, Worcestershire whose buildings were occupied by the Admiralty from October 1939 until July 1940. They learned their lessons in staterooms still bedecked with tapestries — one of which, of course, commemorates the Battle of Blenheim, fought in 1704 in Bavaria, Germany. After the school moved back to its own premises following the construction of air-raid shelters at the Admiralty, Blenheim, like Cornbury Park, Charlbury, was taken over by the War Office.

The county was early in 1939 designated a reception area for evacuees from London, most of whom were children or mothers with babies or toddlers. Already by the autumn of 1939 Oxfordshire County Council Education Department had 58 per cent more children on its books than it had had in July. In addition to the 'official' evacuees billeted in Oxford and Oxfordshire homes, there were tens of thousands of unofficial evacuees: people who simply left London to stay, perhaps with relatives, in the comparative safety of Oxfordshire. Then the population of Oxford itself was further swollen by staff from London hospitals and government departments moving into colleges.

Sir William Beveridge with some of the evacuees who were housed in University College for a time during the war

London University medical students took over Keble, Wadham and St Peter's Hall. Balliol became host to the Royal Institute of International Affairs and St John's to the Director of Fish Supplies (causing Oxford to be dubbed the centre of the fishing industry). The largely masculine atmosphere of the colleges was suddenly transformed by a feminine invasion of women clerks. As for Oxford University, it seems to be capable of withstanding temporary emergencies. It emerged more or less unscathed from the Civil War in the 17th century and it did much the same in the 20th century.

But for an account of the life of a wartime student, Philip Larkin's first novel, *Jill*, is the book to turn to. He wrote in the introduction to the original Faber and Faber edition: 'This was not the Oxford of Michael Fane and his fine bindings, or Charles Ryder and his plovers' eggs. Nevertheless, it had a distinctive quality.' (Michael Fane was the hero of *Sinister Street* by Compton Mackenzie, and Charles Ryder, of course, was the hero of Evelyn Waugh's *Brideshead Revisited*.)

As for the evacuees, there were of course good and bad host families. But spare a thought for the six-year-old boy from Poplar in London's East End who was killed in bed when a dummy bomb fell from an RAF plane and crashed through the roof of a house in Stanway Road, Oxford.

The Floods of 1947

Who might he have been, that half-smart gent I remember from the floods of 2007 in Botley Road? A solicitor, an estate agent, a banker? He was wading along through the water in shirt, tie and the top half of a smart suit; his bottom half was covered by a pair of boxer shorts. He was carrying his trousers, shoes and socks. He also wore a smile on his face in keeping with the spirit of bonhomie that reigned in West Oxford during that memorable inundation.

Had he been clad like that in the great flood of 1947, the smile would have been absent. For the great difference between that flood and the one that followed 60 years on was that the former arrived in March, in a near-freezing city still suffering from wartime rationing and at the tail end of a particularly snowy winter. Wading about with bare legs would have been unthinkable. In the winter of 1946-7 buses and even whole houses in Oxfordshire disappeared in snow drifts. In Oxford itself there were milk and bread shortages. Then, just as people thought the worst was over, came the thaw. Then the rain. Then more rain, then more. One writer described the county as resembling 'one large lake' after both the Thames and the Cherwell rivers burst their banks.

Rosamund Road, Wolvercote, 1947

By 15 March 1947 Wytham was completely cut off and in Wolvercote 200 homes were flooded. Among the worst affected Oxford areas were Hinksey, St Ebbes and Osney. With the ice and snow up river melting and the rain still falling, water left many Oxford houses awash. One family was sitting round their fireplace when water rushed in through the door, swirled round the furniture and put the fire out. More than 3,000 households were affected in the city of Oxford alone. Lord Mayor E. A. Smewin opened a special flood relief fund for the needy.

In many cases, there was little time to take furniture upstairs, so the pieces floated about. In one house, hens took up residence in a bathroom. The owner said they didn't seem to mind too much as they laid double yolkers! A power station in Lower Cherwell Street, Banbury, was swamped, causing the town to lose electricity. When the Cherwell and the canal merged to form one large watercourse, the mainline railway was left under 2ft of water. In Chipping Norton, gas was cut off when the gas works flooded. In Burford the church floor was flooded with 11 inches of water. Still worse followed. Hurricane force winds hurtled across Oxfordshire, bringing down trees and power cables.

In 1947 there were still people around who could remember the other big flood— November 1894. In that year one man paddled down Great Clarendon Street in a bath tub, and water poured in torrents into houses in Grandpont, Hinksey, Osney and Jericho. Abingdon was described as Venice without the gondolas. The other great flood was in 1774 when the old Henley Bridge, dating back to 1234, was swept away.

Leafing through *The Oxford Times* cuttings it seems that there have been floods every few years in the city, with levels of water that used to occur once every 20 years now appearing once every five years. Let's just hope the next flood does not strike in winter!

Alice and Adenauer

It was just seven years after the end of the Second World War and anti-German feeling was still, apparently, running high in Oxford, not least among some sections of the university. In December 1952 that astonishing and wonderful old man Konrad Adenauer (1876-1967), then aged 76 and the chancellor of West Germany, made his first state visit abroad—to Great Britain. He met Winston Churchill, recently re-installed in Downing Street, and the dying King George VI in Buckingham Palace.

Then he took a trip to Oxford, where he visited Balliol—at which college his nephew Hans had been an undergraduate—and New College. He was also scheduled to visit Oriel, but here unpleasantness set in: a group of students at the gates became so abusive that the police directed the official cars through Canterbury Gate and into Christ Church instead, where, of course, there was no official welcome for him. An undergraduate showed him Gladstone's rooms and pointed out the statue of Dean Liddell, the father of the real-life Alice in Wonderland. The student began to explain that the Deanery Garden was at the centre of an important English children's book when Adenauer suddenly stopped and smiled, quite unruffled by the demonstration he had witnessed, and astonished everyone present, British and German alike, by reeling off long quotations from the book. The undergraduate wrote later: 'Dr Adenauer stopped, turned and, putting his hand on my shoulder and with a twinkle of triumph and delight in his eye, started quoting to me from *Alice's Adventures in Wonderland* in German.'

I learned all this from *Adenauer: The Father of the New Germany* by Charles Williams (Little, Brown and Co., 2000) upon which I have at last embarked after living with it, unopened on my shelf, for ten years or so. At 538 pages, excluding Notes and Index, I found reading it is quite an undertaking too—and so, by way of light relief and by complete coincidence, I was last week also reading *The Alice Behind Wonderland,* by Simon Winchester, from OUP.

Several times a year it seems that someone somewhere writes a book about Alice (there was that recent film, too), but Winchester's book makes more than most of the 'affair' that Alice is said to have had with Prince Leopold, fourth son of Queen Victoria, who was a popular undergraduate at Christ Church and went on to become the Duke of Albany in 1881. Interestingly I learned that Alice called her second son Leopold (and the prince was his godfather), and Leopold called his daughter Alice.

Perhaps, as well as being able to quote chunks from *Wonderland,* Adenauer would have known something about Leopold's successors, though their history is not in Winchester's book. Prince Leopold's son, aged 16, went off to become ruler of Saxe Coburg Gotha and subsequently fought on the German side in the First World War.

He was deprived of his British dukedom under the Titles Deprivation Act of 1919; and Leopold's grandson also fought for Germany in the Second World War.

Certainly Adenauer, who had just re-established Germany as a sovereign state and set it on its way to becoming the economic powerhouse of Europe, would have known about the history of the handwritten manuscript copy of *Alice's Adventures Underground* (as the book was originally called). The author Charles Dodgson (Lewis Carroll) gave it to Alice. She eventually sold it at Sotheby's in the 1920s for £15,400 to help pay taxes following her husband's death. It went to the USA, but after the Second World War it was brought back to England and presented to the Archbishop of Canterbury 'as an expression of thanks to a noble people who held Hitler at bay for a long period single-handed'. Now it is on display at the British Museum.

Oxfam

My first Christmas card landed on the doormat on Armistice Day. The excuse for its ridiculously early arrival was an invitation scrawled inside it to a Christmas party. But it was an Oxfam card and it set me thinking about those thoughtful and intelligent people of Oxford who, during the war, exercised their minds to help civilian victims of war regardless of which side they were on.

Somehow it is hard to imagine Oxfam starting up anywhere other than in Oxford—though I suppose it could have been called Camfam had it started in Cambridge—but in fact it began life in 1942 as the Oxford Committee for Famine Relief, one of a

The original Oxfam shop, Broad Street

number of such committees set up to fight poverty and hunger among civilians in war-torn Europe, particularly children in Greece. The original Committee was formed at a meeting of a group of Quakers, academics and other social activists on 5 October which was held in the Old Library at the university church of St Mary the Virgin under the chairmanship of Canon Theodore Richard Milford. Its original purpose was to persuade the British government to allow food through the Allied Forces' blockade for distribution by the Red Cross.

After the war many of the other UK committees wound down their activities, but the Oxford Group continued to relieve poverty and starvation in various parts of Europe, notably in Germany. That the Oxford committee continued to exist is thanks largely to the activities of its remarkable first honorary secretary, Cecil Jackson-Cole (born 1901)—who is surely not now nearly as famous as he should be. He remained honorary secretary until he died in 1979, and his concern was to link the worlds of business and charity, bringing the management skills of the former to bear on the latter.

He was the founder of the Oxford estate agency Andrews—which is still today owned by charitable trusts set up by him. And charities which he founded through his Voluntary and Christian Service Trust (VCS) include Help the Aged (1961); the Anchor Housing Trust (1968); and Action Aid.

Jackson-Cole, or CJC as he was universally known, decided in 1948 that there was an ongoing need for a famine relief organisation—in peacetime as well as wartime—and he persuaded the rest of the committee to support him. The organisation then started collecting and distributing clothes, and widened its scope beyond Europe. After the birth of Israel that year, for instance, it helped relieve hardship among Palestinians. Also in 1948 the first charity shop was opened at 17 Broad Street—where it still thrives, which also served in the early years as the administrative headquarters.

The Committee did not change the name to Oxfam (presumably one of the first uses of this clumsy but catchy technique of abbreviating and then joining together two words) until 1958, when it was registered as a charitable company limited by guarantee. As the charity grew under its new name, its offices began to spread somewhat haphazardly into buildings throughout the city centre, until the organisation moved into a single block in Summertown in 1962. There it remained until 2005, when it moved to its present headquarters off the Eastern By-pass.

Now, as a result of that first seed planted in Broad Street, Oxfam has about 750 shops in the UK and has become the nation's biggest High Street retailer of secondhand books. It has £300 million in turnover and employs nearly 6,000 people worldwide. Speaking on a purely personal level, I wonder why anyone ever buys new clothes, even for wearing at that Christmas party, when you can buy such high quality at Oxfam.

3. The Changing City
Everyday Life Through the Centuries

Unlike other English towns of a similar size, Oxford's social history has long been governed by its schizophrenic personality: with half of it feeling it owes allegiance to Gown; and the other half to Town.

Sometimes this split has resulted in total breakdown—notably during the St Scholastica's Day riots of February 1355 (see Chapter 2), which resulted in over 90 dead in a city of about 5,000 inhabitants. But for centuries the schizophrenia manifested itself simply as a simmering inferiority complex on the Town's part, and a superiority one on the Gown's. As well it might, since the Crown nearly always took the Gown's part in any showdown. For instance, as a result of the St Scholastica's Day riot, King Edward III ordered the Mayor and Corporation to shuffle in procession to the University Church of St Mary on February 10 (the anniversary) every year ever after, and pay the vice-chancellor 63 pence (5s 3d, one penny for every man killed on the Gown's side, but nothing for the 30 killed on the Town side).

Curiously, this unusual state of affairs sometimes resulted in Oxford as a whole doing rather well. For instance, Dr John Radcliffe, physician to King William III, left money to the university—and that money eventually benefited the city as well, as the trustees of his will in 1758 donated £4,000 towards building a hospital, namely the Radcliffe Infirmary.

The city's infrastructure developed more slowly in Oxford than elsewhere, partly because the university looked askance at the very idea of railways arriving here at all. For years Gownsmen seem to have wanted to hold back progress while Townsmen were always keen on modernisation.

Certainly townspeople were unusually vociferous about local affairs. For instance they came close to rioting over the introduction of motorised buses in the early 20th century—though I suspect that there they objected to the way many university people wanted to keep the old horse-drawn trams on purely sentimental grounds, seeing them as quaint.

Interesting, though, that the man largely responsible for introducing those buses, William Morris, later Viscount Nuffield, went on to establish the motor industry here—and he became Oxford's greatest benefactor ever with both Town and Gown benefitting from his largesse.

In 1992 Oxford found itself host to two universities, when the former polytechnic acquired that status. Nevertheless relations between Town and Gown have probably never been more harmonious than now—even if some of the age-old squabbles refuse to go away; for instance, the one about Townsmen allegedly charging too much rent, or refusing to repay deposits. Some things never change.

Poor Relief

Ambivalent attitudes towards immigration are nothing new. Nor apparently is the instinct (perhaps unworthy) of those already settled in a place to try to maintain the status quo.

In 1582, for instance, when the growing number of people seeking poor relief was beginning to cost the better-off an uncomfortable amount of money in rates, councillors in Oxford ordered all people who had come and settled in the city during the previous three years to leave, unless they could prove that they were able to support themselves.

In Banbury, some 50 years later, the parish vestry threatened to withhold relief from anyone who refused to wear a special pauper's badge. By the end of the 17th century mobs of hungry people gathered in Banbury, Chipping Norton and Charlbury demanding cheaper bread. In Oxford women pelted millers and bakers with stones. Historian Anthony Wood, hardly noted for his social conscience, wrote in 1694 that some people starved to death in Oxford.

Things were no better from a poor person's point of view during the next century either. In Deddington in 1797 a scruffy crowd of hungry people boarded a canal boat laden with flour and only let the miller have it back when he agreed not to send it out of the county to the industrial Midlands, where it would fetch a higher price. Instead they insisted that he sell it to them at a very much reduced rate.

By the beginning of the 19th century 20 people out of every 100 were seeking assistance. The Napoleonic Wars and the gathering momentum of the Industrial Revolution only seemed to make matters worse in both the city of Oxford and its surrounding county. The old Poor Laws were totally inadequate and inappropriate for dealing with a problem caused by increasing population, enclosures of land and continually rising prices. Particularly vexing for anyone at the bottom of the social ladder — at any rate in the early 19th century — was the fact that their plight seemed to have nothing to do with the economic state of the county as a whole.

When traveller Arthur Young visited Witney in 1768, he remarked that the town 'was threatened with the utter loss of every means of giving bread to its numerous poor'. When he revisited the famous blanket-making town in 1809 he found that the wool business was once again in fine fettle but that the poor were not benefiting from the boom. He wrote: 'The masters and fabrics may flourish but it cannot be said that the labouring hands do the same.' The number of people employed in the mills had fallen from 500 to 140.

The so-called Poor Laws, which in 1601 placed the responsibility for the poor on parish vestries, meant that the parish where someone was born could usually be held responsible for his or her maintenance. Laws of Settlement introduced later required that anyone coming to live or work in a new parish should have a certificate stating where he was legally 'settled' — usually place of birth but sometimes the place of apprenticeship, or a place of residence for a certain amount of time.

It was thanks to these laws that the sad place of Stonelands, otherwise known as Sworn Lanes or Leys, or even Foresworn Lains (possibly meaning forsworn layings-in) thrived outside Burford for several centuries. It was a disreputable ale house in six acres of land which, due to a quirk of history, was not listed as the responsibility of any parish, or for that matter any county. The net result was that unmarried women swarmed here to give birth, since their offspring would then have no parish of birth to which overseers of the Poor Laws could send them back.

But there was some hope for those down on their luck. Way back in the 15th century the well-to-do were already helping the poor in Oxfordshire on a charitable basis. William and Alice de la Pole founded almshouses in Ewelme in 1437 and ten years later Richard Quatermaine also founded some in Thame. In the 17th century John Holloway, a Witney clothier, founded almshouses for six poor blanket-weavers' widows. In 1640 Henry Cornish founded some for eight poor people.

Effective reform came in 1834, when the county was divided into eight Poor Law Unions with workhouses in Banbury, Witney, Chipping Norton, Thame, Henley, Woodstock, Headington and Bicester. Great play was made by the better-off between the deserving and undeserving poor. But the workhouses lasted nearly a hundred years, until the last were closed in 1929.

Public Health

For much of the past thousand years or so, Oxford's public health and welfare policy has consisted largely of the better off—particularly members of the university—making themselves scarce in times of pestilence and, whenever possible, shifting the poor and infirm into someone else's parish.

Until 1771, the city was composed of 11 parishes, each with its own Board of Guardians and workhouse. Parishioners 'belonged' to their parish, and were expected to show loyalty to it, in a way that is difficult to comprehend now; and paupers were 'thrown on' their parish for their maintenance.

There was already a hospital for lepers in Cowley—St Bartholomew's—in the 12th century. It was founded by Henry I in 1126-8 and had 12 brethren working under one chaplain, who also officiated at the nearby chapel. In 1327, Edward III gave St Bartholomew's to Oriel College as a rural retreat for scholars so that they might 'use the wholesome air in times of pestilential sickness'. In 1536 it became an almshouse, and in 1770 (more than 100 years after it suffered severe damage in the Civil War) it was incorporated into Oxford City Charities.

The Radcliffe Infirmary opened in 1770, and the Oxford Medical Dispensary and Lying-in Charity a few years later, but they were for paying patients, or people who had managed to obtain vouchers from subscribers to the charities.

Most early histories of Oxford deal with frequent epidemics of smallpox, plague, typhus and other infectious diseases—during many of which the university would close and the fellows would flee into the surrounding countryside. But in 1771 the United Board of Guardians was set up and immediately built a workhouse (House of Industry) in what is now Wellington Square but was then called Rats and Mice Hill after a heap of rubbish there, mentioned by 17th-century historian Anthony Wood, and much infested by such creatures.

The two-storey stone workhouse was originally home for 200 paupers, but in 1790 a nursery and a ward for elderly and infirm people were added. By 1861, or 100 years after its foundation, the workhouse was overflowing and a new one was built by order of the Oxford Poor Law Board for 330 paupers in Cowley Road. It opened in 1865 and became known as the Cowley Road Hospital. It was built on an 11-acre site bought from Magdalen and Pembroke Colleges and comprised three parallel blocks designed by Oxford architect William Fisher, the middle one of which boasted a 90-ft tower complete with a weathervane and housed the master and matron. An infirmary, fever wards and a chapel were added soon after it opened. Inmates at the Cowley Road

Cowley Road Hospital

Hospital were classified according to age and sex; infirm and able-bodied. There were also primitive maternity wards, and casual dormitories for tramps and vagrants.

During the First World War, the workhouse became the Cowley Section of the Third Southern General Hospital—which had its HQ in the Oxford University Examination Schools—and was used by wounded servicemen. Following the 1929 Local Government Act, it was reclassified as a Public Assistance Institution. During the Second World War part of it was used as an Emergency Medical Services Hospital, even though there were still 220 old people living there and 15 maternity beds.

With the birth of the National Health Service, the Public Assistance Authority transferred its ownership to United Oxford Hospitals. In 1958 its director, the pioneering Dr Lionel Cosin, succeeded in reducing the average stay there from a year to 35 days. This was achieved by establishing a halfway house and a day hospital in the grounds, the first institutions of their kind in the country. The *Encyclopaedia of Oxford* by Christopher Hibbert (Macmillan, 1988) notes that, despite its workhouse origins, 'considerable regret accompanied its closure in 1981 and subsequent demolition'.

Washing and Water Supply

For centuries the great and the good in Oxford had an aversion to washing on the grounds that it opened the pores and let in diseases such as cholera, typhoid or smallpox. Indeed it was the great, including dons and doctors, who went unwashed just as much as the people whom Thackeray famously described as the 'Great Unwashed'.

For instance, the 17th-century Oxford scientist and architect Robert Hooke seldom washed any part of himself other than his feet. And of course the fact that there was a tax on soap until 1853 didn't help matters either. Only in the late 18th century and early 19th—probably in the wake of spas and sea bathing becoming fashionable—did the idea gain credence that washing was wholesome and that open pores let poisons out rather than in.

Bath Street, in East Oxford, is so named because St Clements Bath was opened there in 1827. The proprietor was a Mr A. H. Richardson, whose grand plans were illustrated in Nathaniel Whittock's illustrated book of Oxford buildings published a year later. The designs for the baths included a splendid portico for the street entrance, and steps down to the river for the use of customers arriving by boat.

But whether the baths were ever actually built in so grand a manner is a moot point. Graeme L. Salmon, in his excellent book *Beyond Magdalen Bridge: The Growth of East Oxford* (Oxford Meadow Press 2010), writes: 'The grand classical facade was probably never built. Inside the cover of a Bodleian copy of the prospectus is a manuscript note from 1907 indicating that a Mr T. J. Carter who had lived in New Street opposite the baths for 60 years did not remember seeing the elaborate facade.' In any case the baths never gained the hoped-for popularity and they closed in 1877. But while they lasted they contained: plunging baths, dressing rooms, warm baths and showers, a saloon complete with periodicals and newspapers, and a swimming school, quaintly described in the prospectus as a 'School of Natation'.

Mains water came to Oxford comparatively early. In the 17th century a London lawyer called Otho Nicholson devised a system for catching water from springs above North Hinksey and sending it to his elaborate Carfax Conduit in the city centre via lead pipes. His system replaced an earlier one devised by the monks of Osney in the 13th century which had fallen into disrepair. Nicholson's North Hinksey Conduit House, with its original 17th-century roof over a reservoir, is now in the the care of English Heritage. The Carfax Conduit, dating from 1617, was given to Lord Harcourt in 1787 after it became a traffic hazard. It now stands as a sort of folly in the park at Nuneham Courtenay.

A sewage system of sorts existed in Oxford in the early 19th century; but all the drains emptied into the Thames or its tributaries. Unsurprisingly cholera was a constant threat. There were serious epidemics in 1832, 1849 and 1854. But things were evidently less bad in Oxford than in London, where the Great Stink occurred in the hot summer of 1858. So bad was the smell that plans to move Parliament and the Law Courts to Oxford only failed to materialise because the weather broke. Disraeli, then leader of the House of Commons, described the Thames as 'a Stygian pool reeking with ineffable and unbearable horror'. Not until John Snow, a London doctor, proved that cholera was communicated by water infected with sewage, rather than being carried on the air, was clean water taken seriously. An efficient sewage system was put in place in Oxford in the 1870s.

But washing continued to be viewed by some with suspicion. I remember hearing of an elderly—and presumably smelly—don in the early 20th century who reckoned that washing destroyed 'the natural oils'. One of his pupils told me that the soap in his room needed dusting every now and then.

Carriers

One early bone of contention between Town and Gown in Oxford concerned exactly who should be allowed to carry goods about.

In 1448, Oxford University announced that students and other members of the university could only have their books and belongings carried to and from the city, or between lodgings within it, by its own licensed carriers. The ruling, which dubbed the university carriers 'privileged persons', caused simmering discontent for centuries, particularly as the city, in turn, began appointing its own licensed carriers.

Even in the 18th century ugly street brawls about exactly who should be allowed to carry whose baggage were not uncommon. In 1731, matters came to a head when a carter called Barnes, who ran his wagon without university licence, was summoned to appear before the vice-chancellor's court. He refused to answer the summons and, according to the historian Thomas Hearne, was 'removed by habeas corpus to London where, no one appearing against him, he was dismissed immediately'. Townspeople made much of his triumph. He re-entered Oxford on his wagon 'in a triumphant manner, with a laced hat, as if he designed to insult the university'.

From then onwards Oxford traded with its neighbouring countryside and market towns by using hundreds of carters, though farmers and shepherds herded their own livestock to market. By 1846 there were 300 wagons regularly plying their trade in and around the city. The carts took passengers or goods wherever they were directed. Sometimes large consignments of eggs, butter, cheese and so on were loaded aboard a country carrier's cart for delivery to a market trader in Oxford. Carriers also undertook errands, such as shopping for particular items, for country people living in outlying villages. In Oxford city centre the carters could be hired at such pubs and inns as The Crown in Cornmarket Street, where there was always a lively bustle of humanity as the carts vied for space with the London coaches.

Another source of income for carters was laundry. Washerwomen set up cottage industries in the clean air of the countryside, with city dwellers, whether Town or Gown, dispatching their dirty linen by cart. Even the advent of the railway did not put a stop to the carters. They met the trains and transported passengers and goods to final destinations. Only the rise of the motor car and the introduction of buses finally killed them off.

The Oxford Canal

Industry came to Oxford by water at the beginning of the 19th century. Until then the city was little more than a market town playing host to a university which had gained a reputation for decadence.

Curiously enough, it was a mill that supplied the university with an essential product which felt the first effects of the Industrial Revolution in Oxford, namely Wolvercote Paper Mill. Originally owned by nearby Godstow Abbey, the mill passed through a number of hands following the Dissolution of the Monasteries, but it was already supplying Oxford's burgeoning printing industry by the 17th century. It was bought by the first Duke of Marlborough, who evidently had a good eye for business as well as soldiering, in about 1715. Almost 100 years later his successor installed Oxford's first coal-fired steam engine there.

Some might be surprised at the sheer extent to which great landowners fuelled the changeover from agriculture to industry. It was again the enterprising Duke of Marlborough who was the moving spirit in supplying Oxford with coal. The duke

financed the building of Duke's Cut at Wolvercote. It enabled coal to be transported by barge from the Thames to the paper mill. Until 1952, when the mill became oil-fired, more than 100 tons of coal passed that way each week.

The Duke had also been instrumental in bringing the canal to Oxford in the first place. He was part of a group supporting the construction of the Oxford Canal between 1769 and 1790. The influential group included Lord North (Prime Minister and one-time MP for Banbury), the university and the City Corporation. The last stretch of the 91-mile long canal stretching from Hawkesbury, near Coventry, was completed in 1790. On 1 January that year, the Lord Mayor welcomed the first barges into the canal basin at New Road. The bells of St Thomas the Martyr rang out and a band played. The purpose of the canal, which cost its supporters £307,000 to build, was to provide the city with coal from the Midlands. Previously the coal had been expensively shipped from the north-east to London, transferred to river barges, and then ferried up the Thames to Oxford.

Inhabitants of Oxford must have been made of stern stuff until the arrival of the canal. Not only was the weather colder but fuel was scarce. Even after its arrival things were not necessarily much better. In 1795 the canal froze over for ten weeks and coal ran out. Ice-breakers, pulled by ten horses each and full of men employed specially to rock them, only broke through in March.

Despite the arrival of the railways in Oxford in the mid 19th century, the canals lingered on. Coal wharves lined the Oxford Canal until after the Second World War and breakable goods, such as pottery from the Midlands, continued to be transported by waterway. Road transport put the final nail in the coffin of the canal's commercial life. It is ironic that the New Road canal basin, opened with such fanfare, should have been filled in and used as a car park. The basin was bought by that arch-industrialist Lord Nuffield in 1937 as a site for his major gift to the city: Nuffield College.

The Coming of the Railways

Powerful influences combined, more or less by chance, to ensure that the railways came to Oxford comparatively late.

When the first line to Didcot and thence to London was proposed in 1837, the Chancellor of the University was the Iron Duke himself (Wellington), who was opposed to all railways as a matter of policy because they might encourage the lower orders to 'move about'. Allied to him were other authorities of both Town and Gown. The university grandees feared for the morals of undergraduates, and their own influence over them, if 'young gentlemen' were able to travel to London too easily.

The town had a more practical objection. It feared that the arrival of the railway would mean fewer people paying tolls to cross Folly Bridge, which in turn would leave the City Corporation short of funds with which to pay the £8,750 still owed for rebuilding it. Town and Gown were joined in their opposition by the Oxford Canal Company, anxious to protect its own interests. The proposed route of the Great Western Railway line in from Didcot was to run alongside the then muddy track called Cowley Road and end up near Magdalen Bridge. The major landowner, Christ Church, scuppered the plan by objecting to it. So powerful was the opposition that successive bills for the Oxford Railway were turned down by the House of Lords in 1837, 1838 and 1840.

The breakthrough came, as breakthroughs usually do when vested interests stand in the way of progress, when the university discovered that more and more undergraduates were in any case taking the one-and-half-hour stage-coach trip to Great Western's station at Steventon, and then continuing by train to the races at Ascot.

The university dropped its opposition to an Oxford line on condition that its university police (the bulldogs) could enter any station or depot and forbid undergraduates from travelling by train, whether or not they had paid their fare. In the enabling Act of Parliament of 1843 this proviso was written in. Presumably, therefore, it still applies.

The first railway line into Oxford was opened with great bustle and excitement on 14 June 1844. The line eventually ran along what is now Marlborough Road and terminated at Western Road.

Rewley Road Station

A prime difference between the Crystal Palace, originally constructed for the Great Exhibition in London's Hyde Park, and its offspring, the former Rewley Road Station in Oxford, was that one lasted just six months on its original site, and the other lasted 147 years. Both experienced a reincarnation: the former at the Sydenham site to which it had been banished at the end of the 1851 Great Exhibition; the latter at the Quainton Railway Society's Buckinghamshire Railway Centre, near Aylesbury, where it flourishes to this day as a visitor attraction for train buffs.

Many will remember the station. As little as ten years ago it stood on ground now occupied by the Said Business School. By then the Grade-II listed building was in an advanced state of romantic decay, having done time since 1951, when it closed to railway passengers, fulfilling such unromantic roles as a tyre depot and car hire garage.

Rewley Road station

It had opened 100 years before that, in 1851, the same year as the Great Exhibition. The engineers who built it, Charles Fox and John Henderson, of Stafford, were the same men who had also developed Joseph Paxton's designs for the Crystal Palace which, sadly, burned to the ground, on its Sydenham site, in 1936. Paxton, a pioneer in the use of glass and iron in construction, started his career as head gardener to the Duke of Devonshire at Chatsworth. Later he became an investor in Britain' burgeoning railway network, often working closely with railway tycoon Thomas Brassey of Heythrop Park, who constructed the Oxford-Bletchley line for the Buckinghamshire Railway, which line the Rewley Road station served.

The station engineers, obviously not unaware that the Great Exhibition would attract a lot of day trippers from Oxford, borrowed so many of the construction techniques used in the palace that the magazine *The Structural Engineer* commented in 1975: 'Until recently it had been thought that no trace of the Crystal Palace structure remained. Strictly speaking, none does, but something very similar has survived.' It then went on to describe the Paxton-like work at Rewley Road. The construction included ironwork such as decorative columns that doubled up as drainpipes, as well as a mass of decorative motifs.

The magazine continued. 'Almost more telling as a comparison than the structural components are the remains of the decorative iron cladding at Oxford which were clearly made from the same casting as in the Exhibition Building.'

The Rewley Road station was constructed at a cost of under £7,000, a price which included not only the station itself but also a large timber yard, a train shed, water tower, and a coal yard which remained in use until the mid 1990s. The ticket office was believed to have been brought from the Great Exhibition after closure.

The station was built next door to the Great Western Station, which stood on the site of the present station, and had opened a few years previously. During the Great Exhibition the two companies competed wildly with each other for passengers. The Buckinghamshire Railway charged 3s 6d for an excursion to London, stating that the journey from Rewley Road to Euston would take just one and three-quarter hours. In the event the journey took two-and-a-half hours. Little change there, then.

Trams and Buses

Anyone moaning that there are too many buses clogging up Oxford's city centre streets these days should spare a thought for their predecessors of 1912. In August that year there was no public transport in Oxford at all. For some decades horse-drawn trams, trundling along tracks, sunken into the surfaces of St Giles and the Woodstock Road, had been in daily use. Then the drivers went on strike over 6d a day, and two colourful Oxford entrepreneurs, the future lawyer and MP Frank Gray and the future motor magnate William Morris, decided that it was time for Oxford's transport to be upgraded.

Some say that the trams, one of which was until recently seeing active service as a chicken coop in Yarnton, only survived as long as they did because they were remembered with such nostalgic fondness by generations of former undergraduates.

Be that as it may, there was nothing sentimental about the derision with which the town (as opposed to gown) viewed the trams, or the way in which Gray and Morris stirred up popular feeling, breaking the law in the process, in order to introduce a motorised system.

The two defied the city corporation (predecessor of the council) by putting a couple of motor buses on the streets without a licence. The public bought tickets in bulk from such shops as grocers and newsagents, who received a commission on sales—and could therefore be deemed to be conniving at the running of the illegal buses.

Only a small proportion of the crowd, which alternately jeered a poor old horse and its tram, and cheered the motor bus, was able to board the first bus bound for the city centre. It was so full from the start that it did not need to stop at any of the stops en route, where more crowds cheered its progress. However, among those who did board the bus was a police inspector. Gray and Morris told him, melodramatically enough, that 'this bus will continue to run and any force to stop it will be met by force'.

The dignified policeman calmed the situation down by declaring that he hoped no force would be necessary but he noted that 'You [Gray] and Mr Morris take full responsibility for this breach of the law and anything which may result.' The inspector had apparently boarded the bus with a valid pre-bought ticket, though there was some argy bargy when it was discovered that his sergeant had got on without one.

The population of Oxford was exercised over this matter of trams to an astonishing degree. Perhaps this was because of a perceived scandal, namely that the chairman of the city watch committee was also a director of the National Electric Company which had been given an option to provide electric trams. The company had let the option lapse and then the committee had calmly given it another one to provide a mixed electric and petrol system. But having whipped up popular feeling, Gray and Morris were faced with a dilemma when they received a note from the city solicitor. It informed them that he had been instructed by the watch committee to apply for warrants of arrest against not only them but also the bus conductors and drivers. The two decided on further defiance and, amazingly, won the day. They called a mass meeting at which the behaviour of the populace so cowed the authorities—they tried to torch a horse-drawn tram—that the corporation gave in.

The Postal Service

In 1635, Charles I appointed Thomas Withings as Postmaster General with the stipulation that the London-Bristol mail should run through Oxford. But after the Civil War that route ran via Newbury and Reading instead. The effects of this potentially damaging move to Oxford's economy were alleviated slightly in 1709 when a branch of the so-called Cross Post from Exeter to Chester via Bristol was extended to Oxford and Wantage.

Not until 1784 did regular mail coaches operate, with the cost of a stamp depending on the distance travelled. By the early 19th century two coaches a night were leaving The Angel Inn in High Street at 11.30 p.m. for London, one via Henley and one via High Wycombe. The distance from Oxford to London was reckoned as 57 miles. Early post marks therefore (stamped on to the envelope, not stuck on) contained the figure 57 and customers paid accordingly.

Pillar boxes appeared in Britain in 1855, to replace the 'receiving houses' where letters could previously be handed in. Oxford has 13 Victorian post boxes —six pillar boxes and four wall boxes —according to a recent count, with the venerable hexagonal model in Park Town being the oldest.

After the introduction of the penny post, Oxford was given the postal number 603 and letters posted here were overstamped with a Maltese cross containing that number. However, in 1871 the Oxford office was by mistake issued with an overstamper, or obliterator, marked 613. Letters marked with the wrong number were still being sent out two years later and are much sought after by collectors.

Another Oxford postal peculiarity occurred in 1859 when Oxford University's much respected debating society, the Oxford Union, suffered a bout of stamp pilfering. The Post Office granted the society permission to overprint its penny stamps with the initials OUS between wavy lines as a precaution against theft. This was the only time the Post Office has given such permission, and even that was withdrawn in 1870.

Running parallel to the penny post in Oxford and Cambridge was an inter-college message service whereby the colleges issued their own stamps. This was only brought to an end in 1885 when the Post Office complained that the system infringed its monopoly.

Just two years after the Penny Black stamp was introduced in 1840, the main Oxford post office at 123 High Street was destroyed by fire. A temporary office was opened in the old Town Hall, and extended in 1865, until the new office in St Aldates, with its beautiful panelled Postmaster's Room upstairs, was opened in 1879.

When the foundation stone of the ornate building by architect E. G. Rivers was laid, the postmaster gave out a few facts and figures about the postal services in those days. They make interesting comparison.

In 1879 there were four deliveries and six collections a day in Oxford, and the postmaster said there were still people about who could remember when all letters for Oxford addresses were carried by just one postman. But by 1879 there were 121 postal employees, of whom 87 worked at, or from, the main post office. The number of letters and packages which had to be sorted and delivered each week was 240,000, of which just over a third were delivered in Oxford and its immediate neighbourhood.

That compares with 1 million packages a day handled by the 400 postal workers at the sorting office at the Oxford Business Park in Cowley, before it departed for Swindon.

The Fire Service

Oxford's first recorded major fire occurred in 1138 when the entire town was apparently burned to the ground. Then, no sooner had the inhabitants built it up again than it was torched once more, this time by King Stephen in 1142. He was filled with wrath following the escape of the Empress Matilda, his rival for the English crown. Famously, she dressed in white to match the snow and escaped from Oxford Castle, flitting across the flooded and frozen Thames.

Indeed, life in early Oxford seems to have been one long conflagration. The city caught fire again in 1190, when St Frideswide's Priory and the church, then standing on the site of what is now the cathedral, went up in flames; and then, once again, rioters deliberately set the place alight in 1236. It is a wonder that any very early buildings, such as the crypt in the castle or St Michael at the Northgate, still survive!

Oxford suffered more deliberate fires during the Civil War when the King's forces caused hundreds of thousands of pounds of damage by burning down much of the western part of the city as a defensive measure.

In 1654 Oxford Corporation—forerunner of the city council—bought its first fire engine and began to enforce rigorous regulations, which required parishes to keep firefighting equipment such as buckets, ladders, hooks and so on to hand. After the Great Fire of London of 1666, during which many scholars and townsmen hurried up the tower of the University Church to view the strange glow in the eastern sky, two more fire engines were brought into service. From the early 19th century until the 1880s Oxford University had its own fire service.

Indeed, in 1845 nine of the city's 15 fire engines were owned by the university or by individual colleges. The other six were owned by the city, the county, Oxford University Press, the parishes of St Mary the Virgin and St Michael at the North Gate, and the Sun Insurance Company, whose mark can still be seen on some Oxford buildings.

Notable fires during and after the 19th century included two, in 1857 and 1863, which nearly destroyed the wonderfully Venetian Gothic grocers Grimbly Hughes which, some will remember, stood in Cornmarket Street until 1959. It had mahogany or marble counters and chairs upon which customers could sit and watch their bacon being sliced—a very different shopping experience to the supermarkets that ousted it.

Amazingly, though, given the city's record, the city and county disposed of their fire engines in 1854, leaving only a private as opposed to public firefighting force. Not until 1870 when two people died in a fire was the public volunteer service restored, operating in conjunction with the police. Then the Volunteer Brigade opened its headquarters at a new fire station in New Inn Hall Street in 1873. The 60 volunteers moved to George Street in 1896 and became professionals in 1940. The headquarters of the fire service moved to Rewley Road in 1971.

Oxford's Weather Station

Oxford has the oldest weather station in Britain, the Radcliffe Meteorological Station, dating from 1772. It is in the garden of Green College beside the Observatory building and next door to the old Radcliffe Infirmary in Woodstock Road. It has been keeping continuous records of the city's weather since 1815, and more spasmodic records from even before then.

In 1768 Dr Thomas Hornsby, Savilian Professor of Astronomy, approached the Radcliffe Trustees for money to build the Observatory; but he must have had a personal hobby of recording weather himself, since irregular observations exist from 1767 until his death in 1810.

The money the Trustees had at their disposal came from the fortune of Dr John Radcliffe (1662-1714) who entered University College to study medicine in 1675 and went on to become London's most fashionable—and expensive—physician. And this despite the fact that when he originally set up in practice in Oxford he had no equipment except a few phials and a skeleton. He became physician to William III in London and by 1707 was said to have amassed £80,000—not so much by his medical skill as by his famous wit, for which rich patients were happy to pay. For instance he once told the King, when examining the royal swollen ankles: 'I would not have your Majesty's two legs for your three kingdoms.'

The Observatory was originally designed by Henry Keane but was completed after his death by James Wyatt. Decorations on the 108 ft octagonal tower, completed in 1794, very much reflect the earlier interest in weather on the site. It is crowned with a copy of the Tower of the Winds, a structure that stood in ancient Athens and was built between 150-100BC by Andronicus of Cyrrhus. The reliefs depicting the winds were carved by John Bacon the Elder, who also carved the familiar lead sculpture of Hercules and Atlas holding aloft the globe.

Britain's Meteorological Office was originally established, under the auspices of the Board of Trade, by Robert FitzRoy (1805-65), who had been captain of HMS *Beagle* on her second voyage (1831-6) to Tierra del Fuego, during which Charles Darwin, as the official naturalist on board, formed his ideas for *The Origin of Species*. FitzRoy's brief was to investigate the possibilities of weather forecasting, mainly to protect ships and their crews.

The Met Office's weather station at Benson dates from 1853—when, incidentally, the mean daily maximum temperature in December was 3.7° C. The coldest December I could spot was that of 1890 when the highest mean daily temperature was 0.2° C. Ironically, Britain had a colder climate in the years before the establishment of the

Met Office, namely 1550-1850, sometimes known as the Little Ice Age. The winter of 1813/14 was the last year the Frost Fair was held on the Thames in London. As for White Christmases, they were far more common until 1752 when Britain at last adopted the Gregorian calendar, in step with the rest of Europe. Until then Christmas fell twelve days later, in early January, when of course we are still likely to experience our most wintry weather.

But further back in history, the Christmas of 1141 must surely have been exceptionally cold in Oxford. That year the Empress Matilda found herself holed up in Oxford Castle while her rival for the English throne, Stephen, besieged the place from two large mounds called Jews Mount and Mount Pelham. Food was running low before she finally escaped, dressed in white so as not to show up against the snow. She crossed the frozen waters of the Thames and Castle Mill Stream on her way to Abingdon. All I can say is that they must have been good at making white clothes in those days. Even sheep, which look white enough normally, always appear a sort of grey against a background of snow.

Oxford's Breweries

Orwell's Ministry of Truth could not have done better: Morrells changed its name to Morrells of Oxford at precisely the moment the company ceased to brew beer there. The day in 1998 when American burger and beer boss Michael Cannon bought the business and then sold off its Lion Brewery in St Thomas Street for redevelopment as luxury flats brought to an end an Oxford brewing tradition stretching back some 900 years.

Shortly after the Norman Conquest, Robert d'Oilly, appointed Lord of Oxford by William I, installed a brewery in his castle, which was built to control the Upper Thames. Records show that this brewhouse was "renewed" in 1267. From the earliest Middle Ages, beer was brewed in the city's monasteries of Osney and Rewley — where the brewhouse building survived until 1850 when it was pulled down to make way for the railway — and in colleges of the university.

After the Town versus Gown riots of St Scholastica s Day on 10 February 1355, control of brewing in Oxford came under the control of the University Chancellor rather than, as before, the joint control of Mayor and Chancellor. According to the *Enyclopaedia of Oxford*, by the time of the first Poll Tax in 1381, there were 32 people listed as brewers in the city. They were men of substance, from families that often supplied mayors and aldermen of the town. What with the production of beer and the high quantities of wine imported from Bordeaux, then ruled by English kings, medieval alcohol consumption must have been prodigious. Many of these brewers were also vintners, inn-keepers, maltsters and such like. By 1700, thanks to rising prices of raw materials and high taxes on hops and malt, most of the small breweries had disappeared and familiar local brewing names began to crop up.

The Swans Nest Brewery, founded on the Thames near Oxford Castle, passed to William Hall in 1781 and became Hall's Brewery. By 1926, when it was taken over by Allsop, it had moved to the site now occupied by Modern Art Oxford. Ind Coope eventually acquired Allsop and revived for a short while its bottling plant at the Eagle Brewery in Park End Street.

When Mark and James Morrell bought the Lion Brewery in St Thomas Street in 1803, beer had already been brewed there by the Tawney family since 1597. Headington Hill Hall, later home to disgraced tycoon Robert Maxwell before becoming part of Oxford Brookes University, was bought by the Morrells in 1831 and remained in the family until 1953.

Colleges gradually gave up brewing their own beer, though The Queen' College was still brewing its Chancellor Beer until the Second World War.

Victorian Photography

Why did the Reverend Charles Lutwidge Dodgson, maths don at Christ Church and author of *Alice in Wonderland*, choose the pen name Lewis Carroll? Because Lewis is an Anglo-Saxon version of the Germanic sounding Lutwidge—a derivation of Ludwig—and Carroll is Latin for Charles. He was fascinated with the business of expressing almost anything in an unexpected way and would, I am sure, have been intrigued by modern technology—mobile telephones and, above all, digital cameras. In his day, cameras never lied.

But while Dodgson was photographing many of the people of Victorian Oxford, most notably, of course, Alice Liddell, daughter of the Dean of Christ Church, who first heard of her adventures during a boat trip to Godstow in July 1862, another photographer was busy recording its architecture. He was Henry Taunt (1842-1922), who, in 1871, became official photographer of the Oxford Architectural and Historical Society, publishing his best-selling A New Map of the River Thame the following year. He joined the staff of an Oxford photographer well known to Dodgson, called Edward Bracher.

The world of photography was itself a sort of wonderland for many Victorians, a new technology greeted with greater awe than we now treat innovations. By 1868,

Taunt was publishing a shilling series of photographic views of Oxford, which are now collectors' items. The Oxford views were so successful that he set up his own business at 33 Cornmarket, moving to larger premises at 9-10 Broad Street in 1874, where he stayed until the lease ran out in 1894. Then he moved to 34 High Street until 1906 when he started conducting his business solely from his Cowley home. He set up a studio and laboratory in the garden, complete with storage for thousands of glass negatives. He took many of his photographs from his houseboat, a familiar sight on the Thames, which at that time was becoming Oxford's major scene of leisure activities, such as punting.

Modern books reproducing Taunt's works include Malcolm Graham's Henry Taunt of Oxford (1973) and his more recent book, comparing Oxford's scenes of then and now. As for Dodgson, he would have loved the business of freezing images in time. As he said, the stories he told on that Golden Afternoon when he, Alice, her sisters, and another clergyman, rowed down the river 'lived and died like summer midges'.

The John Radcliffe Hospital

With great foresight (as it turned out) the Reverend G. B. Cronshaw, then treasurer of the Radcliffe Infirmary, bought the land upon which the John Radcliffe Hospital stands in 1919, following a public appeal. The Infirmary was overcrowded and he guessed that much more space would eventually be needed, not least to continue the fight against tuberculosis.

With this end in mind, the British Red Cross Society gave £15,000 towards the cost of the land, originally part of the Headington Manor estate, to develop facilities for tuberculosis—and the first building to go up on the site was indeed the pavilion-style Osler, which opened in 1926 with 40 beds dedicated to the treatment of that disease. The £15,000, incidentally, was money left over from wartime appeals, and the hospital was originally intended as a war memorial.

The Osler building was named after Sir William Osler (1849-1919), the somewhat eccentric Canadian physician who, when appointed Regius Professor of Medicine at Oxford in 1904, gave a speech on gerontology in which he seemed to approve of Anthony Trollope's ideas, contained in his book *The Fixed Period*, which envisaged men retiring at 67—and then being 'peacefully extinguished' by chloroform after having enjoyed a contemplative year off. No one seems certain, even today, whether or not Osler was joking. But be that as it may, he was the founder of the Oxfordshire branch of the National Association for the Prevention of Tuberculosis and, to a large extent, the pioneer of the modern teaching hospital, insisting that doctors learn their trade by seeing and talking to patients rather than from books and lectures. He said that he hoped his tombstone would read: 'He brought medical students into the wards for bedside teaching.'

Sadly, the John Radcliffe today occupies only about half the land originally purchased in 1919, thanks to money worries forcing the governors to sell building plots from time to time over the years. For instance, a particularly large chunk was sold in the early 1930s to finance expansion at the Infirmary. The crying need for funds was also at the root of the sale of the Infirmary's Sunnyside estate in Cowley, which Dr Ivy Williams had given in 1922 as a convalescent home for Infirmary patients. To compensate for its loss, the second building to go up on the Manor site (in 1930) was a convalescent home with 30 beds, also called Sunnyside.

After the Second World War, seemingly endless discussions about a new teaching hospital got under way. As usual, financial constraints caused delay and it was not until 1971 that Phase 1, consisting of a maternity unit with 180 beds and cots, opened.

Phase II, which took over many of the Infirmary's departments and cost £30 m to build, opened in 1979. And the West Wing—with its children's hospital, facilities specially designed for teenagers, eye hospital, neurosciences unit, and day surgery unit—did not open until 2007. But then, as Sir William Osler said: 'Shut out all your past except that which will help you weather your tomorrows.'

Woolworth's: End of an Era

Misty eyed, we all remember the demise of dear old Woolies, RIP, in November 2008. But Oxford's original city-centre Woolworth's in Cornmarket Street stamped on the site of the old Roebuck Hotel, a coaching inn of the 18th and 19th centuries. Woolworth's bought and demolished the historic building in 1922, opening for business on the site of the present Boots in 1925.

Then the chain store did much the same again in 1939, when it bought another venerable old coaching inn, the Clarendon Hotel (formerly the Star Inn, where the exiled Louis XVIII of France stayed in 1808)—which it demolished in 1954, before re-opening with great panache in 1957.

The gap between the dates of purchase and opening was not purely due to the war. It was also due to one of the bitterest planning battles Oxford has ever seen. Woolworth's had applied to pull down the Clarendon Hotel, where many of Evelyn Waugh's characters in *Brideshead Revisited* were wont to breakfast, and were refused permission. Woolworth's appealed to Harold Macmillan, then Minister of Housing and Local Government, who overturned the refusal. The university, which had set itself against the notion of the city centre becoming 'commercial', was unamused by the decision of Mr Macmillan who, after all, was a former student of Balliol. Dons threatened to vote against his honorary doctorate—the offer of which was consequently dropped. They forgave him later, though, when he became Chancellor of the University.

The day before the new store re-opened for the public, the great and the good of the city were summoned to a sumptuous luncheon in the new cafeteria, with waiters in tails dancing attendance. I know this because a be-tasselled menu has miraculously survived in *The Oxford Times* archives. In that age of post-war austerity, they drank Krug Champagne 1949, Macharnudo Fino sherry, Chateau Kirwan 1945 or Meurault Charmes 1945, and Hines Grande Fine Champagne Cognac. They ate Les Hors d'oeuvres des Gourmets, Le Homard Americain, Le Faisandeau Rôti and much more besides. How the world has changed: in this age of television cooks constantly telling us about good British food, it is easy to forget that not long ago all fancy English restaurants wrote their menus in French—so convinced was the nation at large that its reputation for the worst food in Europe was well-earned.

The new store at 52-53 Cornmarket then opened to the public on Friday, 18 October 1957, with its giant pick 'n' mix sweet counter, its mezzanine cafeteria, its tea for 6d a quarter pound, ladies' nylons at 2/9d, or pillow cases at 2s, single sheets 6/6d. That branch of Woolworth's lasted until 1983 when it in turn was sold to a property company and demolished to make way for the garish Clarendon Centre, which stands there now—named after that 17th-century man of letters Lord Clarendon, who must be spinning in his grave.

Sadly, the Clarendon Hotel was much older in parts than was suspected at the time. Its 12th-century vaulted cellar, still underneath Cornmarket, may have been responsible for the recent fiasco on the road's surface when granite paving, imported from China, cracked and had to be removed by the council at high expense.

Palm's Delicatessen

So sad, the sight of that empty shop in the very middle of Oxford Covered Market, which still bears the name of Palm's Delicatessen. I well remember queuing up with my father in the 1960s, along with plenty of other people of central European origin, to be sold sausages, ham, or sauerkraut by Mrs Loisl Palm herself—a lady who had a real love of sausages; who really *understood* them, if you know what I mean.

Mr and Mrs Palm were refugees from Czechoslovakia. They arrived in England in 1938 and moved to Oxford the following year, setting up shop originally in two market stalls, before moving to the now empty shop where they stayed until the early 1970s when they retired, selling the business to successors who eventually closed it down so recently.

But theirs was one of the first such shops to open outside London, and it flourished partly because of the large number of continental academics, many of them scientists, who flooded into Oxford in the years immediately preceding the Second World War, and longed for the kind of food they had left behind.

Champion of such scientists was Frederick Lindemann (1886-1957), widely known as The Prof, who during the war became Churchill's most trusted—though somewhat eccentric—scientific adviser, created Baron Cherwell in 1941 and Viscount Cherwell in 1956. He was born in the German spa town of Baden Baden, where his American mother was taking the cure. He was the second son of a rich father from Alsace who had emigrated to England in the early 1870s and had married the equally rich Olga Noble, from Connecticut. He was educated in Scotland and at Berlin University where he made extraordinary contributions to low-temperature physics, and where he also developed a certain haughty manner and forthright opinions, for which he later became famous, developing into one of those people often described in obituaries as 'not suffering fools gladly'. In 1919 he became Professor of Experimental Philosophy at Oxford University, and head of the Clarendon Laboratory. His chair was attached to Wadham College, though he decided to live at Christ Church where he had also been elected to a studentship.

As a bachelor he lived in spacious rooms in Meadow Buildings, painted entirely white, with hideous furniture; a chauffeur in full uniform drove him frequently to Downing Street in his Armstrong Siddeley for conflabs with the PM. He persuaded the Imperial Chemical Company (ICI) to provide funds for scientists who had fled from Germany and other Nazi occupied countries, notably Sir Francis Simon and Kurt Mendelssohn (who first liquefied helium in Britain), and the Hungarian Nicholas Kurti, who later became famous for applying science to his cooking (Molecular and Physical Gastronomy, he called it). In 1969 Kurti gave a talk at the Royal Society entitled 'The Physicist in the Kitchen' during which he demonstrated the recently invented microwave to make a reverse Baked Alaska which, of course, was cold on the outside and hot on the inside. Such experiments went hand in hand at the Clarendon Laboratory during the war with radar research and work on the separation of uranium isotopes for the Tube Alloys Project, code name for the hydrogen bomb.

At the end of the war, Baron Cherwell was a keen advocate of two highly controversial ideas with regard to Germany: firstly, he backed the policy of bombing civilians in order to 'break the spirit of the German people'; secondly, he backed the proposal of US Secretary of the Treasury Henry Morgenthau to de-industrialise Germany so that it could never again re-arm itself.

As for Palm's, which provided fodder for many of those brainy refugees, it began selling food from further afield than Europe: it was the first shop in Oxford to stock avocado pears, sweet potatoes and yams. I even remember admiring a tin of candied grasshoppers on sale there. But sausages were the main stock in trade, with Mrs Palm sometimes standing with hands on hips and informing like-minded customers, 'Today they are particularly beautiful.' Occasionally she would ring up my father to tell him when an unusually lovely specimen had arrived in town.

Oxford United Football Club

Whatever you may think of the roller-coaster ride that Oxford United Football Club has enjoyed in its 115-year history, the fact that it still exists at all, let alone has an all-seater stadium the like of which early supporters could not have imagined, is surely something of a miracle.

It started in 1893 as one of several small clubs in and around Oxford. Its first match, as the tiny village club of Headington United, was probably against the United College Servants Wanderers, resulting in a 2-1 defeat. Its founders were a 49-year-old football-playing vicar of Headington, which, incidentally, did not become part of Oxford till 1929, the Reverend Scott Tucker, and a younger, local doctor called Dr Hitchings, who

was anxious to provide healthy exercise for the young men of Headington. A report in the St Andrew's (Headington) Church magazine of November 1893 read: 'The cricket season being over, Mr Hitchings, with his customary zeal for the young men of the parish, has inaugurated a football club.'

That first match was played on a makeshift pitch at Headington Quarry, and the club continued to play at various places around the parish for the next 30 years or so. Not until 1925 did it find a permanent home at the Manor Ground, which until then had been known as Mattocks Field after the company that grew roses there. Public-spirited shopkeepers bought the Manor Ground for the use of Headington people as a sports field. They placed a covenant on the land, stipulating that it should remain an 'open playing' field forever; then they formed a company, the Headington Sports Ground Ltd, to manage the football, cricket, tennis and bowls clubs. Admission to the uncovered enclosure on match days was 6d, the ground 4d, ladies and boys 2d, and season tickets 4s.

United's early difficulty, immediately after the move to the Manor, was the fact that it shared the ground with the Headington Cricket Club—and the seasons overlapped. Eventually the cricket club moved out and in 1960 the football club became Oxford United. Since then the club won promotion to the top flight and won the League Cup, in 1986, under the ownership of disgraced tycoon Robert Maxwell; but it has since plummeted to the Conference League.

The more recent history of the Kassam Stadium, at Minchery Farm, is almost as colourful as that of United itself. Work got under way to build the stadium in 1996. Then contractors walked off site complaining of unpaid bills, leaving the thing half-built for the next four years. In 1999 Firoz Kassam appeared on the scene as 'the only buyer in town', to quote former city council leader and the Lord Mayor of Oxford, John Tanner. He paid £1 for the club and undertook to complete the stadium, though with only three sides instead of the four originally envisaged.

As for the old Manor Ground, it was sold in 2001 for development as a hospital despite the existence of the old covenant. Of all the original clubs founded by Headington Sports Ground Ltd, only the Bowls Club remained, other than Oxford United itself. The Bowls Club was therefore the only organisation able to enforce the covenant. After lengthy negotiations its committee allowed the development.

4. The University
From Medieval to Modern

Like a fragile flower struggling to survive in less than fertile soil, Oxford University came into existence sometime in the middle of the 12th century. But ironically enough, it was the riots between Town and Gown of the 13th century—which so nearly destroyed it forever—that were ultimately the making of it. For with Crown and Church officially backing the scholars against their adversaries, the young university began to thrive. The prestigious degrees it conferred soon put it on a par with such established continental seats of learning as Paris, Bologna and Padua. As well they might, since a master's degree from Oxford could take as long as 18 years to achieve.

Education was at first almost entirely theological, with the university being seen by many bright boys from comparatively humble backgrounds as a way into the Church and thence, with luck, on to jobs of real power in the government of the realm. Only during the second half of the 15th century did Humanist ideas from Europe begin to change the character of the place, attracting more sons of gentry and nobility with careers in law, diplomacy or politics in mind.

Early undergraduates lived in academic halls. There were 69 of these in Oxford in 1444, of which only St Edmund Hall still exists today. Out of these halls grew the colleges, with University, Balliol, Merton, Exeter, Oriel, The Queen's College, and New College all coming into existence in the 15th century.

Originally chancellors of the university were appointed from above down by the Bishop of Lincoln, into whose diocese the town fell until 1542—when the Oxford diocese was created following the dissolution of the monasteries. The earliest recorded chancellor was someone called Geoffrey de Lucy, who was installed sometime before 1216, but the best known early holder of the office was Robert Grosseteste, who went on to become Bishop of Lincoln himself. Gradually the Masters wrested control of the university from the bishop by obtaining the right to elect their own chancellor, and this independence helped them weather the religious storms of the 16th century, a process helped along by the great interest that Elizabeth I took in its affairs.

Again in the 17th century Oxford emerged from the Civil War comparatively unscathed, though some say that even to this day it is less rich than Cambridge as a result of backing the losing, Royalist horse and becoming for a time capital of Charles I's England. Lord Protector Oliver Cromwell became chancellor in 1650, which helped the university survive the rigours of Puritanism; but, strange to tell, the university's worst period of decline came in the 18th century, when too much ease and comfort set in. (Edward Gibbon, 1737-84, author of *The Decline and Fall of the Roman Empire*, famously described his days at Magdalen as 'the most idle and unprofitable' of his whole life.) And as the university's reputation dropped, so did student numbers, with many aristocrats preferring to take the Grand Tour rather than come up to Oxford.

In the 19th century, several commissions were set up in an attempt to make the place mend its ways—which it did. The 1877 Royal Commission swept away the requirement for dons to be celibate, with the result that the population of the city as a whole grew considerably. In 1878 the first hall of residence for women was established (Lady Margaret Hall); eventually in 1972 five men's colleges. The last remaining single-sex women's college, St Hilda's, began admitting men in 2008.

According to the University Calendar, student numbers stood at 3,110 undergraduates in 1890. By the start of the First World War there were just 1,400 undergraduates, and even this figure reduced to 369 by 1918. Today there are more than 21,000 students at Oxford, of whom about 11,750 are undergraduates. Competition for places at Oxford is now stronger than ever before, with more than five hopefuls applying for every undergraduate place. Applications have increased by more than 55 per cent in ten years, while the number of places on offer has remained about the same.

University authorities and politicians continue their fencing match about the number of admissions from state schools. More than half of Oxford's undergraduates (57.7 per cent) now come from state schools. However, that still means that 42.3 per cent come from independent schools, while only 7 per cent of UK children are educated privately, though this figure rises to 15 per cent for all A Level entries.

Sir Thomas Bodley

One of the most spectacularly suitable tombs of the great and the good to be found in Oxford must be that of Sir Thomas Bodley (1545-1613) in Merton College Chapel. The Baroque black and white alabaster monument was carved by Nicholas Stone, master mason to James I and Charles I, with pillars made of marble books.

But what, I wondered, would Sir Thomas have thought of the now not uncommon sight of a an iPad sharing a table at the library named after him (the Bodleian of course) with a vast tome that once upon a time must surely have been anchored to its desk by a chain? Intrigued and astonished, yes; bewildered, probably not. For Bodley was a career diplomat and linguist, a true European, interested in the dissemination of knowledge across borders. He retired in 1598 and dedicated the rest of his life to rebuilding the University Library.

It certainly needed rebuilding, too. He said at the time: 'in every part it lay ruined and waste.' Most of the destruction had occurred in the reign of Edward VI, when commissioners in the name of religion had burned, sold, thrown out, or given away the contents of the library to such an extent that only a 'great desolate room' remained. In 1556 the university even sold off the shelves. Bodley offered to 'bring back the library to its proper use, and to make it fitte, and handsome with seates, and shelves and Deskes'.

Bodley came from a Devon Protestant family which had been forced to flee the country at the start of the reign of the Catholic Queen Mary. His early education was in Frankfurt and Geneva; but on the accession of Elizabeth the family returned to England and he went up to Magdalen College in 1559. After taking his degree he became a Fellow of Merton—which incidentally has Oxford's oldest library, complete with chained books—where he lectured on Greek and natural philosophy. Then in 1583 he was summoned to London to serve the Crown. He was sent on missions, sometimes secret, to destinations including the Netherlands, Germany and France—though it

QVOD FELICITER VORTAT
ACADEMICI OXONIENS
BIBLIOTHECAM HANC
VOBIS REIPVBLICAEQVE
LITERATORVM
T. B. P.

seems he always hankered to get back to Oxford and start the work that was to make him famous. He wrote in his autobiography: 'I concluded at the last to set up my Staffe at the Librarie dore in Oxon; being throwghly perswawded, that in my solitude, and surcease from the Commonwealth affayers, I coulde not busie myself to better purpose.'

The first university library had been housed in a room above the Congregation Room at the University Church of St Mary the Virgin—but it had had a precarious existence. It consisted largely of books donated by Thomas Cobham, Bishop of Worcester 1317-27. When the bishop died his relatives pawned the books to pay debts and funeral expenses. They were soon redeemed though, and deposited in Oriel College. Then in 1337 the University Vice-chancellor decided that the books were

University property—and scholars took them away by force and put them back in the room at St Mary the Virgin.

The room proved inadequate when Duke Humfrey of Gloucester, younger brother of Henry V, gave a collection of books and manuscripts to the university; so a larger room was assigned to them over the Divinity School which was then being constructed. The Duke died in 1447 and so never saw the library named after him, which was not completed until 1488. Now only a very few books from Humfrey's collection has found its way back to the Bodleian after the ravages of Edward's reign, though these include one (*The Epistles of Pliny*) which contains his autograph.

Historian Thomas Fuller (1608-61) wrote that Duke Humfrey was the founder of the library; Bodley, the re-founder; and Edward VI the confounder. Certainly, though, Bodley set about his work with skills that any modern businessman would recognise and even imitate. For instance he initiated the fundraising idea of sponsorship. He created a Benefactors' Book, bound in vellum and displayed prominently, in which the names of anyone donating anything worthwhile was written down in large writing for all to see. He also negotiated an agreement with the Stationers' Company, whereby the company agreed to send the library a copy of every book entered in their register.

But the Bodleian was certainly never a 'lending library' in the modern sense. Even Charles I, when resident in Oxford, was refused permission to read a book off the premises; and the same went for Oliver Cromwell too.

Perhaps Bodley would have seen the electronic revolution as a way of allowing scholars and others to gain information without removing precious books. All the same, his tomb would hardly be the same if those pillars were composed of reading devices set in stone.

The Royal Society

Oxford in the 17th century played a key role in the nation's intellectual life. One central figure was the warden of Wadham College, John Wilkins (1614-72), who was a founder of the Royal Society in 1660 under the patronage of Charles II. Wilkins was also a great peacemaker in difficult political times, gathering around him a group of scientists and free thinkers which included Christopher Wren, Robert Boyle, Robert Hooke and Henry Oldenburg, fellow founder of the Society.

Wilkins became warden of the college in 1648 at the early age of 34 after Parliamentary Visitors had unceremoniously ejected the previous incumbent (for being a Royalist) along with 13 other Fellows; the college, founded in 1610, immediately prospered as a result, attracting students from Royalist and Parliamentarian families alike.

The warden's lodgings became the regular meeting place for scientists who later formed the nucleus of the Royal Society; he even encouraged independent, free-thinking individuals who were not members of the university at all—such as Robert Boyle—to join the group.

In 1656 Wilkins married Oliver Cromwell's younger sister, Robina, the widow of Peter French, a canon of Christ Church, who had died the year before. Wilkins thereby gained access to the government and was given rooms in Whitehall. He also became one of the few people in history to become successively head off both a college at Oxford and then at Cambridge. In 1659, shortly before his death, Oliver Cromwell arranged for Wilkins to become master of Trinity College, Cambridge. But what must have appeared at the time to be astonishingly good fortune turned out to be less rosy a year later when Charles II was restored. Wilkins was then thrown out of Trinity for being a Parliamentarian! Such was the Snakes and Ladders game of life in those days.

A close friend of Wilkins and frequent visitor to Oxford and Oxfordshire was the diarist John Evelyn (1620-1706). He gave Wilkins a transparent beehive, ornamented with statues, in order to enable him to observe the insects going about their daily business. Also a friend of Charles II, some say that Evelyn may have been partly responsible for Charles II's espousing the cause of science in the first place. Evelyn accompanied the King on his visit to Oxford in 1681 when Charles inspected the Sheldonian Theatre with a view to calling a Parliament there. During his visit he watched workmen building the Science Museum next door. To this day the museum is decorated with the monogram of two intertwined Cs and the Roman numeral II—for Charles and his wife, Queen Catherine of Braganza.

Incidentally, Evelyn obtained his family fortune through the possession of a monopoly on gunpowder production during the reign of Elizabeth I. And the first English recipe for the production of gunpowder, brought to these shores from China by Arab traders, was published by the 13th-century Oxford friar and scientist Roger Bacon.

Gargoyles and Grotesques

Like misericords, gargoyles offer an extraordinary insight into the medieval mind, since their carving gave scope to individual craftsmen's weird imaginings of the unworldly realms of heaven and hell, occupied by angels and devils, as well as the worldly site of kings, bishops, and unruly persons from the lower orders. Oxford is particularly full of these strange stone creatures.

Charles Dodgson (Lewis Carroll) was particularly fond of showing Alice Liddell (daughter of the Dean of Christ Church, and, of course, the original inspiration

for Alice in Wonderland) the gargoyle near her house which shows an unfortunate, presumably in hell, condemned to grin for eternity: a miniature devil has been entrusted with the job of holding the mouth in the grinning position forever.

The word 'gargoyle' comes from the old French word *gargouille* which meant throat. The English verb to gargle comes from the same root. The word is appropriate as an architectural term because it describes an object which swallows rainwater off the roof of a building and spits it out into the street, sometimes by way of a pipe in its mouth, rather than allowing the water to cause damage by running down the walls.

Apart from gargoyles, the city is also rich in grotesques. These are like gargoyles but perform no practical function; some of the weirdest feature at Magdalen College where cavorting labourers, animals and mermaids find themselves frozen in stone forever.

Some of these grotesques though, strange to relate, are not medieval at all. They were carved in the late 1970s, time having blurred the originals, by sculptors Percy Quick and Pat Cooley at a time when many of us found it reassuring that such skills were still extant in the modern world. The figures sometimes commemorate Oxford characters too. The mitred bishop holding up his hand in blessing of the passers-by on the High Street is none other than the William of Waynflete who founded the college in 1458.

Amazingly, traces of pre-Christendom survive in the gargoyles and grotesques of Oxford. A friend of mine once set about counting effigies of the Green Man in Oxford and says she found a dozen. A good example of this pagan figure, force of fecundity and earthly fruitfulness, may be found at Magdalen, just before the corner of Longwall Street. Green Men from the 13th century stare down from the roof of Merton College chapel; yet more decorate the tomb of St Frideswide in Christ Church Cathedral. All in all the weird creatures provide a fantastic record of pre-Reformation Britain—and Oxford has had the wherewithal to keep them in good nick!

Academic Gowns

Poor degrees from Oxford have marked the start of many a remarkable career. I might mention Evelyn Waugh, who went off to the pub at Beckley to drown his sorrows on hearing of his third-class degree, or even John Ruskin, who at least obtained a double-third. Perhaps all such people, obvious possessors of huge intelligence, vow between gritted teeth that they'll show 'em.

Certainly the future Lord Curzon (1859-1925) did something of the sort. On learning of his third, he said: 'Now I shall devote the rest of my life to showing the examiners that they have made a mistake.' Then he went on to become Viceroy of India, among other things. One reason for his poor degree may well have been that, as an undergraduate at Balliol, he was far too busy with politics to do much in the way of academic work. In any case, his busy-body aloofness, which within weeks saw him making speeches at the Oxford Union (of which he later became president), won him few friends.

It must have been sweet indeed for him to don the splendid robes of Chancellor of Oxford University in 1907, complete with a gold tassel on his mortarboard, and walk into the Sheldonian Theatre to be enthroned.

Those robes were (and are) at the pinnacle of a complicated array of academic gowns that dates back to the 13th century. In 1222, for instance, the Archbishop of Canterbury decreed that all Oxford students and academics (he called them clerks) should go round in gowns described as *cappa clausa*, loose hooded capes with a hole for the head and a slit in front for the arms.

Academics remained hoodies even after the hood went out of fashion elsewhere in 15th-century England. And just as Oxford University itself came into being when some English students at the University of Paris fled here, the mortarboard seems also to have arrived here from the French capital where it was introduced to the university in about 1520. Mortarboards were decorated with a sort of bump at their centre to which, in the 18th century, was added a tuft or tassel.

In 1770 it became official university policy for anyone judged to be of noble birth to wear a gold tuft, or 'toff', which in turn gave rise to the present slang word for an aristocrat. The snobbish dress-code, only abandoned in the late 19th century, gave rise, too, to tuft-hunting, the habit of less exalted people seeking out the company of gold-tassel wearers.

Over the centuries, founders of colleges and faculties laid down instructions for what amounted to uniforms, in addition to different gowns for holders of different degrees, until by 1636 confusion reigned. An ineffectual attempt was then made to fill a chest with an example of each robe then in use, all clearly labelled. Not until 1956 was the confusion cleared up. Then D. R. Venables, of the clothes shop Shepherd and Woodward, drew up a pattern book of robes and gowns that was finally approved by the university.

As for Lord Curzon, he reckoned one jibe, penned in Oxford, did him more harm than any subsequently coined. It ran:

'My name is George Nathaniel Curzon,
I am a most superior purzon.
My face is pink, my hair is sleek,
I dine at Blenheim once a week.'

When in Oxford he lived at St Giles House, 16 St Giles, now part of St John's College. It was built in 1702 and was described by Pevsner as 'the best house of its date in Oxford'.

Sir William Blackstone

One curse of Oxford University's corrupt old days in the 18th century, when it seems that much of the historic institution was devoted to high living and low thinking, was that relatives of founders of various colleges had the automatic right to fellowships.

By the 18th century there were so many such claimants at All Souls College, all saying that they were somehow related to Archbishop Chichele—who had founded the place some 300 years earlier in 1438—that they were threatening to bring the whole college into disrepute and ridicule.

That was where Britain's foremost jurist, Sir William Blackstone (1723-80), stepped in to save the day. He became bursar of All Souls and wrote his 'Essay on Collateral Consanguinity' to thwart efforts from kith and kin trying to climb aboard the gravy train.

Blackstone's legal career got under way with surprising lack of success when he first practised as a barrister in London. Then he returned to Oxfordshire to become Recorder of Wallingford in 1749. He began lecturing at Oxford University in 1753 and became principal of New Inn Hall (forerunner of the present St Peter's College) in 1761.

But it was his four-volume *Commentaries on the Laws of England*, based on his Oxford lectures, which brought him immortal fame. Written as a beautiful piece of literature, the book had an extraordinary reception among educated English laymen. It was accepted as an authoritative revelation of the law and of the unwritten constitution.

Sir William, whose portrait by Gainsborough hangs in the Middle Temple, lived in Wallingford, just a few steps distant from the redundant church of St Peter, where he is buried. His fame and influence were even greater in the US, after the American victory in the War of Independence, than it was in Britain.

His *Commentaries* became the chief source of knowledge of English Law and even played their part in the drafting of the Declaration of Independence.

In 1976, many American lawyers visiting Britain on the 200th anniversary of the Declaration stopped off on the journey from London to Oxford to visit the grave in Wallingford. Even now a steady trickle of American lawyers visits it.

The grave is easy enough to find. You approach Wallingford from the Crowmarsh end, cross the bridge and turn left into Thames Street to the lovely Georgian St Peter's. The church was rebuilt in the 18th century, the original one having been ruined by Cromwell's troops in 1642 or 1643.

It seems that the church was rebuilt thanks to the influence of Blackstone, though he did not pay for the work as is sometimes suggested. The distinctive steeple, designed by Sir Robert Taylor, with its octagonal turret and spire, is a Gothic version of Wren's St

Bride's in Fleet Street. It cost £2,179 and Blackstone contributed £80. Blackstone also contributed to bringing the clock to St Peter's from Horse Guards Tower in Whitehall. One face manages to show 61 minutes thanks to a mistake by its maker.

Amazingly, the Diocesan Pastoral Committee recommended its demolition in 1967—such was the degree of official vandalism in the 1960s. Now we can only be grateful that the Georgian Gothic building with its distinctive spire is in the hands of the Churches Conservation Trust and is used for musical recitals throughout the year.

Real Tennis

People have played tennis in Oxford since at least 1450. In that year townsmen Thomas Blake, a skinner, William Whyte, a barber, and John Waryn, a glover, were brought before the beeks (literally in one case), namely the Chancellor of the University Gilbert Kymer and Professor Beek, for the criminal offence of tennis playing.

They had been playing 'the Game of Kings', now known as real (royal) tennis, which still thrives in the city at a court in Merton Street—where it has been played since at least 1595, though the present court dates only from 1798.

I gather this information from a truly excellent book by Jeremy Potter: *Tennis and Oxford*, published in 1994 by Oxford Unicorn Press. He remarks of real tennis: 'Humanists in the sixteenth century recognised it as an ideal combination of physical and mental exercise. Philosophers have been eloquent in its praise. Parallels have been drawn with chess. It is fitting therefore that Oxford should have played a significant role in the long history of this game.'

The game of tennis originally came from France, where it had spread like wild fire; hence the French derivations of 'tennis' from *tenez,* meaning *hold,* and 'deuce' from *deux* or two. But earlier forms of tennis, with few rules, had been played in courts and quads, and even in great halls in monasteries and university colleges on both sides of the channel, long before formal rules for the *Jeu de Paume,* as it was often called, were codified.

By the early 16th century Town and Gown authorities had given up the struggle against real tennis. By the 17th century Christ Church don John Locke (1632-1704) was even using tennis to illustrate a metaphysical point when he wrote: 'A tennis-ball, whether in motion by the stroke of a racket or lying at rest, is not by anyone taken to be free agent.'

Courts sprang up all over Oxford, in colleges and in the town. Old tennis balls have been discovered in the rafters of the halls at Merton and Wadham, and lodged in the walls of various college quads and courtyards. The Oriel Square Court was founded even before the Merton Street one, but fell into disuse in the 19th century. It was played upon by kings and princes including Charles I (during the Civil War the Parliamentarians issued a pass to allow a tennis outfit, tailored in London, to be taken to Oxford for him to wear!), Charles ll and even Edward VII when he was an undergraduate.

The name of the game now being played at Wimbledon was long in doubt; so much so that the tournament is simply known as The Championships—without specifying exactly what they are championships of! In time the two versions of the game were differentiated by calling one Real Tennis and the other Lawn Tennis. Rules of the latter were codified in England in the late 19th century and internationally by the International Lawn Tennis Federation, a meeting of 12 national associations, meeting in Paris in 1913. The Federation is now known as the International Tennis Federation. It moved its headquarters to UK during the Second World War.

But back to real tennis in Oxford. The Merton Street court is home to the Oxford University Tennis Club. Its most famous professional, who rented it from Merton College, was the father of Oxford historian and antiquarian Anthony Wood (1632-95), who lived next door in Postmasters Hall. His successor, Alan Oliver, who played lawn tennis for Oxfordshire before taking up real tennis, told me that former professionals had run the club on their own account, and even now the tennis club is open to Town as well as Gown.

Barges and Boathouses

Hanging on the walls of the lounge in the Randolph Hotel are a set of pictures that conjure up a certain elegant but now vanished Oxford. They are pictures by Sir Osbert Lancaster depicting scenes from Max Beerbohm's only novel *Zuleika Dobson*, a satire published in 1911. The book tracks the progress of Zuleika in Oxford. She is so beautiful that even the bearded stone emperors outside the Sheldonian sweat as she passes by in a landau. As for the undergraduates who see her during Eights Week, they all commit mass suicide by jumping in the river.

The stretch of river into which they jump is of course downstream from Folly Bridge, where all the old college barges were moored for about 80 years. Many of the barges were originally the state barges of the London City companies which were bought and brought to Oxford in the late 19th century when organised rowing became an established part of university life. They served as clubrooms, dressing rooms and

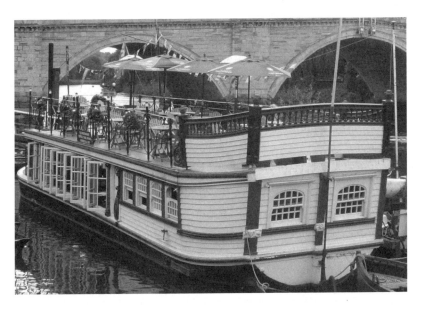

grandstands for the various colleges when the social scene was as important as the rowing itself. Elegant Edwardian parties happened aboard them, although it should be noted that their sanitary arrangements were far from satisfactory.

The very first Oxford barge was built by boatbuilder King in 1815. Despite his calling he had no premises with a river frontage so a barge seemed the ideal solution to his problem. By 1830 colleges were hiring barges from him. The first university barge was towed into place from London in 1846 when Oxford University Boat Club bought the Merchant Taylors Company barge. After that individual colleges started to buy second-hand, or have their own barges built by such boat builders as Salters.

Serious oarsmen and women however deplored them as they made still narrower a stretch of river which many already maintained was too narrow for serious practice. Christ Church, which owns the stretch of river bank below Folly Bridge, was the first college to replace its barge with a permanent boathouse in bright red brick. One by one the other colleges followed suit: a highly visible symptom of the changing character of Oxford from a place of cool detachment to one where results (winning) are all important.

The chaotic but elegant races that Zuleika came to watch were Bumping Races held during Eights Week in high summer. These were the only races held on this stretch of river; the team competing annually against Cambridge had to go to Henley to practise. Bumping, which entails each college boat attempting to bump the one ahead of it, started in 1815 when Brasenose is recorded as becoming the first head of the river.

As for Zuleika, the Oxford she represented is now as dead as the undergraduates who died for love of her. By the late 1950s nearly all the college barges had fallen into decrepitude and were fast disappearing — in some cases, literally under water. Now only one or two remain on different reaches of the river, converted into raffish residences.

Victorian Architecture

Much of Oxford's university architecture still retains a Victorian atmosphere: clubby and proud, reflecting the great 19th-century university reforms and building programmes.

Balliol College, for example, is an ancient foundation in Victorian disguise. Its architecture breathes the indomitable British virtues embodied in such sayings of Benjamin Jowett (its eminent master 1870-93) as 'effortless superiority' — something he hoped his students would achieve — and 'never apologise, never retreat, get it done and let them scream'.

Across Broad Street is another medieval foundation dressed in 19th-century clothes, Exeter College. It dates from 1314 when it was built just inside the city wall and next to a small city gate called the Turl. Its reconstruction in morally uplifting Gothic was largely the work of Sir George Gilbert Scott in the 1850s. The exquisite 17th-century chapel that his so-called 'Early Decorated' version replaces was apparently so well built that it had to be destroyed with gunpowder.

Members of the Pre-Raphaelite Brotherhood, William Morris and Edward Burne-Jones, both came up as undergraduates to Exeter in 1852. In 1857, under the leadership of Dante Gabriel Rossetti, they set about coating the interior of the Union Library, recently completed by architect Benjamin Woodward, with dreamy Arthurian murals.

But the apogee of all things Victorian in Oxford is that great cathedral in wrought iron, the University Museum, recently renamed the Museum of Natural History. A leading personality in its construction was John Ruskin. He took a huge interest in the building of this wonderful construction from the moment that Woodward won the competition to build it in 1854.

His efforts to 'exalt the dignity of labour' by solemnly handing shovels to his students and books to Woodward's workmen, were less than altogether successful. His somewhat effete students, including Oscar Wilde, were unimpressed at being told to dig up the road at Hinksey. However, his efforts at uplifting the workers were not a complete failure. Woodward's men were imported from Ireland. Ruskin made sure they

The Museum of Natural History, Victorian masterpiece

'began each day with simple prayers from willing hearts' and Ruskin's encouragement of the workers to express themselves bore fruit: too much fruit in one case.

A man named O'Shea turned out to be an extremely gifted sculptor but his work was deemed insubordinate by some singularly stuffy committee members and he was dismissed. But even after the sack he continued to carve parrots and owls, representing members of convocation, on the main porch. He was finally made to deface his own work. Then funds ran out and there was no money left to make good his hack marks —

which may still be seen today. So much for Ruskin's ideas about the Dignity of Labour in that Victorian climate.

Nevertheless, he was delighted with the building, perhaps the only one in existence which really gives solid form to his architectural ideas expressed in *The Stones of Venice* and *The Seven Lamps of Architecture*.

T. G. Jackson

Who designed the Bridge of Sighs in Oxford, or the ornate New Examination Schools, or the former High School for Girls in St Giles, with its apparently perfect Georgian lines, or the Military College in Temple Cowley, or the chapel at Balliol, the cricket pavilion in the University Parks, or the restoration of Carfax Tower?

When most of us think of Oxford architects we think of 17th-century geniuses such as Wren, or Hawksmoor, or of other nameless, medieval masters from an earlier, ecclesiastical age. The name of Sir Thomas Graham Jackson (1835-1924)—christened 'Oxford Jackson' by William Whyte in his book of that name—seldom springs to mind. Yet he was far more prolific than any of his predecessors and when accepting an honorary degree in a ceremony carefully choreographed by Lord Curzon (that most superior purzon, as the unkind ditty ran), the Professor of Poetry even announced that he 'might most rightly be called the creator of modern Oxford'.

When Jackson died aged 88 in 1924, *The Oxford Magazine* mourned him as 'Oxford's most distinguished architect since Wren'. Certainly he had been responsible for giving Oxford, and indeed Cambridge to some extent, not to mention several public schools including Radley, a sort of Victorian overlay that contributes greatly to the feel of the place: clubby, even elitist, mainly masculine; the very feel perhaps that now puts off state-school sixth-formers from applying to Oxford University. Yet that atmosphere, following the great reforming commission of the university in the mid 19th century, did not come about by mistake. It was deliberately nurtured, though to be fair, the great reformers such as Benjamin Jowett wanted to spread the public school spirit to all, not only to those who had actually been to public schools.

In this spirit, Jackson was commissioned to design the Non-Collegiate Building next door to his magnificently eclectic New Examination Schools. Whyte points out: 'It was intended to provide inexpensive education for those excluded from Oxford by the high cost of college living.' Wags were quick to note, though, that its walls were of rubble while those of the New Examination Schools were ashlar. *The Oxford Magazine* commented that if this was intended 'by some occult symbolism to signify the relation of the Non-

Collegiate students to the University, then 'it is neither fair nor courteous to hint that the relation is that of the rough to the polished'.

Extraordinary as it may seem now, all things Victorian fell out of fashion shortly after Jackson's death, and despite his fame in life he was almost entirely forgotten for some 60 or 70 years. Worse, he was actually decried, with Peter Levi describing him as 'the only really preposterous architect'. Anyone who has been to Venice will realise, of course, that the Bridge of Sighs in Oxford is actually modelled on the Rialto: but did you know that such a symbol of the city was dreamt up by Jackson and not built until 1913?

The Bridge of Sighs

The Pitt Rivers Museum

Next door to Ruskin's University Museum stands the Pitt Rivers Museum. And some say that the door leading from the University Museum to the Pitt Rivers Museum became the inspiration for John Tenniel's drawing of a door in *Through the Looking Glass*, surmounted by the words 'Queen Alice', where Alice was exasperated by the insubordination of a footman in the shape of a frog in livery.

Pitt Rivers himself was born in 1827 as Augustus Lane Fox. He assumed the additional surnames of Pitt Rivers in 1880 when he inherited a fortune from his great-uncle George Pitt, the second Baron Rivers. His collection of objects from around the world grew originally out of a study he had made of how weapons evolved and improved. Then, as a result of this study, he began collecting early firearms before extending his interest to other categories of interest. As a senior army officer, travelling to the farthest flung outposts of the British Empire at its zenith, Pitt Rivers had ample opportunity to collect things. The rooms of his London home were soon bulging with 'specimens' from all over the world: weapons, costumes, looms and, eccentrically, human remains.

From the beginning, Pitt Rivers saw the educational importance of museums and wanted his things to go on public display. In an 1892 paper to the Society of Arts he wrote: 'The knowledge of the facts of evolution, and of the great processes of gradual development, is the one great knowledge that we have to inculcate, and this knowledge can be taught by museums.' So he decided a home should be found for his collection.

First it went to the Bethnal Green branch of the South Kensington Museum of Natural History, then to the main museum, before being offered to Oxford University on condition that a separate building be constructed to house it. The Pitt Rivers Museum was therefore built in 1884, when General Augustus Pitt Rivers defined one of its main purposes as 'to illustrate the arts of Prehistoric times, as far as practicable, by those existing savages in corresponding stages of civilisation'. Hardly politically correct language, these days.

Another condition of the new museum building was that someone be appointed to teach on subjects connected with the museum. The first person to hold this post was Sir Edward Tylor, who thus became the first teacher of anthropology at a British university. He was succeeded by Henry Balfour, who had the job as curator of the museum from 1891 to 1935. Throughout that long period he continued to add to the General's collections, corresponding with many people in colonial service overseas, until the museum (like the General's house before it) began to bulge at the seams.

Writing in the magazine *The Ashmolean* on the Pitt Rivers' 100th anniversary in 1984, Helene La Rue, then the museum's ethnomusicologist, said: 'His purpose in excavating was not mere acquisitiveness; through a careful study of the sites and everything found on them, he tried to discover how past peoples lived, interpreting his finds through analogies to the so-called 'primitive societies' that he knew.'

And finally, to mark the museum gaining its new premises, in 1990 it handed back some of the skeletal remains in its care to the Australian aboriginal communities—who had requested the human remains of their ancestors to be returned.

Women Students

Change comes to Oxford University in strange ways. William Ewart Gladstone, for instance, originally opposed women being allowed to take their place in academic life, and yet his daughter Helen became Principal at Newnham College, Cambridge, and in 1887 Gladstone planted a tree there in her honour. Gladstone was involved with the Royal Commission into Oxford's affairs in 1850. At best it set the climate for the changes which brought women to Oxford in 1879, when Lady Margaret and Somerville colleges opened as halls of residence for women.

Women's admittance occurred thanks to a group of liberal dons who formed the Association for the Education of Women (AEW) in Oxford in 1878. Lady Margaret Hall and Somerville started out under the academic control of the AEW. The difference between the two was that the first was strictly Church of England and the second was inter-denominational.

Alongside these two residential halls grew up, in typically Oxfordian haphazard fashion, the institution that eventually became St Anne's College. It catered for the largest group of would-be women undergraduates—those living in private homes. The Society of Home Students was formed and administered by Bertha Johnson, wife of All Souls academic Arthur Johnson, from her North Oxford home. Mrs Johnson championed the notion that young women should live in cultured homes rather than take up collegiate life. Amazingly, despite its early roots, St Anne's did not become a college until 1952.

St Hugh's College was founded by Elizabeth Wordsworth as a society for women students in 1886 and moved into its present purpose-built buildings in 1916, having been recognised as a college in 1911.

Oxford's other college founded for women, St Hilda's, owes its existence to that redoubtable advocate of women's education, Dorothea Beale, principal of Cheltenham Ladies College. She founded it in 1893 expressly to help women from Cheltenham to take advantage of the new educational opportunities in Oxford.

The university lagged years behind the foundation of the colleges, however: women were not allowed to take degrees until 1920, although they had been allowed to sit exams and be classified for about 25 years before that date.

Refugee Academics

Some brilliant Jews whom Oxford rescued from Hitler are aiming to found some sort of lasting memorial—a scholarship perhaps—to commemorate the extraordinary role Oxford played in the years before the war when the university offered sanctuary to several Jewish academics fleeing Nazi Germany.

The most famous of these was Albert Einstein (1879-1955), the first German Jewish scholar to take up an academic post at Christ Church. He arrived in May 1931 and was soon afterwards offered a studentship (fellowship) at the college, for an 'emolument' of £400 a year.

Einstein was a protégé of Frederick Lindemann, later Viscount Cherwell (1886-1957), who famously toured the continent in style during the 1930s (some say in a

Einstein's blackboard, 1931, Museum of the History of Science

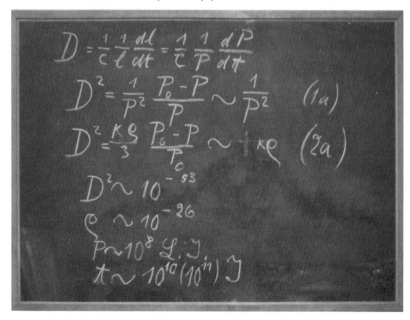

Rolls-Royce; others an Armstrong Siddeley) in order to search out Jewish academics and offer them posts in the relative safety of Oxford.

Einstein's studentship was scheduled to last five years. However, he left after only two, having stayed in his accommodation at Christ Church for three periods between 1931 and 1933. Then, still concerned about the Nazi threat, he departed for Princeton. He asked that his annual £400 be used to assist other Jewish émigrés; and Lindemann—who of course later became famous as Churchill's wartime scientific adviser, universally known in Whitehall as 'the Prof'—did indeed use the funds to bring brainy Jews, mainly scientists, away from Hitler's horrible regime.

Sad to say, though, Einstein's appointment at Oxford also serves to show up some ambivalent attitudes in England towards helping persecuted Germans. When the Dean of Christ Church, Henry White (1859-1934), offered Einstein his research studentship, he immediately received a letter from J. G. C. Anderson, Professor of Classical Art and Archaeology, fulminating against Einstein's appointment as 'unpatriotic', and stating that the college founders had never intended emoluments to go to foreigners. Professor Anderson wrote on 2 November 1931: 'The University cannot carry on its work without a very large Government grant, and yet a college can pay out money to subsidize a German.' Happily, not a lot of notice was taken of Anderson. The Dean wrote: '[Einstein's] attainments and reputation are so high that they transcend national boundaries, and any university in the world ought to be proud of having him.'

I was reminded of all this when I dropped into Oxford Town Hall for the exhibition called 'Persecution and Survival: The Paul Jacobsthal Story' on an extraordinary archive, kept for years in dusty boxes at Oxford's Institute of Archaeology, that tells the tale of the life and times of another German-Jewish academic: archaeologist and expert on Celtic art, Paul Jacobsthal (1880-1957). Jacobsthal was thrown out of Marburg University in 1935 '*aus rassischen Gründen*' (on racial grounds) and together with his wife Guste came to Oxford, helped through the formalities by friends, including classical archaeologist John Beazley, with whom he had already published a work on Greek vases.

His huge collection of photographs had been confiscated by the Nazis, but in Oxford he set about rebuilding it. In this he had the help of many former colleagues in Germany who continued to correspond with him at great risk to themselves. The problem for them was that German pre-history was a hot political potato. The Nazis wanted archaeological evidence of Aryan supremacy. Part of Jacobsthal's legacy is refusing to supply it.

The Discovery of Penicillin

Three men shared the Nobel Prize for the discovery of penicillin: one was born in Scotland, another in Australia, and the third in Germany. But it is apt, somehow, that the Oxford memorial to the team that isolated and purified a mold on the *penicillium notatum* fungus, the so-called 'miracle drug' hailed by many as the greatest discovery of the 20th century, should lie between the Danby Arch (the entrance to the University Botanic Garden) and the High Street, alongside the Rose Garden, which is also a memorial to the team—because herbalists from the time of the English Civil War had long suspected that some mouldy substances killed bacteria on wounds.

Alexander Fleming (1881-1925) was the Scots-born receiver of the 1945 prize for Physiology or Medicine, but his name does not appear on the Oxford memorial. Indeed, when he telephoned the German-born prize-winner Sir Ernst Boris Chain (1906-79), having read that the team at the Oxford University Dunn School were researching his accidental discovery of penicillin back in 1928, Chain exclaimed: 'Good God, I thought he was dead.'

The Australian was the team's leader, Howard Florey (1898-1968), a former Rhodes scholar at Magdalen College who went on to become Baron Florey and the Provost of The Queen's College, whose Florey Building, in St Clements, designed by Sir James Stirling, now commemorates him.

Fleming, a scientist at St Mary's Hospital, Paddington, who served as a captain in the Medical Corps during the First World War, had observed in an article in *The Lancet* that antiseptics probably killed more soldiers than did infection or septicemia. He wrote in later years: 'When I woke up just after dawn on 28 September 1928, I certainly didn't plan to revolutionise all medicine by discovering the world's first antibiotic, or bacteria killer. But I guess that is exactly what I did.'

But it was the teamwork of the researchers at Oxford that brought a number of disciplines together to cultivate the mould, and isolate its antibiotic agent. Chain worked out the natural antibiotic's molecular structure, later confirmed by X-ray by another Oxford Nobel Prize winner, Dorothy Hodgkin (1910-94). Chain, a Jewish graduate of Berlin's Friedrich Wilhelm University, left Germany in 1930. Towards the end of the war he learned that both his sister and mother had perished in the camps.

The first human guinea pig upon whom penicillin was tried was an Oxford policeman, whose illness went into remission. The Oxford team planned to smear their overcoat linings with the precious penicillin culture in the event of German invasion in order to continue growing it elsewhere.

Restoring the Emperors' Heads

'Beware of falling angels', read a famous notice in a decaying Venetian church some years ago. But what is less well known is that many of the great classical buildings of Oxford were in a similarly dangerous state of picturesque decay during the 1940s, 1950s and even 1960s.

In 1965 for instance, a notice in Broad Street telling passers-by to 'beware of falling heads' would not have been altogether out of place, for in that year the university authorities pronounced the 13 so-called Emperors' heads outside the Sheldonian Theatre to be so decayed and dangerous as to need replacing altogether, rather than restoring. The heads have only been known as Emperors since Max Beerbohm described them as Caesars in his book *Zuleika Dobson*, published in 1911. In Wren's accounts for the Sheldonian they are described as 'termains', which may derive from the Roman god Terminus, protector of boundaries and boundary stones. Sir Christopher Wren commissioned William Byrd, a stonecutter with a yard in nearby Holywell Street, to carve the original 14 heads, completed in 1669.

Sadly, after 200 years, they had become so decayed that in 1868 new ones were made; but they chose poor-quality Headington freestone or Milton-under-Wychwood stone. In addition, they were almost immediately daubed with paint by undergraduates during commemoration week, and the process of removing the paint started off such a rapid degeneration that another 100 years later the second generation of heads were in worse condition than some of their prececessors still surviving in Oxford gardens. By the middle of the 20th century John Betjeman was comparing the heads with 'illustrations in a medical textbook on skin diseases'.

In 1968 the Royal Fine Art Commission took the view that a final attempt at restoring the heads should be made before commissioning a third generation. Three heads were consequently taken away for experiments—which unfortunately failed. So Oxford sculptor Michael Black was commissioned to carve one head to see whether substitutes could be made which would preserve the spirit of the old ones. He tracked down all the original, pre-1868 heads and also studied closely the 17th-century prints of the Sheldonian Theatre by the university engraver David Loggan, before producing his prototype.

His head won approval and in 1970 he started work on the remaining 12 using Clipsham stone. The wall, piers and railings were restored at the same time and the new heads were installed in October 1972 at a total cost of just under £27,000. Much of the cost of the new heads was met by the Oxford Historic Buildings Fund, set up in 1957 as a result of an urgent appeal to stop the decay of the city's best edifices, including the Sheldonian, the Bodleian, the Old Ashmolean and many of the best college buildings.

Already in Wren's time Duke Humfrey's Library had been declared dangerous but by 1957 it was perilous, as was Selden End, the room above Convocation House, due partly to shrinkage caused by the installation of central heating. The Oxford buildings had been haphazardly kept standing for centuries (American author Nathaniel Hawthorne wrote in the 19th century: 'If you strike one of the old walls with a stick a portion of it comes powdering down. The effect of the decay is very picturesque') but the total neglect during the Second World War meant that solution had become urgent.

Sir Isaiah Berlin

Isaiah Berlin (1909-97) was born in Riga, Latvia. When he was six his Jewish family moved to St Petersburg, Russia, where he witnessed the 1917 revolution. In 1921 the family moved again, this time to England, where Isaiah was sent to St Paul's School, and then up to Corpus Christi College, Oxford, where he obtained a First in Greats. Then he took another Oxford degree, this time in PPE, and got another First in that—after less than a year on the course.

He was then elected to a prize fellowship at All Souls in 1932; became a Fellow of New College; Chichele Professor of Social and Political Theory; and the founding President of Wolfson College. For 65 years, therefore, apart from a wartime spell in US, he was one of the best known—and certainly one of the wittiest—figures in Oxford.

But since his death, from a Town point of view (i.e. from where I am sitting) the heated debate going on (for instance in the pages of *The Times Literary Supplement* and *The New York Review of Books*) about Sir Isaiah's reputation and standing provides an interesting insight into Gown life—particularly mid 20th-century Gown life at All Souls, where dons, unbothered by students, live together and eat meals together in sometimes waspish propinquity. Life in that august place, a world apart, was apparently full of precious egos, easily bruised, petty snobbery, and college politics taking on an importance almost as great as world politics.

There is the story of historian A. L. Rowse (towards whom Berlin now stands accused of behaving duplicitously) coming down to breakfast one morning, cross about a bad review in *The Times* of his latest book. 'You see the way the upper classes resent that I have been able to rise into their midst entirely by my own merit.' To which the Warden of the college, John Sparrow, looking up from breakfast, replied: 'Rowse, whatever gives you the impression that only the rich detest you?' Charming and comforting somehow to learn that such brainy men (they were all men, of course) could be as silly as the rest of us.

But one of the best stories about Isaiah Berlin links him with Churchill. Isaiah Berlin's reports from Britain's embassy in Washington during the war were so entertaining that Churchill asked to meet him; but thanks to some mix-up Churchill found himself having lunch with the American songwriter Irving Berlin instead. Bewilderment set in when the conversation turned to work in progress...

Modern Architecture in Oxford

Why was there such a delay in Oxford adopting any modern architecture? Nikolaus Pevsner wrote in *Buildings of Oxfordshire* that the first truly 20th century buildings in the city appeared more than half way through it. Maybe it was because of the innate conservation that Matthew Arnold described back in the 19th century: 'Beautiful city! so venerable, so lovely, so unravaged by the fierce intellectual life of our century, so serene! ... whispering from her towers the last enchantments of the Middle Age'.

Pevsner was heralding two small buildings, both by Michael Powers of the Architects Co-Partnership, dated 1957 and 1958: 'These, one can hardly believe it, were the first buildings at Oxford in the language of the 20th century. It beats even Cambridge.' The two buildings were an approach to the Master's Lodging at Corpus Christi and a small range at St John's, which Pevsner praised as 'an intelligently planned group of polygons without anything mannered'.

Very shortly after the Powers achievements, dons stuck two toes in the water. In 1960, Arne Jacobsen arrived in town from Copenhagen and started building St Catherine's College, at the same time that the traditional-style Nuffield College was

completed. Pevsner wrote: 'This, a whole college built by one man to one design, makes Nuffield College look even more absurd. This style of much glass and a minimum of mass which flourished in progressive countries in the 1930s is not dead; that St Catherine's shows.'

Pioneers in the business of departing from the antique were architects Powell & Moya who brought us in the 1960s Wolfson College and the lovely picture gallery at Christ Church. The reasons why Oxford University suddenly embraced the architectural modern world are enigmatic: a sort of latter-day enlightenment perhaps, waking it up out of its cloistered introspection, or more probably simply *force majeure* in the shape of ever-increasing student numbers.

But Oxford had been ruminating the great sea change before it happened. The 1951 Epstein statue of Lazarus, who, of course, rose from the dead, looks quite at home in the 16th-century New College chapel; as do the abstract stained-glass windows by John Piper in the chapel of mock-medieval Nuffield.

Pioneers in the world of concrete were Arup Associates. They were responsible for the jutting concrete beams at two separate buildings at Somerville and, in the early 1970s, for *The Oxford Times* Newspaper House in Osney Mead, which Pevsner describes as 'one of the best commercial buildings'. After which Oxford became known for some of the finest modern architecture, including for instance John McCormack's extensions at both St John's and Wadham College.

Maybe a case not of Lewis Carroll's mock turtle, but of Aesop's tortoise and the hare…

5. The Colleges
Academics and Eccentrics

Back in the 12th century, when Oxford University was just flickering into precarious existence, Masters, licensed to teach, began to gather groups of scholars around them. They hired rooms in the city, mainly in the area around the church of St Mary the Virgin, in which to deliver their lectures; and they lived, usually together with their students, in houses scattered about the town. These houses gradually developed into academic halls which, typically, were run by enterprising graduates for profit. They thrived in the city from the 12th century until the 17th, by which time they had almost—but not entirely—been replaced by colleges. (Despite its name, St Edmund Hall, the last survivor, became a college by Royal Charter in 1957.)

But even after the foundation of the earliest colleges, most scholars continued to lived in academic halls. Astonishingly, as late as the mid 15th century about 1,450 of the university's then population of 1,600 lived in halls. This was because the founders of the earliest colleges intended them for graduate students, not undergraduates.

Only with William of Wykeham's foundation of New College in 1379 was any provision made for undergraduates to live in colleges. He stipulated that 70 places at the college should be made available to boys from his school at Winchester. Thereafter, all succeeding colleges founded between then and the mid 16th century, with the exception of Lincoln (1427) and All Souls (1438)—namely Magdalen (1458), Brasenose (1509), Corpus Christi (1517), Christ Church (1546), Trinity (1555) and St John's (1555) — provided for undergraduates.

The regulation of academic halls, i.e. the maintenance of discipline over unruly and often drunken scholars, was an uphill task for the early university authorities; one that was only tackled—and then only partially—when the university began to emerge as a formal corporate body. The concept of the colleges also becoming independent, permanent communities continued that process.

They were modelled to a large extent on monastic communities, with their cloisters and quads. Indeed five colleges, which had been overtly founded by monks, perished following the 16th-century dissolution of the monasteries. These so-called monastic colleges were: Gloucester College (founded 1277), which stood where Worcester stands today, near Gloucester Green bus station; Durham College (1291), which was replaced by Trinity; Canterbury College (1362), now absorbed into Christ Church; St Bernard's College (1437), re-founded after the Dissolution as St John's; and St Mary's College, which had only recently been completed in New Inn Hall Street when it was dissolved.

A sixth college, Corpus Christi (1513), was originally begun as an outpost for the monks of St Swithun's, Winchester, but luckily was eventually founded as a secular college instead by Richard Foxe (who was commemorated for centuries by a tame fox being kept on the premises).

A number of colleges, notably women's, were founded in the 19th century; then there was a gap until 1952 when St Anne's received its Royal Charter. Since then Oxford has reacted to a changing world by establishing such institutions as Green Templeton College (2008), specialising in environmental studies, and Kellogg College (1990), which caters for part-time graduate students and promoting lifelong, flexible learning.

Confusingly, though, *private* halls, as opposed to the old *academic* halls, reappeared in the 19th century and still survive today, notably in the shapes of the Roman Catholic Campion Hall and St Benet's Hall.

Queen's College

The Queen's College, as it is properly known, was founded in 1341 by Robert Eglesfield, the sixth college to be built in the city. He was chaplain to the wife of Edward III, Queen Philippa. But the building we know today was largely built in the early 18th century by the Oxford family of Townsend, probably working to designs by Nicholas Hawksmoor. The screen and cupola, containing a statue of Queen Caroline, was not built until the 1730s and is modelled on the Luxembourg Palace, Paris.

Mr Eglesfield laid down strict rules about how members of his foundation—fellows, chaplains and 'poor boys'—should behave. He regulated almost every detail of their lives, laying much stress on their eating habits.

Evidence unearthed by archaeologists , called in to survey the site of the college' s new Senior Common Room dining room and underground kitchen, shows just how much fish, rather than meat, they ate in those days. Indeed, twice a week (Wednesdays and Fridays), the dons of yore ate no meat at all.

The chairman of the UN Inter-governmental Panel on Climate Change—who recently jointly won the Nobel Peace Prize—would certainly have approved of the dietary habits of these medieval dons at Queen's College, Oxford. And Dr Rajendra Pachauri recently called on us all to stop eating meat for just one day a week, suggesting that halving our meat consumption would reduce greenhouse gases more than if we halved our car use.

The Oxford Archaeology dig unearthed the western and eastern walls of the 14th-century west range. They found the area in Queen's College that had been a kitchen in medieval times. Within the structure they found animal and fish bones, medieval pottery and a fossilised cat. They also discovered just how important communal dining was in those days for the well-being of an Oxford college.

The founder also stipulated in the statutes that all possessions of the college, including livestock, should be marked with the college crest of a flying eagle, so perhaps the archaeologists' most interesting find was a piece of 14th-century tile that appears to bear part of that crest.

Sarah Parker, spokesperson for architects Berman Guedes Strettons, who were charged with building the new dining room and kitchen, said: 'The tradition of communal dining, once central to building college communities, has somewhat ebbed away. This is partly as a result of the relaxing of collegiate rules and competition from the food outlets of Oxford. Queen's College, however, is determined to create a facility that makes it the most desirable place for its members to eat.'

Queen's College home bursar, Lind Irving-Bell, said of the new building work: 'It is exciting to be providing state-of-the-art facilities that will allow the great dining traditions of Queen's to continue well into the future. I am sure that our predecessors would approve.' Even today college members are summoned to meals by the clarion call of a trumpet, though the instrument used now dates only from the 17th century.

As to fish eating though, eels made up much of the medieval diet. Sadly, Oxfordshire rivers now contain only about one per cent of the eels that they once did. And, of course, at Christmas the scholars made up for their meatless days by feasting on a boar's head - as they still do (even though Christmas Eve was designated a meatless day).

Magdalen College

Three bishops of Winchester founded colleges at Oxford. They probably had the funds as during the Middle Ages their home city was Europe's richest bishopric.

Magdalen College is the second oldest of the three. From its inception the college has been no stranger to controversy. Its founding bishop, William of Wayneflete (1395-1486), was Chancellor of England in 1457 when he closed the old hospital of St John to found Magdalen on the site, apparently helping himself to all its endowments in the process.

The hospital, which is still commemorated each June with a sermon preached from Magdalen's open-air pulpit in St John's Quad on the Sunday nearest to St John the Baptist's day, had existed for more than 250 years before the college's foundation on 12 June 1458. William of Wayneflete, who also oversawmuch of the building of Eton College for Henry VI, borrowed many architectural ideas for Magdalen from those used by his predecessor William of Wykeham, bishop of Winchester at New College in 1379, as indeed did Richard Fox, the last of the episcopal trio from Winchester, at Corpus Christi in 1516.

The chapel at Magdalen was finished in about 1478. It was described by Christopher Hobhouse, in his classic 1939 book, *Oxford* (Batsford), as 'certainly the most beautiful of all the colleges'. Built some 100 years later than the one at New College, the Wykeham plan is evident. There is an ante-chapel set at right angles to the choir and a great east wall, left austerely windowless.

Magdalen found itself at the centre of national politics in 1686 when James II, who had already managed to install two Catholics as heads of Oxford colleges, took a step too far by trying to foist one on Magdalen. The presidency of the college was not in his gift and he lost the battle. Some say it was the beginning of the end for him.

The college buildings apparently did not wear well. In 1724 no less an architect than Nicholas Hawksmoor announced that he had plans to rebuild the whole college as the old buildings were 'so decrepit'. Quite what happened to Hawksmoor's plans is unclear, but in the 1730s a fellow of the college called Edward Holdsworth drew up some grand, classical plans — and actually completed one wing of his scheme, which still stands on the banks of the Cherwell and is known as the New Building.

The drastic plans do not end there. James Wyatt destroyed the original roofs in both Magdalen and New College chapels and in the 1830s the embellishments at Magdalen's were actually put up for auction in the college stables. But we must not carp. Damage to the architecture could easily have been much worse. Even the quadrangle only narrowly escaped demolition in the 19th century. Hobhouse recounts how, in 1822, a senior fellow named Dr Ellerton returned from holiday to find workmen busy pulling down its north side for what would now be described as 'health and safety' reasons. Someone had alleged that the structure was dangerous. We have Dr Ellerton to thank for saving the east cloister and rebuilding the north side, though in less picturesque style than the original.

However, 19th-century students bribed stonemasons to carve one of the beasts in the quad in the likeness of the above-mentioned Dr Ellerton. The joke was that as time went by he began to resemble that creature more and more.

Still interested in sculpture, Magdalen, celebrated its 550th anniversary by placing in its grounds a permanent sculpture by Mark Wallinger—the artist who won the Turner Prize with *State Britain*, a recreation of Brian Haw's anti-Iraq War demonstration in Parliament Square.

Magdalen College's Last Supper

The painting of *The Last Supper* returns to the college ante-chapel after being on tour to various Leonardo exhibitions worldwide. It belongs to the Royal Academy but is on long-term loan to the college. Ever since its arrival in Oxford in September 1992, stretched on a vast metal drum and packed into a specially constructed wooden crate with 20 people in attendance, it has been attracting a steadily increasing number of visitors, some returning time after time. Such is the magnetic draw of Leonardo.

Not that this painting is by Leonardo da Vinci, though it is of momentous importance all the same. It is by the Lombard artist Giovan Pietro Rizzoli, known as Giampietrino (active 1495-1549). He was a pupil of Leonardo who, luckily for posterity, copied onto canvas the original work—namely the fresco in the refectory of the Milan monastery of Santa Maria delle Grazie—a few years after it was completed in 1498.

Luckily, I say, because the original did not survive the ravages of time well. This picture therefore became an essential crib for art experts restoring the original at the end of the 20th century; sadly, it had not only suffered through time but also thanks to Napoleon's troops throwing unsavoury things at it during their occupation of Milan, and also thanks to a stray Allied bomb hitting the monastery during the Second World War, thereby leaving the fresco for a time open to the elements.

As if that were not bad enough there were the alterations perpetrated by the monks of Santa Maria delle Grazie too. At some stage they evidently installed a door beneath the fresco, obliterating Christ's feet in the process. So, all in all, thank God for Giampietrino (even though a fairly acrimonious debate still rumbles on among art experts about how true to his copy the restoration of the original fresco has been).

Magdalen was truly grateful to receive the painting, with the then President of the College Anthony Smith declaring: 'Word rapidly passed through the college and through Oxford generally and ever since that moment there has been a steady trickle of visitors, me returning again and again, to view the work which Sir Ernst Gombrich described as "one of the great miracles wrought by human genius".'

The great Austrian-born art historian E. H. Gombrich (1909-2001) was at the installation ceremony in March 1993 and lectured to a packed ante-chapel of college members and guests, after which the Bishop of Winchester (who holds the office of Visitor to the College) blessed the painting and the choir sang an anthem specially composed for the occasion.

Interestingly, Sir Ernst began by saying how much Leonardo would probably have disapproved of his talk. He began: 'It is unlikely that Leonardo would have approved of my attempts to talk about his work or its copy. After all, he was the author of the

so-called *Paragone*, the comparison or rather the contest of the various forms of art.'
Then he reminded the audience that Leonardo wrote: 'Your pen will be worn out before
you have fully described something that the painter may present to you instantaneously
using his science. And your tongue will be impeded by thirst and your body by sleep
and hunger, before you could show in words what the painter may show in an instant.'

Leonardo chose the version of *The Last Supper* story according to St John despite
the fact that, unlike the story according to the other three gospels, it does not mention
the Eucharist. What he portrays instead is the moment after Christ has said, 'Verily,
verily I say unto you that one of you shall betray me.' And the twelve diners (in addition
to Christ) looked at one another 'and began to be sorrowful, and to say unto Him, Is it
I?' And Judas Iscariot knocked over the salt!

The ante-chapel in which the Giampietrino picture usually hangs dates from
about the same time as the painting, although it was much altered just before Victoria's
accession to the throne by Lewis Cottingham (1787-1847). But anyone wanting to see
a really Victorian version of *The Last Supper* could do worse than visit the Church of St
Thomas of Canterbury in Elsfield. Inside they will find the newly restored mosaic of the
subject as translated by Antonio Salviati (1816-90), who had perfected a way of mass-
producing mosaic tiles. Obviously based on Leonardo's fresco, the mosaic nevertheless
has a chalice in front of Christ rather than the everyday crockery that the monks of
Santa Maria delle Grazie would have recognised.

Brasenose College

Strange old college Brasenose, with old being the operative word. It takes its name from
the bronze sanctuary knocker in the shape of a lion's face and attached to the main gate
of the medieval Brasenose Hall, first recorded in a document of 1279. In the Middle
Ages, colleges and halls were places of safety for fugitives of the law. Anyone fleeing the
hue and cry could claim safety by entering such places, and grabbing hold of the door
knocker constituted 'entering'. So often did such runaways avail themselves of the lion-
faced knocker that its nose became brazen with wear. Hence the name.

The knocker itself disappeared in the 1330s when academics fled the city to
Stamford in search of somewhere more peaceful than Oxford, which at that time was
riven not only by town and gown riots but also by battles between students from the
north and south of England. Edward II (wisely from Oxford's point of view) disapproved
of the move, with its threat of scattering the seeds for breakaway universities, and
ordered the disgruntled dons back to Oxford, a move they took with ill grace, leaving

their knocker behind. Amazingly, it remained in Stamford, gracing the front door of Brasenose House, until 1890 when the original dons' successors bought the building and took the knocker back to Oxford. It now hangs above the college high table.

The present Brasenose College was founded in 1509 by the Bishop of Lincoln and a successful lawyer called John Sutton. At about that time, almost 200 years after the original knocker disappeared, a new 'brazen nose' door knocker was made, complete with a caricature of a human face. It is still in the college's possession and is also represented in an Oriel window in the hall, along with portraits of the two founders.

Brasenose has a quaint 'tall story' about the tallest man in England: during the reign of James I John Middleton left an impression of his enormous right hand on a panel in the cellar. Quite a celebrity in his day, the dons apparently wined and dined him at Brasenose when he was on his way back to Hale from a bout in London, where he achieved fame at court by beating up the King's wrestler.

The so-called 'Childe of Hale', whose portrait survives at the college, achieved some notoriety in an age when the average height of a man was very much smaller than now, as evidenced by the low-door lintels in many 17th-century buildings. Tales of his huge height lengthened after his death and, by the time the diarist Samuel Pepys visited the college some 50 years later, and paid a butler two shillings to see the hand outline, they had him down at 9ft 3in.

But John Middleton must have started turning in his extra-large-size grave (in Hale, Lancashire) when in 1979 investigators from *The Guinness Book of Records* measured his print and decided that he was probably a fraud, a mere stripling at just 7ft 8in.

In Victorian times, when many were keen to exaggerate the age of the university in much the same way as their forbears had been keen to exaggerate the height of John Middleton, the legend grew that the original Brasenose Hall was founded by the 9th-century philosopher John Scotus.

Such proud rumour-mongers, keen to show how much older Oxford was than Cambridge, also believed that King Alfred founded the whole university and reckoned that the college's full name of King's Hall and College of Brasenose bore them out. Some people will believe anything.

Corpus Christi College

Re-roofing the hall at Corpus Christi College concentrated attention on Oxford's connections with Catherine of Aragon (1485-1536). The work brought into sharp focus the remarkable frieze, high up under the rafters, which contains the unfortunate Queen's heraldic device: a pomegranate ('Granada' in Spanish) and the date 1516. The date is remarkable because the college was not officially opened until March 1517.

But Catherine's connections with the college go back way beyond its foundation. Its founder Richard Foxe (1447-1528) negotiated her marriage contract with Arthur, Prince of Wales, elder brother of Henry VIII. She was first married to him (by proxy) in Burgos when she was 11 in March 1497—though she had known for as long as she could remember that it was her destiny to marry the prince of a cold place called Gales.

Then she was married to him again, in person this time and at St Paul's Cathedral, when she was 15, on 14 November 1501. Prince Arthur swaggered out of the bed chamber the next morning demanding beer; but whether or not the marriage—which lasted until Arthur's death on 2 April the following year—was ever consummated is unknown; the none-too-delicate subject later featured prominently in Henry VIII's unsuccessful applications to the Pope to have his own marriage to her annulled.

The Earl of Oxford, who as the Great Chamberlain of England was the only person outside her circle of Spanish ladies to be allowed to see her that morning, reported that the atmosphere was sombre. It probably got more sombre, too, after the princess, used as she was to the warmth of her native Granada, was sent off to live out the winter months of her short marriage at cold, old Ludlow Castle in the Welsh Marches.

Be that as it may, in happier days when she was married to Henry—and before he started clamouring for a divorce in order to marry Anne Boleyn—she used often to visit Corpus Christi when Henry was hunting at the Royal Palace in Woodstock. And she presented the college with its greatest treasure: the gilt Pomegranate Cup, made in about 1515.

Catherine was something of an intellectual, following in the footsteps of her husband's grandmother, Margaret of Beaufort, and concerning herself in the affairs of both Oxford and Cambridge. She was particularly interested in the education of girls and consulted Juan Luis Vives (1493-1540), the Valencia-born Doctor of Law at Oxford University, about the education of her daughter, Princess Mary. Vives resided at Corpus when in England and dedicated his book on women's education to her.

Catherine must have heard something of Oxford even before she arrived in England, for Richard Mayhew, the second President of Magdalen College, was one of the embassy sent to fetch her from Spain to be Arthur's bride. Even today, 16th-century tapestries adorn the President's Lodging, depicting the betrothal of Catherine and Arthur.

Probably she loved the place. Certainly, when the Bishop of Lincoln (in whose diocese Oxford then lay) reported that a certain former Oxford student and son of an Ipswich butcher, Thomas Wolsey, was founding Cardinal College (now Christ Church), she was anxious to see the foundation. In 1525, she did so. She visited the shrine of the 8th-century Saint Frideswide in what is now Christ Church Cathedral. She also visited the Holy Well at Binsey, where Frideswide is reputed to have summoned forth the water. Then Wolsey accompanied her to Corpus where she presented the Pomegranate Cup, before going on to dine at Merton.

What would she have thought of plans to allow elder daughters to succeed to the throne ahead of younger males? Probably not a lot, though as she was enlightened and educated—indeed, the perfect wife for a king—she would have accepted the received wisdom of the time: that not producing a male heir was somehow her fault.

Christ Church's Old Tom

Great Tom, somehow the very embodiment of the timeless voice of Oxford's soul, has been expressing joy—and sorrow too (with clapper muffled)—at great royal and national occasions since Christ Church was founded in 1546; and perhaps even longer, since before that it hung in the great medieval abbey of Osney which, for five years, was Oxford Cathedral.

But in that year college chief carpenter John Wesburn undertook the heavy responsibility of removing the eight bells—called Hautclere, Douce, Clement, Austin, Marie, Gabriel, John and, biggest of all, Great Tom—from the tower of poor old doomed Osney, and reinstalling them in the college chapel that had just been upgraded to cathedral status. The bells were moved across Oxford by a carter called Mr Willoughby of Eynsham.

During the reign of the Catholic Mary Tudor (1553-8) Great Tom underwent a gender change and was renamed *Mary*—an event that was then conveniently forgotten about during the reign of Protestant Elizabeth when he/she/it again became known as Tom. The bells ordered the daily life of Christ Church to such an extent that already by 1583 new machinery, such as bell wheels etc., were needed, along with new clappers. Then in 1612 the bell was recast, possibly to get rid of a 'Papist' inscription.

By 1680 there were eleven bells in the Cathedral tower, including Great Tom weighing more than 7 tons and with a diameter of nearly 7 feet. In that year ten bells were rehung. However, Great Tom was set aside and eventually installed, 14 years later, in Wren's Tom Tower over the college gate where, happily, it still resides. It 'spoke' loud and clear on Restoration Day, 29 May 1684. (Restoration Day, commemorating the date when Charles II was restored to the throne in 1660, was until 1859 one of three days of British monarchical importance celebrated in the Anglican Prayer Book. The others were Guy Fawkes Day and 30 January when Charles I was executed in 1649.)

In 1852 Greenwich Mean Time was introduced to the whole nation, but some Oxford dons decided not to be hustled and bustled about by it in the 19th century; instead they went on using their old Oxford Time. Which is why, even today, Christ Church operates five minutes behind everyone else. Great Tom still rings out its unheeded curfew 101 times every evening at 21.05—or, as those old slow coaches on the other side of the college gates would call it, 9 p.m.

But why does Great Tom ring out 101 times every evening? Answer: it tolls once for each of the 100 students (the equivalent of Fellows in other colleges) who were on the original 1546 foundation, and once more for the studentship created by the Thurston bequest. William Thurston, apparently unconnected to Oxford, in 1664 left £800 to something called the King's College, Oxford. Both Oriel and Brasenose reckoned he meant them, but the Archbishop of Canterbury, sitting in the Court of Arches, awarded the money to Christ Church.

Great Tom's deep tones have a special role for royal jubilees: in 1897, when Victoria celebrated hers, two new bells were added to the ten already hanging in the cathedral).

Christ Church Riots

Christ Church, the largest Oxford college, may have been the *alma mater* of several of Britain's prime ministers, but it has also seen its share of bad undergraduate behaviour.

In 1870 Dean Henry Liddell (father of the real Alice, of course) had to deal with a bout of student rowdiness. Members of the Christ Church Society stole all the statues from the library in protest against the dismissal of a friendly porter called Timms. Worse, they lit fires between the statues, damaging an early Aphrodite and Eros. Shades here of Betjeman's poem 'Varsity Students' Rag':

> 'And then we smash'd up ev'rything, and what was the funniest part
> We smashed some rotten old pictures which were priceless works of art.'

Liddell remarked that if this vandalism had been committed by Town, not Gown, everyone would have demanded the severest punishments. In fact a solicitor was consulted and the threat of legal action, not to mention thunderous publicity from

The Times, shamed the perpetrators into giving themselves up. According to Judith Carthoys, archivist at Christ Church since 1994, in her informative *The Cardinal's College* (Profile Books), Edward Marjoribanks, the first to enter the library, was among three undergraduates expelled.

Liddell said: 'Young men of large fortune have little to fear from such penalties as we can impose. Their parents often look without severity, or even with a half sympathy, on acts similar to those in which they formerly took part themselves, and by long traditional habit take a sort of pleasure in hearing of practical jokes played within the precincts of a college.' But he was indulgent; convinced that this was simply a prank that had gone too far. (In other words, a little as though a P. G. Wodehouse character had by mistake hurt a policeman while trying to take his helmet on boat race night.)

Another occasion was in 1893, during the so-called *belle époque*, or *naughty nineties*. It was the 21st birthday of Sunny, 9th Duke of Marlborough, but the Blenheim Row, as it came to be called, came about as a result of a few Christ Church undergraduates, who had been invited to the ball, painting the college red—and a good many other colours too.

They became cross after the Dean, Francis Paget (1851-1911), and Senior Censor Sampson imposed petty restrictions on them (concerning getting back in good time etc.). The petulant undergraduates painted slogans reading 'Damn the Dean' and 'Damn Sampson' on the doors and walls of the Great Quadrangle, and even cut the bell-rope of Great Tom, the ancient bell used to toll curfews, originally brought to Christ Church from Osney Abbey when the college was founded in 1546. Then they circulated a paper comparing the college to a prep school and complaining of 'Puritan principles. Venial porters. Indifferent dons.'

The next summer something similar occurred again: all the windows in Peckwater Quad were smashed following a Bullingdon Club dinner; and Sampson, shocked to the core, stood down after 16 years in the Censor's job. Judith Carthoys, again: 'In spite of the relative benevolence towards undergraduate antics, the Blenheim and Bullingdon rows damaged Christ Church's reputation, and numbers dropped for a brief period in the mid-1890s. Up to 50 sets of rooms stood empty, a far cry from the overcrowded state at the end of the previous century.'

As for the 9th Duke of Marlborough, he gave another party for his 60th birthday. No one this time tried to stop undergraduates staying out late. The only trouble was that the Duke forgot how old he was: he gave it in 1930 when he was still 59.

Green College and the Radcliffe Observatory

Sir Christopher Wren, one time Savilian Professor of Astronomy at Oxford University, who was, of course, better known for his architectural masterpieces, including the Royal Observatory at Greenwich, was of the opinion that an adequate observatory 'could be placed as well in a garden as a tower' and need consist only of 'a little house of boards'.

Interesting, then, that Oxford is blessed with the Radcliffe Observatory, now part of Green College in Woodstock Road, and described by Pevsner as 'architecturally the finest observatory in Europe'.

How this remarkable building came into being is described in a fascinating new book called *A History of the Radcliffe Observatory*, published by Green College and edited by Professor Jeffery Burley and Kristina Plenderleith, in which we learn from various academics of the building's 'career', as it were, over its 225 years of existence.

Architectural historian Geoffrey Tyack, for instance, introduces us to its birth. Roger Bacon is said to have studied the stars from an eyrie on the old Folly Bridge; but the study of astronomy at Oxford had no official standing until 1619 when the Savilian chair was founded.

The first professors carried out their observations from the top room of the gate tower of the then newly built Schools Quadrangle at the Bodleian. Then Professor Edmund Halley built a sort of observatory on the roof of his residence in New College Lane (which, I gather from Mr Tyack, is still there).

Not until 1768 did anyone see a way of obtaining enough money to build a proper observatory to house such instruments as 15 ft long telescopes. Then Professor Thomas Hornsby approached the trustees of Dr John Radcliffe for the money to build one. Dr Radcliffe, physician to anyone who was anyone at the turn of the 17th century, including King William III, had in 1714 left a fortune to Oxford University so large that it had already enabled it to build the Radcliffe Camera and the Radcliffe Infirmary.

The land upon which the observatory was built was then a quiet country area outside the city which had been leased by the 4th Duke of Marlborough from St John's College. The duke was a keen astronomer — his observatory and instruments are still in Blenheim Palace — so he willingly gave up the land. Henry Keene was first employed to design the observatory but he was superseded, for unknown reasons, by James Wyatt. It was completed in 1795.

In 1935, the building, by then a magnificent anachronism, ceased to be an observatory and became part of the Nuffield Institute for Medical Research. In 1977, it became part of Green College.

Ruskin College

On 22 February 1899, appropriately enough George Washington's birthday, the recently rebuilt Oxford Town Hall found itself bedecked with the Union flag and the Stars and Stripes. Inside, local bigwigs of the Labour Movement read out messages of goodwill from such national leaders as the chairman of the Independent Labour Party, Keir Hardie.

The occasion was the opening ceremony of Ruskin Hall, the forerunner of Ruskin College, which had come into being with the avowed intent of educating working-class men—and women—to achieve social change.

It had nothing to do with the artist and reformer John Ruskin, who was then in his 80s but who nevertheless wished it well. It was named after him as a friend of the movement.

Ruskin Hall was the brainchild of two American students at Oxford University: Charles Austin Beard, aged 24, and Walter Watkins Vrooman, 29. They had met for the first time in late 1898, but such was the success of their project that barely five months later the first students at Ruskin Hall—not to be confused with the John Ruskin School of Drawing and Fine Art, which was founded by Ruskin in 1871—were studying at the Hall's first premises, leased from Balliol, at 14 St Giles.

From the start, Ruskin Hall, which became Ruskin College four years later, was something of an enigma in Oxford. Closely allied to the Labour Movement and seeking

help from local and national trade unions and cooperative societies, it was nevertheless the product of middle-class reformers. Mr Vrooman might claim, as he did in an 1899 interview, that 'We have no 'ism to teach, we have no party and no creed', but it soon became clear that his project was yoked to the emerging Labour Party. Workers needed educating to equip them to seize the reins of power, and they knew it.

By 1902 there were 96 classes going, and Ruskin had branch halls in Manchester, Liverpool and Birmingham. There were also 1,800 students enrolled on correspondence courses. Much of this early success was due to Mrs Vrooman, 20 years Mr Vrooman's senior, whom he had married in 1897. She was rich and funded her young husband's scheme to the tune of about £2,000 a year, another £1,000 coming from the Labour Movement and from individual sponsors of individual students.

By 1909 the college was seen as a provider of future Labour leaders, bent on reform, but because Oxford University, seen as a bastion of a hierarchical social system, continued to have a great say in the running of the college, trouble was inevitable. That year the students went on strike over the sacking, or at least forced resignation, of the principal, Dennis Hird, who was accused of teaching socialism and atheism—exactly what some students who formed something called the Plebs' League in 1908 wanted him to do!

All residential students were sent home with their return fares paid. Some say that this was a blessing in disguise since they were then able to lobby their sponsor organisations for support. Yet when the students returned the place was more, not less, closely linked to the university in that students were offered the chance to sit for the university's Diploma in Economics and Political Science. On the other hand, the college's governing body came to consist solely of representatives of working-class bodies, such as the Trades Union Congress.

In 1913 the college's present red brick, neo-William and Mary headquarters in Walton Street was built. After the Second World War demand for places soared and the college acquired the 18th-century mansion and grounds called the Rookery in Old Headington. In 2008 Ruskin College sold its Walton Street building to Exeter College for £17 million. It moved its headquarters to Headington in 2012.

6. Around Oxfordshire
Towns and Villages

If you drive, or better still take a boat, from Kelmscott in the west (at 73 metres above sea level), where the Thames enters Oxfordshire, to Henley in the east (at 32 metres), you will find yourself travelling through some of the most varied landscape in the south of England, with the changing colour of the architecture around you reflecting the different local building materials. And the same is true if you journey from Banbury in the north, through west Oxfordshire—which tourist authorities are increasingly trying to call the Oxfordshire Cotswolds—to, say, Uffington, in the shadow of the White Horse, carved long ago into the chalk of what are still sometimes called the Berkshire Downs.

This intense variety of landscape is because the county lies at the meeting point of several geological features that are more typically found in neighbouring counties. For instance, the limestone of the Cotswolds overflows out of Gloucestershire in the west; and in the Chilterns, to the east, the flint does likewise out of Buckinghamshire. In the Vale of the White Horse the downs are overlaid with a bed of chalk about 220 metres thick, supporting rolling grassland and spinneys of beech. The buildings here are of brick, or chalk and rubble, with timber frames, reflecting the lack of indigenous stone. By contrast, the deep yellow-ochre ironstone used to build the villages in the north of the county—and also found in Northamptonshire and Warwickshire—looks, if possible, even more like solidified honey than its Cotswold counterpart. Famous quarries, for instance at Burford, Taynton, Headington and Wheatley, contributed the stone to construct the quintessentially English-looking towns and villages of Oxfordshire, along with the important buildings of Oxford and even London—notably St Paul's Cathedral.

Much of present-day Oxfordshire was prosperous for hundreds of years following the Norman Conquest—as the many lovely stone churches attest—thanks to its ability to produce that staple English export: wool. Until, that is, the 19th century, when Australian sheep, with their merino wool, started mercilessly out-fleecing their cousins back home. Widespread poverty then set in, with much of the rural population migrating to towns, though even here jobs were scarce as labour-saving machinery was introduced into such traditional industries as blanket-making in Witney.

On top of these troubles, the ancient forest that had for so long covered much of the county and provided common land was felled and enclosed for cultivation. The names of the three villages of Milton-, Ascott- and Shipton-under-Wychwood are poignantly evocative here because, following the Disafforestation Act of 1853, Wychwood Forest was destroyed. Even now much of rural Oxfordshire is remarkably sparsely populated—though not poor. Houses are expensive and the county, thanks to the M40 and M4 motorways, is within range of weekenders, and even commuters, from London.

Around Oxford itself, the story over the past 40 years or so has been one of brain replacing brawn. Much of the site of the old Morris car works in Cowley is these days occupied by a high tech business park; BMW's sleek Mini plant now employs about 5,500 workers (or associates, as it calls them), which is a far cry from the 30,000 who worked in Oxford's car industry in the 1970s. Since the Second World War the county has also managed to become a centre of the money-spinning motor-sport industry. In this context something called a technical centre at Leafield overlooks bumps in a field—all that remains of Henry VII's hunting lodge which, of course, was then set deep in the forest.

Old Marston

Many undergraduates in the early 19th century probably spent more time out hunting than studying dreary old books. Among such was one Jack Russell (1795-1883), a student at Exeter College, who seems to have been much preoccupied with catching foxes. Hacking about in Marston one day in 1819 he came across a milkman with a dog called Trump, whom he bought in order to train him to flush out foxes that had gone to ground. As a result, this dog became the ancestor of the Kennel Club registered breed now named after Mr Russell.

Marston's name derives from Marsh Town. Until 12 November 1971, when the bridge carrying Marston Ferry Road across the Cherwell was opened, the area was remarkably isolated for somewhere within the Ring Road. Indeed, the only link between North Oxford and Cherwell Drive until then — only 35 years ago but already as remote-seeming as the ancient Romans, at least to anyone stuck in a Marston Ferry Road traffic jam— was by the ferry which had existed at Marston since at least 1279.

Yet the present bridge was not quite the first to be built at Marston. General Thomas Fairfax, commander of the Parliamentary forces laying siege to Royalist Oxford from his headquarters at Headington Hill, built a temporary one there in 1646. He planned to use it in an attack on the city which would have led to hand-to-hand fighting in the streets. In the event, the King surrendered and the bridge was not used.

The treaty ending the siege of Oxford was signed at the Manor House, Ponds Lane, near St Nicholas Church, in what is now often called Old Marston to distinguish it from New Marston which has grown up on its southern side. The Manor, now known as Cromwell's House, belonged in the 17th century to the Justice of the Peace and sergeant-at-law Unton Croke, relative of Richard Croke to whom there is a splendid alabaster memorial dated 1683 in St Nicholas Church.

Despite the lack of a road bridge, Oxford had long been trying to expand towards Marston. Nine years after Mr Russell came across Trump, the church of St Clement was built at the Headington end of Marston Road. It was built at a time when Newman was curate of the parish. It is of unusual Georgian Gothic design and contains a north window removed from St Martin's, Carfax, when all but its tower was pulled down in 1896. Its east window, incidentally, is by someone called J. H. Russell.

For a fleeting moment I wondered whether he could be one and the same gentleman as our terrier fancier. But no. Mr Jack Russell took holy orders and went off to become vicar of Swimbridge, near Barnstable, Devon, thereby explaining why said terriers are sometimes called Parson's terriers. There is a pub in that village called the Jack Russell. It seems that the Reverend Jack Russell, a founder member of the Kennel Club, crossed Trump with Devon hunt dogs to achieve his end of creating a working dog capable of facing up to a fox underground. He must be turning in his Swimbridge grave at the very notion of a hunting ban — even if it is being largely ignored.

Hampton Gay

Not much romantic decay left in Oxfordshire these days. What with spiralling house prices during the past decade, and bankers with bonuses burning holes in their pockets still favouring the county even now, there is hardly a decent ruin to be found anywhere; they've nearly all become bijou residences for better or for worse (too often the latter, in my opinion).

But anyone who loves the romance of a good ruin could do worse than head for Thrupp, north of Kidlington, and take a walk along the canal to Shipton-on-Cherwell, before turning right along a footpath across a bridge over the Cherwell to Hampton Gay, where the ruined Elizabethan manor house stands forlorn among humps in the grass, denoting where the vanished village once stood, across a field from the lonely church of St Giles.

Here is a ruin for the connoisseur, complete with thick-stemmed ivy trees growing through fine stone window frames that would look exaggerated in a Hammer horror film. Lovely. I took the walk of, say, a couple of miles at most on a suitably lowering November day, and found myself lost in wonder at how such a short ramble could encapsulate so much historic tragedy, pathos even.

Hampton Gay, so called because Hampton is derived from a Saxon word for Home Farm, and de Gay was the name of the lord of the manor following the Norman Conquest, was the scene of desperate misery long before that tragedy. It was a victim of early enclosures, carried out by the then lord of the manor, the owner and occupier of the now-burned out house, Vincent Barry, whose monument still adorns the church.

In 1596, faced with starvation, a miller's man named Richard Bradshaw, of Hampton Gay, became a ringleader of an agrarian revolt in which a number of villagers planned to murder Barry and his daughter.

The plot was foiled when Roger Symonds, the village carpenter, spilled the beans to Barry. Ringleaders (probably including Bradshaw) were hanged, drawn and quartered in London, but their deaths were not altogether in vain, for the mighty Lord Norreys opined: 'Some order should be taken about inclosure ... so that the poor may be able to live.'

As a result, the Tillage Act of 1597 was passed. It ensured that all Oxfordshire land that had been put over to pasture since the accession of Queen Elizabeth should be once again ploughed and cultivated. How many people lived in the village before the enclosures is unknown, but now, beside the church and the ruined manor there is only a farm and a few cottages.

The manor, shaped in the classic E of the best Elizabethan houses and still complete with a battlemented central porch with carved lintels, was destroyed by fire and abandoned in 1887, when it was already some 300 years old and the property of

Wadham College, Oxford. Some imaginative souls said that the destruction came about because the place had been cursed on Christmas Eve 1874, when the 2 p.m. Paddington to Birkenhead express crashed on the nearby Cherwell Line, which had opened in 1850. They remembered how on that occasion the inhabitants of the manor had refused to give shelter to the wounded and dying. Among the 34 people who died, when the carriage in which they were travelling fell off the bridge, were two children now buried in the churchyard—their names unrecorded because no one ever came forward to identify them.

Walking back towards the Oxford Canal (opened in 1790) I saw a CrossCountry train whizz past Shipton-on-Cherwell manor, once a recording studio belonging to Richard Branson. The last time I had seen the ruined manor was from the window of one of those trains when the same tycoon, who owned CrossCountry, was showing off the tilting SuperVoyager trains to the local press.

Great Tew

Talk about Romantic Decay. Some of us remember Great Tew, possibly the prettiest village in Oxfordshire, some 30 years ago when many of the cottages had 17th-century timbers (some still covered in bark) poking through their rotting thatch, and parishioners in flat caps took turns to serve warm beer through a hatch in the Falkland Arms pub, because the Lord of the Manor was tardy about appointing a full-time publican.

Great Tew's first benefactor was the undeniably Romantic Lucius Cary, second Viscount Falkland, who before the Civil War used to gather around him at Great Tew all the wisest and cleverest people of his age to discuss art, classics, religion, beauty and, of course, politics. Edward Hyde, first Earl of Clarendon—Chancellor of Oxford University and, indeed, Lord Chancellor of England—wrote in his best-selling account of the English Civil War, *The History of the Rebellion*:

'In this time, his house being within ten miles of Oxford [in fact Great Tew is a little further] then contracted familiarity and friendship with the most polite and accurate men of that university; who found such an immenseness of wit and such a solidity of judgement in him, so infinite a fancy bound in by a most logical ratiocination, such a vast knowledge that he was not ignorant in any thing, yet such an excessive humility as if he had known nothing, that they frequently resorted and dwelt with him, as in a college in purer air.' He added: 'Nor did the lord of the house know of their coming or going, nor who were in the his house, till he came to dinner or supper, where all still met; otherwise, there was no troublesome ceremony or constraint, to forbid men to come to the house, or to make them weary of staying there; so that many came thither to study in a better air, finding all the books they could desire in his library, and all the persons together, whose company they could wish, and not find in any other society.' Such lovely prose, no wonder the proceeds of the book funded the building of Hawksmoor's Clarendon Building in Broad Street, Oxford.

But the point here is that all these clever, rational people wanted one thing only: that peace should prevail in Britain—and yet their efforts came to nothing and Civil War broke out. At the first battle of Newbury on 20 September 1643, Lord Falkland declared: 'he was weary of the times and foresaw much misery to his own country and did believe he should be out of it ere night'. Which he was. He rode out on the Royalist side and was instantly shot dead.

He had been brought up in Ireland where his father was Lord Deputy and he could afford to keep open house, and to bring all sides together in the worsening political and religious climate of the time, thanks to an inheritance from his grandfather, Sir Lawrence Tanfield of Burford. His house was an earlier one than the great house now standing in Great Tew, and the landscape of the village has been altered by a later landscape gardener, namely John Claudius Loudon.

Great Tew later passed to descendants of steam engineer Matthew Boulton. It fell into disrepair when reclusive Boulton descendant, Major Robb, decided to guard it against the modern world. Since his death in 1985 it has been largely restored—though much Romantic Decay may still be found there; even if the place has sprouted a car park, and the pub, sold off by the estate in 1978, has gone gastro.

Chipping Norton

Like Dick Whittington, the theatre at Chipping Norton has prospered on its journey over the past 35 years, ever since founders John and Tamara Malcolm obtained planning permission to create it in 1974. As with Dick, whenever disaster loomed—in the shape of threatened financial cuts from the Arts Council in 2008, for instance—the theatre company has (so far at least) always managed to 'pick itself up, dust itself down, and start all over again'. Now the pantomime at Chippy has become an established part of the Christmas ritual for thousands of West Oxfordshire people: children, parents and grandparents alike.

But what, I wondered, while waiting to order a drink in the bar, would the original builders of the theatre in Spring Street have thought of it all? For it is housed in a former Salvation Army Citadel, opened by the Army's commandant, General Herbert Booth, and his lieutenant, Major Oliphant, in August 1888—and thereby hangs a tale. Foundation stones on the front of the building and in the auditorium read: 'These stones were laid by one hundred of those who through great persecution boldly and conscientiously served their God.'

The persecution the Sally Army troops suffered in Chipping Norton, according to a report in *The War Cry* of April 1888, came at the bony hands of something called the Skeleton Army: a macabre bunch of ruffians, at that time numbering several thousand throughout the south of England, which some publicans had founded earlier in the decade to object to the Salvationists' anti-alcohol teaching. In Chipping Norton they formed processions behind a coffin and clashed with the Salvation Army mercilessly. *The War Cry* reports their 'organised attacks', and adds that 'not only are the male soldiers of the corps kicked and beaten during the whole of the time they are making their way to their barracks, but the same treatment is extended to the women'. The Salvationists triumphed, though, and announced later: 'We have opened fire on this town in right good earnest. The work of God has gone on in a most marvellous manner in spite of every foe.' The Citadel remained in operation until 1962.

Then the building, designed by engineers who had also been responsible for building Victorian music halls, suffered the indignity of being used as a furniture store for a few years until it was discovered, deserted, by the Malcolms. Both of them Royal Shakespeare Company actors, they immediately saw its potential.

In 1973, within two days of learning that it was for sale, they had persuaded an anonymous benefactor to lend them the money to buy it. Then more money poured in from trusts, councils, individuals, and fundraising ventures and appeals. A grant from the Gulbenkian Foundation the following year enabled the charitable theatre company

to buy the cottage next door for conversion into a bar and gallery. In 1990 the other neighbouring house, 7 Goddard's Lane, was bought with the help of a fundraising campaign. It now houses a day-time box office, rehearsal studio, green room, dressing rooms and administration offices.

The theatre reopened 1996, after an investment of more than £1 million raised from public and private sources, including £678,000 from the National Lottery.

Perhaps General Booth, the Methodist who founded the Salvation Army in 1878, would wish the theatre well. After all, his brainchild still marches on and helps thousands of homeless people, particularly at Christmas, even without its citadel. Incidentally, Oxford University very much took the Sally Army to its heart. It granted General Booth an honorary doctorate after the Army built a fortress-like citadel in Castle Street, Oxford, in 1888. This was demolished to make way for the hideous county council offices in 1970.

Witney

King Charles II set up the Hudson's Bay Company by Royal Charter in 1670 to explore and trade with the native people of North America, and in particular to exploit the lucrative fur trade which was then largely dominated by the French. Already in 1681 the charter was proving good news for the people of Witney. In that year the company ordered its first 45 pairs of blankets from blanket maker Thomas Empsome.

But good news for Witney was bad news for the Canadian beaver. Over the next 300 years the Witney Blanket Weavers' Company developed the famous Hudson's Bay Company points blanket. Such pure wool blankets, woven from the wool of Cotswold sheep and much prized by native Americans, were edged with coloured points, or stripes, which indicated their weight, size, and exactly how many beaver pelts they were worth. In effect, the blankets, with their traditional design of brightly coloured stripes top and bottom—recalling the points system—became a sort of money between the British and Canadian people.

One reason why the Witney industry survived so long against competition from the North of England mills, which were nearer the coal fields that supplied the necessary energy, was that labour relations in Witney were comparatively good. William Cobbett, on his *Rural Ride* of 1826, famously ranted against the Witney blanket bosses, saying that new machines had put hundreds of home workers in outlying cottages out of work; but there is no record of Luddites destroying machinery in Witney. However, the death of Edmund Wright, who introduced the water-powered loom at New Mill in the first

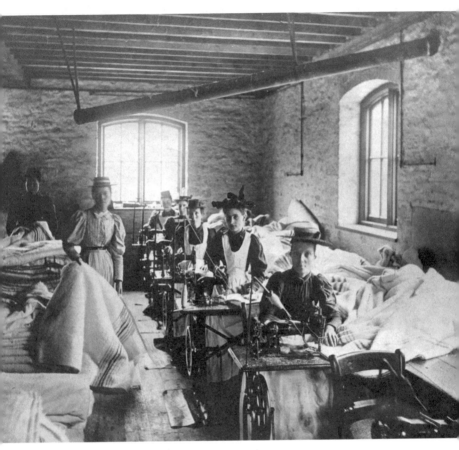

Early's blanket factory

decade of the 19th century, may seem suspicious: he fell into his own wheel and some say his ghost still haunts the place.

As recently as 1935 Ethel Carleton Williams, writing in *Companion into Oxfordshire*, noted that on the approach to Witney the visitor was greeted with the sight of blankets stretched on poles to dry. She added: 'A visit to Witney without seeing a blanket factory would be like watching a performance of *Hamlet* without the Prince of Denmark.'

But in 2002, the last factory (Early's) finally closed, out-fleeced by the sheep of Australia. The town which held its own against the great mills of Yorkshire for so many centuries has now seen most of its mills redeveloped for industries contributing to the knowledge-based economy.

Taynton

Before the Reformation, masons' skills had been in constant demand from churchmen; but with the dissolution of the monasteries many were forced to lead wandering lives. Luckily, their skills never died out.

For Cotswold masons, quarrymen and sculptors came into their own after the Great Fire of 1666: it was decreed that London, including St Paul's cathedral and many of the 89 other churches burnt down, should be reconstructed in stone, rather than highly inflammable wattle-and-daub.

So where did the stones used to build St Paul's Cathedral in London come from? Sir Christopher Wren used many of the stones from the earlier medieval cathedral on the site, but many others came from Taynton and Burford. The stone was loaded on to barges and transported down the Windrush and Thames to St Paul's Wharf, or it was transferred from wagon to barge at the bridge at Radcot.

Wren, of course, was in overall charge of the classical plans for St Paul's — an extraordinary departure from the familiar Gothic of the old cathedral — but master masons, such as members of the Kempster and Strong families, carried out the work. Kempsters managed the quarries at Upton; Strongs managed those at Taynton. The Lords Commissioners in London signed up Thomas Strong as a principal contractor for St Paul's, and he laid the first stone for its foundations on 21 June 1675. He was the grandson of Timothy Strong, who was already building in London and Oxford as early as 1617. In 1630, he built the south front of Cornbury Park, in Charlbury, for Lord Danby.

The St Paul's accounts for April 1678 show that Timothy Strong had 35 masons working for him on the site. He died in 1681, and left the business to his brother Edward, who became a supplier not only of Oxfordshire and Gloucestershire stone but also stone from Portland (so not all the stone for the new cathedral was shipped from the Cotswolds).

Edward hit the big time and retired to Hertfordshire as a country gentleman. There, he wrote his *Memorandums of Several Works on Masonry done by our Family*, noting that he had the 'felicity of seeing both the beginning and finishing of that great edifice' of St Paul's.

Christopher Kempster, who had worked with Wren to build Tom Tower at Christ Church, Oxford, retired to Upton, and is buried at Burford. Accounts show that he was still working at St Paul's in 1707, at the age of 80, when the dome was finished.

Burford

Burford church is proud to display some amazing carvings of native Brazilians. The carvings are the very first representation in this country of native Americans, and one of the earliest in Europe. Any earlier ones are two-dimensional, whereas the Burford effigies are in light relief. The memorial is dated 1569 and is carved in a strange style, quite unlike most Tudor stonemasonry. Professor Virginia Rau, of Lisbon University, has identified the Americans as members of the Tupinamba cannibal tribe, who lived in the early 1500s at the mouth of the Amazon.

But why should they appear on a tomb in Oxfordshire? The carvings can actually be traced back to Henry VIII's barber, Edmund Harman (1509-88), who had the monument put up to himself. There is an excellent pamphlet by Michael Balfour, *Edmund Harman: Barber and Gentleman* (available from the Tolsey Museum, Burford), which suggests that either Harman was engaged in American trade, or else the stone carver, almost certainly a Dutchman called Cornelis Bos, had seen a similar design in the Spanish Netherlands and decided to use it.

A look at the life of Edmund Harman shows that the modern business of exploiting contacts is as nothing compared to the kind of very personal sycophancy that comparatively humble people had to employ at Henry's court in order to better themselves. As the king's barber, a trusted position which, after all, entailed approaching the royal neck with a razor, he was sought out by many of the great and the good of the land, all hoping that he would whisper a word in the royal ear about them and their little business schemes. He was a member of the Privy Chamber, a group of about 15 servants whose job it was to attend to the king's comfort.

In 1538, he was in such high favour as to be included in a list of persons at court who were 'to be had in the King's most benign remembrance'; and this benignity translated itself into material reward in the shape of Burford Priory, which he was granted along with other Oxfordshire land in Taynton, after the Reformation. He even stood as second witness at the signing of the king's last will and testament in 1546, though Harman wrote his own signature in capital letters, almost childishly as though he were practically illiterate and not at all used to putting pen to paper. He also appears with the king in Holbein's last painting, now in the Barber's Hall in London, which, incidentally, the diarist Samuel Pepys acquired more than 100 years later.

Whether Harman actually lived much at Burford Priory is uncertain, but Fisher's 19th-century *History of Burford* maintains that two statues on either side of the front door represent Hercules (presumably a nickname) and a man covered with hair—a reference to both his name, Hairman, and his job. In fact, Harman's name seems to be derived from Hermann. He apparently had German antecedents who had moved to London to oversee trade from the Hanseatic states.

But Herman did well to remain in favour. Powerful enemies gunned for him, including Dr John London, Warden of New College 1526-42, who wanted him burned as a heretic. In the end Dr London himself was convicted of perjury and thrown into jail, where he died.

Filkins

Goodfellows Farm in Filkins (south of Burford and north of Lechlade) was a great Tudor house, which was much improved and enlarged during the first half of the 20th century by the left-wing politician, lawyer, one-time pacifist and diplomat, Sir Stafford Cripps, who lived there 1921-39.

The son of a prosperous London lawyer and conscientious objector, Sir Stafford was an ambulance driver in the First World War. At the start of the Second World

War, Churchill, who was anxious to bring the Russians into the conflict on the Allies' side, appointed him Ambassador to Moscow. His thinking was, presumably, that such a prominent left-winger with strong communist leanings would help the cause. Sir Stafford became Leader of the House of Commons in Churchill's wartime government, and President of the Board of Trade and Chancellor of the Exchequer in Clement Attlee's post-war Labour administration.

Sir Stafford also did much for the community of Filkins. For instance, he agreed to underwrite the cost of building the council houses in the village — much beloved of Pevsner— in order to ensure they were constructed in vernacular style using local stone from nearby quarries— and he proved that it was possible to build in such a way within budget! He also paid for a swimming pool for the villagers, which is still in use, and a village centre which now houses the community shop.

Then during the Second World War many buildings of architectural merit were inhabited by the armed forces, including Goodfellows Farm which was occupied by Land Army girls. But sadly almost nothing remains of the moated house, as it burned to the ground in the cold winter of 1947. Miraculously, no one was killed. But flames spread so rapidly that the girls had to flee in their night clothes, with some climbing on to the roof to be rescued by firemen, and others jumping from the windows. A newspaper reported: 'Some had to walk in the snow without shoes. Villagers found accommodation for them for the remainder of the night and lent them clothes.'

Now the site of the house is occupied by workshops belonging to the Morley family, where Ben Morley heads a company which repairs, exhibits and sells harps, as well as staging recitals and master classes. Morley Harps certainly qualifies as a 'long-established business'. Until the late 18th century, the only harps made were comparatively simple folk harps which have a very limited range. Then a French company, led by Sebastian Erhard in Paris, invented the double-action pedal harp, with 46 strings which could raise the range by a semitone or tone. In the aftermath of the French Revolution, following the execution of many of the company's aristocratic customers, M. Erhard relocated his business to London where he trained and employed the Morleys' ancestor. In due course M. Erhard returned to France, but the Morleys' business, which acquired a showroom in South Kensington and manufacturing plant in Wood Green, continued to prosper. It moved to its present 12 acres in Filkins in 1987.

The 400 acres around continue to be farmed by the Cripps family. And as local historian Richard Martin, who runs a clothes business called Cotswold Woollen Weavers on part of the site of Goodfellows, has said, it is Stafford Cripps' intangible legacy rather than the tangible one which lives on: 'He was a forthright Christian and he promoted self-help. And even today people come into the village to work, rather than leave it, each day.'

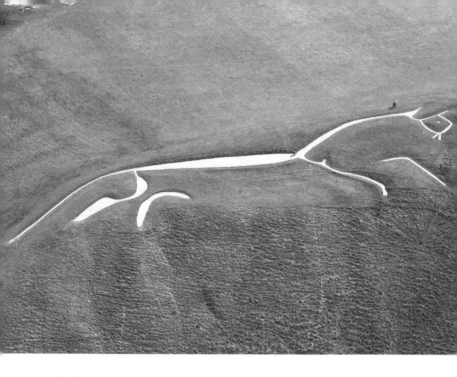

Uffington

Some say that the very heart of England may be found in Oxfordshire. The White Horse at Uffington, 374 ft long and carved out of chalk 800 ft up, lies alongside the nation's oldest artery — the Ridgeway. Is it really a horse? Or is it a dragon? Maybe it is the same dragon that St George killed, according to folklore, on the nearby, flat-topped Dragon Hill.

G. K. Chesterton, in his epic poem 'The Ballad of the White Horse', confused the issue: he equated, figuratively speaking, the Danes, whom King Alfred defeated nearby in 871, with a dragon that was holding England captive. To him, the White Horse represented the best of British, something that was old even before the Romans arrived. He begins:

> 'Before the gods that made the gods
> Had seen their sunrise pass
> The White Horse of the White Horse Vale
> Was cut out of the grass.'

He was probably right. Most recent dating techniques have established that the White Horse is at least 3,000 years old, that is about 1,000 years older than was previously supposed. It was perhaps originally carved by the Celtic tribe living at nearby Uffington Castle, that extraordinary Iron Age hill fort, the impressive banks of which were once surmounted by a wooden structure. What is certain is that the White Horse is by far the oldest chalk carving in Britain.

That it survived at all is thanks to periodic scouring since time immemorial. Until about 1880, when it was in serious danger of becoming completely overgrown, a Scouring Fair was held every seven years. G. K. Chesterton would have us believe that Alfred himself, that 'oft defeated king' who was born in nearby Wantage in 849, ordered the fair to commemorate the turning-point victory over the Danes. Whatever the truth, the fair became a scene of local revelry over the centuries, described in 1859 in 'The Scouring of the White Horse' by the author of *Tom Brown's Schooldays*, Thomas Hughes, who was born in Uffington in 1822.

Apart from scouring the horse, there were wrestling matches in Uffington Castle, and cheese-rolling competitions down the steep sides of an extraordinary ditch called the Manger.

Why the fair came to an end is almost as mysterious as why the horse was carved in the first place. Conjecture has it that the answer to the first question is that the local landowner refused to pay for the fair; and the answer to the second is that the horse was a representation of Epona, a horse goddess — unless, of course, the horse is really a dragon.

Abingdon

Abingdon has been known for at least the last 250 years for its custom of throwing buns from the County Hall as a way of celebrating royal and national events.

The word 'jubilee', from which we derive the verb 'to jubilate' (from the Latin *jubilare)*, dates right back to the Old Testament and the book of Leviticus. It stems from the Hebrew word for Ram, because Jubilee years were proclaimed by the blowing of Ram's horns—which is why trumpets still figure strongly in celebrations now. In Leviticus, jubilees marked every 50th year. During them, Hebrew slaves were freed, debts were written off, and houses and lands that had been sold in the open countryside were supposed to be given back to their original owners or heirs.

The concept of a Silver Jubilee is comparatively modern, possibly reflecting Silver Weddings. Had Silver Jubilees been celebrated earlier in Britain, the first after the Norman Conquest would have been Henry II, that remarkable Duke of Normandy who ended up reigning over territory from Hadrian's Wall in the north to the Pyrenees in the south. He lived much of his life at the Royal Palace of Woodstock, which stood near to the present Blenheim Palace, and ruled for 35 years. He negotiated peace after the bloody civil wars

between his mother Matilda and cousin Stephen. He was also the first to be crowned King of England, rather than the older and more tribal-sounding King of the English. He negotiated peace terms with Stephen at Wallingford, under the terms of which Stephen would be allowed to reign until his death and then Henry would take over. Members of the House of Plantagenet that he established proved remarkably long-lived. Henry III reigned for just short of 56 years (1216-72), and Edward III reigned for 50 years.

The next opportunity for Abingdon bun fun at a Silver Jubilee could have been 1785, the 25th anniversary of George III's reign. But the first actual recorded chucking of 'cakes' as they were then called (I hope penny teacakes, not squidgier items) by bigwigs, such as councillors and so forth, onto the populace in the square below happened on the occasion of the coronation of King George III in 1761. The throwers were back in 1810 to celebrate his Golden Jubilee. Whether there would have been any such frolics for his Diamond is unknown since the poor king, mentally ill, died in January 1820—just a few months short of his 60 years on the thrones of both Great Britain and Hanover.

Queen Victoria, Britain's longest serving monarch to date, overtook George III in the longevity stakes in 1896, but requested that any celebrations be delayed until her Diamond Jubilee the following year; on which occasion there was certainly much bun throwing. The jubilations knew no bounds, the two-day holiday having been declared a festival of the British Empire. Throughout much of the globe—coloured pink on the map—free meals and plenty of beer were made available for all and sundry. And grander banquets were held with much pomp and ceremony for grander people. In Oxford new bells were installed at the Cathedral to ring in the Jubilee.

The first Silver Jubilee was celebrated with bun throwing in 1935 when George V had been on the throne for 25 years. The second was that of his granddaughter, the present Queen, which was celebrated 42 years later in 1977. So 2012 marks only the second 60-year reign in English history.

In terms of longest reigning European monarchs, Victoria is in third place with 63 years. Louis XIV, who came to the French Bourbon throne in 1643 aged four, holds the record at 72 years, and Emperor Franz Joseph of Austria and Hungary, who died in 1916, comes in second at 68 years. So that's a lot of coronations and jubilees and a lot of buns, since the County Hall was built in 1678-83.

Wallingford

Little remains of Wallingford Castle now to show its past, pivotal importance. But one building that would have been there even when King Henry V and Queen Catherine visited Wallingford in 1419 is the George Hotel, formerly known as the George and Dragon, built a year earlier. It would almost certainly have been used to accommodate some of his courtiers.

After her husband's death, this beautiful Catherine, as widow of Henry V, retired to Wallingford Castle. Her son, Henry VI, was educated there, and it was there too that

Owen Tudor seduced her. At the end of the Wars of the Roses, when Henry VI's wife, Queen Margaret, was imprisoned at Wallingford Castle, the Lancastrian cause seemed lost — until, that is, Catherine and Owen's grandson (father of Henry VIII) took the throne as King Henry VII Tudor.

So Henry VIII owed his very existence to an intrigue at Wallingford involving his great-grandmother Catherine.

But Henry VIII ran into his own trouble with the Constable of Wallingford Castle, Henry Norreys. Norreys had long been a favourite of the King's. In 1519 he was created Keeper of the King's Purse and Bailiff of Ewelme. In 1523 he became Bailiff of Watlington and in 1535 Constable of the castle of Wallingford, then in royal hands. Certainly he helped Anne rise to power and plotted against Cardinal Wolsey and against the king's first wife, Catherine of Aragon.

Then in 1535 a courtier called Sir Francis Weston told Queen Anne that Norreys was in love with her. Was he really in love with her, and did she really countenance his love enough to carry on a dangerous liaison with him? We will never know for certain.

But Anne then had a word with Norreys, joking about how he was waiting to 'step into dead men's shoes'.

The mere rumour of this liaison was enough to drive Henry VIII, that despot and ogre, to murderous paroxysms of jealousy. Talk about loose words costing lives! Court tittle-tattle was rife and inevitably reached the ears of the King. Was it then by design or mistake that Anne dropped her handkerchief during a jousting tournament? Certainly it was unwise of Norreys in the circumstances to pick it up, wipe his face with it, and then courteously give it back to her on the tip of his lance, driving the King apoplectic with rage.

'Put not your trust in Princes,' Norreys may well have quoted from the psalms (as Lord Stafford famously did of Charles I in the next century when he received notice of his own forthcoming execution), for it seems unlikely that such an experienced courtier, knowing the King's vengeful personality, would have done more than carry on a playful repartee with her. But Norreys was arrested, tried in Westminster Hall, found guilty and executed five days later on 17 May 1536. Anne Boleyn herself suffered the same fate a couple of days later.

But Anne's daughter, Queen Elizabeth I, believed in Norreys' innocence and in that of her mother. She created Norreys' son first Baron Norreys of Rycote.

The Thames Towpath

Strange, I have always thought, as I walk to work of a morning, that a sign on the path alongside the Thames at Osney, reads 'No Horses'. Supposing I wanted to tow a barge? After all, is that not what a towpath is for?

But thereby hangs a tail. For centuries, arguments raged as to ownership of and access to the riverbank, with landowners often insisting on charging tolls for horses and pedestrians alike. Even today, I gather from a book by Joan Tucker, *Ferries of the Upper Thames* (Amberley), which is packed with an astonishing amount of research, that the river remains for a large part the property of private landowners. They possess not only the riverbank on their land but also the river bed up to halfway across it—though the water itself is now the responsibility of the Environment Agency. The public has no automatic right of access, and in many parts of Oxfordshire you can only get to the Thames—except with the permission of a landowner—by following a lane that once upon a time led to a ferry; and many of these have now also been subsumed into desirable, and private, riverside properties.

Before the Reformation, even before the Norman Conquest, when much of the Thames was controlled by monasteries and priories who owned the many water mills, it seems that boats were towed along not by horses but instead by gangs of men called 'bow hauliers' or 'haylers', who hung about and hired themselves out on an ad hoc basis.

Amazingly such gangs continued to exist, and to compete with horses for work, well into the 18th century. A clergyman, John Fletcher, wrote: 'How are they bathed in sweat and rain. Fastened to their lines as horses to their traces, wherein do they differ from the laborious brutes? Not in an erect posture of the body, for in the intenseness of their toil, they bend forward, their head is foremost, and their hand upon the ground.' He adds: 'The beasts tug in patient silence and mutual harmony; but the men with loud contention and horrible imprecations.'

Only gradually did the horses win the battle for work as, with the coming of the Industrial Revolution, barges became larger. Official towpaths became necessary and were negotiated with landlords by various commissions set up to make the Upper Thames more navigable. But often this meant that the horses had to cross the river by ferry because one landlord refused to let horses over land on his side of the river.

In the mid 19th century there was one ferry for every mile on the Thames between Kew and Lechlade. By 1955 only five were left: Bablockhythe, made famous in Matthew Arnold's 'The Scholar Gypsy'; Temple, near Henley; Cookham, where two ferries operated; and one at Benson. Now there are none.

The general pattern for the development of crossing points on the Thames was: first a ford (sometimes with a man there to give customers a piggy back); then a ferry; and finally, if traffic justified it, a bridge. Radcot and Newbridge vie for the honour of oldest bridge across the Thames, but Lechlade and Wallingford are not far behind. Typically, a crossing place was controlled in medieval times by a monastery which had a hostel nearby for travellers. Many pubs near bridges these days are the successors of such hostelries. Wallingford was from earliest times an important crossing point, and William the Conqueror built a castle there to guard it. The first stone bridge was constructed in the early 12th century.

Between the wars it was realised that the towpath was no longer needed for navigation and was falling into serious, even dangerous, decrepitude. The idea of creating a long-distance path for hikers was then mooted, but did not finally become a reality until 1989 when the Thames Path was declared a National Trail. It took all those decades to work out alternative bridges and routes to replace the numerous old ferries.

So that is why horses are not allowed. The towpath is not a towpath. It is a footpath. Silly me.

7. County History
The Rich and the Poor

When the Romans started their settlements here in about AD 43, the area that was in due course to become Oxfordshire was already defined as the point at which the territories of three major British tribes converged (the Catuvellauni, the Dobunni and the Atrebates). The Romans of course built roads, notably Akeman Street; and settlements grew up along them, such as Alchester (2 miles south of modern-day Bicester) and Dorchester-on-Thames—which in time became one of England's earliest centres of Christianity under the missionary St Birinus, who in the 7th century became the first Bishop of Dorchester. The bishopric was transferred to Lincoln shortly after the Norman Conquest.

By the 11th century, Oxfordshire began to feature as a resort of kings. Canute of Denmark and England was crowned in Oxford in 1018, together with Queen Emma, the widow of the Saxon King Ethelred. And in 1109 Henry I decided to build a wall around his hunting lodge at Woodstock—an estate that was to remain in royal possession until given to the Duke of Marlborough after the Battle of Blenheim in 1704. Some of the first skirmishes of the 17th-century Civil War took place in Oxfordshire. Banbury became a byword for Puritanism, while Oxford became King Charles' capital of England.

By and large peace and prosperity ruled in the 18th century, sadly giving way to strife and poverty in the 19th. And then, as elsewhere, men returning from the First World War found it hard to regain the jobs on the land they had left. But at least in Oxfordshire many were able to find work at the new Cowley car works established by William Morris, later Viscount Nuffield. I know of one former blacksmith, back from the war, who took to bicycling from Burford in order to work there; the irony was that it took him a decade or more to save up enough money to buy a car for himself.

Then in 1974 we had the farce of redrawing Oxfordshire's traditional county boundary. Until 1974, the whole Vale of the White Horse district had been a natural part of Berkshire; this poor county suffered the indignity of losing much of its territory to Oxfordshire, including its former county town of Abingdon. Since then the Vale has sat rather uneasily within the new Oxfordshire, since it is situated to the south of the Thames which, for 80 miles and (possibly) 1,000 years, has formed the frontier. So uneasily, indeed, that many writers and historians, including the producers of the revised Pevsner Guide to Berkshire in *The Buildings of England* series (published by Yale in 2010), and also *An Historical Atlas of Oxfordshire* (Oxfordshire Record Society, also 2010), have blithely continued to define their respective counties by the pre-1974 boundaries.

The next fiasco from the County Council came shortly after the beginning of this century, when some employee there took it into his or her head to announce that Oxfordshire would become 1,000 years old in 2007. This startling piece of news was based on research at Oxford University showing that in 'about 1007' a place similar to what was to become known as Oxfordshire was divided into 24 hundreds for administrative purposes; therefore, so the reasoning ran, it must have already existed as a whole.

Any excuse for a party. An organisation with the singularly uninspiring name of 'Oxford Inspires', which describes itself as the 'cultural development agency of Oxfordshire', then went ahead with helping to arrange all sorts of fun events; including one that involved beaming the message 'Celebrating a Thousand Years of Oxfordshire' onto one of the mighty cooling towers of Didcot power station. This in spite of the fact that Didcot has been a part of Oxfordshire for a mere 33 years, i.e. since those boundary changes of 1974.

King Alfred

Wisdom, wealth and a spirit of ancient English unity—the authorities of Oxford University could not resist the heady concoction that King Alfred represents, particularly as he was born in Wantage.

William Camden, the 17th-century historian and antiquary, decided that Alfred had founded the university in the 9th century. He came to that conclusion as a result of a practical joke: fellow academics had included a fake account of the university's founding among his historical documents.

Nevertheless, the idea caught on like wildfire and became more or less received knowledge in the 18th and 19th centuries. Nonsense, of course, as we now know, but the good result for Oxford was that the most famous archaeological find associated with his reign over the West Saxons, the Alfred Jewel, was given to the Ashmolean Museum. It is inscribed with the words: 'Alfred ordered me to be made.' Some say that it might represent King Solomon, that king of wisdom, with whom Alfred's earliest biographer, Asser, liked to associate Alfred. In any case, several replicas have been made of the brooch, including one given to Hitler by Unity Mitford.

What is clear is that of the two towns claiming Alfred as a son, Wantage and Winchester, the former has the better claim: he was born there in 849. But it was an Oxfordshire sculptor, Sir Hamo Thornycroft, who lived in Combe, who did much to promote the cause of Winchester. He carved the huge statue of the scholar king there in 1901. The statue at Wantage was carved by a relative of Queen Victoria, Count Gleichen, to celebrate the millennium of Alfred's birth. However, it was not unveiled until 1877 when the Prince and Princess of Wales visited the town to celebrate the occasion. Apparently, a public subscription needed to commission the statue had not raised enough money. Not until Robert Lloyd-Lindsay, later Lord Wantage, supplied the cash was it erected.

And what of those cakes? Dickens, in his *Child's History of England*, makes it clear that Alfred's noble, scholarly mind was thinking so deeply about his poor subjects being chased through the land by those wicked Danes that he let the cakes burn. Whether true or not, the story is certainly ancient, much earlier than Dickens' time.

In any case, Alfred has been credited with almost everything great in British history and myth—juries, the navy, even the British Empire.

Radcot Bridge, 1387

Canoeing about upstream from Radcot, near Witney, way back in the 1960s, I remember meeting a stonemason working on the bridge over the River Thames. He told me that cars were a menace and that he never went in them himself. As someone who had been camping out over a Bank Holiday weekend and had managed to see hardly another human being, let alone a car, his remark struck a chord with me.

Radcot Bridge must be one of the oldest bridges spanning the Thames, containing as it does a Gothic niche for a holy statue. The stonemason told me that the statue, stolen during the Reformation, had commemorated the battle, but I neglected to ask him which. He meant, of course, the Battle of Radcot Bridge of 16 December 1387, which decided the course of history during that unhappy century.

In the course of the battle, Robert de Vere, 9th Earl of Oxford, defeated by Thomas of Woodstock, Duke of Gloucester, made his horse leap over the parapet and into the cold river. He shed his heavy armour and sword (found later by his enemies who presumed him drowned) and escaped, eventually, to France. He was condemned to death in his absence by the aptly named Merciless Parliament.

Lord Oxford was the favourite, and possibly homosexual lover, of poor Richard II who heaped lands and titles upon him. He became Marquess of Dublin for life and also Duke of Ireland. His defeat at Radcot Bridge meant that Richard's power was temporarily taken from him by his uncle, Thomas of Woodstock—so called as he was born in 1355 at the royal hunting lodge of Woodstock that stood near the present Blenheim Palace. Richard II was the son of the Black Prince—Edward Prince of Wales—who was also born at Woodstock in 1330, and whose residence, when in England, was at Wallingford Castle.

The Black Prince, incidentally, was the first Englishman with the rank of Duke. He was granted the Duchy of Cornwall. Richard was crowned when only ten years old upon the death of his grandfather, Edward III, and de Vere, just five years older than the king, attended as Lord Great Chamberlain of England.

Robert de Vere lived in exile together with Michael de la Pole, whose English residence had been at Ewelme. He, too, had incurred the wrath of Richard's powerful enemies, many of whom had enjoyed power during the King's minority. Richard, to some extent, turned the tables on Thomas of Woodstock in 1397 when the latter was murdered in Calais by Nicholas Colfox, a 'Lollard' follower of the Oxford academic John Wycliffe, who believed that the Catholic Church needed root and branch reform.

Robert de Vere was killed by a wild boar in 1392. Richard had his body brought back to England three years later and organised an elaborate funeral at Earl's Colne, Essex, which annoyed his enemies to such a degree that it contributed to the King's downfall. He was imprisoned at Pontefract and died on 14 February 1400.

As for that stonemason, he must be long dead, but I always think of him when I take the old packhorse route across Radcot Bridge. For centuries it carried Cotswold wool to Southampton for export.

Reformation in Abingdon, 1538

Relations between the inhabitants of Oxford and that other former county town eight miles downstream along the Thames, Abingdon, were for centuries on the fractious side.

That wonderful fishing ground for historians of the late Saxon and early Norman periods, *The Chronicle of Abingdon Abbey*, dating from the mid 11th century, notes that the people of Oxford were required to pay the monks of the ancient Benedictine Abbey, founded way back in the 7th century, a hundred eels a year in return for permission to build a navigation channel on church land.

Immediately following the Norman Conquest, Oxford started to rise in importance under the iron rule of Robert d'Oilly, appointed governor by William I, while Abingdon Abbey, around the gates of which the town grew up, saw its Saxon abbot unceremoniously sacked and replaced with an unpopular, brash and unruly Norman version. It also found itself required to support 30 knights instead of the dozen Saxons it had previously supported.

Then came some great and prosperous days which, in a holy sort of way, ran parallel to the rise of academic Oxford. As early as 1100 Henry I appointed a learned Italian doctor as abbot, known only as Faritius. Monk numbers increased from 28 to 80 and grateful patients gave the monastery lands including the manor and church of St Mary Abbots in Kensington, London. Even now Kensington and Abingdon still mark the connection by annual mayorial visits.

Instead of Town and Gown troubles as in Oxford, Abingdon experienced what might be called Town and Cowl riots. In 1327 the townspeople rebelled against the rigid control of their trade by the bureaucratic monks. They invaded the abbey, burning and looting it. Later, led by the vicar of St Helen's, they tried (again unsuccessfully) to throw off the abbot's yoke. The pretext for trouble this time was that they wanted their dead to be buried in their own churchyard rather than the abbey cemetery.

All this, of course, was as nothing compared to the disasters in store for the monks when they got to the 16th century—9 February 1538, to be precise—when the last abbot, Thomas Rowland, signed the Deed of Surrender to Henry VIII, packed his bags and left the great monastery along with his 34 monks. They probably closed the great gate, housed in the lovely Gatehouse which was then about 100 years old and which, of course, still exists, quietly behind them in order not to attract too much attention to the fact that they were bringing to an end some 900 years of history.

Abbot Rowland and a few servants and monks moved to Cumnor Place, his country house, which the King had graciously granted to him for life together with a generous pension, paid for out of the plunder gained from ruining the abbey. He knew what was good for him all right since he knew what happened to monks who refused to leave quietly. The abbot of that other great Berkshire abbey of Reading, for instance—Abingdon was of course part of Berkshire until the county reorganisation of 1974—had been hanged, drawn and quartered for not signing the deed quickly enough.

All the same, Abbot Rowland, returning to Abingdon today, would be astonished to see the whirling town alongside the few remains of the abbey. The scarcity of eels in the Thames would probably surprise him almost as much as the quantities of cars.

The Burford Levellers, 1649

Burford still celebrates an annual Levellers' Day in May. But who were the Levellers and what were they doing in Burford?

The Levellers were members of the cavalry of Cromwell's New Model Army, victors of the English Civil War. Some say that it was King Charles himself who coined the name Leveller as a term of abuse, meaning people who wanted to 'level men's estates,

destroy property or make all things common', but three months after the King's execution these Levellers were now paid-up followers of Cromwell. The actual Civil War may have come to an end but dissension about how the country should be governed was rife, with the Levellers, now hailed by some as the world's first socialists, calling for far more in the way of democracy than Oliver Cromwell was prepared to countenance.

In 1647 there was some dissension in the New Model Army, so Cromwell said he would call a General Council of the Army to discuss their future. The council would have consisted of two officers and two men from each regiment. Had such a council been called, it would have discussed something called 'The Agreement of the People' which proposed, among other things, a single-chamber parliament and freedom for accused persons to refuse to answer incriminating questions (as in the Fifth Amendment of the US Constitution).

Then in 1649 the Army were in Salisbury, on their way to Ireland (where Cromwell's troops committed horrendous cruelties). On May Day itself 800 troopers mutinied and refused to continue their journey for a variety of reasons, foremost of which was that they were owed a lot of money in back-wages. Some of the mutineers were also protesting against what they saw as the broken promise from Oliver Cromwell. As a result of the mutiny the soldiers appointed their own new officers, though there was no single leader. Then they marched north in the hope of picking up support along the way.

Arriving in Burford, they only appointed a few sentries because they had been led to believe that no action would be taken against them until their grievances had been discussed. But during the night of 13 May 1649, 2,000 horsemen under the commander in chief of the Parliamentary forces, General Thomas Fairfax (1612-71), attacked from one direction and Cromwell from another. Many of the New Model Army mutineers escaped, and one man on each side was killed in the skirmish; the remaining 340 were locked in the church for three nights.

We have lasting evidence of one such prisoner. He was called Anthony Sedley, and he carved his name on the lead lining of the font in Burford church: 'ANTHONY SEDLEY 1649 PRISNER' [sic]. Sedley escaped with his life. Others were not so lucky. On 17 May Sedley would have been among the captives herded up on to the church roof to watch three of his fellows—Cornet Thompson, Corporal Church and Private Perkins—put against the churchyard wall and shot. They were deemed by a court martial to have been the ringleaders.

A fourth ringleader was forced to preach a sermon, which he did 'howling and weeping like a crocodile', according to an excellent sheet on the whole incident called 'A Burford Trail', published by the Burford and District Society.

The Duke of Marlborough, 1712

New Year 1712 was not a happy one for the great Duke of Marlborough (1650-1722), commander of the allied forces against the French during the Wars of the Spanish Succession, and heroic victor of such momentous battles as Blenheim, Ramillies, Oudenarde and Malplaquet. He started the year in real trouble. On New Year's Eve his political foe, Robert Harley, Earl of Oxford, (1661-1724), had persuaded Queen Anne to dismiss him from all his military posts, and on New Year's Day his sacking was duly published in *The London Gazette* for all to read.

It is surely some measure of the greatness of this astonishing man that he accepted his downfall with the same sort of calm equanimity with which he accepted the ebb and flow of fortune when conducting military operations: simply re-evaluating his position, cool as a cucumber.

Among the many commiserating letters from the great and the good—including monarchs and princes—was a note from an Oxfordshire neighbour called Sir Thomas Wheate, who lived at Glympton, not far from Blenheim (where building work had ground to a halt). He offered the Duke some beagles; and the Duke, ever courteous, replied: 'I am very much obliged to you for being mindful to my want of beagles, though I am yet at a loss where to keep them; however I should be glad to know where they are, and if the huntsman will undertake to keep them till I have a proper place, and upon what terms, to which I shall pray your answer at your leisure.'

Apt that, because the Duke, throughout his life, had been accused of running with the hare and hunting with the hounds when it came to whether or not he wanted to see James II, his erstwhile master, restored to the British throne. Indeed he sailed so close to the wind of treason on this account that he had even seen the inside of the Tower of London in 1692—when he was imprisoned there for five weeks, accused of treachery. He was released when an incriminating letter about the restoration of James and the kidnap of William was judged to be a forgery—though there can be no doubt that Marlborough continued to correspond with Jacobites, until his death.

The fact is, to mix metaphorical animals, he was as wily as a fox; and as good at looking after his own interests. But luckily his own interests were compatible with the business of ensuring that Louis XIV of France never achieved hegemony over the whole of Europe—something that was definitely seen as against British interests.

All the same, he was a true European rather than a little Englander. For instance, extraordinary as it may seem to modern minds, he continued on friendly terms with his nephew the Duke of Berwick, the illegitimate son of his own sister Arabella Churchill and James II, even though he became a marshall of France and one of Louis XIV's best military commanders. He also worked closely in his earlier career with the German Duke of Schomberg, who was created an English Duke and was Dutch William's second in command at the Battle of the Boyne in 1690.

But despite the international mix-up of the protagonists involved in the wars, it is extraordinary how many of those personalities had Oxfordshire connections. For example the Duke of Shrewsbury, one of the people who signed the letter to William inviting him to invade, lived at Heythrop; Lord Oxford had been educated at a small school in Shilton; Lord Clarendon, the brother of Queen Anne's mother Anne Hyde, lived at Cornbury Park, Charlbury; and of course the great Duke himself was given Blenheim by Queen Anne.

And why was Marlborough disgraced in 1712? Lord Oxford maintained that Marlborough—by that time by far the richest man in England—had illegally received £60,000 from the contractors operating army bread wagons, and that he had also received two and a half per cent of British money paid to foreign troops. He found it necessary to go into voluntary exile in 1712 but was greeted as an old friend when the King of Hanover became King George I of Britain in 1714. After all, his continued correspondence with the Jacobites was merely an 'insurance policy' taken out by a man who applied the same kind of ruthless caution to his politics as he did to his warfare.

The Marquesses of Blandford

Many a Marquess of Blandford has found himself in trouble while living in the waiting room, as it were, before moving into Blenheim Palace. Book collector George Spencer-Churchill (1766-1841), for instance, who became 5th Duke of Marlborough in 1817 aged 51, really knew how to spend money. At the auction of the Duke of Roxburghe's library in 1812 he calmly bid £2,260 for a first edition of Boccaccio's racy *Decameron* (published in 1471). To give an idea of the enormity of that sum, the annual wage bill for 75 staff at Blenheim at the time was £786. The Marquess (he was the first to style himself thus, instead of using the French spelling Marquis) moved into Blenheim on his father's death with much expensive ceremony. Unfortunately, bailiffs soon appeared on the scene and put paid to all that. All his books were sold at a loss—with his *Decameron* fetching just 875 guineas. At his death in 1840, the Annual Register at the Palace remarked: 'He lived in utter retirement at one corner of his magnificent palace, a melancholy instance of the results of extravagance.'

The next son, also George, while Marquess of Blandford, seduced a young girl called Susan Law, who bore him a daughter, after his brother dressed up as a

John Marquess of Blandford, later 7th Duke of Marlborough

clergyman and performed a mock marriage service. The judge in a subsequent court case concerning the matter uttered some choice remarks about Lord Blandford's moral character.

Yet another George, while a married Marquess and heir to the 7th Duke, scandalised Victorian England by eloping with Edith, the wife of the Earl of Aylsford. The two set up house together in Paris where a son, Guy, was born. They styled the boy Lord Guernsey as though he were the heir of Aylsford, but the House of Lords disallowed the claim. What really caught the public imagination in all this was the involvement of the Prince of Wales, the future Edward VII, who was accused firstly of having had an affair with Edith himself and, secondly, of having taken Lord Aylsford off to India in order to leave the coast clear for Lord Blandford.

Blenheim itself, thanks to the extravagance of the 5th Duke, would probably have parted company with the Churchills had it not been protected by entailments. Entailments, which required each successor to an estate to only inherit on condition that they passed it on to the succeeding generation, were outlawed in England in 1925.

But, interestingly enough, given the long line of spendthrift Spencer Churchills, it was the upright 7th Duke of Marlborough, described by historian A. L. Rowse as 'a complete full-blown Victorian prig', who caused the greatest sell-offs at the palace. When Marquess of Blandford and MP for Woodstock, he had sponsored the worthy Blandford Act through Parliament. This allowed the subdivision of rural parishes. But when he became Duke he warded off money worries by persuading the Lord Chancellor to push through the Blenheim Settled Estates Act which enabled him to break the entailment.

Under the hammer went the Marlborough Gems, the Sunderland Library, Raphael's Ansidei Madonna, Van Dyke's equestrian portrait of Charles I, to name but a few treasures. Incidentally, the man who bought the *Decameron* from the 5th Duke was Earl Spencer. He had bid £2,550 for it at the Roxburghe sale.

As for Marquesses of Blandford, the family now living at Blenheim might be called Godolphin were it not for the fact that William Godolphin, Marquess of Blandford, died of drink without heirs back in 1731. He was the son of the elder daughter of the first duke and duchess, Henrietta, who had married the Earl of Godolphin.

As it happens, Blenheim and the Dukedom went to the descendants of her younger sister Anne, who was married to Charles Spencer Earl of Sunderland. The name Churchill was added to the surname by the 5th Duke.

Jethro Tull

Why would a pop group founded in 1968 take the name of an Oxfordshire agriculturist born in the 17th century? I wondered this as I stared at a cairn commemorating an international ploughing competition, apparently held in a field at Warborough in 1956 and inaugurated, according to a grandiose tablet, by the Duke of Gloucester. Apt that, I thought—admittedly in a post-prandial haze, having just eaten excellent fish and chips at The Cricketers in Warborough—since Jethro Tull lived for many years down the road in Wallingford and across the Thames in Crowmarsh Gifford.

Jethro Tull (1674-1741) was the son of a Berkshire gentleman farmer, also called Jethro, of Basildon, and went up to St John's College, Oxford, aged 17, but apparently never graduated. Instead he entered Gray's Inn, where he is still listed as the son and heir of Jethro Tull of Howberry, Oxfordshire. Upon becoming a barrister he took a long tour of Europe, but instead of simply looking at the art and architecture, as was the wont of young men on the Grand Tour, he studied methods of agriculture.

On his return to Howberry he worked so hard with his experiments that, in the words of one 19th-century Berkshire history: 'By intense application, vexatious toil, and too frequently exposing himself to the vicissitudes of heat and cold in the open fields, he contracted a pulmonary disorder, which, not being found curable in England, obliged him a second time to travel, and to seek a cure in the milder climates of France and Italy.'

Back in England he found himself severely financially embarrassed and forced to sell Howberry. He moved to a smaller place called, ironically enough, Prosperous Farm, at Shalbourne, near Hungerford, where he adapted his inventions for the new soil conditions he found. His neighbours persuaded him to write a book called *Horse-hoeing Husbandry* 'on the principles of tillage' in 1733; these ideas were taken up by landowners who profited greatly, but he faced incredible opposition and vituperation from labourers and farmers who reckoned his labour-saving ideas would put them out of work.

He himself appeared not to prosper from the book. It seems he had trouble working with others and, according to the 19th-century 'Notes on Basildon': 'His expenses were enhanced in various ways, but chiefly by the stupidity of the workmen employed in

constructing his instruments, and in the awkwardness and maliciousness of his servants, who, because they did not or would not comprehend the use of them, seldom failed to break some essential part or other, in order to render them useless.'

Berkshire claims Jethro Tull as its son, since he was born and is buried in Basildon and, of course, Wallingford was part of Berkshire until the county boundary changes of 1974. But, as a matter of fact, he lived much of his life on the Oxfordshire side of the river at Howberry, near Crowmarsh, where he carried out his agricultural experiments and earned his name as the 'Father of British Agriculture'. Here he perfected his seed drilling method to replace the old system of simply scattering seeds and hoping that they might germinate, thereby increasing yield eightfold and revolutionising the business of ploughing. In the words of my 1927 edition of *Chambers Encyclopaedia*, 'his work was ere long recognised as epoch-making'.

But why was the pop group named after him? Leader of the group Ian Anderson has explained that in the beginning the band used to change its name each week. During the week that the agent by chance called it Jethro Tull the group was asked to play the Marquee Club. Then the name stuck.

Mutiny of the Oxfordshire Militiamen, 1795

Among those gathered to witness the horrific execution by firing squad of a poor Witney blanket weaver turned soldier and another poor man from Chipping Norton on 13 June 1795 was Jane Austen's brother Henry. In 1793 he had taken a break from his Theological studies as an undergraduate at St John's College, Oxford, to join up with the Oxfordshire militia; and by the time of the riots that led to these dreadful events he had risen to become regimental paymaster.

National and European politics intrude remarkably seldom into the sedate world of Jane Austen's books, but of course these were fearsome times for ordinary people to be alive, and with revolution raging across the channel in France the ruling classes were terrified that more of the same might break out here.

Each county was expected to raise a number of men to serve in the militias, with officers by and large selected by the Lord Lieutenant according to set property requirements for each rank—which did not come cheap either, with a colonel expected to show he obtained at least £1,000 a year from land, not trade.

However, with wars in France and the Netherlands going badly and food riots at home, these property requirements were sometimes relaxed, and Henry Austen was accepted as a 'Gentleman to be Lieutenant', which meant that he performed the duties of someone of that rank without formally holding it. Militias were usually posted away from their home counties—so that should riots break out as a result of perceived injustices, such as land enclosures, the soldiers would be less likely to side with the rioters (who might of course include members of their own families).

There was a particularly poor harvest in the summer of 1794 followed by a particularly cold winter. So by June 1795 the Oxfordshire Militia Regiment found itself billeted in appalling conditions at East Blatchington, near Seaford in Sussex, from whence they could see grain being exported from the port of Tidemills. With near starvation rife in the English countryside, this sight apparently brought about a spontaneous mutiny in the ranks of the Oxfordshire Militia. Several dozen soldiers marched to Seaford in a 'disorderly manner', took over the bread and flour there, and sold it off at reduced prices. Ringleaders were arrested and court martialled in Brighton, with four young men sentenced to be flogged and two, former blanket weaver Edward Cooke and Chipping Norton man Sam Parish, condemned to death.

The day before the execution—at least according to the Reverend John Dreng who was apparently present at the event—Mr Cooke wrote to his brother: 'I am going to die for what the regiment done. I am not afraid to meet death for I have done no harm to no person and that is a great comfort to me.' Even the High Sheriff of Sussex was deeply affected by all this. He wrote to the printer of *The Reading Mercury* on 12 June: 'I am proceeding to the execution of the two poor fellows.'

Thousands of regular soldiers and militiamen were marched to Goldstone Bottom, near Hove, to witness the punishment. They were there both to see an example set and to quell any disorder that might easily have arisen since Sussex people were overwhelmingly sympathetic to the prisoners. Messrs Cooke and Parrish were first made to witness the floggings. Then they were made to kneel on their own coffins and were shot by ten comrades who had been selected from among the other mutineers. Then the assembled audience were made to march around the bodies.

The High Sheriff wrote again the next day: 'I am just returned from the ground where two soldiers were shot this morning, about quarter past eight. One of them knelt down upon one coffin and one upon the other, and they both instantly fell dead. Though left there, lest there be any remains of life, a firelock was left close to the head of each immediately after.'

As for Henry Austen, he resigned his commission with the Oxfords in 1801. All the same, his sister must have learned much information about the militia from him. For example there is George Wickham who appears as a lieutenant of the '-----shire Militia' in *Pride and Prejudice*, some of her descriptions could well be based on the experiences of these poor Oxfordshire militiamen.

The Rural Poor, 1891

How much can you believe of what you read in the press? More, perhaps, these days than was the case in 1891 when a national newspaper sent a 'special correspondent' to West Oxfordshire, then judged to be a particularly poverty-stricken area, to look at the condition of the rural poor.

In Woodstock and outlying villages, the reporter from *The Daily News* found many people still seething with indignation from the enclosures of common land that had been depriving them of a livelihood for 100 years or more. He wrote: 'I confess that it made my blood boil to drive about Blenheim Park, and see how the labouring poor have been defrauded of what belongs to them.' Everywhere in the series of articles (with sub-titles such as 'Ducal Land-Grabbers' and 'No Harvest Home') there is a germ of truth, but the special correspondent's views are certainly not balanced and his quotations are not attributed; something which I, for one, would not get away with now.

For instance, the special correspondent quotes an unnamed 'influential Liberal of Woodstock' as saying: 'Look there, the Duke of Marlborough has no business whatever with that land, but as Lord of the Manor, he just simply takes it, and nobody dares oppose him.' Presumably he is referring to the strip of land between the park wall and the A44 west of Woodstock. The correspondent continues: 'The thing looked plain as a pikestaff. There was the park wall bounding the Duke's private property. Between the wall and the road was a space of waste land, common property. The transfer from public to private ownership is begun by sticking up a notice, 'All persons depositing rubbish on this land will be prosecuted — Marlborough.' A little further on comes the next stage, and a low stone wall skirts the road and shuts in the open land. It is now the Duke's and if people want it for allotments he has no objection to let it to them at five-and-20 shillings an acre.'

Of course, the correspondent does his case no good by failing to balance his report by quoting the Duke of Marlborough on the matter. But it is undeniable that poverty among Blenheim tenants and workers in the post-enclosure era, when the estate itself was on its uppers, was very great. In 1832 acute distress prompted 36 villagers of Combe to petition the Duke for allotments, which he granted on condition that half the land was used to grow potatoes.

This was a time when the Dukes of Marlborough had little money and the National Union of Agricultural Workers was just coming into being; a time when many cottages, even occupied ones (for many were abandoned), were falling into rack and ruin. *The Daily News* fanned the flames. Its point was that, despite owning land enclosed by a wall at least 9 miles long, the Dukes 'have generation after generation been gobbling up piece after piece of the common lands of the poor'.

RAF Benson

Work to establish the new airfield next to the south Oxfordshire village of Benson, with its imposing collection of Georgian buildings, began in 1937 and finished in 1939. Its establishment on land previously farmed by the Walter family meant the destruction of the 18th-century Lamb pub, which stood near the present Crash Gate No 6. In 1942 it also meant the destruction of the quirky KCB (Keep the Countryside Beautiful) cafe and filling station on the Old London Road that had long been popular with flying crews, whether British, US or Polish. It moved to Mill Lane where it remained until the end of the war.

Much of the operation carried out from RAF Benson during the Second World War was only declassified in the late 1990s. The secrets then revealed involved the activities of the Photographic Reconaissance Unit (PRU), which arrived at RAF Benson in December 1940.

Thousands of flights set out from here on expeditions deep into Germany. Their missions were to photograph potential targets before bombing raids; and then to photograph them again afterwards to assess the damage—both dangerous operations from which many pilots did not return. It was careful analysis of photographs taken by PRU pilots from RAF Benson which established that the Germans were developing their V1 and V2 weapons at Peenemunde, Holland. Other dangerous flights included sorties to check out German shipping movements and coastal defences.

In their book *Benson, A Century of Change: 1900-2000*, Janet Burt and Peter Clarke write: 'Taking, developing and analysing thousands of photographs involved huge numbers of people, some based at Mount Farm, Berinsfield, and Chalgrove, others at Medmenham, near Marlow.' They also quote an account of the actual business of photographing a target by Pilot Officer Gordon Green: 'The technique of high altitude photography from a single-seater like the Spitfire was largely a question of experience, for a great deal depended on being able to judge where the cameras were pointing. One flew alone to the general area of the target and then tipped the aircraft on its side to check one was properly lined up.'

It is no secret, though, that RAF Benson became home to the King's Flight—later of course the Queen's Flight—in 1939 when a Lockheed Hudson was lodged in A Hangar for the sovereign's use. The Air Ministry had already agreed to pay to fly members of the Royal family about in 1936, but the Flight moved from Hendon to Benson three years later. There was then a four-year period during the war when the Flight was based in Newmarket, but in 1946 George VI formally approved the reconstitution of the King's Flight at Benson. It consisted of four Viking aircraft.

In 1960 the aircraft of the Queen's Flight were painted all over in fluorescent red; the distinctive flying machines became quite a familiar sight over Oxfordshire until the Flight was disbanded in 1995. Janet Burt and Peter Clarke write: 'There can surely never have been such well-maintained aircraft as these. Unsurprisingly, both the old Andover aircraft and the Wessex Mk2 helicopters in 1983 had completed over 10,000 hours' flying and continued to break all previous records for longevity.'

8. Houses and Parks
The Architectural Heritage

'England is like one big park': so said a young nephew of mine from Ireland, as we drove from Woodstock to Burford. I saw what he meant: surely any foreigner would get that impression if their first introduction to England was rural west Oxfordshire: apparently a land full of rich people, all living in big houses set in parks behind walls built of Cotswold stone. We had left Blenheim behind—where the boy had said that the statue of the Great Duke, wearing his toga and standing on top of the Column of Victory, looked like a priest blessing his congregation. We had then turned down a narrow lane to get a glimpse of Ditchley before driving on to Charlbury; we were just passing Lee Place on our right and Cornbury on our left when he made the remark.

But the point is that the comment would have been as apposite almost anywhere in rural Oxfordshire. Houses open to the public to the east of Oxford include Stonor, Mapledurham and Greys Court; to the west, in addition to Blenheim and Ditchley, there is the exquisite Lodge at Sherborne, and of course Buscot, both now in the care of the National Trust (to name but two). To the north are Broughton Castle and Sulgrave Manor; and to the south Milton Manor and Kingston Bagpuize House. And this remark would not have seemed entirely inappropriate even in much of Oxford itself, what with the stunning college architecture, and the existence of such green open spaces as Christ Church Meadow or the Deer Park at Magdalen.

Extraordinary, really, that so much of the county still appears as parkland, even though many of the great houses are no longer private homes (though many are; and some that weren't are becoming so again); and of course most of us, despite how things appeared to a young visitor, live in 19th- or 20th-century suburbs—certainly not grand parks.

All the same, Oxfordshire is so rich in architecture that it is possible to find an example from almost every period you care to seek out. My nephew, for instance, was interested in the mosaic at the Roman villa at North Leigh, but was a little sniffy about Norman churches, explaining that some Round Towers he had been shown in Ireland during a school project were older. I had to match him with the pre-Conquest Saxon church of St Michael at the North Gate, Oxford's oldest building.

But it is not only the grandest great houses and parks, redolent of old-fashioned splendour and designed by architects like Vanbrugh and Gibbs, that impress visitors. Tourists are also attracted by countless smaller manor houses, often with whole villages huddled at their gates. Sometimes, as for instance at the lovely village of Lower Slaughter, the manor has even turned into a hotel for them to stay in.

For rural life in Oxfordshire has probably changed more since the Second World War than during the preceding two or three centuries. The comforting sight of a manor (complete with squire), a vicarage (complete with vicar), a church and a pub is more or less gone forever. As few as one in five pre-war vicarages in England remain vicarages today, and pubs continue to close at an alarming rate, with most survivors in rural Oxfordshire going 'gourmet'. Very few people living in pretty villages nowadays are dependent on the land for their living, but the rural idyll lives on; there is no shortage of people with no land to range over who nevertheless possess a four-wheel-drive vehicle.

But another surprising paradox is hidden here: beneath this change, there is no change. For much of Oxfordshire's agricultural land is still owned by the families that have owned it for generations. It has been estimated that 69 per cent of Britain's acreage is owned by 0.6 per cent of the population. In the Cotswolds, as my nephew noticed, that is very apparent.

Vanbrugh House

It was so sad, the sight of that strangely beautiful building at 20 St Michael's Street, Oxford, known as Vanbrugh House, which the City Council left empty for a decade; now it is to become part of a new 22-room hotel.

But why is it called Vanbrugh House, and how did it come to be built in the first place? According to a 1920 publication by the Oxford Architectural and Historical Society, the reason is clear: it states unequivocally, 'There seems no doubt that No 20 St Michael's Street is a minor work of the great 18th-century architect Vanbrugh, the designer of Blenheim Palace. The enormous Doric order, the apron blocks and heavy keystones to the windows, which have no architraves, are all characteristics of his heavy and monumental manner.' Nikolaus Pevsner, though, is less sure. He wrote: 'It is a bit of a joke and must be by an imitator of Blenheim.' Later he even refers to it as 'almost a parody of Blenheim'.

I gather this information from a booklet (*Vanbrugh House, Oxford*, 1982) by Edward Hibbert, who for 40 years was a solicitor with Marshall and Galpin, the law firm that occupied the building for more than half a century, and who, together with his brother Christopher, edited that mine of local history, *The Encyclopaedia of Oxford* (Macmillan, 1988). He explained that whether Vanbrugh designed the building or not, he certainly had close connections with it; for the house was home to three generations of the Peisley family of Oxford builders, from the late 17th until the mid 18th century. Mr Hibbert wrote in his booklet: 'Opinions differ as to whether the design was by Sir John Vanbrugh. Bearing in mind the close working relationship between Vanbrugh and Peisley at Blenheim it is quite possible that Vanbrugh drew some sketches for the stone front of the building and may well have stayed or dined with Peisley.'

The building behind the magnificent facade dates from the 17th century. Its cellars contain remains of the city walls, which ran along the north side of St Michael's Street to the North Gate, near which stood the infamous Bocardo Prison, miserable final home of the martyred bishops Latimer and Ridley, and archbishop Cranmer, which was demolished in 1771.

In 1671 the house was leased by the City Council to Matthew Jellyman, who was appointed jailer of the Bocardo Prison; and in 1680 this lease was renewed at a rent of two shillings a year plus 'a couple of good fat pullets'. It was this lease that was later assigned to Bartholomew Peisley I (who built the senior common room at St John's, completed the library and chapel at St Edmund Hall, and became involved in supplying Headington stone for St Paul's Cathedral). Bartholomew Peisley I (1620-92) is likely to have designed the two beautifully panelled rooms and a fine 17th-century staircase.

Then it was Bartholomew Peisley II (1654-1715) who, as master mason working under the direction of Sir John Vanbrugh, built the grand bridge now spanning the lake at Blenheim. His daughter, Mary, married Henry Joynes, the clerk of works at Blenheim 1705-15. A report from the Treasury to the Duke of Marlborough dated September 1710 states: 'The great arch of the bridge is keyed and has succeeded to admiration, which Peisley the builder is very proud and overjoyed at, it being a great and nice piece of work.'

Bartholomew Peisley III (1683-1727) completed the transformation of the facade of Vanburgh House in about 1721. Diarist and librarian Thomas Hearne described Mr Peisley as 'a noted wealthy mason' and his widow—who later married the president of Trinity College—as 'a very pretty woman'.

The new hotel, which planners have approved, will comprise numbers 20-24 St Michael's Street. North Gate Hall, the imposing former United Methodist Free Church at number 18 (next door to Vanbrugh House) was designed by local architect J. C. Curtis and built in 1871. It is also City Council owned and contains remnants of a bastion of the medieval city wall. It remains empty and, according to a Heritage Assessment by the council's own Heritage and Specialist Services Team, shows 'clear signs of lack of maintenance'.

Shotover Country Park

Anyone concerned about the debates over the environment and the freedom to roam should perhaps spare a thought for the medieval inhabitants of Oxfordshire. From the Norman Conquest until the end of the 14th century, about a third of England was covered by Royal Forest, that is land set aside for the King's hunting pleasures, where special forest law pertained and where only the King and his aristocratic cronies could hunt.

Oxfordshire was typical, with Shotover Forest extending to 15 square miles in size, stretching from the escarpment of Shotover Hill right down to Oxford's Magdalen Bridge in the east, and Wychwood Forest, with the royal palace and park of Woodstock (now Blenheim) at its core, in the west.

It seems that William the Conqueror and his son William II, famously killed in a hunting accident, had much more concern about the animals living in the forests than about the common people living there. Horrible punishments including death and mutilation were regularly handed down by the forest courts for anyone with the temerity to interfere with the King's game or to harm his trees without permission.

Blinding, for example, was a common punishment for killing a hare. In short, what a person could or could not do in the royal forests, or where they could or could not roam, was severely controlled. But the land and game were probably better preserved than they had ever been before or since.

Royal Forest as a form of land management was introduced from the continent by William I, but the term forest did not have its modern connotations. It simply meant grassland, woodland, heath or wetland that was capable of supporting deer and game. Its history provides an insight into English land management over the centuries. Kings soon realised, for instance, that their forests were a wonderful source of revenue. They charged their forest subjects for pannage (feeding pigs on acorns) and agistment (grazing) and drew money from fines imposed in the forest courts (swainmotes).

Unfortunately, Shotover Forest suffered mismanagement during Cromwell's Commonwealth when Sir Timothy Tyrrell was Keeper of Shotover. There was already not all that much to mismanage since Charles I had cut down many of the oaks to use to defend his Royalist capital of Oxford during the civil war. It is ironic that it was his efforts at imposing his ancient rights which had largely contributed to the unrest that caused the war. But Shotover Forest ceased to be a royal forest in 1660.

The eminent jurist Sir William Blackstone (1733-80), who was the recorder of Wallingford, an Oxford University professor and author of the seminal textbook *Commentaries*, made a detailed study of forest law and its courts. Inhabitants of such land could manage it and subsist off it in strictly circumscribed ways. For example, common people could graze domestic animals there, in carefully managed areas, or grow vegetables (usually using the strip farming method), and trees were carefully pollarded, thus preserving the trees themselves as well as providing fuel and building materials.

The lovely, gnarled old Shotover oak in Shotover Country Park, the remains of the old royal forest now managed by Oxford City Council, is an example of such a pollarded tree. It was until recently thought to have been about 250 years old but is now thought to be more than 400. Experts say that pollarding long ago probably prolonged its life.

Garsington Manor

Would not Lady Ottoline Morrell, and indeed her husband Philip, have been sad that their beloved Garsington Manor is no longer being used as a setting for opera. Probably they would have been grateful for the efforts of the late Leonard Ingrams who founded Garsington Opera, bringing to a close the spirit of 'open house' that has reigned for about 100 years since 1915, the year the Morrells bought the house.

Keenly aware that they were living through a war which would change Britain forever, they turned the lovely house and gardens into a refuge for conscientious objectors, while continuing to entertain the foremost writers and thinkers of the age. Lady Ottoline wrote of Garsington: 'It was indeed a ravishing decor, recalling to one a Watteau or a Fragonard, a Mozart opera, an Italian villa, a Shakespeare play or any of the lovely worlds that poetic art has created.'

Ottoline was a half brother of the 6th Duke of Portland and a cousin of the late Queen Elizabeth the Mother. Philip was the son of an Oxford lawyer, related to the beer family, whose company had been solicitors to Oxford University for a century or more. The odd pair—she often to be seen by astonished villagers charging round about in a pony and trap, with orange hair and wearing Turkish trousers; he conventional enough—bought the Elizabethan house from the family of a farmer who had let it deteriorate. They were welcomed into the village with much ringing of the church bells. Philip's family had owned land and cottages in the village for generations.

Philip Morrell (pronounced in those days to rhyme with Durrell) lent Bertrand Russell, Ottoline's long-time lover, rooms in the old Bailiff's House. He, in turn, had no objection to lending the rooms to the conscientious objectors to whom Philip was able to offer farm work, an offer which saved them from harassment, since it was deemed by the government as being of national importance.

Almost every great literary figure of the age—W. B. Yeats, Lytton Strachey, Virginia Woolf, T. S. Eliot, Aldous Huxley, Siegfried Sassoon—visited Garsington, but it was perhaps D. H. Lawrence who summed up best what it meant to many of them, a symbol of all that the war was changing, 'of old things passing away... this house of the Ottoliones—it is England'.

Nuffield Place

Of all the great benefactors who have endowed Oxford with money—I might mention Dr Radcliffe, I might mention Cardinal Wolsey—one stands alone for the sheer scale of his generosity—Lord Nuffield. His home at Nuffield Place, off the Oxford-Henley road and reached by following a sign to the nearby young offenders' institution, gives a unique insight into the unassuming way of life of this extraordinary man and his wife. It also preserves a slice of the 1930s. William Morris, later to become Lord Nuffield, was born in Worcester in 1877 but moved to Oxford when he was three. He started in business aged 16 with £4 capital, making and repairing bicycles in James Street, Oxford. He then went on to found a car manufacturing empire.

Nuffield Place was originally built in 1914 and has a Lutyens look to it, with slightly continental-style shutters and an overhanging roof. This is not surprising, since its architect, Oswald Partridge Milne, was a pupil of Lutyens. The 1930s flavour comes from the fact that Lord Nuffield, then living in the nearby converted golf clubhouse, bought it in 1933 and set about making it his own.Some details, that he would probably never have imagined would interest visitors 70 years on, are fascinating: the cocktail cabinet, the tiles in the bathroom. Even the reproduction antique furniture made by Cecil A. Halliday of Oxford, manages to shout 1930s.

Lord Nuffield made almost a career of giving. He said once: 'The worry which comes from giving is very great.' In all, he gave away about £30 million in his lifetime, and the place where he thought about the work, giving very precise instructions as to how the money should be spent, was at this house, often while gardening.

There is the story of how a motorist stopped to chat one day while Lord Nuffield was clipping the hedge. The motorist asked him what sort of a chap Lord Nuffield was. 'Oh, he is not so bad when you get to know him,' he replied. 'Was he paid well?' 'It's enough, and there is some left over for others.' The stranger then proceeded to tip him half a crown! I am indebted to the excellent guidebook of the house for that tale, itself a piece of history since it was produced and donated by the Nuffield Press, the only remaining commercial organisation to carry his name.

Lord Nuffield died in 1963, but Nuffield Place is open to the public on certain Sundays through the year.

Mapledurham House

Could Mapledurham House, on the banks of the Thames, have been the inspiration for Toad Hall in Kenneth Grahame's *The Wind in the Willows*? Certainly the house in E. H. Shepard's illustrations resembles it and we know that Shepard rowed up and down the Thames near Reading, on the boundary between Oxfordshire and Berkshire, seeking inspiration. But any resemblance might merely show that the house inspired Shepard's illustrations, and not necessarily Grahame's text.

In any case, the Elizabethan house, built in 1588 by Sir Michael Blount, has other literary associations. South Oxfordshire has always been comparatively rich in followers of the old religion (recusants), and the persecuted minority helped each other wherever possible. The Blounts were a recusant family. They added the chapel to Mapledurham at about the time of the Catholic Relief Act of 1791. The family is also connected by marriage to that other great south Oxfordshire recusant family, the Stonors, of nearby Stonor Park, where St Edmund Campion's *Decem Rationes* was secretly printed in 1581, the year of his execution.

In the early 18th century, the poet Alexander Pope was also a frequent visitor to Mapledurham. The sisters Teresa and Martha Blount became his particular friends, with Martha becoming his heiress. Pope's father, a successful London draper, was a Catholic. The precocious Alexander was therefore ineligible to go to university. Apart from some help from priests, he was largely self-taught in both Latin and Greek. But Pope's translation of Homer's *Iliad* made him rich. In the house at Mapledurham may be seen classical landscape paintings that belonged to him, and in the garden stand two urns designed by William Kent that came originally from Pope's villa at Twickenham.

Much of Pope's work on the *Iliad* was also carried out at Stanton Harcourt, in a tower overlooking the church. It was while Pope was working there that he heard the sad tale of lovers from the village who were struck dead by lightning while lying in each other's arms, a fact recorded by a plaque on the church wall.

Ditchley Park

Ditchley Park, near Charlbury, was built in 1722 to designs by James Gibbs—architect of the Radcliffe Camera. But by 1933, when the 17th Viscount Dillon died, it had only one decrepit bathroom—apart, that is, from the bath in front of the fireplace in the saloon where Lord Dillon used to wash!

Ditchley was therefore in sore need of money to bring it back to glory. And Ronald and Nancy Tree were exactly the kind of American rich that Ditchley needed: charming, talented, leisured, gilded, they bought the superb mansion and lavished their cash and their design on the house. Their spending was to rival the 18th century for its extravagance combined with 'good taste'.

Anglo-American Ronald Tree was the son of an English property developer. His mother was the daughter of Marshall Field, the founder of the Chicago department store of the same name. Ronald Tree edited the *Forum Magazine* in New York 1922-6. Then he became an investor until the Wall Street Crash of 1929. An aesthete to the core, he was bi-sexual. In England he found his true vocation. He became Conservative MP for Harborough in 1933 and Churchill gave him a job in the Ministry of Information.

His wife Nancy, from Virginia, was a niece of yet another Anglo-American, Nancy Astor, who became Britain's first woman MP. Otherwise known as Nancy Lancaster, Mrs Tree was a doyenne of interior design and the owner of the company destined to develop into Colefax and Fowler.

Both husband and wife were urbane and witty, and Ditchley soon became a magnate for the internationally rich and famous, including Cecil Beaton, assorted lords and ladies and, most famously, Winston Churchill. The great days of Ditchley in modern times were during the 1930s when not only its rooms, designed by William Kent, were restored in bright colours (leading the way in interior design), but its gardens and grounds were restored and, probably, the last parterre in Britain was built there by Sir Geoffrey Jellicoe.

Their neighbours at Blenheim had of course also relied on American money, from Consuelo Vanderbilt, for restoration. And they were frequent visitors to Ditchley: Churchill, his wife Clementine and their daughter Mary appear no fewer than 13 times in the visitors' book for the period between 9 November 1940 and 28 September 1942. The reason for their numerous visits was that Churchill had been advised that his country retreat of Chequers would be too vulnerable to Nazi bombs on clear nights for his safety. He therefore wrote to Mr Tree: 'Would it be possible for you to offer me accommodation at Ditchley for certain weekends when the moon is high?'

After the war, Ronald Tree—always known as Ronnie—divorced Nancy and took himself and his new wife, American Marietta Peabody FitzGerald, whom he had met at the Ministry of Information, off to Barbados where he founded the Breakers Hotel, still a haunt of the super-rich. There he established the habit of the rich to winter in the Caribbean, a habit which had been pioneered by Anthony Eden and, of course, Ian Fleming.

Blenheim Palace

Every month the Duke of Marlborough sends off his Quit Rent standard to the Queen at Windsor in payment for the Royal Manor of Woodstock, granted to his forbear in 1705 by Queen Anne, when the park was given—with Parliament's approval—to John Churchill, the great duke.

Building of the palace began in the summer of 1705 with the architect John Vanbrugh laying the first stone, followed by seven gentlemen each hitting it with a hammer and throwing down a guinea. An observer noted: 'There were several sorts of musick with the three morris dances: one of young fellows, one of maidens, and one of old beldames. There were about 100 buckets, bowls and pans, filled with wine, punch, cakes and ale. From my lord's house all went to the Town Hall where plenty of sack, claret, cakes etc. were prepared for the gentry and better sort; under the Cross eight barrels of ale, with abundance of cakes, were placed for the common people.'

If only things had continued in so happy a vein. Vanbrugh, who from the start had considered Blenheim 'much more as an intended monument of the Queen's glory than a private habitation for the Duke of Marlborough', was six years later putting about the quip to hundreds of unpaid workers that the palace was a 'monument of ingratitude'. The root of the trouble was that it was not clear who had engaged Vanbrugh, the Duke or the Queen. When the Queen and the Duchess were the closest of friends this had not mattered, but when the Duchess was ousted from favour, matters took a turn for the worse. Of course, the absence of any contract led to trouble and payments from the government to meet the bills dried up.

In 1712, the Queen ordered work to stop and the half-built palace stood forlorn and deserted. At court, the duke was accused of embezzlement and dismissed from all his posts. Not until the accession of George I in 1714 did work recommence. Such was the row with Vanbrugh that the palace was never finished; the Stable Court remains incomplete, so when Vanbrugh wanted to visit the palace in 1725 he was not allowed into the park.

The same fate, incidentally, befell another hero. Lord Nelson, together with Emma Hamilton and Sir William Hamilton, were not admitted by the 4th Duke in 1802. Nelson's successors, incidentally, were granted a pension of £5,000 forever, though this was abruptly halted in 1946, showing that what the state has granted it can also take back.

Capability Brown at Blenheim and Nuneham Courtenay

Lord Randolph Churchill, father of Sir Winston, sat well back in the cushions of his comfortable coach and remarked complacently: 'Finest view in England.' He and his young American wife, Jennie Jerome, had just passed through the main Blenheim gate from Woodstock; she had gasped at the splendour of the view of the Baroque palace reflected in the lake.

That view was artificially created by architect Sir John Vanbrugh, who designed the palace, and Lancelot Brown (universally known as Capability Brown), who designed the landscape. Noblemen of the 18th century spent much of their time (and money) in reorganising the relationship between man and nature. Blenheim, with its continental, heavily Palladian palace set in its very English park, is a prime example of the art of playing God.

Another may be found at Nuneham Courtenay. An earl moved here simply because he liked the view—but thought he could improve it. Earl Harcourt, a courtier so correct in matters of etiquette that he was employed to teach Royal manners to Georges II and III, moved to Nuneham Courtenay (previously spelled Newnham Courtenay) in 1760 from his ancient family home at Stanton Harcourt. When the earl arrived in Italy on the Grand Tour he realised that back in Oxfordshire he owned the perfect place by the Thames for a Palladian villa. He read the words of Palladio himself describing such a place as: 'being seated on a hillock of most easy ascent, at the foot of which runs a navigable river and on the other side surrounded by several hills that seem to form an amphitheatre'. The beautiful stretch of river forms one of Britain's most accessible of 18th-century landscapes, having long been a destination for people taking boat trips out from Oxford. Indeed Charles Dodgson (Lewis Carroll) and his boatload of girls, including Alice Liddell, had rowed out to Nuneham a weekend or two before the famous expedition to Godstow when Alice first heard of her adventures in Wonderland.

The only trouble with the earl's perfect place was that it already contained an ancient village in the way of the view. No problem. He moved it, transplanting the villagers (except one old lady who begged to stay in her cottage) to its present position on the Henley-Oxford road. Sadly, the connoisseur earl died by falling down a well at Nuneham while trying to rescue a dog.

His son was of a different stamp. He was a Republican follower of Jean-Jacques Rousseau, who came to stay at Nuneham, and concurred with Rousseau's ideas about the Noble Savage. He stayed out in the woods, denounced hereditary aristocracy, gave away the royal portraits in the house, and had the coronets taken off his coach.

However, his wife rebelled and he softened his ideas. Soon he was employing Capability Brown to 'naturalise' his park. He would even have built a fake castle had not the opportunity to acquire the Gothic Carfax Conduit, that had for centuries stood in the middle of Oxford, not arisen. In 1787 he erected it in the landscape instead of a folly.

Cotswold Wildlife Park

To a child of three, I suppose, there is nothing so very extraordinary about a rhinoceros strolling about in Oxfordshire; it is just another fact to take in: interesting, but perhaps marginally less so than a ride on a miniature train, or the prospect of an ice cream.

I thought about this when introducing my granddaughter to the rhinos at the Cotswold Wild Life Park, near Burford—which I think is really just as interesting for grown-ups as it is for children. But what is extraordinary, at any rate to me, is

that children might have seen exotic animals from faraway places walking about in Oxfordshire, in Woodstock to be precise, almost 900 years ago.

According to historian William of Malmesbury (*c.*1080-*c.*1143), writing in his *Chronicles*, King Henry I 'was extremely fond of the wonders of distant countries, begging with great delight from foreign kings, lions, leopards, lynxes, or camels, animals which England does not produce. He had placed there also a creature called a porcupine, sent to him by William of Montpelier.

I gather this information from a lovely book called *Woodstock and the Royal Park: Nine hundred years of history* (Chris Andrews Publications Ltd). Henry I's grandson, Henry II, Count of Anjou and son of the Empress Matilda, ascended the English throne in 1154 under the terms of the Treaty of Wallingford, signed the previous year, which made him the heir of King Stephen—and brought to an end the civil war between Stephen and Matilda. He immediately set about building a stone palace at Woodstock to replace the wooden one of his grandfather. It stood across the lake—created in the 18th century by damming the river Glyme—from the present Blenheim Palace in a place now marked by a stone block that was put there in 1961. Whether or not he kept the menagerie is not certain, though his son Richard I is recorded as owning a crocodile; but what is known is that foreign animals were living in the park in early medieval times until they were transferred to the Tower of London in 1252.

A menagerie then remained at the Tower until 1835 when the animals were moved to Regent's Park to form the basis of London Zoo. The sight of the animals on the road to London must have been a source of wonder to villheins peering out of hovels; and indeed their presence at the Tower must have added a sort of surreal quality to the last days of those imprisoned there and awaiting execution.

Little wonder, though, that the Norman kings were able to gather up wild beasts from all over the known world. After all, Henry II and Eleanor of Aquitaine (both buried in Normandy) between them ruled lands which stretched from Hadrian's Wall in the north to the Pyrenees in the south. Their Norman relatives were kings of Sicily from where they made sorties across the Mediterranean to Tunisia—where lions roamed until the 19th century.

As for the Cotswold Wildlife Park, it was opened it to the public in 1970 by owner John Heyworth, exhibiting 230 creatures from 40 different species. To me Bradwell Grove, the Georgian Gothic revival house at the centre of the park, dating from 1804 and designed by William Atkinson, forms a link to the earlier menagerie at Woodstock Palace—which I fondly believe may have been at least partly built in the Gothic style.

Rousham and Enstone Water Features

How to find yourself a *bona fide* hermit to roam your garden was a problem besetting many a well cultivated person with an eye for the Romantic during the 18th century. Many such people, having employed landscape architects to construct water grottoes or caves, then felt a compelling urge to find a hermit to live in them. Some even took to advertising in newspapers—though such action apparently gave rise to lively dinner party debate about whether a proper hermit would be likely to take a daily newspaper.

Water grottoes first made their appearance at water sources in Britain in the early 17th century but became progressively more fashionable over the next 150 years or so, as William Kent's work at Rousham, for instance, illustrates. The owner of Rousham House, Charles Cottrell Dormer, tells me—disappointingly enough—that there never was a hermit employed there as far as he knows.

Nevertheless, perhaps the most extraordinary water gardens, complete with perhaps the most extraordinary hermit ever, existed not far away in Enstone. Thomas Bushell, one-time secretary to the Lord Chancellor, Francis Bacon, created the Enstone Marvels there. These were water gardens, near where the Harrow pub stands today, which were so marvellous that King Charles I and Queen Henrietta Maria visited them on 23 August 1636.

Dr Robert Plot (1640-96), first Professor of Chemistry at the University of Oxford, and the first keeper of the Ashmolean Museum, described the event in his 1677 *Natural*

History of Oxfordshire: 'a Hermite [who rose] out of the ground, and entertain'd them with a Speech; returning again in the close down to his peaceful Urn. Then was the Rock presented in a Song answer'd by an Echo and after that a banquet presented also in a Sonnet. 'The rock in question was 'so wonderfully contrived by Nature herself, that [Bushell] thought it worthy all imaginable Advancement by Art'. Indeed the Queen graciously allowed the rock to be named after her. She did this after watching two fountains of rose-coloured water rise into the air, each suspending a golden ball. The King helped himself to one of the balls and found inside it a portrait of the Queen carved in ivory.

Dr Plot laments that during the Civil War ('the late unhappy wars') the garden 'with all the ingenious contrivances about it' fell into decay. Mr Bushell, however, was apparently an eccentric of the first water. Long before he contrived his Enstone Marvels he went about in a coat entirely covered in buttons, like a sort of pearly king; and when Francis Bacon fell from favour Mr Bushell took himself off to the Calf of Man, the highest point of the Isle of Man, and became a hermit in earnest, living on herbs.

He wrote: 'The sudden fall and death of my late Lord Chancelour Bacon, in King James's reign, were the motives which persuaded my pensive retirements to a three years' unsociable solitude in ye desolated isle called the Calf of Man, where in obedience to my dead lord's philosophical advice, I resolved to make a perfect experiment upon myself, for the obtaining of a long and healthy life.'

Better times did befall him. He was an expert in mining and in minerals and Charles I put him in charge of the Royal Mines of Wales, in which capacity he minted money and sent it to the King in Oxford.

Sulgrave Manor

Ask any of the very knowledgeable guides at Sulgrave Manor who owns the place, and they will answer: 'You do.' Then they will explain that you share it with not only every other Briton alive today but also with every American. For the Manor is in a way a celebration of Britain's 'special relationship' with USA— as the Union Flag and the Stars and Stripes flying alongside each other over the lawn bear witness.

It is a lovely place all right, in an area sometimes called Banburyshire: in Northamptonshire, in fact, but still so close to Oxfordshire as to have an OX postcode; a region so rural that until the late 1950s it had no electricity. When I last visited, we found members of a local club playing croquet in front of the house, and we felt we had reached the very heart of England and Englishness. It was intriguing, therefore, to see the Stars and Stripes repeated in the coat of arms over the front door on the Tudor porch, which was built in 1539.

The central part of the house dates from the 16th century and is furnished entirely with things dating from that period; there is even a painting of President Washington, one of a series, similar to the portrait of him that adorns every dollar bill. And outside in the Colonial Garden there are tobacco plants to remind you that George Washington made his fortune from that particular weed, using—it cannot be denied—slave labour.

In truth, the connection to the first US president George Washington (1732-99) is at best described as remote but is still interesting. He was the great-grandson of John Washington (1632-77) who emigrated to Virginia in 1656. And this John, who came from a cadet branch of the family, was himself the great-great-grandson of the builder of Sulgrave Manor, Lawrence Washington (1500-83). Remote indeed: how many of us can even give the surnames of our 16 great-great-grandparents? All the same, there the connection is, however slight, and it would be churlish to carp.

Lawrence Washington was a successful wool merchant who had himself emigrated from County Durham, where the senior branch of the family owned Washington Old Hall. He was a cousin of the Spencers, ancestors of Princess Diana and owners of the two nearby great houses of Althorp and Wormleighton; and he bought Sulgrave, formerly the property of Northampton Priory, for £321.14s.10d. from Henry VIII after the dissolution of the monasteries. He was keen to hang on to it, too, and in this context one story—or perhaps legend—that refuses to go away is the one about how, during the reign of Mary I, the Washington family gave shelter to the Queen's sister Princess Elizabeth who, so the story goes, tried to escape from Woodstock where she was held captive.

Strange to think, though, that during the time that Lawrence Washington lived in the house the New World had only recently been discovered. To him, his wife Anne Pargiter from nearby Greatworth and their 11 children it must have seemed as exotic as Outer Space now seems to us; unknown but full of opportunities which, at that time, were being mainly exploited by Spaniards and Portuguese. Names such as Florida (land of flowers) and Brazil (named after a kind of wood) might have been familiar to them, but they could not possibly have imagined that one day both a capital city and a state would bear their family name.

Eventually, the manor that once belonged to the ancestors of George Washington was sold to a charity, established for the purpose in 1914, on behalf of all of us. The purchase commemorated Washington's rural English roots and at the same time marked 100 years of peace between the two nations—since the Treaty of Ghent, signed in 1814, which ended the war of 1812.

Faringdon Folly

Dyeing the birds in the garden vivid colours, reminiscent of parrots in the Amazon rainforest, is what springs to mind when thinking about Faringdon House. The strange operation seems to sum up the eccentric life of Lord Berners, owner of the house in the 1930s and builder of its extraordinary folly. Those years just before the Second World War, like those before the First, seem to have produced, for a rich few, a certain decadence as Europe hurtled towards Armageddon. In 1935, Lord Berners, famous for letting Penelope Betjeman's horse join the tea party in the drawing room, set about emulating 18th-century aristocrats by building a folly in the grounds.

Follies, usually specially built ruins, were popular with early landscapers for adding a twist of romantic decay to the well-ordered views they constructed. There are about 1,200 in the country. Lord Berners' own creation seems to have come about because it was built on Folly Hill, and obviously needed a folly. Even he, however, did not employ a hermit to occupy his expensive 140 ft whim of stone, as had some nobleman 150 years earlier.

He told his architect friend, Lord Gerald Wellesley: 'The great point of this tower is that it will be entirely useless.' He took off on holiday hoping to see a gothic extravaganza when he returned. In fact, the construction, which met with much opposition from what passed for planners in those pre-war days, was too plain for his liking and so he set about adding false battlements and an octagonal room on top. Patriotism crept in here too. On Guy Fawkes night 70 years ago he let off not only fireworks, but also dozens of doves painted red, white and blue.

Now the last large-scale folly in the UK, it is open to the public on the first Sunday of the month from Easter to October. It offers views north across the Thames Valley and southwards to the Berkshire Downs. Not having climbed the folly myself, I am not sure whether Lord Berners' sign at the top is still extant. It read: 'Members of the public committing suicide from this tower do so at their own risk.'

Kelmscott Manor

Perhaps no part of Oxfordshire has undergone less change than its western extremity, particularly that lonely reach of flat meadow, with the low hills of the Cotswolds around it, with which William Morris fell in love in 1871. But he would be astonished to see it now, all the same. What, for instance, would he think of the quantities of cars which these days poke their way down narrow roads to the riverbank at Kelmscott, the house into which he moved that year?

Morris believed that the downtrodden poor, at that time suffering from the effects of the Industrial Revolution, which had driven millions out of the country and into the polluted towns, could be improved by surrounding them with beautiful and practical products of good workmanship. Yet, of course, he would have hated cars, objects which he would surely have seen as destroyers of that natural world he loved.

The green message contained in his book *News from Nowhere* somehow strikes a doleful chord for any modern motorist arriving at Kelmscott with the belief that small is beautiful. The social reformer, poet and design guru described a journey up the Thames from Oxford to Kelmscott: 'The smallness of the scale is everything, the short reaches and the speedy change of the banks give one a feeling of going somewhere, of coming to something strange, a feeling of adventure which I have not felt in bigger waters.'

Obviously no motorist could experience this feeling and anyone arriving by boat will be greeted by the sight of dozens of unnatural-looking cars!

Morris rented the Manor there that first year of 1871, together with fellow member of the Pre-Raphaelite Brotherhood, painter Dante Gabriel Rossetti. Later he bought the Elizabethan house, which he described as a 'heaven on earth', and kept it as his country home until his death in 1896. The 600 or so designs for wallpapers, fabrics and tapestries which he created are still among the nation's top sellers—and the harmony in the relationship between the man-made house and its natural surroundings influenced them.

For instance, he wrote of the tiled roof on the house: 'It gives me the same sort of pleasure in their orderly beauty as a fish's scales or a bird's feathers.' The guiding principle in the design of both house and garden was that nothing should be allowed to intrude that was not both beautiful and useful.

Nevertheless, the early years of Morris's life there were lived in a stormy state of continuously heightened emotion as part of a *ménage à trois* consisting of himself, his wife Jane and Rossetti, who painted the beautiful Jane so often that her whimsical look has become known as the 'Rossetti look'. Jane Burdon was the daughter of an Oxford ostler. Her rags-to-riches story began when Rossetti spotted her in the audience at the theatre—a converted gymnasium in Oriel Street—and persuaded her to model for him. Then she met and married Morris.

Poor Rossetti became increasingly insane, and finally departed, leaving William and Jane Morris sad, disillusioned, but still convinced of the truth of their ideas.

Wychwood Forest

The last silent and hauntingly beautiful remnant of the old Royal Forest of Wychwood, part of the Cornbury estate, still the county's largest piece of broad-leaf forest, opens to the public on Palm Sunday, thereby fulfilling a long-standing tradition.

Since time immemorial, inhabitants of such villages as Leafield, Finstock, Milton, Shipton and Ascott-under-Wychwood, all bordering the forest, have made their way to its heart on Palm Sunday to visit a well near the lakes called Wort's Well. Right off the beaten track, it may be approached from Hatchings Lane, Leafield, and then by walking for more than a mile through forest that for centuries supplied oak to build ships for the Royal Navy. Usually on Palm Sunday the forest is carpeted with bluebells. The tradition is that visitors to the well take with them bottles. They gather wild liquorice growing around the well and mix it with the well-water to produce a cure-all medicine. Local historian John Kibble wrote in 1928 that prayers were said around the well.

Charles I first gave Cornbury to Lord Danby, the man who founded the Oxford Botanic Garden. It passed to Lord Clarendon, whose *History of the Revolution* about the English Civil War raised money enough to finance the Clarendon Building in Oxford, and whose grandson, Viscount Cornbury, scandalised America as Governor of New York and New Jersey by cross-dressing. In the 17th century Lord Clarendon planted more than 2,000 trees at Cornbury.

But much of that work was undone during the Industrial Revolution when in 1856-8 1,970 acres of forest were enclosed and grubbed up. Subsequent owners of the estate have included the du Cros family, the beer barons Watney, and the City investment family Cayzer, which hit the headlines recently with a family tussle over the £629 m Cayzer Trust. The beer connection is interesting since the word 'wort' means either the unfermented malt in beer, or any herb or vegetable. Might not the name 'wort', therefore, when applied to the well, not refer to the liquorice as the base ingredient of the medicine?

The 6,500 acre forest, with its lakes and tracks that resemble medieval roads, alive—as in hunting days of yore—with deer, can be easily missed altogether by anyone driving near Charlbury. Get out of the car, though, and walk, and you quickly see why west Oxfordshire has the status of the least populated district in the south-east, though entry to this primeval world is restricted to a well-marked right of way on all days but one each year, thus preserving the meadow saffron, herb paris, purple orchid and adder's tongue for which it is known.

After your walk, a pint of beer in the Navy Oak at Leafield slips down easily enough; and then you can take in the church at Finstock, where T. S. Eliot was baptised.

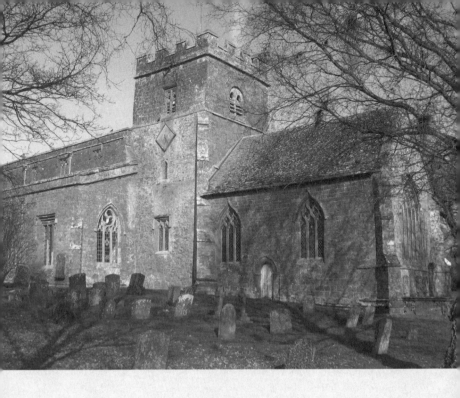

9. Churches and Religion
Centuries of Faith

One of the earliest seeds of Christianity in England, from which the faith was destined to spread throughout the realm, was planted in what is now Oxfordshire soil. For, according to the Venerable Bede, the missionary Saint Birinus baptised King Cynegils of Wessex at Dorchester in 635. The former Roman stronghold then became one of the earliest Christian sites in Britain, with St Birinus establishing his cathedral there. He became the first Bishop of Dorchester, using the place as a central base from which to spread the word.

In undertaking missionary work in England, the Italian priest Birinus was following in the wake of St Augustine, first Archbishop of Canterbury, who a generation earlier had been sent by Pope Gregory the Great to start converting England. Like so many tender plants, the original bishopric had to fight to survive, flickering in and out of existence for a couple of centuries while the Danes rampaged about. But it was formally re-founded in 880 and then continued as the centre of a diocese stretching from the Thames to the Humber until the first Norman bishop, Remigius, relocated to Lincoln in 1072. Oxfordshire then remained without a cathedral for 530 years, until Henry VIII, by then head of the Church of England, established his new bishopric of Oxford in 1542.

It is the sheer antiquity of Christianity that makes church-crawling so particularly rewarding in Oxfordshire. For instance, the lovely abbey at Dorchester that we see today was founded in 1140, and though not a trace of the original cathedral survives, it is nevertheless somehow apt that the great Jesse window, depicting the ancestry of Jesus, should be here of all places; for the way the churches multiplied in Oxfordshire is very like a family tree, with mother churches giving birth to daughter churches, and a complicated network of relationships developing.

Between the 10th and 12th centuries a change occurred: our familiar parish churches began to appear. No one knows how most churches came into being, or exactly who paid for them, but by the end of the 12th century the parochial system was firmly in place. It depended on a curious mixture of ecclesiastical and lay power. All churches were controlled by the bishop, but the *advowson*—the right to appoint a rector to the living—belonged to the landowner, which by medieval times might as easily have been a monastery, or an Oxford college, as a squire living in the nearby manor. The living—which was supposed to provide for the upkeep of a priest—came from tithes: namely the compulsory payment of a tenth part of all parishioners' produce. It was paid to the rector, even though he usually appointed a vicar (from the Latin *vicarius*, meaning substitute) to do all the actual work. Tithe barns still exist, for instance at Great Coxwell and at Enstone.

There was a building boom in post-Conquest Oxfordshire, and even now many Oxfordshire churches are basically Norman, though of course nearly always—Iffley being the notable exception—overlaid for better or worse by later alterations caused by the vicissitudes of history. Wandering around churches surely provides the best possible insight into the mindset—not to mention the economic well-being or otherwise—of Oxfordshire people through the ages.

For instance, the 17th-century Puritans were deeply suspicious of the new Baroque style of the University Church in Oxford, thinking it to be far too Roman Catholic-looking. Yet when the Oxford Movement did indeed lead the Church of England closer to Rome in the 19th century, it was the Gothic style that was once again favoured by such architects as Scott, Pugin, Butterfield and Street, all of whom were active in the county.

St Cross Church

Oxford's long history of secularisation continues. Now St Cross of Holywell, one of the city's oldest churches, has become an archive for storing historical documents appertaining to Balliol College.

The church, in existence since at least 1100, was originally a chapel connected to the church of St Peter-in-the-East. In 1266, Merton College acquired the lordship of the manor of Holywell, together with both churches. Then, almost 700 years elapsed before Balliol became Merton's tenant of the manor house adjoining the churchyard in 1930, which it still is.

But what, I wonder; would some of the illustrious people buried in that churchyard think of this occurrence? The composer of Anglican Church music Sir John Stainer (1840-1901), for instance, is commemorated in a splendid stained glass window; an Oxford professor of music and a churchwarden here, he did much to restore St Cross in the late 19th century.

Then there is Kenneth Grahame (1859-1932), author of *The Wind in the Willows*, who had such a long but largely unhappy relationship with Oxford. The epitaph on his grave at St Cross, written by his cousin Anthony Hope, reads: 'To the beautiful memory of Kenneth Grahame, husband of Elspeth and father of Alastair, who passed the River on the 6 July 1932, leaving childhood and literature through him the more blest for all time.'

Also buried at St Cross are such Oxford luminaries as: Regius Professor of Medicine Sir Henry Acland (1815-1900); poet and novelist Charles Williams (1886-1945); and Williams' fellow member of the Inklings—the group of friends who included C. S. Lewis and J. R. R. Tolkien who met weekly in the Eagle and Child pub, in St Giles—H. V. D. Dyson (1896-1975), a Fellow of Merton.

The close association of Merton and Balliol exemplified here dates back to the University's very earliest days. Balliol was founded in the 13th century by John de Balliol who, after insulting the Bishop of Durham (the story goes), was whipped at the door of Durham Cathedral and told to perform an act of charity—which he did by founding Balliol. After his death, his widow Dervorguilla became patroness of the college (formal statutes date from 1282) but only allowed undergraduates to study there. Anyone wanting to continue studying had to make other arrangements—which usually involved moving to Merton College.

Merton originally leased Holywell manor house, which was largely rebuilt in 1516, to rectors of St Peter-in-the-East. Then 1531 it was let to the prominent and much-persecuted Roman Catholic family of Napper, many of whom were priests, who remained there until the second half of the 17th century. By the 19th century, it appears on maps as a Penitentiary for Women, meaning that it was a home for unmarried mothers who, as it happens, had the job of laundering college linen.

Under Balliol's £3 million scheme to turn the church into a Historic Collections Centre, it remains a consecrated building. Certainly Balliol have a lot to preserve after almost 800 years. For example, many scholars believe that the manuscripts bequeathed to it by William Gray, Bishop of Ely, in about 1450, constitute the largest single medieval collection to survive in England. And I hope St Cross's own treasures, including a 1569 chalice and an alms dish of 1683, will be kept on display.

St Frideswide

The church of St Frideswide in Botley Road, consecrated in 1872, was designed by Samuel Sanders Teulon and described by Pevsner as 'typical Teulon in its ruthlessness'. Vicars of this church have certainly included a few robust characters. The first vicar to take the job was Oxford boxing blue G. L. Kemp, who floored an intruder in the belfry with a blow to the chin.

The vicar from 1933 to 1976 was the Reverend Arnold Mallinson, a noted antiquarian and collector of coins. He somehow embodied a peculiarly (and slightly mad) Oxford spirit, borne of a mixture of medieval Catholic whimsicality and Protestant Victorian values—the 'Anglo-Saxon Attitudes' at which Lewis Carroll used to poke fun.

And indeed St Frideswide's has a strong Alice connection as it contains a wood carving by Alice known as the Alice Door. Carved originally for the mission church of St Frideswide in Poplar, East London, built in 1890 but closed in 1953 following wartime damage, it depicts Oxford's patron saint sailing down the Thames on her way to found the Priory of St Frideswide on the site of what is now Christ Church.

The Reverend Mallinson with the Alice Door

The door was presented as a gift to St Frideswide's, Osney, in 1954. Framed in a Gothic arch, the carving has a Pre-Raphaelite feeling; perhaps unsurprising since Alice's tutor was none other than Ruskin himself, who admired the style. The carving somehow mirrors the ten-year-old Alice's own river journey from Christ Church to Godstow on the 'Golden Afternoon' of 4 July 1862 when Lewis Carroll first told her the stories of her *Adventures in Wonderland*. The Alice Door in St Frideswide's manages to lead the imagination straight back to 19th-century Oxford and back further to the Middle and Dark Ages, missing out altogether the Classical renaissance.

In 1950 the Reverend Arnold Mallinson also became Perpetual Curate of St Margaret's, Binsey. At Binsey, he was bothered by a real case of bats in the belfry, and advertised for a stuffed owl with which to frighten his antagonists. He was immediately inundated with dozens of the birds, some large, some small; some in glass cases, some not. One wonders whether his proposed cure for the problem would be lawful these days, now that no one may disturb the protected creatures in any way?

Black Bourton

All acts of official vandalism—I might mention the destruction of railways by Beeching, or the neglect of the canals in the early 20th century—pale into insignificance when compared to the wanton destruction perpetrated by that old ogre Henry VIII during the Reformation.

It is always comforting therefore when medieval works of art, inefficiently desecrated by the King's 16th century henchmen, re-emerge like so many ghosts from another world. This happy event occurred at the church in Black Bourton in west Oxfordshire (sadly, no longer served by the Oxford-Fairford railway line) where in 1931 some exquisite murals were discovered beneath the whitewash. It is fitting somehow that these figures should step forth in Black Bourton. The village owes its sombre name to the fact that the surrounding land once belonged to Osney Abbey (itself dissolved in the Reformation, of course) and the monks who farmed it used to wear black habits.

The frescoes date from 1275 and are resplendent in golden ochre and rich red. Among the best preserved are a curious Tree of Jesse, similar to the Jesse window at Dorchester; a Saint Christopher; the Coronation of the Virgin; and the Baptism of Our Lord, with the water of the Jordan depicted by an almost modern-looking curve around Jesus' waist. The nave at Black Bourton has been increased in height since the frescoes were painted, so a blank space appears between them and the roof.

Exactly the same has happened at Bloxham church, where more figures from a spiritual age survive into our own secular times. The Last Judgement depicted here must have kept the parishioners in fear and trembling about what awaited them if they misbehaved in this life. The jaws of Hell open up in a sort of grimace to receive the souls of the wicked dead who rise from their graves on the north side. As if in apology for the desecrations of the past, Bloxham church also contains the extraordinary pre-Raphaelite east window designed by William Morris and his friend Edward Burne-Jones. It provides a vivid contrast between the Victorian idea of spirituality and the medieval one.

Miraculously, despite the ravages of the Reformation and of Oliver Cromwell a century later, Oxfordshire still has some great frescoes left behind. There is a frightening Last Judgement in Combe church, where red devils goad sexy-looking women into the fires of Hell. A whole gallery of frescoes re-emerged from beneath peeling plaster in 1858 at Chalgrove church. The paintings, dating from 1350, provide anyone who cares to look with a fairly good idea of how a church would have looked before the Reformation, although sadly they have faded over the last century and a large memorial plaque obliterates two scenes.

Hints of everyday life in the 14th century crop up in unexpected places too. In North Stoke church, for instance, a scene of the Stoning of Saint Stephen depicts a basket, containing the stones, that is probably exactly like the one the artist's wife would have used for the shopping. Thankfully, King Henry's destruction was incomplete. He himself could have learned from the murals at tiny Widford church where three kings living meet three kings dead who say: 'As you are now, so once was I. As I am now, so will you be.'

South Leigh

Enter the church of St James the Great in South Leigh and you suddenly find yourself in a place reminiscent of pre-Reformation England. For the walls are covered with paintings that carry you back to the Middle Ages as if travelling on the back of the archangel St Michael—who is depicted here with his arms and legs covered in a feather outfit to match his wings.

I was astonished by the bright medieval art gallery, but it soon became apparent why the place is not better known. A question hangs in the air: when does what one expert calls 'restoration' cross a line and become what another calls 'repainting'? I have pondered this at Roman villas in North Africa, where rebuilding appears to be under way.

My guidebook to Oxfordshire, edited by Arthur Mee and published in 1942, is unequivocal. It says of the South Leigh paintings: 'The greatest treasure of the church is in its 14th and 15th century wall-paintings, happily rescued from coats of whitewash. In spite of long oblivion it was possible to restore them line by line, and the quality of the drawing and their wonderful escape make them famous in the story of such recoveries'.

But after the war we all seem to have become more sceptical. Pevsner, in his Oxfordshire volume of *Buildings of England*, published in 1974, is almost dismissive. He writes of the paintings: 'C15, mostly heavily restored in 1872 by Burlison and Grylls.' And the very good guide booklet for sale in the church, by Valerie Hirst, explains: 'They have been restored many times, most recently in 1992. They are a dramatic and unique representation of an early church's teaching to village people who were unable to read and write.' And that, surely, is the point.

However 'heavily restored' the paintings in their present form might be, they provide an extraordinary insight into the medieval mindset—which must have been constantly influenced by church interiors like this. That St Michael, for example, depicts him weighing souls. The Virgin Mary intercedes on one side by dropping rosary beads into the scales, and devils try to haul them down on the other—a frightening story to an illiterate England. Roger Rosewell, in his book *Medieval Wall Paintings*, says: 'An original painting of his scene may be seen below a later and larger Victorian over-painting made in 1872. An even more frightening picture shows the seven deadly sins spewing from the jaws of hell.'

South Leigh church was in the parish of Stanton Harcourt until 1869, and it was the first vicar of the separate parish, Gerard Moultrie, who discovered these murals beneath the whitewash.

Back at Stanton Harcourt, though, is an extraordinary and direct connection to the battle which put the Tudors on the throne, and without which the Reformation may never have happened. For Robert Harcourt was the standard bearer of Henry Tudor,

Earl of Richmond (later Henry VII, father of Henry VIII) who defeated Richard III at the battle of Bosworth Field in 1485. And over his tomb in Stanton Harcourt hangs a sad-looking piece of rag, which is all that remains of the standard that was the rallying point at the battle. According to Arthur Mee, the standard was in 1942 accompanied by a plumed helmet, but there was no sign of that when I visited recently. As for wall paintings at Stanton Harcourt, only a few splashes of colour remain.

St Lawrence, Combe

The Medieval Judgement Day fresco over the transept arch of St Lawrence church, Combe, must surely be one of the best to survive the ravages of Henry VIII and Oliver Cromwell in Oxfordshire. It shows God dividing the good from the bad, complete with devil goading licentious women and naughty priests off to Hell.

And unseemly goings-on were certainly what the devils looked down upon one Sunday in December 1820 when the Reverend Charles Rose of Lincoln College, together with farmers John Bolton, William Harris, William Roberts and Charles Rowles, fought with churchwardens Thomas Bumpus and James Long to turn the rector out of his pulpit in front of the entire congregation causing 'such tumultuous vociferations as were with difficulty put a stop too'.

From that day onwards matters in the village went steadily downhill. On Friday, 27 September 1822, the Rector of Combe, Dr Edward Tatham, who was also Rector of Lincoln College, owner of the living, turned up at the church with three constables, his sons who were exhibitioners at Lincoln, and a few others to break into the church and change the locks. He did this in a bid to lock out the curate Bartley Lee, whom he had previously sacked but who refused to go quietly or even to go at all.

On Sunday, 29 September 1822, up to 500 villagers assembled in the churchyard. When Dr Tatham arrived, supported by gamekeepers supplied by the Duke of Marlborough, lord of the manor and principal landowner in the village, he was forcibly thrown out and the church door forced by the mob which broke in and took possession of the church.

Court cases dragged on for years. In one, Dr Tatham was described as a 'most eccentric and unaccountable character'. In another, it was said that the origin of the dispute was 'some trifling difference between the Doctor's lady (who is a low-bred, vulgar woman) and the defendant', namely the unfortunate Mr Lee whom Tatham was trying to eject from his cottage. Tatham's prospective replacement for Lee, the Reverend Rose, was heralded with 'rough music played on pots and pans wherever he went'.

In fact, the row is now usually thought to have been far more about social conditions than anything else. Some of the cottages in Combe were described in evidence to an early 19th century Parliamentary enquiry as little better then piggeries. Bartley Lee was seen by some as a champion of the labourer, while Tatham was seen as the personification of tyranny. Interesting therefore that Lord Charles Spencer Churchill sided with Lee and was prosecuted along with the labourers.

Churchill

Anyone concerned about the fairness or otherwise of tax bands should perhaps spare a thought for the inhabitants of Churchill, near Chipping Norton: their village was burned to a cinder as a result of an ill-fated tax avoidance scheme.

The tax that caused the tragedy was the chimney tax, introduced by Charles II in 1662 in a bid to be fair, his thinking being that richer people in bigger houses would have to pay more, and poorer people less. The tax was levied at one shilling per hearth, payable twice a year on the quarter days of Michaelmas (September 29) and Lady Day (March 25).

In Churchill the tax backfired, so to speak, when in 1684 an enterprising baker decided to knock his hearth through to next door to enable himself and his neighbour to share the same hearth! Four people died in the ensuing conflagration and at least 20 houses were destroyed, along with several barns and other outhouses. As a result the village was rebuilt further up the hill—of stone this time instead of timber frame and thatch.

The Churchill fire became notorious in the debate about the charge which was never popular, not least because it involved tax inspectors nosing about in people's homes. It was abolished by William and Mary in 1689.

When the village moved up the hill after the fire, the original church of 1348 was left increasingly isolated on its original site. By 1825 the church had become sufficiently run down for the rich but eccentric philanthropist lord of the manor, James Haughton Langston, of Sarsden House, to obtain permission to pull it down. Now only the chancel remains in the old graveyard.

Langston built the present, replacement church of All Saints in the middle of the 'new' village. Its tower is a two-thirds scale replica of Magdalen College tower in Oxford, and Churchill choristers even assemble up on their tower sometimes on May morning to sing in the dawn, like their Oxford counterparts. There is even an outdoor pulpit, similar to the one at Magdalen. Architect James Plowman seems to have enjoyed his brief of bringing Oxford to the country: the buttresses of Churchill church are modelled on those of the chapel at New College and the typically late Georgian interior incorporates a hammerbeam roof modelled on the one at Christ Church. Churchill's church tower is a landmark in this part of the Cotswolds, designated an Area of Outstanding Natural Beauty.

But near it stands a fountain that some think a monument of outstanding unnatural ugliness. It was described in Nikolaus Pevsner's Oxfordshire book as 'memorably ugly'. Put up in 1870 by Julia, Countess of Ducie, daughter of Mr Langston, in memory of her father, it certainly does not seem so bad to me. Indeed, it reminds me of the water conduit removed from Carfax, Oxford, in 1786 to Nuneham Courtenay where, to this day, it does duty as a folly in the grounds of Nuneham House.

Curiously, fire still seems something of a hazard in Churchill. Another serious fire swept through it in September 2007, and scaffolding was necessary for repair work for some time after.

St Peter, Daylesford

A hidden architectural gem of national importance straddles Oxfordshire's border with Gloucestershire. It is the church of St Peter at Daylesford which, until 2001 when it became redundant, was one of the parish churches within the Oxford diocese making up the team ministry of Kingham, Daylesford, Churchill and Sarsden.

Gaining access to this secret jewel of a building, standing like a sort of architectural sleeping beauty in its grove of yews, is not easy; but anyone lucky—or unlucky— enough to get in will soon see the probable reason for the door being so often locked: the place is in a terrible condition, with sizable chunks of what looks like Purbeck marble lying about, and notices on pews warning visitors to beware of falling masonry.

Aptly enough, a notice straight ahead of you when you enter by the south door talks in flowery language of how the 'mouldering hand of time' dealt in such a way with a previous Saxon church on the site, which the first Governor-General of India, Warren Hastings—who retired to nearby Daylesford House—had had to rebuild it in 1816. That church—presumably built in the same restrained Regency style as Warren Hastings' simple tomb in the churchyard, dated 1818—did not last long though.

Poor Warren Hastings, who loved India and Indian culture with all his heart, and employed fellow Indian colonial Samuel Pepys Cockerell (descendant, incidentally of the diarist Pepys) to design Daylesford House largely in the Indian idiom; his tale is romantic but sad. He was born at nearby Churchill from where, as a child, he used to gaze across the Evenlode valley at Daylesford—owned by his family for centuries—and vow to re-acquire it. Having become Governor-General of India he could expect a comfortable retirement and a peerage; instead he was impeached on the (unfounded) grounds of corruption—largely because so many were jealous of the fortunes being made by so-called English nabobs. However, the East India Company, to its eternal credit, built Daylesford House for him.

The church building was replaced in 1859-63 by the present Victorian extravaganza, which is somehow cosmopolitan and urban in its heavy construction, but at the same time beautiful; a sort of *jolie laide* of a building. It was designed by that high priest of Victoriana, John Loughborough Pearson (1817-97), whose renown was so great during his lifetime—his works include Truro Cathedral and the west front of Bristol Cathedral—that he was buried in Westminster Abbey.

The new church was commissioned, apparently regardless of expense, by Harman Grisewood, the benefactor who bought the Daylesford estate in 1853 from General Sir Charles Imhoff, the last of the Hastings family connections. Grisewood replaced the houses along the road leading to the gateway into his park with the Victorian buildings there now—which look almost like a succession of gate lodges. Exactly what Mr Grisewood did for a living I know not, but he was evidently extremely rich. He was a relative of Freddie Grisewood, radio and early TV presenter who was born at Daylesford, and of the Harman Grisewood who became controller of the BBC Third programme; and I am sure he would be turning in his grave if he saw the state of his lovely church now. His grave as it happens is in the churchyard—which is better maintained than the church, though sadly signs of recent vandalism are apparent on one Grisewood tomb where an exquisite Victorian stone angel has been decapitated.

Daylesford House passed from the Grisewoods to Viscount Rothermere, then the steel magnate Heinrich von Thyssen, and is now the home of Sir Anthony and Lady Bamford.

Swinbrook

Six generations of Fettiplaces recline in effigy on stone shelves, like so many passengers in couchettes on a French train, at Swinbrook church, near Burford. But were they really members of an Oxfordshire family?

One of their manor houses was in Widford, which by a curious quirk of history was for more than 800 years an island of Gloucestershire, completely surrounded by Oxfordshire; another was just outside Shilton, which managed to be a detached part of Berkshire for nearly as long. Nothing remains of either house except a few bumps in the ground at Widford, a vanished village now only accessible by footpath, where a hauntingly beautiful chapel of simple Saxon design stands forlorn in a field by the Windrush. The chapel stands where a Roman villa once stood and where, incidentally, some years ago, I was vouchsafed the slightly surreal sight of an old-fashioned electric bar heater standing on a Roman mosaic. Presumably the vicar had put the heater there to warm the place up for one of the services held in the chapel from time to time.

Widford achieved notoriety in 1784. The tearaway Dunsdon brothers were then terrorising the neighbourhood; thriving as highwaymen by taking illicit advantage of the recent construction of the turnpike, now the A40. In a scene reminiscent of the wild west, two of the four brothers, Tom and Harry, rode to the Burford Whitsuntide fair that year and drank and gambled with the best (or worst) of the revellers—though, of course, everyone knew exactly who they were. The Whitsuntide Fair was held from ancient times until 1826 in Widford parish on a plain called Capps Lodge where there was a tavern on the edge of Wychwood Forest. It was a rowdy affair involving the selection of a lord and a lady from among the Burford lads and lasses, who then demanded venison. The demanding, according to the excellent *A Thousand Years of Burford* by Raymond and Joan Moody (Hindsight of Burford), was a habit dating from 1593. Until that year the people had claimed one day's hunting a year; thereafter the day's hunting was commuted to a brace of bucks, demanded annually from the keepers of the forest.

The goings-on of 1784 were particularly unruly, ending with barman William Harding being shot in a brawl with the Dunsdons. The landlord was also shot, though a ha'penny in his waistcoat pocket saved his life. The Dunsdons were captured in the general melee but had to be taken all the way to Gloucester by the constable, since Widford was officially part of Gloucestershire. After they were hanged, their bodies were displayed in irons, hanging from an oak tree on the boundary of the parishes of Fulbrook, Widford and Shipton. The gibbet tree is still there, but on private ground.

Again according to Raymond and Joan Moody's book, baptism records show that the number of Burford illegitimate births rose in February (about nine months after Whitsun) in the late 18th and early 19th centuries; but that probably only tells half the story: anyone born on the piece of land called Sworn Leys, near Shilton, where the other Fettiplace house once stood, would as likely as not be left unbaptised. For though Shilton was a detached part of Berkshire, those particular six acres were officially nowhere—part of no county and no parish. Babies born there were left unregistered and the place was long known as a baby farm. The remains of a mansion was still standing there as late as 1905. It is thought that these strange irregularities of boundaries were rectified by enclosure acts of about 1844.

So were the Fettiplaces Oxfordshire people? Yes, since they owned tracts of land in Oxfordshire and some of them were even keepers of Wychwood Forest. As for that Roman mosaic, it has been covered over in order to preserve it; the heater has gone and so has the vicar, his beautiful vicarage at Swinbrook sold as a private house.

Cote Baptist Chapel

Dusty things, quaint and quirky, full of romantic decay but practically irrelevant to modern life. There is one in the middle of almost every town and village in Oxfordshire, often locked, seldom visited, much loved: a church. Which of us is not a little sad when we come across a particularly beautiful example, only to read a notice on the door telling us that the place is now redundant and in the hands of some worthy outfit that has become responsible for its upkeep?

Cote Baptist Chapel near Bampton has a lively and interesting history. The first chapel was built in 1703, with a replacement in 1756, in the wake of the 1689 Act of Toleration which, in theory at least, granted freedom of worship to dissenters; though in practice they remained second-class subjects until 1829, excluded from local or national government and from English universities.

These 'habits of dissent' were well established in this part of the county. About 150 years before the Reformation the area contained more than its fair share of Lollards— people who followed the teachings of John Wycliffe, Master of Balliol College, Oxford, who had the temerity to publish the Bible in English as early as the 14th century. In any case, it seems that the Nonconformists were unjustly scorned by snobbish clergy of the established church.

In 1738 two Anglican priests told their bishop that the Baptist teacher was 'a man taken from the sheepfold, his followers at best but yeomen, one with the other mean and illiterate'. However, the sheer quality of the 18th-century gravestones at Cote shows that the worshippers here were far from poor or mean. John Piper thought the chapel one of the most beautiful buildings in Oxfordshire and one of his illustrations of it appeared in Betjeman's *First and Last Loves*.

Betjeman of course favoured a great range of Oxfordshire's country churches, including the contrasting south Oxfordshire chapel of St Katherine, Chiselhampton, built in 1762, about which he wrote a poem to help raise restoration funds in 1952:

'How warm the many candles shine
On Samuel Dowbiggin's design
For this interior neat
These high box pews of Georgian days
Which screen us from the public gaze
When we make answer meet.'

In fact, someone called Dowbiggin certainly designed the next-door manor house but no one seems certain that he also designed the church. But the point is that the little church with its box pews and 17th-century pulpit is a monument to times past and a three-dimensional record of local history—and is now in the Care of the Churches Conservation Trust.

Cote Baptist Chapel has now been owned by the Historic Chapels Trust since 1994; and Dr Kate Tiller, Reader Emerita in English Local History at Oxford University, has written a very informative *History and Guide to Cote Baptist Chapel.*

St Katherine, Chiselhampton

Charles Wesley

Whenever you hear the strains of 'Hark! the Herald Angels Sing', it comes as a shock to realise that those stirring words were composed by someone banned from preaching by the Church of England.

Charles Wesley, born December 1707, went up to Christ Church, Oxford, when he was 19. The following year he formed what became known as the Oxford Methodist Group, the foundation of the Methodist movement. His elder brother, John, who had also studied at Christ Church, joined the group a couple of years later in 1729, when he returned to Oxford as a tutor at Lincoln College. The sons of a Lincolnshire rector, who both became Anglican priests themselves, the brothers became known as Methodists by fellow undergraduates when they founded something called the Holy Club, whose members met at regular times to inject 'method' into their religious studies. The very word (from the Greek *methodos*, meaning rule) was coined in Oxford in the 18th century to describe the group's regular habits.

Methodists actually celebrated the tercentenary of Charles Wesley's birth in May rather than December, as that was the month, in 1738, when the brothers experienced a spiritual awakening, or revelation, which resulted in the formal founding of Methodism. After that year they were repudiated as non-conformists by the Church of England and forced to preach in the open air.

Oxfordshire is rich in non-conformist chapels, the Baptist one at Cote dating from the early 18th century probably being the most picturesque, though the baroque Wesleyan converted mansion on Burford High Street is the most splendid, even if the urns on its roof and next to its entrance stairs have long since been removed to Cornbury Park, Charlbury.

Charles Wesley composed some 6,000 hymns, including 'Love Divine, All Loves Excelling' and 'Christ the Lord is Risen Today'. He composed the lyrics of 'Hark! The Herald' in 1739. Originally the first couplet ran:

'Hark! how all the welkin rings
Glory to the King of Kings',

but this was later altered by fellow Methodist George Whitfield. 'Hark! the Herald' was originally sung to a tune also used for 'Amazing Grace', the hymn composed by a former slave ship captain. The familiar tune that many of us bellow out at Christmas was composed by Felix Mendelssohn in 1840 as part of his Festegesang, performed in Leipzig to commemorate the printing press inventor Johann Gutenberg. It was adapted from the song 'Vaterland, in deinem Gauen' (Fatherland, in your Districts) in 1855 by William Hayman Cummings.

Anyone surprised that the lovely carol's lyrics were written by someone banned from preaching in Anglican churches might be equally surprised to learn that Mendelssohn stipulated that the tune should never be used for sacred music. In any case, the Christmas that Wesley celebrated fell on what is now Epiphany, since he lived before the changeover to the Gregorian calendar in September 1752. Epiphany seems to be the one great festival that has faded completely away. Formerly it was celebrated with almost as much merrymaking as the first day of Christmas. Perhaps New Year's celebrations have taken over.

Incidentally, many Oxfordshire people believed, right up until the turn of the 19th century, that on Old Epiphany day, 17 January, the cattle would kneel in their stalls.

Kelmscott Manor

10. The Arts
Writers, Painters, Composers

Oxford has long acted as a magnate for writers and poets. The very air seems to crackle with their thoughts. Way back at the start of the 13th century, one of the university's first chancellors, Robert Grosseteste, composed his long poem 'Le Château d'Amour' here, and shortly afterwards that extraordinary polymath Roger Bacon started rocking the early university establishment with his passion for Arab science and cosmology, along with something called 'angelology'. But sadly his mind was too rich for lesser mortals and he was sent away.

And there we have the beginnings of a paradox that has dogged Oxford for most of its life. On the one hand it encourages original, revolutionary thought; on the other it has in the past all too often found itself identified as the authority against which those rebellious minds pit their wits. Certainly anything approaching academic freedom took a long time coming. There were, after all, those regrettable book burnings in the 16th and 17th centuries, at which even works by John Milton were ordered to be consigned to the flames of a bonfire in the Bodleian quad.

Of course academics, as a general rule, are more concerned with criticising other people's work than becoming artists themselves, but all the same some of the most famous poets associated with Oxford have had a love–hate relationship with it. Shelley was sent down in the early 19th century after quarrelling with his college authorities; and more than a century later even Betjeman left Oxford without a degree. Nevertheless, the heady ferment of ideas that is Oxford has made not only the city, but also the entire district around it, one of the most fertile areas for writers in Britain.

In other areas of artistic endeavour, Oxford has always been more comfortable with itself, happily fulfilling the roles of patron, collector and curator. John Ruskin, appointed professor of fine arts twice (because he resigned the chair first time round in protest against vivisection), figures large here. He founded Oxford's Ruskin School of Fine Art and championed the formation of the Pre-Raphaelite Brotherhood, members of which included William Morris, who first rented and then bought Kelmscott Manor, upriver from Oxford, where he lived with fellow Pre-Raphaelite Dante Gabriel Rosetti. As it happens, the Brotherhood was formed at a party thrown by John Everett Millais in 1848—who also had strong Oxford connections, but of the Town rather than Gown variety. One of his earliest paintings was of the Mayor of Oxford 1842-3, James Wyatt, wood carver, gilder, picture framer and dealer, and his family, who lived above the shop at 115 High Street. Wyatt picked up on Millais when he was just a teenager, staying with his half-brother in Oxford; and Wyatt evidently had an eye for up-and-coming artists, because he also displayed J. M. W. Turner's famous painting of Oxford High Street at his shop, thus dealing with the two most important British artists of his time.

J. M. W. Turner—not to be confused with William Turner of Oxford—was the son of a London barber and wig-maker. Aged 14, he came to stay with his uncle in Oxford in 1789, from which time a whole sketchbook of drawings still exists, along with a watercolour of the city. In later life he frequently painted views of Oxford. We are lucky to be able to view these at the Ashmolean Museum, the oldest museum in Britain, named after the collector Elias Ashmole, who began gathering 'rarities' in the 17th century. And the Ashmolean is indeed testament to Oxford's role as curator of the arts.

But in addition to these more familiar artists, Oxford and Oxfordshire are full of the works of earlier, usually anonymous artists. Who, for instance sculpted the gargoyles, or the fantastic statues of creatures adorning the Great Quad at Magdalen? Or the memorial in Burford church to Edmund Harman, barber to Henry VIII, said to contain the first depiction in England of native Americans? Then there are all the stained glass windows and frescoes. I could go on and on. It is a rich county, all right.

Oxfordshire Writers

Can any county be as full of the shades of dead writers as Oxfordshire? *The Oxford Literary Guide to the British Isles* includes a map of southern England that shows the shire to be knee-deep in such ghosts.

Where to start is the problem. Woodstock is as good a place as any. Here Alexander Pope, who translated much of his *Iliad* in Pope's Tower at Stanton Harcourt, visited Fair Rosamund's Well in 1717 and 'toasted her shade in the cold water'. Fair Rosamund—Rose of the World, said to be the most beautiful woman in Christendom—was the mistress of Henry II (1133-89) and, according to *The Garland of Good Will* by Thomas Deloney (1543-1600), was hidden in a maze here—but was discovered by Queen Eleanor, who followed a silken thread unravelling from her dress. All the 'labyrinthine brickwork maze in maze', as Tennyson described it in his play *Becket*, was unable to save her.

Blenheim, designed by playwright Sir John Vanbrugh, was still being built when Pope visited, but he noted that only one wall remained of Henry II's manor. Walter Scott surmised how this destruction came about in his novel *Woodstock* (1826), set in the Civil War. The manor was occupied then by Henry Lee, ranger of the Royal Woodstock Forest, whose daughter, according to Scott, fell in love with a Parliamentarian soldier. Chaucer's House in Park Street, Woodstock, is probably on the site of the house where Oxford academic John Aubrey said that Chaucer stayed with his son.

Tomb of Alice de la Pole, granddaughter of Chaucer, St Mary's, Ewelme

Now where shall I go? Across Blenheim Park to Combe, I think. The bawdy poet John Wilmot, Lord Rochester, lived near Combe gate in High Lodge (he spent one entire year drunk), having been appointed ranger of the forest by his friend Charles II. American novelist Nathaniel Hawthorne visited the Lodge and described in *Our Old Home* (1863) seeing the canopied bed in which Rochester died, repenting of his wicked ways. (I think the bed was still there in 1960; I remember being shown something called Rochester's cot, hung about with rotting damask, like something out of a Hammer House of Horror film.)

Also in Combe lived Sir Thomas Elyot (1490-1546), writer and early champion of women's education. Jumping fast forward 400 years we also come across short story writer A. E. Coppard, who moved to Combe in about 1914 from Islip (where the saint and king Edward the Confessor was born in 1003).

Now let's flit like a high-flying bird to the Vale of the White Horse—a flight that some might regard as cheating since it only ceased to be part of Berkshire in 1974. Here we alight in Uffington where *Tom Brown's Schooldays* (1857) author Thomas Hughes was born in 1822. He was baptised in the church where his grandfather was vicar. His grandmother later moved to nearby Kingston Lisle. She was a friend of Scott and Dickens and furnished them with much folklore, which they used in their works.

Travelling north again, who could resist coming down to roost at Ewelme, once the home of William de la Pole (1396-1450), Duke of Suffolk, who built the almshouses here? Chaucer is thought to have visited the Duchess, Alice, who was his granddaughter. And Jerome K. Jerome (1859-1927), following the rip-roaring success of *Three Men in a Boat*, moved into a farmhouse here and is buried in the churchyard.

In nearby Nuneham Courtenay the first Earl Harcourt removed a whole village to create a romantic landscape beside the Thames—something deplored by Oliver Goldsmith (1730-74) in his poem 'The Deserted Village', in which Barbara Wyatt, who refused to leave her cottage, is commemorated.

In that little gallop I only scratched the surface of where we could have gone. Indeed, I think there can be few writers of note in the English language who are unable to claim a connection with Oxfordshire.

Shakespeare in Oxfordshire

Long ago, when the world of mass tourism was relatively young, I used to act as tour guide for rich Americans, driving them about in an old Humber Imperial bought for the purpose. In those days—and I am talking here of the late 1960s and early 1970s— the London to Stratford tour was known as 'the milk run', with Oxford cropping up at about midday: just too early for lunch and certainly too early for an overnight stay (as was often ruefully noted by restaurateurs and hoteliers keen to extract dollars from pockets).

Some 400 years earlier, Oxford fared better in that respect. Shakespeare found it an ideal place at which to stay overnight on his frequent journeys between the capital and his native Stratford-upon-Avon. He used to put up at the Tavern at 3 Cornmarket, where he lodged in the so-called Painted Room—which still exists, the painted walls having been rediscovered in 1927.

In my days as a guide, full of the overconfidence of youth, I had no qualms at all about wading into the whole Shakespeare debate, never failing to state as fact all sorts of highly conjectural theories. For instance there was the one, still going strong; about how young Will was caught poaching deer at Charlecote Park in Warwickshire. The tale, first propagated by poet laureate Nicholas Rowe in a 1709 biography, has it that in about 1583 Shakespeare was brought before magistrate Sir Thomas Lucy of Charlecote Park, and charged with the crime.

He was probably fined and possibly flogged; and then he stuck a ribald note on the gatehouse at Charlecote. The result of this foolhardy action was that he was forced to leave the district as fast as possible—and so went to London to seek fame and fortune.

The whole saga achieved credibility through the absurd Justice Shallow, who appears as a figure of fun in both *The Merry Wives of Windsor* and in *Henry IV Part II*, in a way that some say satirises the real-life Sir Thomas. For example, Shallow's coat of arms features 'a dozen white luces' (pike) and the Lucy coat of arms does indeed contain three white pike. Then there is the fact that Sir Thomas was proud of his lineage: his family had lived at Charlecote since at least 1189, and always referred to his coat of arms as 'a very old coat too', the words used by Shallow in *The Merry Wives*.

But the whole fun of talking about Shakespeare is that so few verifiable facts are known about him. And in spouting forth to tourists long ago I was only following in the footsteps of a whole line of Shakespeare scholars. I found out that his father, John Shakespeare, had been an illiterate glover—useful when we reached Woodstock and paid a visit to the glove factory there. I also told tourists about the famous bit of William Shakespeare's will, in which he left his 'second best bed' to his wife Anne Hathaway.

I didn't know the part of the will in which he left 20 shillings to his godson. Had I known that I probably would have leapt (wrongly) to the conclusion that the godson in question was Sir William Davenant, son of the innkeeper of the tavern where Shakespeare used to stay in Oxford.

Handel in Oxford

George Frideric Handel (1685-1759) first came to England in 1710, in a move which, to some extent, presaged the coronation of the German Elector of Hanover as King George I of Great Britain and Ireland in 1714. Unlike the King, though—a divorced nobleman who never even learned English—Handel quickly came to love England and the English him. The son of a barber-surgeon from the German town of Halle, Handel's prodigious musical talent was, fortuitously, recognised by the town organist.

After some years in Italy studying opera, he took up a job at the court of the Elector of Hanover as *Kapellmeister*, but immediately left for London where his opera *Rinaldo* was performed in 1711. Finding himself, reluctantly enough, back in Hanover in 1712, he immediately applied for leave to return to London. And it was in London that he wrote his famous *Water Music* to serenade George I in 1717.

When Handel arrived in Oxford in July 1733 for a week's sojourn here, he was 48 years old and had already been living in London for 23 years. He was greeted with much pomp and ceremony by about 4,000 people who crowded into the Sheldonian Theatre to hear the premiere of his oratorio *Athali*, as well as performances of *Deborah, Esthe,* and *Acis and Galatea. Athali* was to be performed as part of 'The Act' (forerunner of the Encenia in the Sheldonian), and 1733 turned out to be the last of these week-long old-style graduation ceremonies.

On the same occasion Handel was famously offered an honorary degree, which, curiously, he refused. There is still a certain mystery surrounding Handel's reasons for this. Historian Thomas Hearne, who took almost as jaundiced a view of Oxford goings-on as his predecessor Anthony Wood did in the previous century, suggests that Handel refused the degree because Oxford University imposed a small charge for conferring it.

Whatever his reason, music in Oxford continued to flourish. Music groups performed in colleges and taverns. One of these groups developed into the Musical Society of Oxford, which first met at the King's Head tavern, but in 1748 moved to the Holywell Music Room (now the nation's oldest music chamber) which was built to house it.

Handel's famous week in Oxford in 1733 came to be commemorated with a regular week-long Handel festival, called 'Handel in Oxford: A Celebration of the Anniversary of Handel's Glorious Week in Oxford in July 1733'.

Then 60 years later, in 1791, another composer visited Oxford to be offered an honorary degree...

Haydn in Oxford

Joseph Haydn (1732-1809) was born just a year before Handel came to Oxford. Son of a wheelwright, his parents recognised his genius when he was only six and sent him away to study under a schoolmaster, a distant relative, at the small town of Hainburg. Haydn later recalled this master giving him 'more thrashings than food'. However, Haydn's singing voice apparently thrived, for he was noticed by the choirmaster of St Stephen's cathedral in Vienna, where he became a chorister.

He spent most of his life working for the Austrian princely family of Esterhazy, who maintained their own private orchestra at their palace 30 miles from Vienna. But working as a wage slave of the princes, he was forbidden to compose for other patrons or even to sell his works. Despite this, his fame spread and Haydn was eventually able to negotiate better terms. First he visited Paris and then, on New Year's Day 1791, he began his triumphant English excursion, promoted by Johann Peter Salomon, a German violinist and conductor working in England, who arranged for him to give weekly concerts in London.

But it was the musicologist Charles Burney, who had obtained his doctorate in music from University College, Oxford, who suggested that Haydn be offered an honorary degree and promoted his performance at the Sheldonian. For Haydn, this may well have been his finest hour: in Oxford, at the Sheldonian Theatre on 7 July 1791, when he conducted his Symphony no. 92 in G major; it has been known ever since as the Oxford Symphony.

The performance was accompanied by Haydn's acceptance of an honorary Master of Music degree from Oxford University, and it finally confirmed the status of the composer, then in his late 50s, as an international celebrity. As the applause died down he said: 'Thank you very much.' To which the adoring crowd responded: 'What good English you speak.' Maybe Haydn's acceptance of the honorary degree did something to smooth the academic feathers in Oxford—ruffled for more than 50 years since Handel's refusal of the degree.

In fact the 'Oxford Symphony' was not specially composed for the occasion. It had originally been performed in Paris and had then been greeted with much acclaim in London. The story goes that because of lack of time, a symphony was needed that was already familiar to the Oxford musicians. In any case, he had not yet finished any of the 12 'London' symphonies he was writing for his English audiences—so he brought to Oxford one of the most recent of his completed ones.

When Haydn returned to Vienna he was regarded as 'the father of the symphony'. Years later, Napoleon took the city after an intense bombardment in May 1809. But Napoleon ordered a guard of honour to stand outside Haydn's home, where the composer was lay dying.

Shelley in Oxford

In 1810, Percy Bysshe Shelley (1792-1822) came up to University College, Oxford. The university, and in particular University College, has a slightly ambivalent attitude towards the poet. On the one hand the college honours his memory with that extraordinary, almost androgenous-looking nude statue of him set up in the west range of buildings in 1893; on the other it is difficult to forget that he was, in fact, sent down (expelled) after only a year.

His quarrel with the college authorities concerned the publication of a pamphlet called 'The Necessity of Atheism'. He, together with fellow student Thomas Jefferson Hogg (1792-1862)—who became his lifelong friend and biographer—were identified as the authors of the tract and hauled before the beaks, including the dean of the college, George Rowley.

Both refused to answer questions put to them when they were interrogated separately, with Hogg apparently telling the dean: 'If

Letters in which Shelley, famously an atheist, posed as a member of the clergy

Shelley had anything to do with it, he [Hogg] was equally implicated and desired his share of the penalty.' That afternoon a notice appeared on the college board announcing their expulsion due to their 'contumacy in refusing to answer certain questions put to them'.

Thanks to the intervention of his father, Sir Timothy Shelley, Percy Bysshe, who was the elder son and heir to the baronetcy, was offered the opportunity to recant and thereby avoid expulsion; but he refused to do so. Certainly the youthful duo seem to have been a thorn in the side of the authorities for months. Some say that Shelley even posted an anti-God notice on the chapel door.

Shelley wrote his first book, *Zastrozzi*, at Oxford, under the initials PBS. It was a Gothic novel advocating atheism. He and Hogg also wrote a burlesque, purportedly by Margaret Nicholson, the mad laundress who tried to murder George III in Oxford, and 'Leonora'—a manuscript which a respectable Oxford printer called Slatter refused to print. A Mr King of Abingdon was going to print it when the two were sent down.

After rustication, Hogg became a lawyer and Shelley tried to put into practice ideals floated early in the French Revolution: republicanism, atheism, free love, vegetarianism. Shelley eloped with and married the 16-year-old Harriett Westbrook, who eventually drowned herself in the Serpentine in Hyde Park, London; then he married Mary Godwin, daughter of William Godwin and rights of women champion Mary Wollstonecraft, the creator of *Frankenstein*. Shelley lived in Marlow, Buckinghamshire, before moving to Italy—where he drowned in the bay of La Spezia. His body was burned on the beach.

The statue now in University College was originally commissioned from the sculptor Onslow Ford to mark Shelley's grave in the Protestant cemetery in Rome where Shelley is buried. Pevsner, in his Oxfordshire book, comments: 'it is all extremely lush', but at least it is a recognition on the college's part of a poet who thought freely and was way ahead of his time, as evidenced, for instance, in *The Revolt of Islam*.

Curiously enough, the memorial statue is housed in a domed building designed by Champneys, which indirectly calls to mind an anniversary that Oxford is maybe more pleased to remember: a plaque on the High Street indicates that this is the site where Robert Boyle and Robert Hooke performed experiments with an air pump which were closely connected to the founding of the Royal Society 150 years before Shelley came up, in 1660—but that is another story.

Matthew Arnold

I suppose that Matthew Arnold (1822-88), coiner of the phrase 'City of Dreaming Spires', embodies for many of us—who vaguely remember reading bits of him at school—the very essence of Oxford. But some might say that the spirit he affirms is more that of a relatively new Oxford—Victorian, mainly masculine, self-confident, empire-building—than that conjured up by his other much-quoted description of the place: 'Home of lost causes, and forsaken beliefs, and unpopular names, and impossible loyalties.'

Though by no means rich, indeed the reverse, Arnold exemplified a certain energetic but elitist spirit that was sweeping through the minds of educationalists at the time. He came up to Oxford from Rugby, where his father Thomas Arnold (1795-1842) was headmaster, having created the world remembered by Thomas Hughes (born in Uffington 1822) in *Tom Brown's Schooldays*. Thomas Arnold's ideas typically relished the notion of promoting a healthy mind in a healthy body through the medium of organised team sports. Indeed, one of Matthew's brothers, the novelist William Delafield Arnold (1828-59), was one of the four boys who wrote down the 'Rugby Rules', still in force today.

Matthew Arnold came up to Balliol as a scholar in 1841, at a time when Benjamin Jowett (1817-93) was already a Fellow. Jowett of course became Master of Balliol—but demolished much of it in order to produce a college more redolent of his age. Arnold was one of many distinguished students who formed their characters under Jowett's influence: their defining characteristic, at least according to Prime Minister H. H. Asquith (himself one of them), being 'effortless superiority', a phrase that has annoyed members of Balliol ever since.

Other Balliol poets included Hilaire Belloc, Gerald Manley Hopkins and Arthur Hugh Clough—in whose memory Arnold's poem 'Thyrsis' was written, which contains the lines:

> 'And that sweet city with her dreaming spires,
> She needs not June for beauty's heightening,
> Lovely all time she lies, lovely tonight.'

Matthew Arnold all his life lived and breathed the spirit of Oxford. His godfather, John Keble, became a champion of the Oxford Movement; his brother Tom became a Catholic and at one time worked for Cardinal Newman; and his father, a graduate of Corpus Christi, became Regius Professor of Modern History in 1841, the year before he died. Matthew himself became a fellow of Oriel in 1845 and Professor of Poetry in 1857.

G. W. E. Russell, in *Portraits of the Seventies*, described Arnold as 'a man of the world entirely free from worldliness and a man of letters without the faintest trace of pedantry'. His 'man of the world' bit was to earn a living as a school inspector, which involved travelling throughout Britain by train, using the time to fill countless notebooks with erudite observations—in much the same way as Trollope wrote his novels in the train while travelling the country on Post Office business.

But in an Oxford that was changing fast, not only through new building but also through Royal Commissions bringing about much needed university reform, how could he write in lines immediately preceding those about 'lost causes': 'Beautiful city! so venerable, so lovely, so unravaged by the fierce intellectual life of our century, so serene! ... whispering from her towers the last enchantments of the Middle Age ...'? Beats me. Though I suppose parts of it remained, and still remain, 'unravaged'.

As for Jowett, I cannot resist recounting the story of a guide in Broad Street, as described by W. S. Walsh in 1893: 'Those are Professor Jowett's study windows, and there [here the ruffian would stoop down, take up a handful of gravel and throw it against the panes, bringing poor Jowett, livid with fury to the window], ladies and gentlemen, is Professor Benjamin Jowett himself.'

Kenneth Grahame

Kenneth Grahame (1859-1932), author of *The Wind in the Willows*, is surely one of the greatest of graduates that his beloved Oxford never had. Educated at St Edward's School, he had always assumed that he would progress to the university along with most of his contemporaries, as was the custom with the British bourgeoisie at the time. Not only did he not do so, but with that denial most of his dreams and plans for his future life were shattered, for everything he wanted to do required a degree from either Oxford or Cambridge.

His mother died in 1863 when Kenneth was not quite five years old, shortly after the birth of his brother Roland. The death caused his father to turn morosely to alcohol; so Kenneth, along with Roland and his elder sister and brother, Helen and Willie, had to be brought up as orphans by relatives, notably their maternal grandmother in Cookham Dene.

Grahame spent the first five of his seven years at St Edward's School (founded in 1863) at its old site in a pleasant Queen Anne mansion in New Inn Hall Street. Then in 1873 the warden of the school acquired the 100 acres St Edward's now owns in North Oxford at a good price, since at that time it was farmland. Before the move cricket was played on Port Meadow on a pitch that had the advantage of having no boundaries, the object apparently being to slog the ball so far that it was lost—and then simply to run more and more runs.

He did well at St Edward's, despite an unpromising start at the age of nine in 1868. He recorded his early days there: 'The junior form, or class, was in session, so to speak, and I was modestly occupying that position, at the very bottom, which seemed to me natural enough when the then headmaster entered—a man who had somehow formed an erroneous idea of my possibilities. Catching sight of me he asked, sternly, 'What's that thing doing down there?' Then the headmaster exited with the edict that if Kenneth had not progressed to near the top of the class by the end of the lesson he would be severely caned. And the upshot was that even though the rest of the class strove to achieve unheard of heights of stupidity in order to save their classmate's bottom, he simply collapsed into tears of horror and bewilderment. Eventually he did well in the Wild World outside childhood, namely at St Edward's, becoming head boy.

Grahame wrote of his beloved Oxford: 'The two influences which most soaked into me there, and have remained with me ever since, were the good grey Gothic on the one hand and, on the other, the cool secluded reaches of the Thames—the 'stripling Thames, remote and dragon-fly haunted.'

But the Wild World failed to keep its end of the unwritten bargain. When his uncle and guardian bluntly told him that going to Oxford was 'out of the question' and that he should make his own way in the world as soon as possible by taking up a job in the Bank of England, he appears to have taken against the real world of adults—'beyond the Wild Wood'—and cultivated an imaginary one. He wrote of them: 'Possessing all the sinews of war [that is, they had the money and could afford to send him to Oxford] this stiff-necked tribe has consistently refused to part: even for the provision of luxuries so much more necessary than luxuries.' And yet, despite his lack of Oxbridge degree, he rose to become secretary of the Bank of England.

The Wind in the Willows was published in 1908, as the culmination of secret tales he used to tell his son Alastair, born in 1900. Poor Alastair. He was what we would these days call a manic depressive; in addition his eyesight was so bad that he was also what we would call 'partially-sighted'. In one respect only was he luckier than his father: he did go to Oxford, to Christ Church to be precise. But he hated it and in May 1920 made his way across Port Meadow to the railway line and apparently lay down in front of a train—though in kindness, it seems, the verdict was accidental death.

Shortly afterwards Grahame moved from his home in Blewbury (then in his beloved Berkshire; now in Oxfordshire) to Pangbourne where he died in 1932. He is buried in St Cross churchyard, Oxford, with the beautiful epitaph composed by his cousin, Anthony Hope.

Gustav Holst and the Cotswolds

Can you say who composed the music of that favourite carol 'In the Bleak Midwinter', as well as knowing the source of the words? It is indeed a fine pairing, with the words by Christina Rosetti and the tune by Gustav Holst (1874-1934).

The origin of the name is that Gustav's great grandfather came to England from Riga, Latvia, in 1802, where he had been part of the large German-speaking population there. During the First World War he was to drop the 'von' in his name by deed poll. Holst's father, Adolph von Holst, was organist and choirmaster at All Saints Church in the north Cheltenham parish of Pittville, a job he combined with that of music teacher. He married one of his piano students, Gustav Holst's mother Clara, and Gustav's birthplace was at 4 Pittville Road (now renamed Clarence Road), which since 1974 has become a museum dedicated to his life and times.

Clara died when Gustav was only eight. After leaving Cheltenham Grammar School for Boys, Holst failed to gain a scholarship to the Royal College of Music and found himself constantly short of money, bicycling around the villages near Cheltenham, often with his trombone strapped to his back. But he managed to follow in his father's footsteps to become organist and choirmaster, though still only 18, at the lovely church of St Lawrence, Wyck Rissington. It was his first paid job and it kindled his interest in the English choral music tradition which, ever since the Reformation, had remained far stronger in this country than on the continent.

The success of his operetta *Lansdown Castle*, performed at Cheltenham Corn Exchange, convinced his father that it was worth paying out good money for him to go to the RCM without a scholarship. There he met his contemporary Ralph Vaughan Williams, and both were taught by Hubert Parry (1848-1918), who was Professor of Music at Oxford 1900-1908. He composed the music for 'Jerusalem' (words by Blake, of course) and 'Dear Lord and Father of Mankind'.

He became director of Music at St Paul's Girls' School in 1907. A shy, retiring man, he was astonished at the success of his orchestral suite, *The Planets*. According to his daughter Imogen's biography, he was asked to set the hymn 'I Vow to Thee My Country' to music and was relieved to find that it fitted the Jupiter tune in *The Planets*.

Vaughan Williams remained a neighbour. If you follow the signposts to Down Ampney, you will find where Holst's lifelong friend Ralph Vaughan Williams (1872-1958) was born and is buried, after which he named the tune to the hymn 'Come Down, O Love Divine'. He was the son of the Vicar of Down Ampney. In 1911, the Oxford Bach Choir, which has given so many Oxford people their first taste of choral music, gave the first performance of Vaughan Williams' *A Sea Symphony*. In his declining years, Vaughan Williams also composed his *Oxford Elegy*, based on texts from Matthew Arnold.

But back to Holst. At Wyck Rissington there is a plaque on the organ informing us that Gustav Holst, composer of the tune for 'In the Bleak Midwinter', was born not far away in Cheltenham; and in Cheltenham, there is a large bronze statue of Holst.

T. E. Lawrence

Odd people, collectors, and perhaps oddest of the odd are book collectors, a growing band of people, some of them rich, who are prepared to chase after first editions and pay thousands for books signed by famous authors—and thousands more if one famous author has dedicated his book to a fellow author.

Many of the books most avidly collected first saw the light of day in Oxford. Sometimes I wonder if there may not perhaps be a fortune mouldering away in this very newspaper office. I wonder that because it was compositors at *The Oxford Times* who produced the very first, privately published edition of T. E. Lawrence's *Seven Pillars of Wisdom* in 1922.

That particular book is a veritable Holy Grail for collectors. The editions produced by our typesetters were printed on thin, cheap paper (itself made at the old paper mills in Wolvercote) and circulated to Lawrence's friends including Robert Graves, E. M. Forster, Thomas Hardy, George Bernard Shaw, Rudyard Kipling and D. G. Hogarth, who was then keeper of the Ashmolean Museum.

At that time, Lawrence (1888-1935), who had grown up in a house in Polstead Road, North Oxford, the illegitimate son of a Welsh baronet and his erstwhile housekeeper, thought it would be improper to make money out of publication of his war memoirs from the Middle East, particularly as they alleged double-dealing on the part of the Briitish government.

Unfortunately, he quickly ran out of copies of his enormous 300,000 word tome and set about publishing a new 'subscription edition. But how much is one of those elusive Oxford 1922 editions worth? Only two known copies are still out there somewhere. The only copy to be sold in recent years appeared at Christie's, New York in May 2001 and sold for £700,000.

The fascination with anything to do with Lawrence of Arabia stems partly from his much-vaunted agonising during its gestation: the first manuscript was lost or stolen on Reading station in 1919 so he was forced to write the whole thing again! (How much would that manuscript be worth?)

The 'subscription' edition, 170 copies of which appeared in 1926, was illustrated by such luminaries as Colin Gill, Augustus John, John Singer Sargent, and Henry Lamb. It cost subscribers 30 guineas apiece and copies sell today for about £35,000 each.

But what about that fortune lying around our office somewhere? Sadly, it's very unlikely to exist. Lawrence was careful to number every copy he had set.

Flora Thompson

Speaking as someone who almost every week whirls past signs to Juniper Hill and Tusmore Park on the A43—a road called 'the turnpike' in Ms Thompson's day—I have long been meaning to turn off and revisit the remains of her world.

Flora Thompson's trilogy, *Lark Rise to Candleford*, was inspired by the three villages of Juniper Hill, Cottisford and Fringford. So vivid are her descriptions of late 19th-century life in those places that I always find it shocking to see—even through a car window, travelling at 60 m.p.h.—just how the march of time has dealt with them.

Juniper Hill was Lark Rise in the book. Flora Thompson (1876-1947) was born there as Flora Timms, daughter of Albert and Emma Timms. Her father was a stonemason who worked for the same company in Brackley for 35 years. There is a plaque to her on a cottage called The End House, but Mr Greenwood explains that the cottage has been entirely demolished except for one wall. Flora Thompson (Laura in the book) conjures up her Oxfordshire childhood and girlhood: her walk to school in Cottisford (Fordlow) with her younger brother, who was later killed in the First World War; her job in the post office at Fringford (Candleford Green), which shared premises with the blacksmith's forge.

Her literary career started with visits to the public library at Winton, from 1907; then in 1911 she won an essay competition in *The Ladies Companion* for a 300 word essay about Jane Austen. Finally she started sending essays to Oxford University Press about her rural observations, and these were gathered into the trilogy for publication in 1938.

Flora's birthplace in Juniper Hill

Since her time, even the manor, Tusmore Park, abode of a personage as remote from her as any celestial being, namely Lord Effingham, has been rebuilt twice, most recently by Syrian millionaire Wafic Said.

The poignancy of time and change is only increased, at least for me, when you realise that even Thompson's world had only come about through violent change a decade or two before her birth. Villagers, dubbed the Juniper Hill Mob, had rioted against enclosure of the common and the ejection notices that went with it. Among beneficiaries of the enclosure was Eton College, which owned the manor of Cottisford from 1441 to 1885.

Paul Nash

Mistletoe, that mythic and mystic plant that manages to grow between earth and heaven, fascinated Romantic war artist Paul Nash (1889-1946) who lived in Oxford from 1939 until his death.

Already in 1912, while still under the influence of those Oxford artists, the Pre-Raphaelites, he had become fascinated by Wittenham Clumps, producing pictures of them that seem almost to turn the Oxfordshire (then Berkshire, of course) countryside into a sort of dreamscape.

But by the time he and his wife Margaret moved to Oxford, this idea of imbuing landscape with intrinsic moral character, consciousness even, had evolved to an extraordinary degree. His 1941 picture *Totes Meer*, of dead German aircraft, dumped at a tip in Cowley, themselves forming a sort of macabre landscape, sums up his fascination with flying and the idea that monsters of the sky might attack us earthlings (as indeed they did).

It is curious that the sojourn in Oxford of one of the greatest 20th century British artists should be so little recorded. Paul (not to be confused with his younger brother, fellow war artist, John) and Margaret Nash moved to 106 Banbury Road in July 1940 after a long house hunt during which they had 'camped' at the Randolph Hotel and in rooms in Beaumont Street and Holywell Street; it seems that houses in Oxford were at a premium during the war, thanks to people moving out of London.

Portrait of Paul Nash by Oxford Mail journalist Stanley Parker, 1943

Paul Nash founded the Arts Bureau for War Service shortly after arriving in Oxford, and in 1941 was appointed an Official War Artist by the War Artists' Advisory Committee. He soon found himself working for the Air Ministry and then for the Ministry of Information. He wrote: 'In the present emergency, the talent of artists of all kinds, architects, sculptors, painters, writers, and musicians, should be regarded as potential material for war service'.

Sadly for Paul Nash, he suffered an acute asthma attack in Oxford, causing him to spend long periods in the Acland Nursing Home. Naturally, he equated the attack on his body with the attack by Hitler on his nation. In a way presaging James Lovelock's Gaia theory, Nash saw not only his nation but also the world as a whole, as a possessor of real, living personality. For instance, he was almost as interested in natural monsters of the sky as he was in those man-made 'machines of death'—aeroplanes.

Some might say his mixture of dreamy Romanticism and hard, pragmatic patriotism illustrated a way of thinking in wartime Britain that is fast being forgotten. Certainly his war artist work took him to air bases at Harwell and at Abingdon. He wrote that he used his art 'in the character of a weapon. I have always believed in the power of pictorial art as a means of propaganda'.

While living in Banbury Road (like mistletoe it was suspended above the earth 'about the level of the smaller tree tops and the flight of the blackbirds and thrushes') he noted a sad event: out of the blue, a hawk attacked his favourite blackbird. He wrote: 'His buxom brown wife is always flying up here and then from the shrubbery where the nest is to look round, calling plaintively. We have been rather miserable ourselves and nothing much can be done about that.'

He died in July 1946 shortly after this small domestic tragedy; not, as it happens, in Oxford but in his sleep in Boscombe, Hampshire, where he had gone for a short break. His period at 106 Banbury Road is now commemorated by a blue plaque.

John Piper

No one, to my mind at least, has recorded the landscape of the whole 20th century quite as effectively as John Piper (1903-92).

Even at Epsom School, in Surrey, he had been interested in guidebooks, producing his own as a result of bicycling about and visiting churches galore; and this interest was revived with his collaboration with Betjeman in 1938 to produce *Oxon, The Shell Guide to Oxfordshire*—which, curiously enough, excluded Oxford itself, perhaps because Betjeman was about to publish his own *An Oxford University Chest*, which appeared the same year.

Before the war, Piper was also involved in the Recording Britain project launched by Kenneth Clark, who in 1931 had been appointed keeper of Fine Art at the Ashmolean. During the war his reputation was made as a war artist, recording the effects of bombing, particularly in Coventry. Apt, therefore, that his best-known post-war work should be his window in the rebuilt Coventry Cathedral.

Piper lived until his death at Fawley Bottom Farmhouse (known as 'the Bum' by John Betjeman), near Henley on Thames. He moved there with Myfanwy Evans in 1935; and the pair were married two years later, when Piper's divorce from his first wife, Eileen Holding, came through. In his early career he worked as an abstract painter, but just as he was achieving success in that field his interest in architecture and landscape took over— thanks, some say, to his friendship with Betjeman, who lived not far away at Uffington.

His paintings of Blenheim, like those of Windsor (and the Queen Mother had 26 of those, so worried was she that the castle lay in the Luftwaffe's flight path), capture the essence of Englishness; Piper really loved what he saw, but at the same time seemed worried about the future—that is now. How did his lovely pictures of Blenheim come to be painted in the first place? The Duke of Marlborough told me: 'I went out to lunch at a friend's house and saw some paintings by John Piper; then I simply wrote him a letter and asked him to come to Blenheim.' The result was that in 1983 Piper started capturing the spirit of the place in a most beguiling way. Here, for instance, is the Temple of Diana, where Winston Churchill proposed to Clementine Hozier in 1908, and here too are storm clouds lowering in an ominous sort of way above the bridge, with the palace in the background. Churchill said: 'At Blenheim I took two important decisions: to be born and to marry. I am happily content with the decisions I took on both occasions.'

But we are lucky living in Oxfordshire, because so many lesser-known works abound here. I don't know what has happened to the many set designs he produced

Piper tapestry of Green Man, Magdalen Centre, Oxford Science Park

for productions at the Kenton Theatre in Henley, but anyone can go and see windows designed by Piper at St Peter's Church in Wolvercote or, for that matter, at St Mary the Virgin in Turville, or St Mary's in Fawley, or St Paul's in Pishill, or St Bartholomew's in Nettlebed. Then there are tapestries (and a window) at Magdalen College, and yet more windows in Nuffield College —to name but a few.

After visiting the recent exhibition at Blenheim, I for one feel inspired to seek out all these works. In particular I shall go and re-examine the mural at the River and Rowing Museum in Henley. It is on loan from P&O and I saw it first aboard the original liner SS *Oriana* when I was en route for Egypt in 1961. I shall also be one of the first in the queue to visit the museum's exhibition of the Gyselynck collection of Piper paintings. Dorchester Abbey, too, is staging an exhibition entitled 'John Piper and the Church'.

J. R. R. Tolkien

Like medieval seekers of saints' relics, fans of famous authors don't stop at books. Book dealer Rick Gekoski, in 1966 a postgraduate occupant of rooms above those of J. R. R. Tolkien at Merton College, once sold off the great writer's gown for £550.

At that time Tolkien, shuffling about with his pipe and tweeds, was the nearest thing Oxford had to a modern-day celebrity: fans wanting autographs and shouting 'Gandalf lives' in Merton Street must have borne some similarity to pilgrims visiting St Fridewide's well in Binsey several centuries before. *The Lord of the Rings* was published in 1955, but really achieved cult status in the 1960s with the appearance of the paperback edition in the US. But earnest collectors sought out first editions of *The Hobbit*, published back in September 1937.

According to Gekoski's fascinating book about books and their collectors, *Tolkien's Gown* (Constable), the idea for *The Hobbit* sort of jumped out at Tolkien when he was correcting an exam paper. He turned over a page and came across a completely blank sheet. On it, he wrote: 'In a hole in the ground there lived a hobbit.' He said later: 'Names always generate a story in my mind. Eventually, I thought I had better find out what hobbits were like.' Nowadays a first edition of even an unsigned copy of *The Hobbit*, in reasonable condition and with its dust cover (designed by the author) would sell for about £30,000; an inscribed one, about £75,000; an inscribed *Lord of the Rings* about £50,000.

Many of the other books mentioned by Gekoski have strong Oxford connections. First copies of *Brideshead Revisited*, 1944, were inscribed as 'privately printed for the author's friends; no copies are for sale'. The inscription went on to request that no copies be lent 'outside the circle for which they are intended'. What price now for such a book? Gekoski got £16,000 for one inscribed to Graham Greene in 1990.

Oscar Wilde's *The Picture of Dorian Gray* went down a treat in Oxford, described by Gekoski as 'that traditional home for refined homosexuals'. Lord Alfred Douglas, while an undergraduate at Wilde's old college, Magdalen, fell in love with him, and the consequences, leading Wilde to Reading gaol, are well known.

As for selling Tolkien's gown, acquired by his scout who had been asked to clear his rooms, one wonders what market there might be in other garments. Or what about bones? Saintly bones had a price in the old days.

C. S. Lewis

Maybe it was the sight of a large indoor plant placed outside the wardrobe in my room—to make way for the Christmas tree in the dining room—which reminded me of *The Lion the Witch and the Wardrobe* (back to front as it were); or maybe it was the release of the 20th Century Fox film of his Narnia book *The Voyage of the Dawn Treader*—but one way or another I have been thinking about C. S. Lewis (1898-1963) recently.

Or perhaps this cold old winter, tight in the grip of the White Witch, so to speak, reminded me of his poem 'What the Bird Said Early in the Year', inscribed on a plaque in that loveliest of Oxford places, Addison's Walk, in Magdalen College:

'I heard in Addison's Walk a bird sing clear:
This year the summer will come true. This year. This year.
Winds will not strip the blossom from the apple trees
This year nor want of rain destroy the peas.
This year time's nature will no more defeat you.
Nor all the promised moments in their passing cheat you.'

Clive Staples Lewis, always known as Jack to family and friends, was born in Belfast, the younger son of a solicitor. He won a scholarship to Malvern College and then to University College, Oxford, in 1916. He came up to Oxford specifically to train in the Officers Training Corps before seeing active service—and being wounded in April 1918 by an English shell falling short while serving with the Somerset Light Infantry. While training for the army, Lewis made a pact with fellow cadet Edward Moore—known as Paddy—that if either were killed the other would look after both their families. Moore was indeed killed in 1918, aged 19, and, true to his word, after the war, Lewis went to live with the mother of his friend, Jane, and her daughter, Maureen. In 1930 he, Jane, Maureen and his brother Warren moved into the Kilns in Headington Quarry. The Lewis brothers and Jane shared the £3,300 purchase price of the house and large garden.

Whether C. S. Lewis and Jane Moore were lovers has inevitably been the subject of speculation, but suffice to say here that she was 26 years his senior and he referred to her as 'mother'. As for Maureen, known as Daisy, she unexpectedly became a baroness through the family of her father, who was separated from her mother. It was an unusual baronetcy too, which could be passed down the female line, and which she did indeed pass on to her son after her death in 1997. She also inherited a castle, dating from the 15th century, in Caithness. After the death of Warnie Lewis in 1973, she also inherited the Kilns.

In 1956 C. S. Lewis married the American writer Joy Gresham (1915-60) at Oxford Registry Office, and then again, in Anglican form, the next year in the chapel at the Churchill Hospital where she was a patient and believed by many to be dying.

Lewis was elected a fellow of Magdalen College in 1925 having won a First in Literae Humaniores in 1922 and another First in English Language in 1923. (The windows of his rooms in the 18th-century New Building at Magdalen are those with window boxes of flowers—or so I was told when I last visited the college.)

One of his students, John Betjeman, described him as 'breezy, tweedy, beer-drinking and jolly'. Much of his beer drinking was done at the Eagle and Child pub (affectionately called the Birdie and Brat) in St Giles, where the informal group of writers known as the Inklings used to foregather. Other members of the group (of which he was the leading light) included Tolkien and fellow poet and theological writer Charles Williams, who for many years was an employee of the Oxford University Press.

Lewis continued to live at the Kilns as much as he could, even after he was appointed in 1954 to the newly established chair of English Medieval and Renaissance Literature at Cambridge—and swapped Magdalen for Magdalene College. He died at the Kilns and is buried at Holy Trinity Church in Headington. The garden of the Kilns is now a nature reserve.

John Betjeman

What was the ancestry of Aloysius, the famous teddy bear belonging to Sebastian Flyte in *Brideshead Revisited*? Some say that his creator, Evelyn Waugh, conceived him after hearing about John Betjeman's bear, whose name was Archibald Ormsby Gore, 'born' in 1908—two years before Betjeman himself came into the world (1906-84).

Quite why Betjeman's bear was called that, no one knows; presumably Betjeman just loved the name of this distinguished old Welsh family and decided to align his bear to it. He wrote in 1931, 14 years before the publication of *Brideshead*:

> 'There was once an elderly bear
> Whose head was the shape of a pear.
> He sat in deep gloom
> And longed for the tomb
> As he had lost nearly all of his hair.'

In any case I cannot help thinking that Betjeman at Oxford, where I believe the bear accompanied him to Magdalen College in 1925, was far more like Charles Ryder, the narrator, than Sebastian Flyte. He was an observer of grand people rather than actually being one himself.

Like Ryder, Betjeman came from comparatively humble origins in London, the son of a furniture manufacturer; but at Oxford he was intrigued, for instance, by a peer who rushed round a college quadrangle shouting: 'I am as drunk as the lord that I am'.

At Magdalen his first tutor was the Reverend J. M. Thompson, of whom he wrote: 'rumour had it that he had been defrocked for preaching in Magdalen College Chapel that the miracles were performed by electricity'; and his second tutor was C. S. Lewis, with whom he did not get on, and described as 'breezy, tweedy, beer-drinking and jolly'.

He was of course a great analyser of people and places. For instance, he saw three Oxfords: the Christminster of Thomas Hardy's *Jude the Obscure*; Oxford University; and something he called Motopolis, which he abhorred. As to people, he divided undergraduates into two types: aesthetes and hearties. He wrote: 'Hearties were good college men who rowed in the college boat, ate in the college hall and drank beer and shouted. Their regulation uniform was college tie, college pullover, tweed coat and grey flannel trousers. Aesthetes, on the other hand, wore whole suits, silk ties of single colour and sometimes— but only for a week or two while they were fashionable—trousers of cream or strawberry pink flannel. They let their hair grow long and never found out, as I never found out, where the college playing fields were or which was the college barge.'

These were glitterati, either really rich or at any rate able to obtain credit, whom he sometimes called Georgians because they dined at The George, which until the 1940s stood on the corner of George Street and Cornmarket, 'where there was a band consisting of three ladies and where punkahs suspended from from the ceiling, swayed to and fro, dispelling the smoke from Egyptian and Balkan cigarettes'.

Leafing through some of what he would probably describe as 'hack' work (he famously described himself in *Who's Who* as a 'poet and hack' I found it impossible not to marvel at how much the place, both town and gown, has changed in the last 80 years—possibly more than in the preceding 200 years, even taking into account the various Royal Commissions etc. that triggered such dramatic changes in the 19th century as the building of his beloved North Oxford.

He wrote in his guidebook, *An Oxford University Chest* (1938): 'To escapists, to arty people like the author of these pages, the internal combustion engine is, next to wireless, the most sinister modern

invention. It booms overhead with its cargo of bombs, it roars down the lanes with its cargo of cads, it poisons the air, endangers the streets, deafens the ears and deadens the senses.

Betjeman left Oxford without a degree. As for Waugh, Betjeman described him as an 'accurate and learned observer'. Perhaps the two bears, Aloysius and Archibald, were sort of observers of the observers.

Barbara Pym

Barbara Pym (1913-80) had a life of ups and downs when it came to literary success and failure. At the age of 16, inspired by Aldous Huxley's *Crome Yellow*, she attempted her first book, *Young Men in Fancy Dress*, which now resides in the Pym Archives at the Bodleian Library.

Her first published novel was *Some Tame Gazelle*, written in 1935, shortly after she graduated from St Hilda's College, Oxford. It was about two unassuming but churchy spinster sisters in their 50s living in a rural setting, some 30 years before she and her younger sister Hilary did exactly that in Finstock. But it failed to find a publisher until 1950.

Then, throughout the 1950s, Jonathan Cape published her work. That was until 1963, when her seventh book, *An Unsuitable Attachment*, was rejected for being old-fashioned. She and her writing were plunged into the wilderness.

Her fortunes were suddenly revived, however, when in January 1977 both Philip Larkin and Oxford don Lord David Cecil, who lived down the road from Barbara Pym in Wilcote, named her in *The Times Literary Supplement* as 'the most underrated novelist in the country'.

Poignantly enough, in 1981, the year after Barbara Pym died of cancer at Sobell House Hospice in Oxford, OUP published—with proceeds to Oxfam—her *Places: An Anthology of Britain*, which was month-by-month notes on a year in west Oxfordshire, with contributions by well-known authors and poets, chosen by Ronald Blythe.

What of the year she chronicled in *Places*? She prefaced it with the paragraph: 'Every writer probably keeps some kind of diary or notebook, and my own (mercifully less personal and introspective as the years go on) has provided these few observations on the weather and natural surroundings, history and associations of the area.'

For April she noted that four kittens were born in time for a warm Easter; then, immediately afterwards, came the observation: 'Finstock church is neither ancient nor particularly beautiful but it has the distinction of being the place where T. S. Eliot was received into the Church of England on 29 June 1927.'

In August she visited nearby Ditchley Park, open to the public in that month. Bawdy poet John Wilmot, Earl of Rochester, to whom she refers often in *Some Tame Gazelle*, was born there in 1647. She remarked 'that his poems are hymns—to girls' and quotes: 'My Love, thou art my way, my life, my light.' Diarist John Evelyn noted that Ditchley was in his day 'a low timber house with a pretty bowling green'.

After Ditchley, Barbara Pym visited Spelsbury church where Rochester, who died at High Lodge, near Combe Gate in Blenheim Park, then part of the royal estate of

Woodstock, is buried. She wrote: 'In the churchyard outside is the large square-oblong tomb where the Cary family are said to be buried, but the top is broken and there is a scattering of bones (can they be human bones?), dry and grey-white.'

Now the unassuming people of whom she wrote, and the values they represent, are treasured by her many admirers. She spent the last years of her life during the 1970s in Finstock, home of the Finstock Friendly Society which was set up in the 19th century to help villagers through hard times. And in 2006 a blue plaque was put up to her memory on the two sisters' modest home, Barn Cottage. There is even a Barbara Pym Society, which holds a regular annual conference.

II. Customs and Legends
Rural Traditions

It is tempting to peer back at life in pre-industrial Oxfordshire and think of it as a sort of golden age; but take a quick look at the ways in which our forebears used to enjoy themselves on their days off and it becomes immediately apparent just how very different we have become from them—and in a remarkably short period of time too. Basic attitudes to life on earth have changed so much, and overall probably for the better.

Considering how much has improved, I sometimes find it hard to identify with former inhabitants of the county at all. As little as a couple of centuries ago, for instance, bull, bear and badger baiting were commonplace. There was a thriving bull baiting club at Oxford University until 1826, and even parsons were not averse to watching the sport of baiting bears, if the diaries of the Reverend Francis Witts, born in the Cotswold village of Swerford in 1783, are anything to judge by. A completely unsanitised attitude to the grim realities of life and death pertained. Dog fighting and and cock fighting remained popular pastimes, only frowned upon by the authorities because they tended to encourage gambling. Then of course there was the occasional public execution, with spectators getting up early and walking long distances to watch. The last public execution at Oxford Prison, now a hotel, was in 1863.

But how did this huge change in mindset between then and now come about? Until recently, of course, people were compelled—to a far greater degree than now—to make their own entertainment in a world that was not media-dominated; but the great change in the way ordinary people behaved in their leisure time came about in the mid 19th century when many traditional customs began to be frowned upon by an increasingly straight-laced Victorian clergy, aided and abetted by a powerful temperance movement. Morris dancing met with stony disapproval throughout the late 19th century and might well have disappeared had not that great champion of folklore, Cecil Sharp, rescued the tradition. In 1900 he began recording the tunes and steps of the Headington Quarry dancers, thereby saving tunes for posterity that might otherwise have been lost forever.

Time and again Oxfordshire vicars, and indeed others of high social standing, suppressed the old ways on the grounds that they encouraged lewdness, drunkenness, fighting and general subversion—or sometimes even because there was a suspicion of paganism; though locals sometimes found ways of continuing their customs all the same. In Charlton-on-Otmoor, for instance, the Reverend George Riggs removed the extraordinary evergreen statue-cum-crucifix known as 'Our Lady' from the rood screen in 1854; but villagers reinstated her as soon as he had left the village

Oxfordshire also contained a particularly large area of Royal Forest until the 19th century, so enclosure of common land, together with cutting down the old forests, had a more than usually severe impact on old customs. Indeed one reason given for destroying the forest of Wychwood was that it encouraged lawlessness among those who roamed about in it. Certainly the Forest Fair held there was famous for its rowdiness.

Nowadays, though, fairs and customs are comparatively sober events, with the possible exception of May Day in Oxford. Even fairs such as Oxford's St Giles and the Witney Feast are tame compared to years gone by. It all goes to show that customs and traditions themselves change or disappear in accordance with changing ideas about what is or is not acceptable. Hence the cruelty debate which still rages in rural Oxfordshire over fox hunting, with many still claiming that present laws are unsatisfactory.

Michaelmas

About this time of year I often visit a certain walnut tree in open country near my old home in Combe. This is partly because it stands near a favourite mushroom field, the secret location of which I am not about to tell; partly because I like eating walnuts; and partly because I enjoy planting trees. The oldest tree I have planted is now 25 and producing nuts itself.

Seasons change, but none can have changed—or declined—as much as the period leading up to the quarter day of Michaelmas (29 September, the feast of St Michael and All Angels), which for centuries was celebrated with almost as much gusto as Christmas but is now barely given a passing nod, except perhaps at Oxford University where the ensuing term is at least still allowed to bear its name.

The run-up to the feast included Holy Rood Day on 14 September, also known as the Devil's Nutting Day, on which youths and maids would 'go a-nutting', an expression which crops up in songs and plays from the 16th century onwards as a byword for sex and seduction—with a tradition, dating back to the time of Charles II, that a good year for nuts was also a good year for babies.

In Oxfordshire, nuts were a great source of free food for poor farm workers— until, that is, the 1930s, when walnut wood was in high demand for car dashboards and cocktail cabinets. Indeed, my particular walnut tree was once for the axe. Luckily, its trunk was found to be split and it was spared. Michaelmas Eve was known as Crack-Nut Day and nuts were cracked in church.

On Michaelmas Day anyone who could afford it ate a 'stubble goose' —a bird reared that year and prepared around harvest time. It was held that anyone who did not eat one would lack money in the coming year. Printers and publishers held a feast called 'wayzgoose' to mark the changing season and the advent of the period in which they would need to work by candle light.

Michaelmas was sometimes called Pack Rag Day because so many people were busy changing their accommodation and jobs. This was the season of hiring fairs, or mops, which persisted in Oxfordshire until the turn of the 19th century and were not finally killed off until the First World War. Labourers and would-be serving girls turned up to be hired for the coming year. They carried symbols of their trades in their button-holes, such as a piece of whipcord for a carter, a piece of sponge for a groom gardener, or a piece of straw for a thatcher—which was replaced with a piece of ribbon when the wearer was hired. The mops were often followed by a second 'Runanaway Mop' the next week, for those who had either not been lucky first time around, or had found their contract had somehow fallen through.

Oxfordshire mops included those at Abingdon, a hiring fair with a large funfair element on the first Monday and Tuesday after Michaelmas, with a Runaway the following week; Banbury, on the first Thursday after Old Michaelmas (10 October); Bicester, three October fairs known as Hiring, Runaway and Confirmation; Burford on 25 September; Chipping Norton, on the Wednesday before 11 October; Deddington, on 30 September; Faringdon, in mid-October with a Runaway ten days later; Henley, on the first Thursday after 21 September; Thame, on Old Michaelmas Day; Wallingford, on the last Wednesday in September; and Wantage, in mid-October. In Deddington and Stratford (Warwickshire) ox roasting formed part of the feast.

What with the harvest safely home, going a-nutting and a year's wages in workers' pockets, September must have been a merry month for many. So merry that Victorian middle classes worried greatly about the morality of hiring fairs. In Burford, for instance, girls seeking employment transferred to a room upstairs in the Tolsey, away from the young men; and in Banbury they were moved to an upstairs room in Parsons Street.

The Times in 1858 fulminated against mops. It said that drink was the curse of the working classes. Funny that; I thought everyone knew (thanks to Wilde) that work was the curse of the drinking classes.

All Souls Day

Doubtless the Fellows of All Souls College will be up to their tricks again next November, singing their dread song while the port circulates around the dining table on All Souls Day, November 2.

The college was founded by Henry VI and Archbishop Chichele in 1438 to commemorate the Faithful Departed, namely those souls suffering in purgatory, itself a sort of medieval waiting room between here and heaven—or hell, depending on your ultimate destination.

The date of All Souls Day was decided in the 11th century by a hermit who told the Abbot of Cluny that he had heard the groans of a few souls in purgatory. Cluny, in France, was the senior abbey to Fécamp, which in turn held the lordship of the manor of some Oxfordshire parishes—including Cogges near Witney—following the Norman Conquest. The day comes straight after the feast of All Saints, or All Hallows on November 1, which celebrates those souls who have made it to heaven already, without stopping off in purgatory on the way. All Hallows replaces a much earlier pagan festival celebrating the Dead Departed, and is increasingly celebrated nowadays on All Hallows Eve, known as Hallowe'en, on October 31.

But of the many Oxfordshire tales of the things that go bump in the night, one of the creepiest concerns death foretold. The Reverend J. C. Blomfield, rural dean of Bicester in the late 19th century, tells the tale in his History of the Deanery of Bicester. Geoffrey Shaw, a graduate of St John's College, Cambridge, became vicar of Souldern in North Oxfordshire in 1698. He was sitting in his vicarage late one night, having a quiet smoke, when a former fellow student came in and joined him—which was odd, since the gentleman had been dead two years. Odder was the fact that the spectre, a former vicar of Enstone named Nailor, then told him that another acquaintance, a Mr Orchard of Cambridge, was to die very suddenly and that he, Geoffrey Shaw, would then follow suit shortly afterwards.

Odder still, and the fact that set university high tables chattering in both Oxford and Cambridge, was that Mr Orchard did die as predicted, while his servant was out of his room fetching his supper. Oddest of all was that Shaw told his friend, the Cambridge public registrar named Mr Grove, this strange tale before he himself collapsed and died on Sunday, 17 November 1706 while reading the lesson at evensong in Souldern church. And Grove in turn told the tale to several Cambridge dons, also before the death, including the then university vice-chancellor, Dr Balderston.

Blomfield, in his *History*, notes that in the 1890s the Bible from which Shaw was reading at the time of his sudden death was still in the church, complete with a note marking the text from which he was reading at the time. As for the spectre, Mr Nailor, his gravestone in Enstone churchyard reads that he died 'grievously dispirited in the house of the Lord'.

The vicarage at Souldern was made famous a century later by William Wordsworth. He was a friend of the then vicar, Robert Jones, and produced the poem 'A Parsonage in Oxfordshire'. Unfortunately, it seems that the poem is about the vicarage that stood there before being replaced by the present Victorian house.

Christmas

Funny old thing, tradition. Most of us might think of turkey or goose as the traditional food of Christmas, but the dons of The Queen's College, Oxford, know better. They have been stuffing their faces with Boar's Head at a Yuletide feast every year since the 14th century.

The boar's head was an essential part of a grand Christmas, at court, say, or even at a rich squire's manor in the English countryside, right up until the early Industrial Revolution when the old social hierarchy began to break down and wild boars became scarce in England, though they still abound in France where the meat is often eaten at Christmas. The ceremony involves a trumpet fanfare as the head, complete with an apple or lemon in its gaping mouth, is borne into the hall on a gold or silver platter and the Boar's Head carol is sung in Latin.

Trust a college at Oxford, 'whispering from her towers of lost enchantments of the Middle Ages. Home of lost causes and forsaken beliefs' (to quote Matthew Arnold) to keep up the old ways. Presumably, once the Hilary term got under way, those lucky dons who ate the poor old boar this time round must have packed away their memories, along with their Christmas decorations, and be getting down to work again. Unless, that is, they truly believe in lost causes, in which case they will only have got round to celebrating the end of Christmas on 17 January, to be precise.

True to form, Oxford and Oxfordshire people were vociferous in objecting to the introduction to England of the Gregorian calendar in 1752 which, they said, 'robbed' them of 11 days. Right up until the start of the 20th century some people on the Oxfordshire/Gloucestershire border continued to celebrate the Old Christmas Day on 5 January, and therefore the 12th day of Christmas, Epiphany, on 17 January.

One person who has still not accepted the Gregorian calendar, though, is the English taxman. Before Pope Gregory decreed his calendar in 1582 (130 years before England finally accepted it), the start of the new year was 25 March, the feast of the immaculate conception. And that explains why, taking into account the 'robbed' 11 days, 6 April is now the start of the English (and UK's) financial year.

But to return to that wild boar. The academics of The Queen's College claim that their feast has nothing to do with Christmas at all, which might explain why their celebration was not suppressed when Christmas was officially banned by the Puritans 1649-60. The dons claim they are celebrating the miraculous deliverance of one of their number who, out walking one day in Shotover Forest, was charged by a boar. He was wandering about with a copy of Aristotle at the time, so he shoved the volume into the boar's mouth and choked it to death!

And why is the first term in the modern new year called Hilary term? Because its start falls on or near St Hilary's day, 13 January, reputedly the coldest day of the year: in the winter of 1891, a horse-drawn coach complete with passengers and weighing nearly 7 tons was driven along the frozen Thames.

May Day

Could May morning singing from the top of Magdalen College tower date right back to 1509? Possibly. Benefactor of the college King Henry VII died on 21 April that year and 1 May could have been chosen as the day to commemorate him—perhaps combining the Christian Requiem Mass with a much earlier pagan custom of welcoming in the spring. But the truth is that no one knows exactly how, or why, or even when the custom started.

In the 16th and 17th centuries several colleges celebrated May morning, with New College even putting on a rival singing performance from the top of its tower—though historian Anthony Wood noted that this ceremony was stopped 'because Magdalen College men and the rabble of the towns came on May Day to their disturbance'. He went on to describe how, after the New College singing, a crowd of people would form a procession to St Bartholomew's Hospital in the Cowley Road 'with their lords and ladyes, garland, fifes, flutes and drumms to salute the great goddess Flora and to attribute to her all praise with dancing and music'.

In Shepilinda's *Memoirs of the City and University of Oxford*, written in 1737, a particularly colourful practice is recorded: 'The tradition of this is, that once upon a time the tradesmen of this City went all out a gathering May in a morning, in which time their wives made them all cuckolds.'

Then historian John Pointer wrote in *Oxoniensis Academia* in 1749: 'Another remarkable tradition is having a Concert of Music upon the Top of the Tower, every May Day, at four o'clock in the Morning, in commemoration of King Henry VII the Founder of the Tower, being at first a Mass of Requiem, or Mass sung for the Rest of his Soul.'

Garlands still feature in the unique Oxfordshire May Day goings-on at Charlton-on-Otmoor. On May Day the children of the village carry an evergreen garland, sometimes called the 'lady', into the church. It is made in the shape of a cross that manages also to resemble a woman, and is put on top of the beautiful rood screen (the best in the county, according to Pevsner) in the church of the Virgin Mary, and then kept there until the feast of the Virgin on 19 September, when it is replaced.

In Christine Bloxham's book *May Day to Mummers: Folklore and Traditional Customs in Oxfordshire* (Wychwood Press, 2002), she wrote that the woman who 'dressed' the garland in 1980 'talked about giving the lady a waist and putting buttons of wild flowers down her bodice'. A theory about the Otmoor lady is that she replaces, like a sort of ghost, a statue of the Virgin that stood on the rood screen until the Reformation.

In Oxford, garlands, flowers, and music of sorts also formed an important part of the May Day revelries for several centuries. Until the early 20th century, girls made garlands, or crosses, of flowers. They carried them round the city begging for money before depositing them in churches. The boys, meanwhile, set up a din by blowing cow's horns or hollow canes. Even 100 years ago there would have been much playing of tin pipes and penny whistles on May morning, and there was also a procession through Oxford of the brewers' dray horses and carts.

Oak Apple Day

The day of King Charles II's Restoration, 29 May, his 30th birthday, was for more than a century a holiday known as Royal Oak Apple Day, after an Act of Parliament decreed that 'the day be forever kept as a day of thanksgiving for our redemption from tyranny and the king's returning to his government'. Special prayers were the order of the day in churches throughout the land until 1859, when they were removed from the prayer book.

Particularly in Royalist Oxford and Oxfordshire you might have expected some fuss to mark the occasion; after all Oxford was the Royalist capital of England during the Civil War and Charles II, too, called a Parliament here in 1665, having fled the Plague in London. Nowadays, the occasion is only marked by toasts being drunk in a few Oxford colleges; but the custom, until about 100 years ago, was for people to wear a sprig of oak in their lapels or hats—perhaps with a gilded oak apple attached—and for children to run around with nettles, with which to sting anyone not wearing an oak buttonhole.

The oak sprig buttonholes, of course, commemorated the tree in which Charles II, alongside a soldier with the remarkable name of Colonel Careless, had hidden after his defeat at the hands of Oliver Cromwell's forces at the Battle of Worcester in 1651. After that battle, incidentally, Cromwell's soldiers mistook Arthur Jones of Chastleton for the fugitive king and chased him to Chastleton House, where they found his horse but not him. He only escaped capture by hiding in a closet while his wife drugged the soldiers' wine and sent them to sleep!

In Charlbury, home to Charles's Lord Chancellor, Edward Hyde, the Earl of Clarendon (who lived at Cornbury Park), celebrations of Oak Apple Day were especially exuberant. Well into the 20th century, children would go round the houses early in the morning and decorate the knocker or lintel with oak branches. They would call again later in the day and ask for money and, if none was forthcoming, chant 'Shig-shag, penny a rag. Bang his head in Cromwell's bag'.

The reference to Cromwell in that Charlbury ditty is sinister, though. Oliver Cromwell was buried with much pomp in 1658, but three years later his body was dug up and hanged at Tyburn, with the head afterwards cut off and stuck on a pole at Westminster Hall, where it remained until 1684. Not until 1960, the 300th anniversary of the Restoration, was it buried at Cromwell's old college, Sidney Sussex, Cambridge, in an unmarked grave—though to this day no one knows what happened to the rest of his body. Somehow, the macabre event underlines Cambridge's Parliamentarian sympathies, as opposed to Oxford's Royalist ones.

As far as Oxford was concerned, when Charles Stuart set out for England from the Dutch beach of Scheveningen in 1660, the feeling of intellectual release from Puritan repression was nowhere more keenly felt than here, where such men as Robert Boyle, Robert Hook and Christopher Wren formed the nucleus of what was to become the Royal Society under the king's patronage. Indeed, much of the university remained obstinately Jacobite and loyal to the Stuart cause, even after the Crown passed to the Hanoverians. And in Oxfordshire as a whole, Charles was a familiar and popular figure, particularly in Burford where he often attended horse races with Nell Gwyn. Indeed he created their son the Earl of Burford.

There were just a few anti-Royalists, however: antiquarian and historian Thomas Hearne, for example, lost his job as a keeper at the Bodleian when he refused to take the oath of allegiance to George I.

Harvest

If rising food prices are a worry now, spare a thought for the pre-First World War inhabitants of rural Oxfordshire. For them August was a busy but anxious month: joy if the harvest was brought home successfully; otherwise despair and the prospect of real hunger.

The last cart of corn was decorated with flowers, ribbons and greenery, with women and children riding on top of the load singing at the tops of their voices. At the front of the wagon would be a man and woman, dressed in finery, representing the king and queen of the harvest.

Harvest 1958, guessing the pumpkin's weight in Clifton Hampden

In this last respect, though, things were apparently not always what they seemed. *Folk-Lore* magazine in 1902 described an Oxfordshire harvest home of some 70 years earlier: 'On the last night of the harvest, when the load was to be carted, it was the custom to send down to the fields a number of band-boxes containing women's dresses and a good deal of finery for the men and horses. Four young men then dressed themselves up, two to represent women, and they sat in couples on the four horses that drew the load.' Also in that magazine, they noted that in Culham any man who lagged behind the others, and was therefore thought to be lazy, would be told 'he had got the Little White Dog'—though quite why is unclear.

At Sandford-on-Thames the farmer used to provide a gallon of beer to greet the last load—as well he might, since the reapers used to sing a song that contained the lines:

'Our bottles are empty, our barrels won't run,
And we think it a very dry harvest home.'

In fact, few harvest homes in Oxfordshire were dry. In 1872, *Notes & Queries* magazine noted that from 'every house they passed, buckets of water were thrown on them'.

It seems that it was also customary for girls to hide behind hedges and pelt the last load with apples. At Cottisford in the 1880s, as Flora Thompson recorded in *Lark Rise to Candleford*, a King of the Mowers was elected. She wrote: 'With a wreath of poppies and green bindweed trails around his wide, rush-plaited hat, he led the band down the swathes as they mowed and decreed when and for how long they should halt for a breather, and what drink should be had from the yellow stone jar they kept under the hedge in a shady corner of the field.'

Nothing in the agricultural year united a village in a common cause quite like the harvest. Everyone depended on it, from the squire to the smallest child, but a few strange customs to do with hierarchy persisted. For instance, on some farms, if the farmer himself appeared in a field being mowed, he would be given the bumps, that is, thrown up in the air and caught again by the women workers. And if a stranger crossed the field, 'largesse' would be demanded.

Once the harvest was safely home, a harvest supper would of course be on the menu. In Victorian Oxfordshire, however, there were early calls to tame the traditional rowdiness. Already in 1864 a diarist of Lower Heyford, James Dew, recorded that combined harvest suppers, rather than the old single-farm affairs, were coming into fashion—and were far more decorous.

Possible remnants of customs dating right back to medieval times and the tithes (tenths) demanded by the abbots remained till late. The monasteries in pre-Reformation time kept their share of the corn in tithe barns such as the one in Great Coxwell, one of the finest in England, which belonged to the Cistercian Abbey of Beaulieu. Even in the 19th century there was a ceremony about cutting the very last sheaf of corn, which was apparently reminiscent of the way serfs of long ago would tie up the corn that they were allowed to take home for their own use.

Otter Hunting

The otter hunting ban of 1978 was a very different kettle of fish to the more or less ineffective attempt to ban fox hunting in 2004. It had teeth, and the most ancient form of hunting with hounds ceased from one day to the next—despite fierce opposition to the ban from such powerful groups as the British Field Sports Society.

The Cherwell valley—in particular land between Hampton Gay and Rousham—was for centuries (from the 1200s) prime otter-hunting country; and though few would probably now dispute that the practice really did represent the 'unspeakable chasing the uneatable', it reached its zenith of popularity in the years just before the First World War—extraordinarily enough, just at the time that Kenneth Grahame's *Wind in the Willows* gained popularity—and only tailed off as otters became scarce.

Originally otters were hunted for their pelts, then as pests, since they competed with man for fish, and then purely for sport. Even in the elegant gardens designed by William Kent at Rousham, pride of place is given to the grave of an otter-hound called Ringwood, described as 'an otter-hound of extraordinary Sagacity'. And the hound's eulogistic epitaph goes on to challenge otters everywhere not to 'Dare pollute my Ringwood's tomb'. Ironic that, since pollution from fertilisers caused the catastrophic decline of the otter in the 1950s and 1960s.

Prolific Victorian historian of parishes around Bicester, the Reverend J. C. Blomfield, described a Cherwell hunt: 'When the otter is found the scene becomes exceedingly animated. He instantly takes the water and dives, remaining a long time underneath it, and rising a considerable distance from the place at which he went in.' He goes on to make the desperate sequel sound eerily like a small-scale whaling scene: 'Then the anxious watch which is kept of his rising to 'vent'; the steady purpose with which the dogs follow him, and bait him as he swims; the attempts of the cunning beast to drown his assailants by diving while they have fastened on him; the baying of the hounds; the cries of the hunters, and the fierce dogged resolution with which the poor hopeless quarry holds his pursuers at bay, inflicting severe, sometimes fatal wounds, and holding on with unflinching pertinacity, even to the last, form a scene as animated and exciting as the veriest epicure in hunting could desire.'

Victorian diarist George Dew, who lived in nearby Lower Heyford, describes how a visiting pack of otter-hounds, which had already killed 30 otters that year, arrived by train at Heyford in the spring of 1874, with huntsmen dressed in blue uniforms. 'They found an otter in Northbrook and drove him to Enser's Mill at Kirtlington where they killed him after about four hours' hunt, the water at this point being deep.'

Otter hunting was effectively banned in England and Wales because the Countryside and Wildlife Act of 1978 made it an offence to kill or disturb an otter or harm a holt. Few would dispute now that one of the best occurrences of recent Oxfordshire history has been the reappearance of the shy otter in the county's rivers. Let's hope that one day the water rat follows suit.

Smoked Eels

For about a decade now I have enjoyed eliciting Yuletide squeals from work colleagues by the simple expedient of placing an eel on my desk. Once the squawk was so loud that it surprised people working in the advertising department, about 50 yards away. Very satisfactory.

But only this year have I begun to understand the almost mystical joy of eating a smoked eel of, say, 2 feet long: gnawing his vertebrae, scraping his shiny skin for the chewiest bits, savouring his oils, and the rest. I came to this deep understanding at a solitary repast the other day, during which I finished up this year's specimen—bought at the excellent fish market in Osney Mead, opposite *The Oxford Times* office—without anyone else being there to voice their usual comments of mixed disgust and fascination. As with oysters, when you feel you are eating the essence of the sea—so with eels. But with this difference: you find yourself eating the essence of rivers too.

Little wonder that, according to Alexandre Dumas' *Le Grand Dictionnaire de Cuisine*, 'the [ancient] Egyptians placed eels on a par with the gods'. Recent diligent research into medieval compost heaps and latrines at monasteries and colleges has proved, beyond doubt, that for centuries, indeed millennia, the people of Oxfordshire ate prodigious quantities of eels, hauled from the River Thames and its tributaries. So important, indeed, were eels as a source of protein that they even acted as a sort of currency. In the 11th century, according to the Chronicle of Abingdon Abbey, the people of Oxford paid the monks a hundred eels a year in return for being allowed to dig a navigable channel on the Thames at Thrupp, near Radley.

The Domesday Book (1086) records 22 eel fisheries along the Thames, producing 14,500 eels a year in tax revenue. And a mill at Cassington—near the point where the

Evenlode flows into the Thames, just above the toll bridge at Swinford—alone paid rent to the Abingdon monks of 175 eels a year. Now, however, there are few Evenlode eels about, their numbers having fallen to about 1 per cent of what they once were, according to the Environment Agency.

On the Windrush, too, the slippery fellow has fared no better—though Domesday assessed the eel fishery at Taynton to be worth 62s 6d a year. I learned much of this information from *The Book of Eels* (HarperCollins, 2002), a wonderful book by local author Tom Fort, which I took from the shelf after eating my own eel—which, incidentally, had made its first appearance at table, in accordance with tradition, on Christmas Eve.

The cause of the spectacular decline of Oxfordshire eels is easy to pinpoint: namely the spectacular rise of London humans during the 19th century. Between 1800 and 1880 the capital's population grew from under 1 million to nearly 5 million (with all their sewage, along with waste from tanneries, slaughterhouses and the like) going straight into the Thames. The result was that MPs were unable to sit in Parliament during the Great Stink of 1858, and that fish life was all but extinguished at the mouth of the Thames. The elver run up river, and the silver eel run down—which for centuries were sources of food and fun for Londoners—became things of the past, though Londoners continued to enjoy eel pie and jellied eels, thanks to imports.

The picturesque eel baskets, or bucks, as depicted in Tenniel's illustration of Godstow Lock in *Alice in Wonderland* also became things of the past, though Alice herself would have been familiar with eels. In the poem 'You are Old, Father William' the old man balances an eel on the end of his nose. Both Alice and Lewis Carroll compared Alice's art teacher—none other than John Ruskin—to an eel, who taught Alice 'drawling, stretching, and fainting in coils'.

But be that as it may, I predict that telly chefs will soon rediscover the humble eel—though their resulting resurgence will mean more being caught in Holland and Scandinavia, not in the Thames.

Sundials

The business of telling the time was a very haphazard affair until well into the 19th century. Then the introduction of trains, and the necessity for them to run according to a timetable, caused a certain amount of standardisation.

All this exercised the minds of Oxford University dons considerably. They warded off the railway from Oxford's city centre until comparatively late, worrying that trains would enable undergraduates to escape too easily to the fleshpots of London and

generally undermine the dons' authority. And, of course, the cathedral, which is also the college chapel of Christ Church, still officially runs to a different time to the rest of the country—five minutes behind everyone else.

One early sundial, in the form of a column, stands in the quad of Corpus Christi. Built in 1580, it is officially called the Turnbull Dial, after its maker Charles Turnbull, but it is more usually known as the Pelican, after the stone bird that surmounts it. Until 1706 the sundial only worked in summer. That year it was dismantled and placed on a plinth to increase its height and enable it to catch a few rays, even in winter.

From about 1653 the academics at All Souls could tell the time accurately enough, provided it was a sunny day. That year Sir Christopher Wren was made a Fellow of the college and it was about then that he designed the great sundial there, bearing the ponderous motto '*Pereunt et Imputantur*', meaning that the hours pass away and are set down to our charge, a quote, I am told, from Martial's *Epigrammata*. It was originally placed in the First Quad but later moved to its present site in the North Quad. Wren said of it: 'One may see to a minute what it is o'clock, the minute being depicted on the sides of the rays.'

But even without any very accurate means of telling the time, the eternal questions of time and space had bothered minds for centuries, not only in the university but out and about in the countryside, too. But perhaps the oddest manifestation of pre-railway thinking about time and space has nothing to do with the university at all. About half a mile from the village of Wroxton in north Oxfordshire, at the North Newington turn on the A422, is a remarkable signpost-cum-sundial made of Hornton stone and dating (though much restored) from 1686. Each of its four sides bears carvings of male and female hands (identified by rings on the fingers) pointing travellers on their way. It was skilfully restored in 1974 by local stonemason George Carter.

Witney's clock and sundial, on top of the Buttercross—until the 1950s the place where sheep were bought and sold—are successors of those made thanks to a 1683 bequest by William Blake of Cogges. Also in Witney is the single-handed 18th-century clock on the Blanket Hall, similar to the one at Garsington church, where the hours are rung on a bell and the hands tell the quarter hours.

But back to Oxford and those dons preoccupied with the mysteries of time, space—and trains. The Reverend Spooner (1844-1930), warden of New College, when expelling an undergraduate, is alleged to have said: 'You have hissed all of my mystery lectures. Now you must leave Oxford by the town drain.'

Ghosts

Stories of ghosts, witches and things that go bump in the night are alive and well in the Cotswolds. Some have been investigated and chronicled by the wise men of Oxford.

Take the first major battle of the English Civil War, for instance: Edgehill, fought near Stratford on 23 October 1642, with the Royalist cavalry claiming victory under Prince Rupert. Already by December of that year, on Christmas Eve, 'shepherds and other countrymen, together with certain wayfarers' were reporting a ghostly re-enactment of the engagement which had left more than a thousand dead on the field. They had heard 'first the sound of drums afar off and the noises of soldiers, as it were, giving out their last groans'. King Charles I, then living in Oxford, having made the university city the Royalist capital of England, sent officers off to the battlefield to investigate. Amazingly, they reported back after a week 'wherein they heard and saw the aforementioned prodigies distinctly knowing divers of the apparitions, or incorporeal substances by their faces, as that of Sir Edmund Varney and others that were slain, of which upon oath they made testimony to his Majesty'.

Historians noted those quotes in a contemporary pamphlet, 'Seventeenth-century Oxford'. And the 17th-century Anthony Wood took an interest in witches: his papers, now in the Bodleian Library, bear testimony to his investigation of the Camden Wonder, during which a nobleman's rent collector disappeared suddenly. Three servants were hanged for murder, then the rent collector reappeared claiming to have been kidnapped and sold as a slave in Turkey.

Oxfordshire exorcisms over the centuries have involved laying ghosts in ponds. Alexander Pope, who translated much of the *Odyssey* in the tower that bears his name at Stanton Harcourt, wrote of the ghost of a Lady Harcourt who had been murdered in the room he used as a study. He said her spirit roamed about until laid to rest in one of the ponds.

A ghost at the Manor House in Bampton was first laid in a pond. When the pond dried up, it reappeared. This time it was laid in a cask of strong beer and walled up! Other reputed ghosts include a medieval nun at the Weston Manor Hotel, who was apparently burned at the stake. Then there is Cowleas Corner, on the road between Bampton and Clanfield, where suicides used to be buried at dead of night. And many more can be found in J. A. Brooks, *Ghosts and Witches of the Cotswolds* (1981).

Dialect

'That cake was proper unked and he was in a proper swivet you.' If you don't understand what I am talking about, you probably have not lived in Stonesfield, in west Oxfordshire, for the last half century or so. But were (or are) those old words in use throughout the county or just in Stonesfield? I don't know. And a ramble through such online versions that exist of that wonderful work, Joseph Wright's six-volume *English Dialect Dictionary*, has not enlightened me much, though 'unked' is there.

Angie Ware, a reader of this column who comes from a family of Stonesfield-ites that has lived in that village for generations, is intrigued by the dialect still spoken in that softest Oxfordshire accent by some people living there, and she wonders just how local particular words are. For instance, in the language of Stonesfor (as dialect talkers call Stonesfield), 'unked' means horrible, and 'in a swivet' translates as 'in a state' in the standard English most of us speak these days.

She writes: 'In general, Stonesfield folk always added the word "you" on the end of sentences. "Thee" and "thou" were used until the 1940s and 50s and I remember my grandfather using "thee" and "thou" during my childhood in the 1960s when he would regale us with tales of his time on the Somme at the sunken road of Goosycour.' She adds: 'I keep meaning to get out a map of France to find out exactly where the sunken road of Goosycour actually was.'

But perhaps—and this is only a suggestion on my part—it was the name of a particular wartime trench, many of which were called sunken roads and, in some cases, named after London streets.

Be that as it may, she continues with more examples of Stonesfor speak: 'yet'—gate, as in 'shut that yet'; 'quilt'—swallow, as in 'my throat is so sore I cannot quilt'; 'dillon'—runt, as in 'dillon of the litter'; 'provida'—food or vittles, as in 'must get in some provida for the family'; 'twam't'—it wasn't, as in 'it wasn't me that did it'. And 'desables'—state of undress, as in 'he came to the door and caught me in my desables'.

That last one is an oddity since, if it really is antique, it must have originated in Norman French. Most Oxfordshire words are Germanic and originate from the Saxon spoken by the people of Wessex before the Norman Conquest. Most noticeable among these is the word 'bist', second person singular for 'you are' in modern German of course, and also widely used in the Cotswolds and indeed throughout Wessex, notably in Thomas Hardy's novels. Angie Ware noted the word in her list: 'bist'—is/are, as in 'where bist going yous', meaning 'where are you going?' Could it perhaps be an abbreviation of 'Where be'est thou going?' Unfortunately I am no expert.

Experts there are, though, notable among them Joseph Wright (1855-1930), the seventh son of a Yorkshire workman who became Professor of Comparative Philology at Oxford University and edited the famous dialect dictionary between 1898 and 1905. He also created the Dialect Test to capture the vowel sounds of any individual dialect, and so place the speaker's origins. He was a specialist in Germanic languages and Old and Middle English. He was also an important influence on J. R. R. Tolkien. What he must have thought of Oxford English, now sometimes called the Queen's English or Received Pronunciation, which most of his contemporaries at Oxford must have used, is unknown (at least by me).

What I cannot resist, though, are a few more examples of Cotswold Anglo-Saxon speak: 'housen' for houses; 'leaze'—pasture; 'frem'—fresh or flourishing. Some expressions such as 'hopping mad', meaning angry, seem to be making a comeback. Then, of course, there are a few so-called Anglo-Saxon words still in use which are unprintable here.

12. Names from History
Personalities of City and County

Oxford University has a strong personality all its own: elusive; still evolving; perpetually surprised at finding itself on this earth at all, let alone sitting by a river in an English county. For the place is to a large degree a small kingdom of the mind, longing to be self-sufficient but in fact trapped in the body of a humdrum town. It is hardly surprising therefore, since it resembles so closely a human being with a big brain— and of a thoughtful disposition—that it has spawned far more than its fair share of astonishing characters among its sons and (latterly) daughters.

First among them, in terms of time, was Robert Grosseteste, whose name actually means Big Head in Norman French—the language spoken by 12th-century Gown, but not Town—and indeed we know that he really did have a huge head for the size of his body. He became one of the university's first chancellors, setting the scene, as it were, for following generations. He originally studied theology in Paris, but came to Oxford because the ecclesiastical storm caused by some of his ideas was not so great here as there. Theology then, like science now, transcended national borders.

But a certain originality in approach to the business of dealing with the practicalities of life has dogged many an Oxford man ever since. Poor old John Aubrey, for instance, who came up to Trinity in 1642, just as the English Civil War was getting started, was very disorganised, scribbling his notes for his famous *Brief Lives* on any old scrap of paper.

He wrote of the president of Trinity, Dr Ralph Kettle: 'He was irreconcileable to long haire [I am using Aubrey's spelling in all these quotes] ...woe be to him that sate on the outside of the Table ... I remember he cutt Mr Radford's haire with the knife that chipps the bread on the Buttery Hatch.' The doctor's teaching methods were also unorthodox. Aubrey wrote: 'As they were reading of inscribing and circumscribing Figures, sayd he, I will shew you how to inscribe a Triangle in a Quadrangle. Bring a pig into the quadrangle, and I will sett the colledge dog at him, and he will take the pig by the eare, then come and take the Dog by the tayle and the hog by the tayle, and so there you have a Triangle in a quadrangle; *quod erat faciendum*.'

Others featuring in his 426 *Brief Lives* include the poet Lucius Cary, second Viscount Falkland (1610-43), who built Great Tew where (Aubrey wrote) 'his house was like a Colledge, full of learned men'—like Ben Jonson, Edmund Waller and Thomas Hobbes. For Oxfordshire too, like its county town, has long been peopled by strong characters: the Mitfords, Churchills, Clarendons of this world, to name only a few.

Overall, a beguiling and somehow very English sense of the ridiculous has long held sway here, and nobody captures it so well as Charles Dodgson, otherwise known as Lewis Carroll, the author of *Alice in Wonderland* and *Through the Looking Glass*. Perhaps he was thinking of pre-Norman Conquest Oxfordshire when he wrote of Alice looking intently along the road and remarking: 'I see somebody now. But he is coming very slowly—and what curious attitudes he goes in.' To which the White King replied, 'Not at all. He's an Anglo-Saxon Messenger—and those are Anglo-Saxon attitudes.' But then, as Lewis Carroll also wrote, 'Life, what is it but a dream?'

Amy Robsart

Did she fall, was she pushed, or did she jump? Those were the questions preying on the minds of both Oxfordshire villagers and the grandest of courtiers in London, Madrid, Paris and Rome after the body of Amy Robsart was found at the bottom of the stairs at Cumnor Place on 8 September 1560. What was certain was that the beautiful 28-year-old had broken her neck. The reason for all the fevered speculation in places high and low was that Amy was the wife of Robert Dudley, later Earl of Leicester—the acknowledged lover of Queen Elizabeth I. Although many people were imprisoned for asserting that the so-called Virgin Queen was at various stages carrying Dudley's child, she made no secret of her infatuation for him or that, despite the existence of Amy, she had considered marrying him.

Since her husband's rise to royal favour, Amy had spent much of her time away from court, travelling in the country; and in September 1560 she was staying with Sir Anthony Forster and his family at Cumnor. Sir Anthony was chief controller of Dudley's private expenses—a sort of accountant and a family friend. On the fatal day, the family had all gone off to attend Abingdon Fair, leaving Amy and a few other women behind.

After the tragedy, Amy's body was removed in secret to what was then Gloucester Hall (now Worcester College, Oxford), and Lord Dudley ordered Sir Thomas Blount, a distant relative, to mount an inquiry into her death. The Spanish ambassador certainly suspected Dudley; Catholics in Paris and Rome made much of the suspected murder. But people in Cumnor suspected suicide, as Amy's maid reported that she had heard her 'pray to God to deliver her from depression'.

It was noted with glee by conspiracy theorists everywhere that Dudley did not attend her funeral at St Mary's church, Oxford, at which the preacher, Dr Babington, made an unfortunate slip of the tongue. He referred to her as having been 'so pitifully murdered', though in some versions the words read: 'so pitifully slain'. The Reverend Thomas Lever, of Sherburn, wrote to the Privy Council on 17 September of 'the grievous and dangerous suspicion and muttering' about Lady Amy's death which, of course, at least in theory, left the way open for Dudley to marry Elizabeth.

Cumnor Place—not to be confused with the present 18th-century house of the same name—stood south-west of the present churchyard. The 14th-century building, originally belonging to the Abbey of Abingdon, was demolished in 1810.

Nell Gwyn

Burford is forever associated with oranges because it was so beloved by a certain former orange seller described by 17th-century diarist Samuel Pepys as 'witty and pretty'. This was of course Nell Gwyn (1650-87), mistress of Charles II, who often visited the town with the King to attend Burford Races, staying (usually) at the George Hotel in the High Street, opposite the junction with Witney Street, now sadly closed. There was for years a portrait of Nell Gwyn in Burford Priory, but whether the Benedictine monks took it with them when they sold the place recently, I know not.

Nell's descendant, Charles Beauclerk, maintained in his biography of her that she was born in Oxford and that she only moved to London, where her mother became the keeper of a bawdy house (brothel), after her father, a former Royalist cavalry officer in the Civil War, died. Nell Gwyn, of course, had Charles to thank for all her good fortune. She would not have even been able to become an orange seller at Drury Lane Theatre had the King not allowed theatres to come back into existence; during the 11 years of Commonwealth under Oliver Cromwell, 1649-60, they had been banned as 'frivolous'.

The kind of oranges she sold in the theatre would have been kumquats, those little fruits that you eat whole. Before their introduction to England, oranges were only grown here for their scent and blossom. But for centuries, northern noblemen vied with each other to bring something of the south to their cold countries, growing oranges in grand orangeries—witness at Blenheim. The Arabs brought oranges to Europe from China—the name is derived from the Arabic Narandj—and they travelled to such northern climes as Britain from Moorish Spain and Portugal. Marmalade, indeed— that conserve made famous in Oxford—could well have been introduced by Charles II's wife, the Portuguese Catherine of Braganza. Originally, it was made of quince, or *marmelo* in Portuguese. And some orange trees dating from the time of Charles II are still alive today.

Almost certainly, jockeys at Burford races were refreshed between races with oranges. The races reached their height of fame on 17 March 1681, when Charles II was staying with Lord Clarendon at Cornbury Park. He decreed that the King's Plate, usually awarded at Newmarket, would that year be presented at Burford. Burford races were run south of Aldsworth and continued into the 19th century.

Nell persuaded the King to give their eldest son Oxfordshire titles. As a boy of six he became Earl of Burford and Baron Headington. And the child was largely brought up in a magnificent house in Windsor called Burford House. Later, he became the first Duke of St Albans as well as keeping his titles of Burford and Headington.

Hers is a wonderful tale of rags to riches. She referred to herself as 'the Protestant whore' and, ironically enough, oranges—or at least the colour orange, named after the fruit—became associated with Protestantism when Charles' nephew, William of Orange, became King of England after ousting the Catholic James II.

William Buckland

You may have heard of William Buckland, the Oxford don who helped himself to the heart of the King of France—preserved in a silver casket at Nuneham Courtenay— and ate it. He was both a formidable academic and an eccentric of the first water: a clergyman, he became a Fellow of Corpus in 1809 and the first Professor of Geology in 1819, a canon of Christ Church in 1825 and Dean of Westminster in 1825.

But anyone interested in his extraordinary habits, particularly his diet, should turn to the Reverend W. Tuckwell's *Reminiscences of Oxford*. The author was a childhood friend of Professor Buckland's son Frank—and never forgot the food at the Canon's house in Tom Quad. He wrote: 'horse flesh I remember more than once, crocodile another day, mice baked in batter on a third—while the guinea pig under the table nibbled at your infantine toes, the bear walked round your chair and rasped your hand with file-like tongue, the jackal's fiendish yell close by came through the open window, the monkey's hairy arm extended itself suddenly over your shoulder to annex your fruit and walnuts'.

This son, Frank, grew up to become a naturalist only a little behind his father in the league table of Oxford oddities. He went about with his pockets full of glow worms and moss—because he said it was good for them—and he won the disfavour of the Dean of Christ Church when an eagle of his flew into the cathedral during the Te Deum. Stuffier Victorians were left unamused, too, when Frank took Tiglath Pileser, dressed as a student of Christ Church, to a party at the Botanic Garden. The problem here was that Tiglath Pileser was a bear! The Dean told him straight: 'Mr Buckland. I hear you keep a bear in the college; well, either you or your bear must go.'

Professor Buckland did himself no favours with the Catholic hierarchy in Palermo, where he went on honeymoon. When the priests reverently opened up the reliquary to show him the remains of the city's patron saint, Rosalia, he shouted out: 'They are the bones of a goat, not of a woman.'

Then there was the time he visited 'a foreign cathedral where was exhibited a martyr's blood—dark spots upon the pavement ever fresh and ineradicable. The professor dropped on the pavement and touched the stain with his tongue: 'I can tell you what it is; it is bat's urine.' By that time he was well into eating his way through the whole animal creation, declaring that the worst thing to eat was a mole.

As for the incident of the King of France's heart (reputedly Louis XIV's), shown to him by Lord Harcourt, A. J. C. Hare relates in his book *The Story of My Life*: 'Dr Buckland, whilst looking at it, exclaimed: 'I have eaten strange things but have never eaten the heart of a king before,' and before anyone could hinder him he had gobbled it up, and the precious relic was lost forever.'

He ended his days as Rector of Islip, where he is buried, and where Tiglath Pileser raided the sweet shop. Islip, of course, was the birthplace of another King, Edward the Confessor.

Thomas Beecham

As rags to riches tales go—I might mention Lord Nuffield, or even Dick Wittington—the story of Thomas Beecham, founder of the famous Powders company that in 1989 became the multinational SmithKline Beecham, and in 2000 GlaxoSmithKline, must rank among the most spectacular ever.

Thomas Beecham, grandfather of the conductor Sir Thomas Beecham, was born in Curbridge, near Witney, in 1820. He was the son of a depressive shepherd, called Joseph, who had been forced into an unhappy marriage to his mother, Sarah, just two months before his birth, and his only formal education consisted of a year at school from the age of seven.

The school he attended was the National School in Witney, just over a mile's walk away, which the Church of England-based National Society had set up in the Town Hall; then at the age of eight he was sent out to work as a shepherd, earning 1s 6d per seven-day week, and living for the most part in a shepherd's shelter on Curbridge Down.

I read all this in *Beecham's: from pills to pharmaceuticals* (Crucible) by Anthony Corley, a member of the Centre for International Business History at the Henley Business School, who has also, incidentally, contributed nearly 100 entries to the *Oxford Dictionary of National Biography*, mostly on business leaders. He notes that conductor Sir Thomas Beecham wrote that 'the minutiae of commerce never fail to be tedious in narrative', but I can vouch unequivocally that this particular company history is an exception. It is anything but tedious.

High in the Cotswold hills Thomas continued his own self-education, and would surely have endorsed Sir Walter Scott's view that 'all men who have turned out worth anything have had the chief hand in their own education'. As a successful entrepreneur, he wrote later: 'Very early in my teens I took charge of the entire flock and stuck to it until I was twenty years of age.'

In about 1833 he moved to Cropredy, near Banbury, where he worked for a progressive farmer called William Chamberlain and took up residence in a shepherd's cottage on the 400-acre farm. Perhaps he noticed during his lonely upbringing exactly which herbs and plants kept his flocks healthy, or perhaps he picked up information from 'wise women' who picked plants from hedgerows to make potions; anyway he soon earned a reputation for curing animals and humans alike—and also took to casting horoscopes and telling fortunes.

In his words, he started making 'decoctions [liquid medicines] of a human kind'. Then, being the innovator he was, he invented a grinding machine called a 'kibbler' out of old knives and agricultural implements to turn vegetable matter into a sort of dough, which he then fashioned into strips, to be cut into pills, using a board with hollows in it to act as a mould. He peddled these pills around the Oxfordshire markets to which he tramped long distances to buy and sell sheep.

In 1840 he took his first life-changing step: he gave up shepherding and moved into his uncle's three-room cottage in Kidlington. There he concentrated more on pill production, contributing what money he could to the meagre shepherd's wages that his uncle and cousin earned. He also took jobs: first as a postman, collecting and delivering post from nearby Gosford, and blowing a horn around Kidlington as a signal for people to give him letters to take back to Gosford; second as a part-time gardener at the Kidlington mansion Hampden House.

Then he took another momentous step: like many during the Industrial Revolution he moved to Liverpool and then St Helens, in Lancashire—where there were plenty of people feeling unwell. He married the first of three wives (the third of whom claimed he tried to poison her) and in time set up a pill factory. He was joined in the business by his son Joseph—later Sir Joseph—who proved he had a flair for business to rival his father's.

But Thomas Beecham's great talent was for advertising. There is the story (true or untrue) of the Lancashire clergyman who asked the company to supply some free hymnbooks in return for the company displaying an advertisement on the flyleaf. When the books arrived the clergyman was surprised to see no advertisement—until, that is, Christmas, when the congregation found themselves singing:

'Hark, the Herald angels sing,
Beecham's pills are just the thing.
Peace on earth and mercy mild;
Two for a man and one for a child.'

Charles Darwin

The most important event in the evolution of the study of science, not only in Oxford but everywhere else too, was the great British Association debate of 30 June 1860 at the University Museum, Parks Road, between Thomas Henry Huxley (1825-95), known as 'Darwin's bulldog', in the Science corner, and Samuel Wilberforce, Bishop of Oxford (1805-73), in the Church corner.

Charles Darwin (1809-82) had published his earth-shatteringly significant book, *The Origin of Species*, seven months before. But where was he on that fateful day? Answer: he was at Moor Park, near Farnham in Surrey, receiving hydropathic treatment for a debilitating illness at a sort of spa set up there by Dr Edward Wickstead Lane.

I gather this piece of knowledge from a small booklet, just 12 pages long, published by Huxley Scientific Press—a very small Oxford enterprise run by Sophie Huxley (a distant relative of Thomas Huxley) and her husband. It is called *Darwin's Mysterious Illness* and is written by Robert Youngson, a retired doctor and the author of popular scientific books as well as many important medical reference works.

Dr Youngson speculates on what Darwin's malady might have been, describing it as a puzzle unsolved for 150 years. After Darwin's return from his five-year journey of discovery aboard HMS *Beagle* in 1836, he wrote to a friend, Bernhard Studer, in 1847: 'Shortly after my return from my long voyage, I had a tedious and severe illness, and I have never since recovered my strength and suppose I never shall... I appear quite well, but from being a strong man, I am incapable of any continued muscular exertion; or indeed of much exertion of mind, for even conversation, if it excites me, tires me in a very short time, so that I am compelled to live a most retired life.'

Dr Lane described his symptoms: 'When the worst attacks were on, he seemed almost crushed with agony, the nervous system being severely shaken, and the temporary depression resulting distressingly great.' And Charles Darwin's son Francis wrote in his *Reminiscences of My Father's Everyday Life* (*c*.1884): 'For nearly 40 years he never knew one day of the health of ordinary men, and thus his life was one long struggle against the weariness and strain of sickness.'

Dr Youngson examines—but seems to doubt—the possibility of the fatigue being due to Chagas' Disease, described for the first time by Brazilian physician Carlos Chagas (1879-1934). This disease is caused by the South American blood-sucking cone-nosed assassin insect *Triatoma infestans*, or *benchuca*, sometimes called the 'kissing bug' because of its painless bite, which all too often kills its victim through heart failure.

Certainly Darwin was exposed to the attentions of this horrid product of evolution. He recorded an incident that occurred during the *Beagle* voyage in the village of Luxan in the Argentinian province of Mendoza in March 1835: 'At night I experienced an

Cartoons of Wilberforce, Darwin and Huxley

attack (for it deserves no less a name) of the Benchura, a species of Reduvius, the great black bug of the Pampas. It is most disgusting to feel soft wingless insects, about an inch long crawling over one's body.'

But Darwin did not die of heart failure; instead he died many years later, aged 73, of coronary thrombosis. His own doctors and friends suspected old-fashioned hypochondria. He could work for, at the most, two hours at a stretch; then he needed to lie down on a sofa and have a novel read to him. Professor John Tyndall at the Royal Institution remarked that illness allowed Darwin plenty of time 'to ponder a great deal'. Huxley even joked: 'If only I could break my leg, what a lot of scientific work I could do.'

As for that debate at the University Museum between the evolutionists and the creationists, controversy still rages as to the exact exchange of words between Wiberforce and Huxley. It went something along the lines of Wilberforce asking whether Huxley was descended from an ape on his mother's or his father's side; and Huxley replying that he would rather be descended from an ape than a bigoted prelate.

Alice Liddell

The discovery of some Burne-Jones paintings in an unassuming house reminded me once again of the whimsical Victorian Oxford inhabited by Alice Liddell, the inspiration for *Alice in Wonderland*. The St Catherine window in Oxford Cathedral is by the same artist and is dedicated to one of Alice's sisters, Edith, who was the third daughter and youngest child of the Dean of Christ Church, Henry George Liddell.

On the so-called Golden Afternoon of 4 July 1862, when the ten-year-old Alice first heard of her adventures from the lips of mathematics don Charles Dodgson—during a boat trip down the Thames to Godstow—the eight-year-old Edith interrupted the tale 'not more than once a minute'. Also on board the rowing

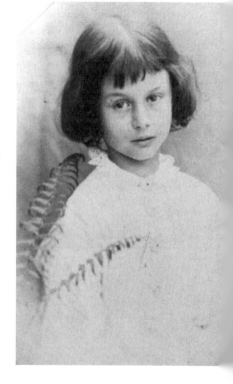

boat was Alice's older sister, Lorina, two years older than Alice and known as the Lory, and the Reverend Robinson Duckworth, of Trinity College. Edith, the red-haired child nicknamed the 'dear little Eaglet' by Dodgson (otherwise known as Lewis Carroll) died, aged 22, in 1876. She was engaged to Aubrey Harcourt of Nuneham Park.

The Pre-Raphaelite window shows an imposing figure standing on ground littered with fritillaries, those flowers which grew so profusely in Christ Church meadow in Alice's day that flower girls sold them by the armful. Apt, somehow, that Edith had been engaged to Aubrey Harcourt, for the story of Alice's adventures as told on the Golden Afternoon was the continuation of one begun on an earlier boat trip to Nuneham Park that had been brought to an abrupt end by rain. On that occasion the whole party had got soaked and Mr Dodgson had had to bang on a friend's door in Sandford for shelter.

Alice remembered: 'If the Dodo hadn't known the way to that nice little cottage, I don't know when we should have got dry again.' It seems that everyone on board had nicknames. Duckworth (obviously) was the Duck. Dodgson was the Dodo because of his stutter. Whenever he introduced himself he would say 'Do-Do-Dodgson'. And of course the Liddell children had often seen the last mortal remains of that vanished bird in the recently-built University Museum (where they remain to this day).

Another work of stained glass by Burne-Jones in Oxford Cathedral is the St Frideswide window of 1859. It shows medieval pilgrims visiting the holy well of Oxford's patron saint at Binsey, the Treacle Well. As Mavis Batey pointed out in her booklet *Alice's Adventures in Oxford* (published 1984 by Pitkin Pictorials): 'The installation of the St Frideswide window in the Latin chapel of the cathedral, one of Burne-Jones's first essays in glass painting, was a great event in the world of Pre-Raphaelite art. 'It was much admired by Dean Liddell, and all Christ Church watched the assembling of the stained glass on the grass behind the cathedral.'

Passing Binsey on the Golden Afternoon, the girls heard of the Dormouse's tale of the three sisters who lived at the bottom of a treacle well. Alice herself, under the tutelage of John Ruskin, became a competent artist. She created a woodcarving of St Frideswide travelling by boat along the Thames on her way to found a nunnery where Christ Church now stands. The carving now hangs in St Frideswide's Church, Osney. It seems fitting, somehow, that more Burne-Jones paintings should come to light in Oxford.

Sir Arthur Evans

Extraordinary how times change, particularly if you are an archaeologist. A century ago when Sir Arthur Evans (1851-1941) was knighted for his services to archaeology at Knossos in Crete, it was perfectly acceptable for a dashing and rich individual like him, hugely knowledgeable but largely self-taught in his chosen profession, to follow a hunch and dig about more or less where he pleased. Now, of course, excavations are carried out differently, with practically every shovelful of earth being sifted and subjected to objective peer review.

Sir Arthur was the son of Sir John Evans, an amateur expert on ancient British coins, and stone and bronze implements, who had made his fortune as the head of the paper manufacturers John Dickinson, of Nash Mills, in Hertfordshire. Evans went up to Brasenose College, Oxford, from Harrow to read Modern History in 1874. After several adventurous years travelling in Europe—notably in Bosnia Herzegovina, where his sketching got him arrested as a spy—he returned to Oxford in 1884 to become Keeper of the Ashmolean Museum. By then, he had become an authority on the already crumbling Ottoman Empire, of which Crete was then a part—and his chief interest was Cretan seal stones, or gems, depicting in miniature aspects of life in Crete from the 27th century BC to the 15th century BC—the period he called the Minoan civilisation.

Now the Ashmolean still has the best collection of seal stones outside Greece— but amazing as it may now seem, he prepared the way for excavating at Knossos by buying the site; so the dig became an essentially private enterprise happening on his own land. He was anxious to pin down the dawn of European civilisation, but modern critics have two important complaints about his methods: first, he dug straight through strata containing remains of much later Roman buildings in order to reach the period in which he was interested; and he reconstructed a certain amount of what he called the 'Palace of Knossos' in such a way that it is now sometimes difficult to see what was actually revealed (rather than built or painted by his team).

Evans bought Youlbury on Boars Hill in 1893 and lived there from 1894 until his death. During the Great Depression, he had Jarn Mound at Youlbury, and its surrounding wild garden, built in order to give work to local people. His house, with its Minoan-style decorations, has sadly burned down, but much of the estate is now a Scouts Activities Centre, since he left land there to the Scout movement. In conjunction with the Oxford Preservation Trust the rest of Youlbury later became a 'private open space'.

Evans remained Keeper of the Ashmolean until 1908. He therefore oversaw the building of the extension to the galleries in Beaumont Street in 1894, most of which were demolished during the recent renovations there. But he evidently had a yearning to play his part in the modern world as well as in the ancient one. In 1909, he put himself forward as the Liberal candidate for Parliament for Oxford University but was persuaded to withdraw by Lord Lansdowne, Unionist leader in the Lords.

Lewis Evans (1853-1930), the younger brother of Sir Arthur, was instrumental in establishing the Oxford Museum of Science in Broad Street. The chairman of the family paper-making firm, he amassed a collection of early scientific instruments; and this collection, including early sundials, astrolabes and mathematical instruments, he gave to Oxford University in 1924. In that year, the upper floor of that lovely 17th-century building was assigned to the Lewis Evans Collection—and Mr Evans himself was given an honorary Doctor of Science degree the following year.

Now the museum occupies the whole building. It was established by statute in 1935, thanks largely to Mr Evans and his friend Robert Gunther, the author of the 14-volume *Early Science in Oxford*—in which, incidentally, he complained that the university paid too little attention to science.

Prime Minister H. H. Asquith

Strange how things repeat themselves, or fail to be resolved, or just continue on and on; call it what you will. A hundred years ago the government of Herbert Henry Asquith (1852-1928), who spent his happiest years living at Sutton Courtenay, was wrestling with the problem of how to pay MPs. True, in those days no one considered paying their expenses out of the public purse; but whether or not to pay them anything at all in the way of wages was the point at issue.

Son of a non-conformist Yorkshire wool merchant, Asquith was a scholar at Balliol College and president of the Oxford Union, and became a Fellow of that college shortly after graduating. He then made a fortune as a barrister before becoming an MP. After serving as Liberal Chancellor of the Exchequer, Asquith succeeded Sir Henry Campbell Bannerman (who died at 10 Downing Street) as Prime Minister in 1908 (travelling to Biarritz to kiss hands with Edward VII who said he was too ill to come home for the ceremony), at the head of a coalition that relied on Labour and Irish support to stay in power.

He presided over Chancellor of the Exchequer Lloyd George's so-called People's Budget of late 1909, which was opposed vigorously, even violently, by Tories and in particular by the House of Lords—which led to the Parliament Act of 1911, reluctantly passed by the Lords under Asquith's threat of swamping the upper house with hundreds of new peers. The Act succeeded in limiting the power of the House of Lords.

The MPs' money question reared its head after the law lords, passing final judgment in a case brought by one Mr Osborne (whether a relation of the Labour chancellor, I know not), forbade trade unions from paying money to any political party—a judgment which left some Labour MPs conspicuously destitute. The problem was tackled in 1911 by allotting each of them a £400 annual salary; and in 1913 an act reversed the Osborne judgement on trade union contributions.

Asquith moved into the seven-bedroom house called The Wharf, Sutton Courtenay (then in Berkshire) in 1913, together with his socialite second wife Margot. The riverside house where weekend guests would include future wartime Prime Minister Winston Churchill, is built on the site of a pub, the Queen's Head, which had earlier served bargees working at the neighbouring mill. About a year later he signed the declaration of war with Germany there, taking Britain into the conflict in which his son Raymond was to die.

The other so-called Liberal reforms that resonate down the 101 years since he became Prime Minister (an office he occupied until 1916, the longest term ever, until superseded by Mrs Thatcher) include the introduction of the first old-age pension at 5 shillings a week for single people over 70 and 7s 6d for couples; an attempt to regulate hours and introduce a minimum wage; and a movement towards Unemployment Benefit and National Insurance.

Asquith's house, Sutton Courtenay

In 1925, Asquith became the Earl of Oxford and Asquith, joining the House of Lords which he had threatened to undermine. He had wanted to become simply the Earl of Oxford, since he was so fond of the place, but many Tories objected. He ran into trouble of the same sort when he endeavoured to become Chancellor of Oxford University. He was defeated from that objective by Viscount Cave, for political reasons.

After his death, Margot was left seriously short of money (probate valued his estate at just £9,345, perhaps £500,000 today) and she sold The Wharf. For a time she occupied a house in Bedford Square, London, which had previously belonged to Lady Ottoline Morrell. The neighbouring Mill House was bought not long ago by the film star Helena Bonham Carter, Asquith's great-granddaughter. Asquith is buried in the church of All Souls at Sutton Courtenay where, unlikely as it may seem, writer George Orwell is also interred.

Unity Mitford

Very few people, I should guess, visit the churchyard of that quintessentially English village of Swinbrook, set in rolling Cotswold country, without pausing to ponder on the short but eventful life of Unity Valkyrie Mitford (1914-48), whose gravestone there—between those of her sisters Nancy and Diana—reads: 'Say not the struggle naught availeth.'

Poor misguided Unity, aged 19, went to Germany for the first time in 1933 as part of the British delegation to the 1933 Nuremberg Rally—and fell head over heels in love with Hitler. She said: 'The first time I saw him I knew there was no one I would rather meet.' The next year she returned to Munich, enrolled in a language school to learn German, and set about stalking her quarry.

Extraordinary as it may now seem, she succeeded in meeting Hitler by simply sitting every day in the front room of a cafe (the Osteria Bavaria), where he usually ate, until after ten months he eventually invited her over for a chat and a cream cake. She wrote to her father, Lord Redesdale: 'It was the most wonderful and beautiful day of my life. I am so happy that I wouldn't mind a bit, dying. I am the luckiest girl in the world... For me he is the greatest man of all time'. Jealous of the English blonde, Hitler's mistress Eva Braun wrote in her diary: 'She is known as the Valkyrie and looks the part, including her legs.'

Unity Mitford became a full-blown Nazi of the worst sort, giving horrible anti-Jewish speeches. MI5 boss Guy Liddel wrote in his diary: 'Unity Mitford had been in close and intimate contact with the Fuehrer and his supporters for several years, and was an ardent and open supporter of the Nazi regime. She had remained behind after the outbreak of war and her action had come perilously close to high treason.'

Following the declaration of the Second World War on 3 September 1939, Unity's father learned that she had attempted suicide in the English Garden, Munich, by shooting herself in the head with a pearl-handled pistol, said to have been given to her by Adolf Hitler. Indeed, her sister, Diana, the wife of the leader of the British Union of Fascists, Sir Oswald Mosley, who had also been in Germany until just before the war, had left for England when Hitler told his admirer Unity that hostilities between Britain and Germany had become inevitable.

Redesdale, according to Richard Griffiths, a former fellow of Brasenose College, Oxford, writing in his book *Patriotism Perverted* (Constable 1998) had pleaded with her by telephone to come home on 6 September—and then heard nothing for two months. Redesdale himself, incidentally, is (according to Griffiths) listed as a warden of The Right Club, a mysterious, extreme right-wing group led by the anti-Semitic MP Captain Archibald Ramsay—who, like Mosley, was imprisoned under the Defence Regulations in 1940.

The Mitford clan, Swinbrook, 1934 (Unity centre seated)

After shooting herself, she was taken to hospital where Hitler visited her and paid her bills. Then she was transported to neutral Switzerland and thence back to England where, on arrival in January 1940, and speaking from a stretcher, she told reporters: 'I'm glad to be in England, even if I'm not on your side.' Back at the family home in Swinbrook, she was treated by Professor Cairns of the Nuffield Hospital, Oxford, and, reportedly recovered sufficiently to have an affair with an RAF pilot officer at nearby Brize Norton.

Even without recent speculation that she bore Hitler's child in an Oxfordshire nursing home (dismissed as gossip by her sister, the dowager Duchess of Devonshire), hers was an odd life all right—surely one of the strangest in the 20th-century history of Oxfordshire.

Blue Plaques

Who cannot have noticed blue plaques, commemorating notable characters in all walks of life, springing up like autumn mushrooms all over Oxford and Oxfordshire? And who cannot also have wondered at some time or another about the how the process works for getting your name in blue.

OXFORDSHIRE BLUE PLAQUES BOARD

Here at the Iffley Road Track the first sub-four minute mile was run on 6th May 1954 by ROGER BANNISTER

UNIVERSITY OF OXFORD

The scheme was the brainchild of the former Lord Lieutenant of Oxfordshire Sir Hugo Brunner, who became its first chairman—a post since occupied by Kate Tiller, the Deputy Lord Lieutenant and Emeritus Reader in English Local History at Kellogg College, Oxford.

The first blue plaque to go up in the county was to Sarah Cooper, maker of the first pot of Cooper's Oxford marmalade, at 83 High Street. The 50th plaque went up at 42 Park Town to commemorate Professor William Morfill (1834-1909) whom Sir James Murray (1837-1915), pioneer compiler of the *Oxford English Dictionary*, described as 'a unique scholar ... whose knowledge of the Slavonic languages was greater than that of any other Englishman, as far as I know'. Murray's own plaque, incidentally, may be found at 78 Banbury Road, his former home and, indeed, workplace.

Most plaques commemorate people, but two commemorate institutions: they are Westfield House, at Aston near Bampton, which between 1937 and 1939 was a refuge for Basque children; and the King's Centre, opposite Newspaper House in Osney Mead, where the Magnetic Resonance Imaging Scanner was invented by Oxford Instruments in 1980.

Outside Oxford, plaques include one at 39 Stert Street, Abingdon, to lottery winner John Alder (1712-80); another to farm labourer Mont Abbott (1902-89) at Biddy's Bottom, Fulwell, near Enstone, who found fame through his memoirs as told to Sheila Stewart in her book *Lifting the Latch*; through to Jethro Tull (1674-1741), agriculturist and inventor of the seed drill, at 19A The Street, Crowmarsh Gifford.

Secretary of the Oxfordshire Blue Plaques Board, Eda Forbes, described how you qualify: 'You must be dead. And you must have been dead for at least 20 years, or, alternatively, it must be at least 100 years since you were born. And you must have lived in the place for at least five years. In Oxford, too, the decision was taken early on that no plaques would go on university buildings. For instance, you will not find a plaque stuck onto Christ Church to commemorate, say, Lewis Carroll.'

The Board meets in April and October each year to sift through nominations for blue plaques, which may be proposed by anyone. Members of the Board include representatives of Oxfordshire County Council; the Diocese of Oxford; Oxford City Council; Cherwell, South Oxfordshire, Vale of White Horse and West Oxfordshire District Councils; Oxford University and Oxford Brookes University; Oxfordshire Chamber of Commerce and Industry; Oxfordshire Architectural and Historical Society; Oxford Civic Society; Oxford Preservation Trust; and the Centre for Oxfordshire Studies.

Ms Forbes explained that the scheme was a purely local one. It is not administered, as many people imagine that it might be, by English Heritage, which took over many similar London schemes (though not that of Westminster) in 1986. Importantly, too, it receives no regular funding—which means that when someone has been considered worthy of a plaque, a search then begins for money to pay for it.

And who was that lottery winner, Mr Alder of Abingdon? He was the landlord of the Mitre Inn who, when given £22 to settle the brewer's bill by his wife, bought a lottery ticket with some of the money. He used his winnings to buy clothes and food for the poor, a new body for the stagecoach called The Abingdon Machine, and a set of bells for St Nicholas church.

INDEX

Abingdon 21, 45, 68, 137-9, 144, 148-9, 209, 218, 230, 239-40, 247, 262

Abingdon Road 26

Abolitionists 38-9

Adenauer, Konrad 46-7

Alfred, King 111, 136-7, 145-6

Alice's Adventures in Wonderland 46-7, 69, 83, 173, 187, 240, 246, 254-5

All Souls 3, 86, 95, 100-1, 104, 230-2, 241

Anglo-Saxon Oxford 2, 23, 25-6, 244

Arnold, Matthew 101, 142, 210-11, 214, 232

Ascott-under-Wychwood 122

Ashmolean Museum 36, 94, 100, 145, 175, 202, 214, 218, 256

Asquith, H. H. 210, 257-9

Aubrey, John 35-7, 203, 246

Balliol College 44, 46, 72, 78, 84, 90, 92, 119, 185-6, 198, 210, 257

Banbury 35, 45, 51-2, 58, 121, 144, 176, 230, 251

Banbury Road 2, 6, 17-19, 21, 217-18, 261

Beaumont Palace 8

Beaumont Street 217, 256

Beecham, Thomas 250-2

Beerbohm, Max 88, 99

Benson 42, 66, 142, 159-60

Berlin, Sir Isaiah 100-1

Betjeman, John 16-18, 99, 114, 198, 202, 218, 222, 223-4

Binsey 10, 20, 23, 33, 113, 187, 220, 255

Black Bourton 188-9

Blackbird Leys 14-16

Blackstone, Sir William 86-7, 165

Blandford, Marquesses of 152-4

Blenheim Palace 43, 85, 118, 137, 151-4, 158, 161, 163-4, 170-4, 203, 219-20, 225, 249

Boars Hill 256

Bodleian Library 25, 28, 29, 37, 39, 55, 79, 81, 100, 118, 202, 225, 236, 242

Bodley, Sir Thomas 79-81

Botley Road 11-13, 44, 187

Brasenose College 10, 30, 89, 104, 109-11, 114, 256, 260

Breweries 30, 68-9, 234

Brideshead Revisited 44, 72, 221, 223

Broad Street 31-3, 48, 70, 90, 99, 127, 211, 257

Buckland, William 249-50

Burford 37-8, 45, 122, 132-4, 196, 199, 202, 230, 235, 248-9

Burford Levellers 149-50

Capability Brown 172-3

Carfax 2, 26, 30, 92, 124

Carfax Conduit 55, 173, 193

Carroll, Lewis, Dodgson

Cassington 239

Catholic Martyrs 32-3

Charlbury 43, 51, 133, 152, 161, 169, 182, 199, 235

Charlecote 205

Charles I 3, 14, 20, 29, 34, 37, 63, 78-9, 81, 88, 114, 141, 149, 154, 165, 175-6, 181, 242

Charles II 3, 12, 19, 28-9, 35, 38, 40, 81-2, 88, 114, 130, 192, 204, 229, 235, 248-9

Chipping Norton 45, 51-2, 128-30, 156-7, 230

Christ Church 1, 7, 18, 29, 35, 39, 46, 59, 74, 84, 87, 89, 96-7, 102, 104, 113-16, 133, 193, 199, 212, 241, 249-50, 254-5

Churchill family 22, 41-2, 46, 73, 97, 101, 135, 151-4, 170-2, 192, 219, 246, 258

Churchill hospital 222

Churchill village 134, 192-4

Combe 146, 158, 188, 191-2, 204, 229

Cooper, Frank 11-12

Cooper, Sarah 12, 261

Cornbury Park 43, 133, 152, 161, 181, 199, 235, 249

Cornmarket 32, 56, 65, 70, 72-3, 205, 224
Corpus Christi College 4, 100-1, 104, 106, 111-13, 210, 241, 249
Cote Baptist Chapel 197-9
Cotswolds 122, 132-3, 179, 193, 213-14, 227, 242-4, 251, 259
Cotswold Wildlife Park 173-5
Cowley 2, 13-16, 42, 52-4, 64, 70-1, 122, 144, 217
Cowley Road 14, 52-3, 59, 233

Darwin, Charles 66, 252-4
Daylesford 134, 194-5
Dialect 243-4
Ditchley Park 22, 161, 169-70, 225
Dodgson, Charles, aka Lewis Carroll 12, 47, 69-70, 83, 102, 173, 187, 240, 246, 254-5
d'Oilly, Robert 2, 4-6, 24, 68, 148
Dorchester-on-Thames 14, 143-4, 183-4, 188, 220

Einstein, Albert 96-7
Elizabeth I 11, 31, 33, 78-9, 82, 113, 125, 141, 247
Emperors' heads 88, 99-100
Enstone 175-6, 184, 231-2
Evans, Sir Arthur 256-7
Exeter College 78, 90, 123

Faringdon 178-9, 230
Filkins 134-5
Fire service 64-5
Floods 4, 7, 13, 44-5, 64
Folly Bridge 4-5, 10, 59, 88-9, 117
Friars 24, 32

Garsington 14, 16, 41-2, 166-7, 242
Grahame, Kenneth 168, 186, 211-12, 238
Grandpont 2, 4, 10-11, 25-6, 45
Great Tew 126-7, 246
Green College 66, 117-18
Gwyn, Nell 235, 248-9

Hampton Gay 124-5, 238
Handel, George Frideric 206
Haydn, Joseph 207-8
Headington 9, 16, 52, 69, 71, 75-6, 99, 120, 122-3, 163, 222, 228
Henry I 11, 14, 52, 144, 148, 174
Henry II 24, 137-8, 174-5, 203
Henry III 28-9, 138
Henry IV 205
Henry V 81, 139
Henry VI 106, 139-40, 230
Henry VII 122, 140, 191, 233-4
Henry VIII 7, 111-12, 133-4, 140-1, 148, 177, 184, 188-9, 191, 202
Hinksey 25, 45, 55, 90
Holst, Gustav 213-14
Holywell Street 32-3, 99, 185-6, 206, 217
Iffley 7, 16, 184
Islip 204, 250

Jackson, T. G. 92-3
Jewish Quarter 26-8
John Radcliffe Hospital 71-2

Keble College 16, 44, 210
Kelmscott 121, 179, 202

Lady Margaret Hall 78, 95
Larkin, Philip 44, 225
Last Supper, Magdalen College 108-9
Lawrence, D. H. 14, 42, 167
Lawrence, T. E. 214-15
Lewis, C. S. 186, 221-3
Liddell, Henry, Dean of Christ Church 46, 114, 116, 255
Liddell, Alice 69, 83, 173, 187, 254-5

Mad Parliament 28-9
Magdalen Bridge 4, 9-10, 14, 54, 59, 164
Magdalen College 16, 27-8, 39, 53, 78-9, 83-4, 98, 104, 106-8, 162, 193, 202, 220-3, 233
Mapledurham House 161, 168

Marlborough, Dukes of 21, 57, 116, 118, 144, 151-4, 158, 164, 171, 191, 219
Marston 18, 123-4
Matilda, Empress 26, 64, 68, 138, 174
May morning 193, 228, 233-4
Merton College 26-7, 31, 34-5, 78-9, 84, 87-8, 113, 185-6, 220
Milton-under-Wychwood 99, 122, 181
Mitford family 145, 246, 259-60
Morris, William, of Kelmscott 90, 179-81, 188, 202
Morris, William, Viscount Nuffield 13, 50, 58, 61-2, 144, 167-8

Nash, Paul 216-17
New College 24, 26, 33, 46, 78, 100, 102, 104, 106-7, 118, 134, 193, 233, 242
North Leigh 162
Nuffield College 58, 101-2, 220
Nuffield Place 167-8
Nuneham Courtenay 55, 172-3, 193, 204, 249, 255

Oak Apple Day 234-5
Oriel College 11, 14, 46, 52, 78, 80, 114, 210
Osney 4, 6-7, 14, 24-5, 30, 36, 45, 55, 68, 102, 113, 116, 141, 187-8, 239, 255, 262
Otter hunting 238-9
Oxfam 47-8, 225
Oxford Airport 21-2
Oxford Brookes University 69, 262
Oxford Canal 5-6, 57-9
Oxford Castle 2, 5-6, 11, 24, 26, 64, 68
Oxford Marmalade 11-12, 249, 261
The Oxford Times 7, 15, 21, 45, 72, 102, 214, 239
Oxford United Football Club 75-6
Oxford University Press 65, 215, 222

Pacifists 41-2, 134
Palm's Delicatessen 73-4
Parliament 3, 28-9, 38, 55, 82, 146, 171, 234-5, 240, 257

Parliamentarians 20, 37-8, 82, 88, 123, 150, 203, 235
Pembroke College 53
Piper, John 102, 198, 218-20
Pitt Rivers Museum 94-5
Poor relief 50-3, 125, 143, 158, 179
Port Meadow 13, 19-21, 212
Postal service 63-4
Public health 52-3
Pym, Barbara 225-6

Quakers 38-9, 47
Queen's College 32, 78, 98, 105-6, 232-3

Radcliffe, Dr John 50, 66, 71, 118
Radcliffe Camera 118, 169
Radcliffe Infirmary 52, 71, 118
Radcliffe Observatory 66, 117-18
Radcot Bridge 132, 142, 146-7
RAF Benson 159-60
Railways 5, 21, 50, 56, 58-61, 68, 126, 188, 240
Reformation 8, 84, 132, 141, 146, 148-9, 188-90, 198, 213, 234, 237
Rewley Road 59-61, 65
Richard III 191
Robsart, Amy 247
Rousham 175, 238
Royal Society 36, 74, 81-2, 209, 235
Royalists 3, 8, 20, 29, 36-8, 78, 82, 123, 127, 165, 235-6, 242, 248
Ruskin, John 16, 84, 90-2, 118-19, 187, 202, 240, 255
Ruskin College 118-20

Shakespeare, William 128, 166, 204-5
Shelley, Percy Bysshe 202, 208-9
Shipton-on-Cherwell 124, 126
Shipton-under-Wychwood 122, 134, 181, 196
Shotover 9, 13, 164-6, 233
Somerville College 95, 102
South Leigh 189-90
St Aldates 25-7, 30, 63

St Anne's College 17, 95, 104
St Clements 8-10, 98
St Cross church 185-6, 212
St Frideswide 1, 7, 10, 23-6, 29, 64, 84, 113, 187, 255
St Giles 16, 18, 61, 85, 92, 119, 124, 186, 222, 228
St Hilda's College 78, 95, 225
St Hugh's College 41, 95
St John's College 17-18, 44, 85, 101-2, 104, 118, 155-6, 163
St Scholastica Day's riots 29-31, 49, 68
Stephen, King 13, 26, 64, 68, 138, 174
Suffragettes 41
Sulgrave Manor 162, 176-7
Summertown 17-19, 48
Sutton Courtenay 257-9
Swinbrook 195-6, 259, 261

Taunt, Henry 69-70
Taynton 122, 132-3, 240
Temple Cowley 11, 13-14, 92
Tennis 76, 87-8
Thames 1-2, 4, 10, 26, 44, 55, 58, 64, 68-70, 121, 132, 141-4, 146, 149, 168, 173, 179, 187, 204, 212, 233, 239-40, 254-5
Thompson, Flora 215-16, 237
Through the Looking-Glass 94, 246
Tolkien, J. R. R. 186, 220-2, 244
Trams 50, 61-2
Trinity College 35, 40, 104, 164, 246, 255
Tull, Jethro 154-6, 262

Uffington 122, 136-7, 204, 210, 218
University College 66, 207-9, 222

Vanbrugh, Sir John 162, 171-2, 203
Vanbrugh House 163-4
Victoria, Queen 10, 18, 46, 109, 114, 139, 146

Wadham College 44, 74, 81, 87, 102, 126
Wallingford 30, 86, 138-40, 142, 147, 154, 156, 165, 174, 230

Waugh, Evelyn 44, 72, 84, 223-4
Weather station 66-7
Wesley, Charles 199-200
Wheatley 122
Widford 189, 195-6
Witney 51-2, 122, 130-1, 156, 228, 242, 251
Wolfson College 100, 102
Wolvercote 17, 20-1, 45, 57-8, 214, 220
Women students 41, 78, 95-6, 104, 118
Wood, Anthony 34-6, 51, 53, 88, 206, 233, 242
Woodstock 2, 30, 37, 52, 112, 137, 144, 137, 154, 158, 171-2, 174-5, 177, 203, 205, 226
Woodstock Road 6, 21, 42, 61, 66, 117
Woolworth's 72-3
Wychwood Forest 122, 164, 181-2, 196, 228
Wycliffe, John 31-2, 147, 198
Wytham 45

Yarnton 20, 61

Zuleika Dobson 88-90, 99

THE PEDESTRIAN HOBBY-HORSE

Denis Johnson's patent specification drawing. In the coloured original the machine is shown painted green with a maroon saddle cover with gold tasselling. As made by Johnson the configuration was broadly in line with this drawing, except that an early modification allowed for a more direct form of steering.

THE PEDESTRIAN HOBBY-HORSE

AT THE DAWN OF CYCLING

BY

ROGER STREET

Artesius Publications

British Library Cataloguing in Publication data: a catalogue record
for this book is available from the British Library
Copyright © 1998 Roger Street
Published by Artesius Publications, East Quartleys, Willow Place,
Bridge Street, Christchurch, Dorset, England, BH23 1ED
Telephone: 01202 483081
First edition 1998
ISBN: 0 9532722 0 6
Typeset, printed & bound by The Ipswich Book Company Ltd.

*To my good friends whose unswerving loyalty and support
has helped me through a thousand dark days*

CONTENTS

		Page number
List of illustrations		iii
Foreword by Les Bowerman		vi
Preface		viii
Chapter 1	*The quest for the medieval Hobby-Horse*	1
Chapter 2	*Karl von Drais and his Running Machine*	13
Chapter 3	*Denis Johnson and his Pedestrian Curricle*	25
Chapter 4	*The Hobby-Horse on the road*	63
Chapter 5	*A Pedestrian Carriage for Dandies, Nobility and Royalty*	89
Chapter 6	*Velocipedes for Ladies*	111
Chapter 7	*The English Hobby-Horse prints*	123
Chapter 8	*An explosion of invention*	141
Postscript		157
Appendix 1	Denis Johnson's patent specification	161
Appendix 2	Surviving early Hobby-Horses in the U.K. and elsewhere	165
Appendix 3	The Hobby-Horse prints	170
Appendix 4	Will of Denis Johnson	179
Select Bibliography		181
Index		185
About the author		195

LIST OF ILLUSTRATIONS

Page number
(alphabet numbers refer to colour illustrations)

Frontispiece
Denis Johnson's patent specification drawing

Chapter 1
Tilting at the quintain — 1
The "Cantering Propeller" — 4
Boney's Cavalry – Ruse de Guerre — 8

Chapter 2
Single and tandem laufmaschines — 14
Army staff messenger on laufmaschine — 15
Karl von Drais on his machine — 16
Leipzig copy of von Drais machine — 19
Draisiennes dites Velocipedes — 22
Draisienne horse-brass — 23

Chapter 3
Marriage licence allegation — 26
Stop him who can !! — A
Johnson, the First Rider on the Pedestrian Hobbyhorse — 27
Signature of Denis Johnson — 28
Horwood's Plan of the Cities of London, Westminster &
  Southwark — 29
Denis Johnson commemorative plaque — 30
Pedestrians Travelling on the New Invented Hobby-Horse ! — E
Every Man on his Perch, or Going to Hobby Fair — B
Child's hobby-horse — 34
Denis Johnson velocipede no. 316 — 36
Jack mounted on his Dandy Charger — E
Denis Johnson velocipede no. 204 – 2 views — 37
Denis Johnson velocipede no. 221 — 38

	Page number
Denis Johnson velocipede no. 100	39
Hobby-horse (National Museum of Science & Technology, Ottawa)	40
Denis Johnson velocipede no. 25 – 3 views	41
Denis Johnson velocipede no. 31 – 2 views	42
Johnson's Pedestrian Hobbyhorse Riding School	43
Hobby-horse (Ipswich Museum) – 2 views	44
Hobby-horse (Royal Museum of Scotland)	45
Hobby-horse copy (Snowshill Manor)	46
Hobby-horse (Museum of Historic Cycling) – 2 views	47
Hobby-horse copy (Ulster Folk & Transport Museum)	48
Hobby-horse (Strangers' Hall Museum, Norwich)	58

Chapter 4

Pedestrian Hobbyhorse	C
Modern Olympics	71
Modern Pegasus or Dandy Hobbies in Full Speed	72
Returning to Hull	74
Military Hobbyhorse	F
Non-steerable hobby-horse	82
Author's replica non-steerable hobby-horse	83
A meeting on the road	G
A Sketching Party	84
Mayfield family hobby-horse	86
Goy's dandy-horse	87

Chapter 5

The Dandies' Rout	92
Enamelled hobby-horse pill box	93
"Hobby" fob seal – 2 views	94
The Right Hon. Robert Lowe M.P.	95
Silhouette of the Rev. Joseph Coltman on velocipede	96
Dandy-horse playing card	97
New Reading – or – Shakespeare Improved	100
Economy – or a Duke of Ten Thousand	105
*A P****e, Driving his Hobby, in HERDFORD !!!*	106
Staffs. pottery jug	108
Willem, Prince of Orange's velocipede – 2 views	109

Chapter 6

| *FASHIONABLE EXERCISE, or The Ladies Hobby School* | 112 |
| *Views of the Lady's Pedestrian Hobbyhorse* | F |

	Page number
Lady's hobby-horse (Science Museum) – 3 views	115
The Ladies Hobby	116
The Female Race ! or Dandy Chargers running into	
Maidenhead	118
The Hobby Horse Dealer	119
More Hobbies, or the Veloci Manipede	G
The New Invented Sociable, or The Lover and his Hobby	H

Chapter 7

The Dandy Charger	124
"Dandy Charger" plate	126
Match against Time or Wood beats Blood and Bone	D
Going to the Races	127
Anti-Dandy Infantry Triumphant	128
Pottery jug	129
Every One His Hobby, plate 1	130
Every One His Hobby, plate 2	130
Enough to make a Horse Laugh !	131
The Pedestrian Carriage, or Walking Accelerator	H
The Chancellors' Hobby, or More Taxes for John Bull	133
The Devil alias Simon Pure	134
Hobby-horse (Museum of Irish Transport)	136
Hobby-Horse Fair	138/9

Chapter 8

British Facilitator, or Travelling Car	142
Grinders	144
Manivelociter, Bivector & Trivector	146
Hobby-horse with suspension spring	148
John Baynes' "land punt"	151
Sievier's Patent Pedestrian Carriage	152
Gompertz's modified velocipede	154
Kent's Marine Velocipede	155

Select Bibliography

Title page of Fairburn's New Pedestrian Carriage	183

About the author

Author on wooden horse	195

v

FOREWORD

by Leslie G. Bowerman

President of the Veteran-Cycle Club 1994-1997
Editor of "Veteran-Cycle Club News & Views" 1987-1997

For the most part authors of books on cycling history fall into two categories – those who reproduce known information, uncorrected myths and all, and those who reproduce known information after excising the myths. We still see new books with the myth of the so-called Comte de Sivrac's 1790 célérifère cited as the first type of bicycle, notwithstanding that Jacques Seray comprehensively proved in 1976 that the célérifère imported by Monsieur Sievrac from England was in fact a horse-drawn carriage.

We can hope, probably in vain, that we have heard the end of the "Leonardo bicycle" now that Professor Dr Hans-Erhard Lessing has manifestly proved that the sketch said to have been in the Codex Atlanticus was neither by Leonardo da Vinci neither was it a bicycle. It was simply somebody's modern-day doodle (with or without original intent to deceive) on a totally unrelated image which had seeped through from the other side of a page.

A valuable service is performed by those who draw together various strands of information already in the public field and present them in an orderly and logical fashion, using skill and judgment to omit what is doubtful or plain wrong.

Roger Street fits into neither of these categories. Appropriately for a scholarly lawyer with a lifetime of relevant experience, he doggedly and meticulously pursues each strand in the subject of his study to its origin. This ensures that he is able to present the reader with much information that is totally new.

Many topics in early cycling history have been worked over again and again and still original truth does not appear. Roger Street, by way of contrast, takes what is recognised as the starting point in cycling history, and surprisingly we realise that it has not been looked at in depth before. He is thus able to present to us a completely new and panoramic view of the start of bicycling, albeit that he is concerned mainly with the British hobby-horse, wisely leaving the detailed study of von Drais and his laufmaschine to Professor Lessing.

Much fruitless academic effort has gone into arguing which type of velocipede, pedestrian or pedal driven, merits what is thought to be the prestigious title of "The First Bicycle". Roger Street sidesteps this esoteric argument, but the story he relates leaves no doubt that the pleasures and pains, the competitive thrills, the companionship of others awheel and the shared experiences are *mutatis mutandis* exactly what we love and tolerate with the latest bicycles today.

In his first chapter, entitled "The Quest for the Medieval Hobby-Horse", Roger Street traces the use of the term "hobby-horse" back to the medieval meaning of s small horse or pony. It is perhaps worth adding – in this day and age when any mention of sex helps the selling of newspapers and books – that William Shakespeare was of course familiar with all the then contemporary meanings of the term "hobby-horse", using it notably in Act IV, Scene 1 of *Othello* to signify a filly that anyone could ride !

This is a delightful book which you will be reluctant to put down until you have been right through, and which you will pick up again and again to savour the atmosphere and sketches of cycling in what Roger points out was an all too brief six months of 1819.

We now have for the first time the complete book of the hobby-horse velocipede.

Nor is it any subject of fair joking, as a thing to be laughed down, if men, because they cannot have wings, acquire a pair of seven-league boots instead, and realise the tales of the Nursery
("Speedy Pace" letter to *Gentleman's Magazine*, May 1819)

PREFACE

The story of the forerunner of the pedal bicycle is both important and highly entertaining. In essence the machine consisted only of two wheels in line supporting a beam on which the rider sat whilst propelling himself forward by pushing with his feet on the ground. Somewhat surprisingly, research into the British, or more specifically English, version of the original continental invention has been limited and no previous book has been devoted to the topic. The author aims to rectify this omission both for the general reader and the veteran-cycle enthusiast.

The hobby-horse was a two-wheeled rider-propelled machine, and can therefore on etymological grounds reasonably be described as the archetypal bicycle (Latin *bis*, twice, late Latin *cyclus*, wheel). Moreover, although it took more than forty years before the idea of adding cranks and pedals to the front wheel of a hobby-horse velocipede became a commercial reality in France, the developmental link between the machine (in its continental form) and the French bicycle (known in England as the "boneshaker") can hardly be disputed. Nevertheless, to avoid possible confusion and controversy, it is probably sensible to acknowledge that the absence of pedals places the earlier item in a category of its own.

Though the two-wheeled machine, even in its hobby-horse form, is generally considered to be still less than 200 years old, there is some tantalisingly fragmentary evidence to suggest that it may have a much longer genealogy. The case for and against is considered in the first chapter. For practical purposes the regular historic period of cycling can be said to date from 1817 in Germany, 1818 in France and 1819 in England. A brief account of the original German "laufmaschine" (which in France became known as the "vélocipède") precedes the detailed story of the English "pedestrian hobby-horse" and the other machines which it inspired.

The contemporary written record is supplemented by a wealth of largely, but not entirely, satirical prints which provide many of the illustrations for this book. Appendices bridge the early Nineteenth and late Twentieth centuries with a list of the hobby-horses still existing in public and private collections in the United Kingdom and elsewhere, and a detailed catalogue of extant prints.

I am deeply indebted to Professor Dr. Hans-Erhard Lessing of Mannheim for much of the material in the chapter on Karl von Drais. I am also grateful to Nick Clayton, Editor of the Veteran-Cycle Club periodical *The Boneshaker,* to Glynn Stockdale, Director of the First Penny-Farthing Museum, and to Les Bowerman, until recently Editor of the VCC magazine *News and Views*, for providing assistance and encouragement generally, as well as to Jim McGurn, author of *On Your Bicycle,* to Pryor Dodge, American author of *The Bicycle*, and to Lorne Shields of Canada, for supplying information. Roland Sauvaget has kindly supplied me with English translations of some French texts. Peter Matthews has helped me to track down the existing Irish hobby-horses. Paul Goldman, until recently Assistant Keeper of the Department of Prints and Drawings at the British Museum, has checked the chapter on the hobby-horse prints and Appendix 3.

I have also received help from the Bibliothèque Nationale, Paris, the Birmingham Central Library, Blenheim Palace, the Bodleian Library, Oxford, the Brighton Reference Library, the British Library, the British Museum, the Cyclists' Touring Club, Godalming, the Guildhall Library, London, Harvard University, Cambridge, Mass., Liverpool Central Library, London Metropolitan Archives, Manchester Central Library, the Mark Hall Cycle Museum, Harlow, the Museum of British Road Transport, Coventry, the Museum of Irish Transport, Killarney, the National Museum of Science and Technology, Ottawa, the Norwich City Library, the Public Record Office, the Salisbury Library, the

Science Museum, the Science Reference Library, the Theatre Museum, the Ulster Folk & Transport Museum, "Velorama" (the National Bicycle Museum of The Netherlands), the Westminster Archives Centre, and a number of other libraries, museums, stately homes and private individuals.

Chapter 1

THE QUEST FOR THE MEDIEVAL
HOBBY-HORSE

The basic idea of movement by means of sitting astride a simplified form of wooden horse on wheels appears to be of medieval origin. It is related to the military exercise of tilting at a post or target known as a quintain. The attack was normally made on horseback or on foot. However a famous Fourteenth century illuminated manuscript in the Bodleian Library, Oxford, *The Romance of Alexander* (ref. MS. Bodley 264), contains a border illustration of a youth on a wooden horse with four wheels, drawn by two of his comrades, tilting at an immovable quintain (the reproduction is from a 1933 collotype facsimile copy of the manuscript also at the Bodleian).

Although this *Alexander* text has apparently been in England since about 1400 it is of Flemish origin and was illuminated by Jehan de Grise between 1338 and 1344 (*The Bodleian Library and its treasures 1320-1700* by David Rogers, 1991). Nevertheless Joseph Strutt in

Tilting at the quintain, 1338-1344 (courtesy of Bodleian Library, Oxford). It seems probable that a machine such as this existed in Europe in the Fourteenth century.

1

the 1833 edition of his *Sports and Pastimes of the People of England* refers to and illustrates this wooden horse under the heading "Running at the quintain practised by the Londoners", and it is quite possible that such a contraption was in use in this country as well as on the continent. The quintain tilter cannot of course be described as riding some sort of primitive bicycle for two reasons. Firstly, he is not propelling himself – though if he were not concerned with holding his lance and charging the target he could presumably thrust forward with his feet in "hobby-horse" style. Secondly, the wooden horse has four wheels, not two. Could it be that we are nevertheless looking at the progenitor of the early Nineteenth century hobby-horse, itself the forerunner of the modern bicycle?

Support for the concept of a "medieval hobby-horse" is to be found in another Fourteenth century illuminated manuscript, the *Sachsenspiegel*, held in the library of Heidelberg University. This contains not one but two intriguing illustrations, one of a man apparently seated astride a beam between two (or perhaps four) wheels, the other of an individual bestriding what is clearly a four-wheeled machine. Both illustrations are reproduced in Jacques Seray's 1988 book *Deux Roues* (at pages 27/28). The images it is said relate to the enfranchisement of a serf by his king. Seray suggests it is an open question whether such a machine actually existed, or whether the representation is symbolic or simply the imagination of the artist. The present author suggests that the combined evidence of both the *Alexander* and *Sachsenspiegel* manuscripts points to the probability of the existence of some form of primitive four-wheeled velocipede in Europe in the Fourteenth century.

According to Ruth Bottomley of the Victoria & Albert Museum : "Large wooden horses on wheels were introduced at the end of the sixteenth century and were big enough for the child to sit on. They perhaps developed from the idea of the tilting seat and proved to be more popular than the hobby-horse because the young child could be given rides ... Some of the horses were pulled along by a string; others were pushed by a pram-type handle ... *Other horses were simply propelled by the feet of the rider*" [the present author's italics] : the quotation is from p.7 of *Rocking Horses* by Ruth Bottomley, Shire Publications, 1991. Ben Jonson's play *Bartholomew Fair* (first performed in 1614) has the toy seller Lanthorn Leatherhead asking the question "What do you buy mistress ? A fine hobby-horse to make

2

your son a tilter ?" In a letter to the author Ruth Bottomley suggests the "hobby-horse" here referred to would have been the ancient stick-between-the-legs type which has been a plaything since Greek and Roman times, rather than a wooden horse on wheels.

It is possible that the Fourteenth century wooden horse pulled by others, and later child's toy sometimes propelled by the feet of the rider, may have developed into an adult rider-propelled vehicle by the Seventeenth century. A small book entitled *A CENTURY of the Names and Scantlings of Inventions by me already practised* written by Edward Somerset, 2nd Marquis of Worcester, in 1655, contains descriptions of a hundred varied inventions he claimed to have "tried and perfected". Although some sound rather fanciful, his Lordship obtained statutory recognition for his "Water-commanding Engine"and is given credit for being "the man who first discovered a mode of applying steam as a mechanical agent" by Charles Partington, the author of an 1825 work on the *Century of Inventions* which included historical and explanatory notes and a biography of Edward Somerset. One of the inventions described by the Marquis forms the 91st "Scantling" (a "scantling" in this context meaning a short summary)and reads as follows :-

> *An artificial Horse, with Saddle, and Caparizons* [decorated coverings] *fit for running at the Ring, on which a man being mounted, with his Lance in his hand, he can at pleasure make him start, and swiftly to run his career, using the decent posture with bon grace, may take the Ring as handsomely, and running as swiftly as if he rode upon a Barbe.*

A fascinating if somewhat problematic account. With our knowledge of the medieval wooden horse it seems reasonable to consider the possibility that the later invention described is a more sophisticated example of the same machine. Although no express mention is made of wheels, it is difficult to imagine how the contrivance could have been anything like "as swift as a Barbe" (i.e. a Barbary horse) without employing them. Whether the article had four wheels or only two, whether it was steerable in any way, must remain matters of conjecture. However if speed was a primary characteristic it may be that there were only two wheels, and the short, straight run to the target suggests steerability might not have been of paramount importance. In any event, the writer of a note in *The Literary*

3

Chronicle and Weekly Review for 22nd May, 1819, who knew of the Seventeenth century "artificial horse", regarded the then newly-introduced velocipede as having "less originality in it than has generally been imagined" – a view not shared by a correspondent in *The Liverpool Mercury* a few days later.

Oddly enough, despite the fact that Charles Partington's book on the *Century of Inventions* came out in 1825, only a few years after the introduction of the hobby-horse velocipede, he ignores this and seeks to relate the 91st Scantling to the various automaton figures constructed in the Eighteenth century by Jacques Vaucanson and others, saying that any person acquainted with them "will readily admit the possibility of making a horse of this description" (one is reminded of the illustrated later "Cantering Propeller" three-wheeled velocipede horse patented by P.W. Mackenzie in America in 1862,

THE CANTERING PROPELLER.

The "Cantering Propeller". Mackenzie's 1862 three-wheeled velocipede horse was driven by a cranked axle with power applied by the feet of the rider.

though this was not strictly an automaton as the motive power came from the rider).

The author's own view is that of the two alternatives the much simpler non-automatic rider-propelled early hobby-horse is the more credible, but there really is not enough evidence to come to any firm conclusion. The point would have been resolved had the Marquis managed to realise his ambition "to leave to Posterity a Book, wherein under each of these Heads the means to put in execution and visible trial all and every of these Inventions, with the shape of all things belonging to them, shall be printed by Brass-plates". Sadly he failed to do this.

The most detailed claim for an actual two-wheeled velocipede substantially pre-dating the known examples is to be found in an article in *Cycling* entitled "From Hobby-Horse to Bicycle" by Fred S. Leftwich B.A., the first part of which is contained in the issue for 21st November, 1896. This states :-

> *The first principle of the bicycle appears to lie in the "hobby-horse", as it was called, of Joseph Patterson, a post-boy in the service of the celebrated post-master Hobson, of Cambridge ... Patterson's "hobby-horse" was merely a miniature wooden horse without legs, mounted on two wheels, and driven along by the rider thrusting his toes on the ground. In 1796, Patterson's son, or grandson, it is uncertain which, constructed several hobby-horses, introducing various improvements on the original, notably a steering gear, which he carried to London, and exhibited for hire in Hyde Park, where they at once became a toy for the entertainment of the exceptionally eccentric few. They gradually gained in popularity until 1804, and Patterson, who owned as many as sixty of these curious aids to locomotion, had acquired a decent fortune, when, owing to a most deplorable fracas arising in connection with a race, in which two gentlemen of quality were killed outright and several others fatally injured, they were by order of the authorities banished from the park, and soon went entirely out of fashion. In 1857 a number of these hobby-horses, in a very bad state of preservation, were discovered in the cellars of an old house in course of demolition on Paddington Green.*

This is a most puzzling item. Not only do we have a non-steerable hobby-horse substantially pre-dating the German invention of 1817 to be described in the next chapter, we also have a steerable variety in use in some numbers in Hyde Park twenty years or so before the foreign machine. The only actual comment following the article in *Cycling* was a letter a fortnight later from James Johnston of the Glasgow Cycling Club, who criticised Leftwich for having omitted any reference to Kirkpatrick Macmillan, the Scottish blacksmith who has been credited with making the first treadle-driven bicycle in about 1840 (a claim now itself hotly disputed in some quarters). In fact the article could have been criticised on a number of other points, and cannot be regarded as recommended reading for anyone interested in acquiring a sound working knowledge of the early history of the bicycle. An obvious inconsistency so far as the Patterson claim is concerned is the reference to Joseph Patterson as having been in the employment of Thomas Hobson (of "Hobson's Choice" fame), as according to the *Dictionary of National Biography* this gentleman lived from c.1544-1631. The "Hyde Park" Patterson (no Christian name is given) is most unlikely to have been a son or grandson of someone living about 150-200 years earlier.

Despite these objections, Leftwich's claim for the Patterson family is so important as to warrant further investigation, particularly in view of the amount of specific detail provided. The author knows of no other reference to Patterson in the Nineteenth or Twentieth century cycling literature, which is itself somewhat surprising. Concentrating on the "deplorable fracas" said to have occurred in 1804, the author carried out fairly extensive research at the Public Record Office in the official records of the Royal parks (of which Hyde Park is one) to try to discover some reference to the banning of hobby-horses. Unfortunately this proved entirely fruitless for the period in question, as did a search in *Palmer's Index to The Times* under various headings for the relevant period, and a lengthy and detailed perusal of every issue of the monthly *Sporting Magazine* (which covers a very wide range of sporting and general topics) from its start in 1792 to 1820. Indeed it was impossible to find a single reference to a hobby-horse velocipede before the "regular historic period", effectively 1819 in England. So as things stand at present the Patterson account can only be labelled "awaiting corroboration". The author's own view is that confirmation is unlikely to be forthcoming, the probability being that the claim is either a complete fabrication or relates to events which occurred at a later date. But he would love to be proved wrong.

The term "hobby-horse" was it seems in regular use from medieval times onwards, but not (if we discount Leftwich) to describe any sort of velocipede until the year 1819. In early times a "hobby" was a small horse or pony and later meanings seem to derive from this.Apart from the well-known stick with a horse's head "ridden" by children, there is the "hobby-horse" figure in olden times worn round the waist by morris dancers. In the late Eighteenth and early Nineteenth centuries the same term was often used to describe an individual's overriding passion (a use popularised by Laurence Stern in his 1759-67 book *Tristram Shandy*). A useful definition from just prior to the English velocipede period, referring to three of these four meanings, is to be found in the 1811 *Dictionary of the Vulgar Tongue* : "HOBBY HORSE. A man's favourite amusement, or study, is called his hobby horse. It also means a particular kind of small Irish horse : and also a wooden one, such as is given to children." One has to be careful to decide which meaning of the word is intended. About four hundred years ago an anonymous author wrote the play *Timon,* on which Shakespeare may have drawn for his more famous *Timon of Athens.* It contains the following lines :-

Dost heare him, Paedio ?
He sayth he rode upon a wodden horse.
That I had such a one ! dost thou know where
Are any wodden horses to be sould,
That neede noe spurrs nor haye ?
Ile aske this strainger.

H'st, master, stay !
Master, what say you to a hobby horse ?

The reference by Gelasimus to the stranger who says he "rode upon a wooden horse" is later explained by his servant Paedio : "But he doth meane a shipp, and not a horse." The stranger who claimed he had "mounted on a wodden horse this day arrived at Pyraeum" had just disembarked at the port of Athens. According to *Brewer's Dictionary of Phrase and Fable* (1981 edition), "Before the days of iron and steel construction a ship was sometimes called a wooden horse." By the opposite analogy the camel is still occasionally referred to as the "ship of the desert". There is no real reason to suppose that Paedio's reference to a "hobby horse" intends to refer to anything other than the child's stick toy, or perhaps the medieval masque accessory.

The *Sporting Magazine* for October, 1795, tells us that "*Walking* Stewart is now *riding* his *hobby-horse* over the mountains of Wales". It is tempting to suppose we have here an early reference to an intrepid velocipedist, but in fact the italics only emphasise that Stewart the well-known pedestrian was simply indulging in his hobby i.e. by trekking on foot over the Welsh mountains. And what is the "curious machine or chair" devised by "an ingenious medical gentleman in the city". Again, the heading "Riding and Walking at the Same Time" in the *Sporting Magazine* for July 1800 suggests, but does not this time expressly refer to, some sort of hobby-horse velocipede. The item is tantalisingly brief. The only further information we are given is that "the invention is well-conceived, and will, no doubt, prove of the highest utility to the aged and infirm, as it is constructed so as to communicate a most pleasant motion, not only to the limbs, but to the body : by riding, at least in a manner quite different from a rocking horse". It is difficult to guess the exact

Boney's Cavalry - a Ruse de Guerre, 1813 (courtesy of David Baldock). Arguably the first "hobby-horse" print - but the "hobbies" shown here are of the type employed by morris dancers, not velocipedes.

form of this "curious machine", but the absence of any reference to wheels or forward movement seems perhaps to indicate some kind of early exercise machine and not a turn-of-the-century hobby-horse.

What must surely be the first "hobby-horse" print is the illustrated *Boney's Cavalry – a Ruse de Guerre or Bayes's troop in French pay*. This was published on 4th May 1813 by Thomas Tegg of Cheapside (of whom more later). The reference is apparently to Napoleon's disastrous invasion of Russia in 1812, which ended in the famous retreat from Moscow and the loss of most of his army. The remaining soldiers are to employ the morris dancers' hobby-horse skirt in an attempt to deceive the opposing forces into thinking the French cavalry is still at full strength. Tegg's comment at the foot of the print is : "As War is Boney's Hobby, then Why not on Hobbies mount his men." But of course we are not referring here to machines of the supposed Patterson type.

Another odd reference occurs in an engraving by Cruikshank published October 1817, of which a copy is in the British Museum. The print is entitled *A Peep into the City of London Tavern* and illustrates a debate on Robert Owen's plan for the relief of the poor which took place on 21st August, 1817. One of the principal opponents of the proposals (on the grounds of their impracticality) was a Mr. Waithman, who is shown holding a document headed "Amendment" and saying : "Mr. Chairman – I rode on my Hobby horse to town this morning for the purpose of opposing the worthy and benevolent Gentleman's Plans..." (which he was successful in doing). The author of the British Museum's *Catalogue of Political Satires*, Dorothy George, suggests that "this may be an early allusion to the velocipede patented in England in 1818". Although as we shall see the German invention referred to earlier was in existence in August 1817 – just – it seems most unlikely that it was in use in London at such an early date. The reference here is probably to an old-established type of horse known as a "hobby" in use in Ireland at about this time, a breed "much valued and admired for their easy paces, and other pleasing, useful and agreeable qualities" according to an article in the *Sporting Magazine* for December, 1792.

There is a verse appearing in the February issue of *The County Magazine* for 1787 which has sometimes been referred to as possibly providing enigmatic evidence for the existence of an Eighteenth century hobby-horse velocipede. It is worth quoting in full :-

A New E N I G M A

> *Though some perhaps will me despise,*
> *Others my charms still highly prize,*
> *(Yet, ne'ertheless, think themselves wise.)*
> *Sometimes, 'tis true, I am a toy,*
> *Contriv'd to please some active boy;*
> *But I amuse each Jack o'dandy,*
> *E'en great men sometimes have me handy,*
> *As witness Mr. Toby Shandy:*
> *Yet seldom I gain many thanks,*
> *Though I serve people of all ranks:-*
> *Lady-painters, lordling fidlers,*
> *And (though I say it) sometimes riddlers,*
> *Who when on me they're got astride,*
> *Think that on Pegasus they ride:*
> *But thus to boast avails me not,*
> *"For O, for O, I am forgot."*

OBSERVATOR.
Whiteparish, Feb. 22, 1787.

It is clear that the answer to the riddle is the word "hobby-horse", and that a number of the word's meanings are being used – the child's toy stick, the "overriding passion" (Toby Shandy's hobby-horse was military fortification), the medieval masque accoutrement (the last line is a quote from Shakespeare's *Hamlet* Act 3, Scene 2, referring to this). The line "But I amuse each Jack o'dandy" is of particular interest in the present context. Another less common name in 1819 for the hobby or pedestrian hobby-horse was "dandy-horse", a reference to the London swells who commonly bestrode the machine. It seems quite a coincidence to find a reference to Jack o' dandy in a 1787 verse about "hobby-horses", and one is almost persuaded to conclude that a two-wheeled adult machine was available for his use at this date. However in the author's opinion, in the light of the existing evidence, it would be wrong to reach such a conclusion.

The "pre-historic" position can be summarised as follows. We know of the existence in medieval times of the simple wooden four-wheeled horse used for tilting at the quintain (and possibly for other purposes), later apparently developing into a child's toy propelled by the feet of the rider. But whether it also developed in the Seventeenth century into the Marquis of Worcester's "artificial horse", which a man being mounted could "at pleasure make him start, and swiftly to run his career", can only be a matter of conjecture. The story of the late-Eighteenth century Patterson non-steerable but later steerable hobby-horse, available for hire in Hyde Park, must be treated with considerable suspicion. It is unlikely that the author of the *County Magazine* "Enigma" had a hobby-horse velocipede in mind, or that such a machine was used by Waithman in London in 1817. It seems therefore that we must look across the water for the genesis of the two-wheeled velocipede.

Chapter 2

KARL VON DRAIS AND HIS

RUNNING MACHINE

The authenticated hobby-horse story starts in Germany in 1817. To be precise on Thursday, 12th June, 1817, in Mannheim, which was the date and place of the first recorded ride (of some nine miles) by its inventor Charles Frederic Christian Louis Baron Drais von Sauerbronn (Karl von Drais was the abbreviation he himself used). Ackermann's *The Repository of Arts* for 1st Feb 1819 contains what is probably the first detailed note on the invention following its appearance in England. The writer states : "The inventor, Baron von Drais, travelled last summer [this should have read the summer before last] from Mannheim to the Swiss relay-house, and back again, a distance of four hours' journey by the posts, in one short hour; and he has lately [in fact at the end of July 1817] with the improved machine, ascended the steep hill from Gernsbach to Baden, which generally requires two hours, in about an hour, and convinced a number of scientific amateurs on the occasion, of the great swiftness of this very interesting species of carriage."

Of course, in its country of origin the machine was not called a "hobby-horse". The first name given to it was a "Loda", which may be a combination of "lo" for locomotive and "da" for dada, the French word for a hobby-horse. The modern illustrations by Joachim Lessing show the machine in its single and tandem forms.

In October 1817 von Drais produced a three-page advertising leaflet describing his invention, which he was now calling a "Laufmaschine" i.e. a "running machine". The well-known illustration of a wavy-haired young rider, identifiable by his uniform as an army staff messenger, also a vehicle plan (both drawn and engraved by W. Siegrist, Mannheim, 1817) are from this leaflet. Professor Dr. Hans-Erhard Lessing suggests that the contemporaneous French translation of this description substituting the word "Vélocipède" (i.e. "quick foot") for "Laufmaschine" shows that the term "velocipede" was coined by von Drais himself. However it is possible that the word was known in Italy some years earlier – a Milan police ordinance of 1811, which cannot at present be dismissed as a forgery, purports to restrict the

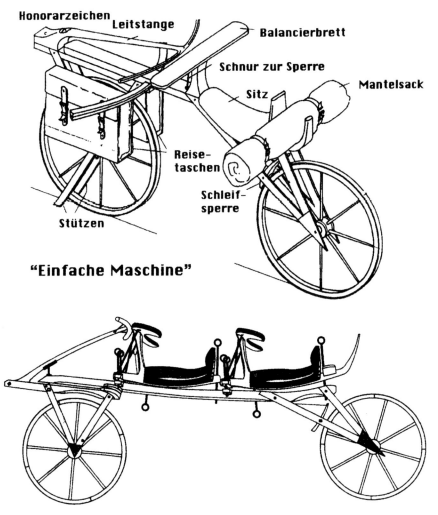

Single and tandem laufmaschines (modern illustrations by Joachim Lessing). The tandem drawing is an attempted reconstruction of what the original might have looked like.

use of "velocipedi" within the city on pain of confiscation of the machine. Further research is in progress.

In recent years there has been considerable German research into von Drais and his inventions, as a result of which we now have a wealth of biographical detail. What may well be the only authentic picture of the inventor is in the possession of the Städt. Reiss-

Army staff messenger on laufmaschine, 1817 (Drais advertising leaflet). Military use of the two-wheeler was contemplated at an early date.

Museum, Mannheim. The illustration is a considerably enlarged portion of a print of an 1819 painting by J.P.Karg of a scene in the Mannheim Castle gardens. Towards the front of the main frame can be seen the letters "v.Dr." i.e. von Drais, and this would seem to be intended to be a portrait of the man himself.

Von Drais' early years were summarised by Hans Lessing in his paper *Karl von Drais' two-wheeler – what we know* read at the First International Conference of Cycling History in Glasgow in May 1990:-

Karl von Drais ... was born in 1785 as the eldest child and only son of a leading official of the margrave of Badenia, in Karlsruhe, seat of the Badenian court. In those times the German speaking countries were split into a multitude of small political entities – with no national patent law at all ! Presumably in opposition to his father, who had studied law and suffered from an epilepsy, young Karl developed mechanical inventive skills. He had no easy boyhood – his mother died when he was fourteen, and before

Illus. of Karl von Drais on his machine, 1819 (courtesy of Städt. Reiss-Museum, Mannheim). Although seeming older than his years, this may be the only authentic contemporaneous illustration of the inventor.

16

that the whole family had to flee the approaching French revolutionary army. Leaving school in 1800 he joined the private forestry school of his uncle and then studied physics and architecture at the university of Heidelberg for two years. In 1810 he was named Forstmeister (district forest officer), but was – with the help of his influential father – able to take paid leave ! This worked well enough as long as his father lived, but later on the envious Badenian civil servants took revenge. The family had moved to Mannheim, also on the Rhine river, and Karl, now 25 years old, started inventing and publishing in the local newspapers.

The precursor to von Drais's radically new Laufmaschine was his less original invention of a four-wheeled "Fahrmaschine" or "driving machine", for which he applied – and was refused – a Badenian privilege in 1813. There is no extant drawing of this item, but von Drais described it as having a cranked rear axle driven directly by the rider's feet. The prototype was a tandem with the front rider steering the front wheels by two vertical struts – which could be let down to serve as shafts for a horse on steep hills or in an emergency. The intended use of the vehicle was to provide : "summer spins for wealthy citizens, mail transport by keepers of post horses, war times transport of the wounded, transport of small loads." Von Drais stated the machine could achieve a speed of two hours' walk within an hour, apparently meaning just four miles per hour, a modest enough but possibly accurate claim having regard to the poor state of the roads at that time. The reasons why the inventor relinquished his first "carriage without horses" are stated by Fairburn in his 1819 *New Pedestrian Carriage* booklet to be that "it required two servants to work it , and was a very complicated piece of workmanship, besides being heavy and expensive".

It appears that for the next few years von Drais abandoned the idea of land transport, concentrating on inventions such as a diving machine, a shooting machine and a method of speed writing. Professor Lessing suggests it may have been the volcanic eruption of the Tambora on the Little Sunda Islands in April, 1815, which indirectly inspired von Drais to invent his two-wheeled Laufmaschine. The eruption gave rise to a worldwide ecological catastrophe in the form of freak weather conditions, which in Germany in 1816 resulted in a bad harvest and famine causing some 40,000 people to emigrate. As Adam Smith had written earlier, did it make sense to feed horses for transport when people were starving ? If we accept this theory, it suggests that von Drais may have been planning his new machine for up to a year before it actually took to the road.

If a volcanic eruption may have produced the *motivation* for a new machine, it is likely that the actual *inspiration* was the activity of ice skating. In his advertising leaflet of October 1817 (as translated in the *Birmingham Commercial Herald* for 20th March, 1819) von Drais states : "On a hard road, the rapidity of the Velocipede resembles that of an expert skaiter; as the principles of the two motions are the same. In truth, it runs a considerable distance while the rider is inactive, and with the same rapidity as when his feet are in motion." An English newspaper put it more succinctly the following year : "The principle of the invention is taken from the *Art of Skaiting*" (*The Courier*, 11th December, 1818). The following limerick by the present author not only records the supposed inspirational moment, but also aims to assist English speakers with the correct pronunciation of the inventor's name:-

> *There once was a Baron von Drais* [pronounced "Drice"]
> *Who observed some swift skaters on ice*
> *"If they balance on steels*
> *Then why not two wheels –*
> *Yes, a Laufmaschine, that would be nice !"*

Von Drais' leaflet is effectively divided into two parts. It starts by describing the machine's advantages (again the quote is from the *Birmingham Commercial Herald*) : "1st, That on a well-maintained post road, it will travel up hill as fast as an active man can walk. - 2nd, On a plain, even after a heavy rain, it will go six or seven miles an hour, which is as swift as a courier. – 3rd, When roads are dry and firm, it runs on a plain at the rate of eight or nine miles an hour, which is equal to a horse's gallop. – 4th, On a descent, it equals a horse at full speed." Comparing his new machine with the long-established horse-drawn vehicle, von Drais says : "As a horse draws, in a well-constructed carriage, both the carriage and its load much easier than he could carry the load alone on its back; so a man conducts, by means of the Velocipede, his body easier than if he had its whole weight to support on his feet. It is equally incontestable that the Velocipede, as it makes but one impression, or rut, may always be directed on the best part of a road."

Leipzig machine. One of a number of unauthorised, albeit modified, copies of von Drais' machine. Note the simplified steering arrangement, also the capacious luggage-carrying baskets.

In the second part of the leaflet Karl von Drais considers the promotion of the item. The protection of his invention was a matter of real concern to him, as at this date there was no unified German state with power to grant patents but only a number of independent dukedoms. We know that in the latter part of 1817 plagiarised designs appeared in Dresden, Frankfurt and Leipzig. The illustration of a Leipzig machine (surmounted by bonnets) appeared the same year in issue no.47 of the German fashion magazine *Modem-Zeitung*.

Von Drais tells us that his personal wish was to obtain patents giving him exclusive rights of exploitation both at home and abroad, but that he did not want to delay the public benefits of his invention. He had therefore decided, whilst reserving his rights, to provide details of the machine in advance of obtaining formal protection, taking the philanthropic view that his own interests should be secondary. The inventor hoped that the public would in turn show good faith by adopting an interim proposal on a voluntary basis, under which he would receive an honorarium of a Carolin for each item made and sold by anyone other than himself. He would then issue a numbered badge to be fixed to the front of the machine as proof of payment. Von Drais said that if the payment of a Carolin presented a difficulty in any particular case he would accept half of this amount. A detailed specification to assist manufacture would be supplied free on demand to anyone applying for a licence.

At this date (October 1817) von Drais was apparently himself making machines to order (although he was uncertain whether he would be able to continue to do so the following year and was hoping that the task could be entrusted to an enterprising manufacturer). He asked customers to specify their inside leg measurement as this would determine the height of the seat of the machine. Von Drais stated that orders would normally be completed within a month, but that he could only guarantee prices for orders placed in the then current year. A standard machine (with badge), including if required provision for carrying clothing, a brake and a stand, was to cost four Carolin. Different prices were to apply in respect of machines with a seat height adjustment, tandems, and three and four-wheeled machines with a passenger seat in front and a rider's seat behind.

Von Drais' leaflet tells us that three or four-wheeled machines were not really suitable for travelling on country roads, and were more appropriate to wide, level promenades in good condition, where even ladies could be carried in comfort as swiftly as a racing sled. There was of course the advantage over the sled of not having to suffer the dust thrown up by the horses, and one could sit in comfort in the open and enjoy the view. For even greater elegance and enjoyment one could have "a silk umbrella against sun and rain" or "a sail to make use of prevailing winds". A lantern could also be supplied on request, obviously allowing the machine to be used at night.

Von Drais' application in 1817 for a Badenian privilege was granted early the following year. He also applied by his patent agent Louis Dineur for a patent in France, which was duly granted in February, 1818. At the same time in April, 1818, that he was giving a lecture and demonstration in Frankfurt, a servant was exhibiting the machine in the Luxembourg Gardens in Paris. The latter event was described in the *Liverpool Mercury* for 24th April, 1818, under the heading "CARRIAGE WITHOUT HORSES. (From the Paris papers.)" in the following terms :-

An immense concourse of spectators assembled yesterday [5th April 1818] at noon, at Luxemburg, to witness the experiments with Draisiennes (a species of carriage moved by machinery without horses.) The crowd was so great that the experiments were but imperfectly made. The machine went, however, quicker than a man running at speed, and the conductors did not appear fatigued. About three, a lady appeared in a Draisienne, conducted by the chasseur [huntsman] of the Baron de Drais, who made with it several turns in the alleys, in the midst of the crowd. The machine, although charged with a double weight, had the same rapidity, and the efforts of the conductor did not seem to be increased. The machine ascended with facility the hillocks which are placed in some parts of the garden. The Draisiennes appear to be convenient for the country, and for short journies on good roads.

The illustrated French print *Draisiennes dites Velocipedes* apparently dates from April 1818. It depicts (translating from the French inscription) "portable and economic horses invented outside France". The Bibilotheque Nationale catalogue of prints describes the scene (again translating from the French) as "German velocipedist guided by a goose". In view of the date it seems reasonable to speculate that the individual caricatured may be the servant of Karl von Drais, followed by another rider, venturing beyond Paris into the open countryside.

In October, 1818, Drais himself travelled to France and demonstrated his velocipede in both Nancy and Paris. A detailed English description of the impact of the Draisienne in France, and elsewhere in Europe, is contained in *On Your Bicycle* by James McGurn, 1987 (in the section "The Running-Machine" pp.14-18). Comprehensive biographical notes on the German inventor are contained in an article by Professor Lessing entitled "Karl von Drais" in *The Boneshaker*, (the magazine of the Veteran-Cycle Club), no.109, Winter 1985. Von Drais died aged 66 years on 12th October, 1851, and more than forty years later in 1893 a monument was erected to his memory at his birthplace Karlsruhe by the German Bicyclists Union.

Draisiennes dites Velocipedes. (Courtesy of Museum of British Road Transport, Coventry). An interesting if somewhat puzzling print. Who was the rider ? Why was he armed with two pistols and a sword ? Who was the second rider only hinted at in the picture ? And why the goose ?!!

It has been suggested that Karl von Drais paid a visit to London around 1818 and had a machine made for him by a mechanic "Knight" (*Vélocipèdes*, Lockert, Paris, 1896, pp. 54/55), and it seems German sources refer to this individual as having improved the Laufmaschine in England. This may be so (we know von Drais came here in 1832, still trying to promote a modified machine) though the present author has never come across any reference to Knight in the contemporary English periodicals or newspapers.

What we do have is an interesting reference in a lecture given by Thomas Davies in May 1837 ("On the Velocipede", reproduced in *The Boneshaker*, no.108, Autumn 1985) to the use of a Laufmaschine made in England at an early date. Davies tells us :-

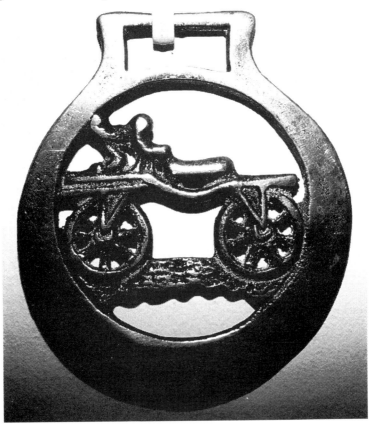

Draisienne horse-brass (author's collection). A modern horse-brass struck in 1976 to commemorate the twenty-first anniversary of the formation of the Southern Veteran-Cycle Club (now the Veteran-Cycle Club).

Soon after the publication of [the von Drais pamphlet], *a German gentleman with whom I was acquainted, named Mr. Bernhard Seine, a native of the City of Mannheim, came to England, about twenty years ago, bringing with him the pamphlet, and he frequently rode about the streets of the city of Bath upon a velocipede made after the construction of the original invention. Mr. Seine did not hesitate to run on his velocipede at a violent rate down some of the steepest streets in that city over the pitching of the road, but I never heard of his meeting with any accident.*

According to the normally reliable Pryor Dodge (*The Bicycle* p.18), "Velocipedes were soon all the rage in the fashionable spa town. For the next few years the gentlemen of Bath rode Draisines in the outlying hills as part of their health regime, making short trips of twelve to fourteen miles and day trips of up to forty." Regrettably, no source reference is able to be provided.

Chapter 3

DENIS JOHNSON AND HIS PEDESTRIAN CURRICLE

Herr Bernhard Seine may have been England's first velocipedist.But the real credit for introducing the machine into this country belongs wholly and solely to another individual, a coachmaker of Long Acre in the City of Westminster, Denis Johnson. At present we know relatively little of his early life, despite the primary importance of his role in connection with the development of the English pedestrian hobby-horse. (An article *The First Bicycle* in *The Wheel World* for September 1883 purporting to tell of the "factory mechanic" Johnson's life and joint invention of the machine with his sister in "a small village on the South Coast of England" is entirely fictitious and should be disregarded.) Regrettably, the majority of the early records of the Worshipful Company of Coachmakers and Coach Harness Makers were destroyed during the Second World War, and those that remain at the Guildhall Library, London, contain no reference to Johnson.

According to the French author Jacques Seray in *Deux Roues*, "it is said he had been trained as a clockmaker or watchmaker", but no authority is quoted in support. It could be that the statement has its origin in an error in *The Repertory of Arts* for January 1819, which in a list of new patents inadvertently refers to Johnson as a watch-maker. Although none of the standard biographical dictionaries contains any mention of our man (even the contemporary *Annual Biography and Obituary* published in London from 1817 to 1837 fails to notice him), the author has contributed an article to the *New Dictionary of National Biography* to be published in 2004.

Johnson's stated age at death suggests he was born in 1760, but as yet we have no knowledge of his place or exact date of birth. Denis Johnson married Mary Newman by licence of the Archbishop of

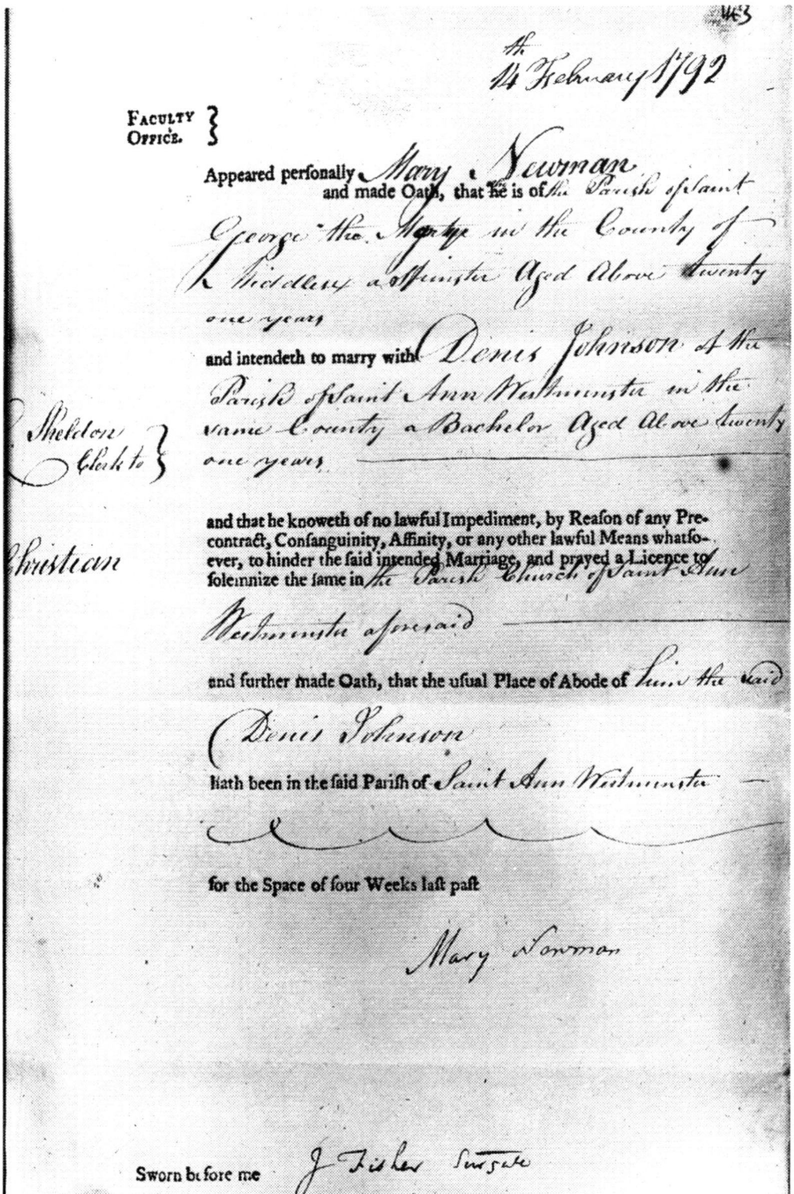

14th February 1792

FACULTY OFFICE.

Appeared personally _Mary Newman_ and made Oath, that he is of _the Parish of Saint George the Martyr in the County of Middlesex Westminster_ Aged Above twenty one years

and intendeth to marry with _Denis Johnson of the Parish of Saint Ann Westminster in the same County a Bachelor_ Aged Above twenty one years

Sheldon Clerk to

Christian

and that he knoweth of no lawful Impediment, by Reason of any Pre-contract, Consanguinity, Affinity, or any other lawful Means whatsoever, to hinder the said intended Marriage, and prayed a Licence to solemnize the same in _the Parish Church of Saint Ann Westminster aforesaid_

and further made Oath, that the usual Place of Abode of _him the said Denis Johnson_ hath been in the said Parish of _Saint Ann Westminster_

for the Space of four Weeks last past

Mary Newman

Sworn before me _J Fisher Surrogate_

Marriage licence allegation, 1792 (by courtesy of Lambeth Palace Library, London). The licence itself was granted the same day as the allegation (and bond) - St. Valentine's Day, 14th February 1792 - and the marriage between Denis Johnson and Mary Newman took place three days later.

26

Canterbury at St. Anne's parish church, Soho (the bridegroom's parish), in the City of Westminster on Friday, 17th February, 1792, when he would have been 31 or 32 years old. The application for the licence was made by Denis's fiancée, as the illustrated marriage allegation shows. Neither party had previously been married. Why the couple decided to pay a fee to avoid publication of banns in their parish churches, why the application was to the archbishop as opposed to the bishop or archdeacon of the diocese, why Mary and not Denis made the allegation (and provided a bond against any "lawful impediment"), must for the moment remain matters of conjecture.

Denis and Mary had two daughters, Mary and Ann, born in 1795 and 1798 respectively. The family lived in Soho for a number of years, certainly until the turn of the century. Presumably Denis was working as a coachmaker, though as yet we have no proof of this. During the 1790s a certain Joseph Johnson had a coachmaking business in Clerkenwell (and he may likewise have lived in Soho). It is possible

Johnson, the First Rider on the Pedestrian Hobbyhorse, 1819 (courtesy of Museum of British Road Transport, Coventry). A more respectful, though not necessarily more accurate, representation of the "famed jockey".

27

that this was a relative of Johnson's for whom he worked for a while, but again this can only be speculation at this stage. In Holden's Triennial Directory for 1799 Johnson has no entry in the business section, but is listed as having a private address in Batemans Buildings, a narrow thoroughfare immediately to the south of Soho Square (then known as King Square), where he is recorded as paying the usual householder rates.

Denis Johnson was in his late fifties when von Drais invented his Laufmaschine, which became known as the Draisienne in France and was soon heard of in England. Johnson's known age seems to tie in with what may be the best extant portrait we have of him, in the colour illustrated 1819 lithograph *Stop him who can !! An English patentee introducing a French hobby-horse – or a bit of a push down Highgate-Hill to Long Acre*. Nevertheless, one can only hope that this caricature (possibly by or after George Cruikshank) does our hero less than justice, as it certainly portrays him in an unattractive light. A less detailed, but more flattering, representation is contained in the illustrated print *Johnson, the First Rider on the Pedestrian Hobbyhorse*, published by Ackermann and dated 1st May. Both drawings depict Johnson as a man of only modest stature.

As a result of a search in the Tabley House papers in the John Ryland Library, Manchester, reported to Glynn Stockdale of the Veteran-Cycle Club, we have examples (see photo illustration) of Denis

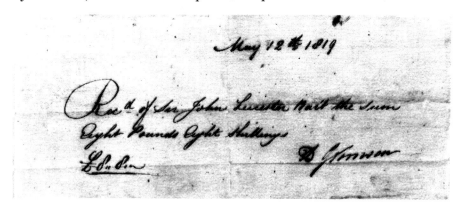

Receipt with signature of Denis Johnson (reproduced by courtesy of the University of Manchester). An account also in Johnson's hand confirms the payment is for "a New Patent Pedestrian Machine".

Johnson's businesslike handwriting and signature. Although there is a gap of more than a quarter of a century, Johnson's 1792 signature in the St. Anne's marriage register is very similar to those of the

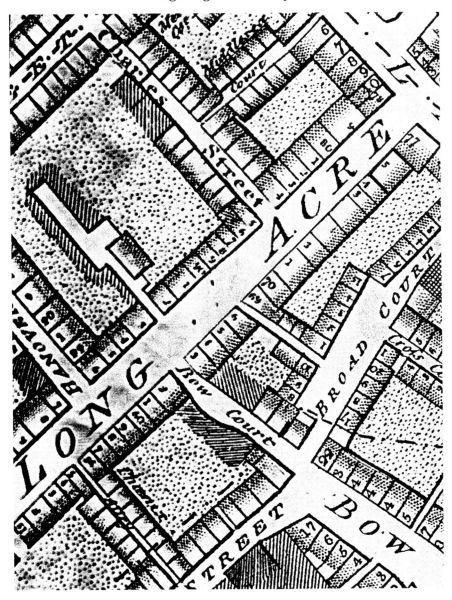

Horwood's *Plan of the Cities of London, Westminster & Southwark* (courtesy of Westminster Archives Centre, London). As can be seen Johnson's premises at 75 Long Acre occupied one of the larger sites.

Tabley House receipts.

The rating records for the parish of St. Martin-in-the-Fields show that Johnson took occupation of 75, Long Acre, in March 1818 (the year is also confirmed by the London trade directories). An extract from Horwood's *Plan of the Cities of London, Westminster and Southwark* shows the street layout in Johnson's day, little altered at the present time. No.75 adjoins the property on the corner of Long Acre and Drury Lane (the parish and city boundary). The site of the long-demolished premises is now part of Acre House, 69-76, Long

Long overdue recognition at Long Acre. The proposed Denis Johnson commemorative plaque hopefully soon to be installed at Acre House. Courtesy of City of Westminster. An interior display is also planned.

Acre, a late Nineteenth century building currently being refurbished for use by the Italian fashion house Balloon SPA as their UK headquarters. At the author's suggestion the Covent Garden Area Trust has applied to the City of Westminster, under its commemorative Green Plaques Scheme, for the Council to erect a plaque on the present building to record that this is the site of Denis Johnson's workshop. The illustrated drawing is by The Royal Label Factory. The Veteran-Cycle Club is sponsoring the proposal.

We do not know exactly how Johnson became aware of the von Drais machine, but we do know that this was his inspiration for devising a more attractive and streamlined version of his own. And it must surely have been Denis Johnson who was the "ingenious coach-builder of this metropolis" who was said to have "procured one of these very useful machines, in which he expects to make some important improvements" (*The Courier*, 11th December, 1818, under the heading "Newly-Invented Carriage"). As a coachmaker Johnson was able to use his professional skills to improve the German machine, particularly by subsisting metal for wood where he thought it appropriate to do so.

It was probably in the Autumn of 1818 (the exact date is not known) that Johnson applied by Petition to be granted a patent. There appears to be no copy of the Petition (or of the required law officer's Report) extant, although the document is referred to in a Warrant dated 6th November, 1818, and in a Bill dated 11th December, 1818, both leading to the Grant of the patent (Public Record Office ref.s HO 89/9 and SO 7/306 respectively). According to a contemporaneous German newspaper (*Oppositions-Blatt oder Weimarische Zeitung*) the patent cost was the then not inconsiderable sum of £100.

A complete copy of the Grant to Denis Johnson of Royal Letters Patent dated 22nd December, 1818 – no. 4321 of 1818 – can be seen on a patent roll at the Public Record Office at Kew (P.R.O. ref. C66/4205). It commences as follows :-

GEORGE the Third by the Grace of God etc. To all to whom these Presents shall come Greeting Whereas Denis Johnson of 75 Long Acre in the Parish of Saint Martin in the Fields in the County of Middlesex Coachmaker hath by his Petition humbly represented unto us that in consequence of a Communication

31

made to him by a certain Foreigner residing abroad he is become
possessed of a certain invention of a Machine for the purpose of
diminishing the labour and fatigue of persons in walking and
enabling them at the same time to use greater speed which said
Machine he intends calling the Pedestrian Curricle That the said
invention or machine is new in this kingdom and hath not been
practised therein by any other person or persons whomsoever to
his knowledge or belief ...

We do not have the name of the "certain Foreigner residing abroad" who communicated the invention to the London coachmaker. Could it have been von Drais himself? This seems unlikely though it cannot at this stage be ruled out as a possibility. Karl von Drais applied outside Germany for patents in Austria (unsuccessfully) and France (successfully), and if he had wanted to could presumably have done so through an agent in England. There is no evidence of any arrangement between Johnson and von Drais under which the German inventor agreed to the English coachmaker proceeding with a patent application in his own name in consideration of financial recompense.

The Grant of Patent was for a term of fourteen years and gave Johnson six months to provide full details of his invention. This he did just in time, the Specification (with drawings) being dated and inrolled on 21st June, 1819 (P.R.O. ref. C 54/9824). The document is reproduced in full in Appendix 1. and is largely self-explanatory. It will be noted that the seat of the machine is adjustable, also that like the Draisienne there is a rest for the rider's elbows and forearms "so as to support himself with the full muscular use of his legs". An important sentence appears towards the end of the document : "The dimensions of this machine must depend upon the height and weight of the person who is to use it, as well as the materials of which it may be formed, consequently no specific directions can be given about them, further than saying that the lighter and more free from friction the whole can be made, and the larger the diameter of the wheels, the better and more expeditious the machine will be."

As depicted in the patent specification drawings (and in many of the prints) the front and rear wheels appear to be the same size, but some surviving machines have a rear wheel slightly larger than the front one – for example the Science Museum's exhibit has a 25.5"

STOP HIM WHO CAN !!.— an English Patentee introducing a French hobby-horse — or a bit of a push down Highgate-hill to Long Acre.

Stop him who can !!, 1819 (courtesy of the Pryor Dodge Collection). We know that Denis Johnson was a skilled velocipedist, so this depiction of him on a machine causing mayhem on Highgate Hill seems unfair. If the artist is Cruikshank, he may well be recalling his own escapade on the same hill described in Chapter 7. Note absence of arm rest - a machine ridden by Johnson would in reality have had one.

A

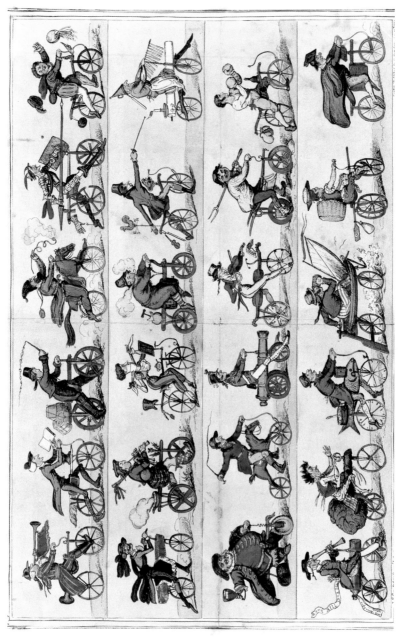

Every Man on his Perch, or Going to Hobby Fair (by courtesy of the National Museum of Science and Technology, Ottawa, Canada). Three of the hobby-horse riders are depicted on imaginary three-wheelers appropriate to their trades.

B

PEDESTRIAN HOBBYHORSE.
McIobson, Puttenier, 75.Long.Acre.

Published at Ackermanns.

Pedestrian Hobbyhorse, 1819 (author's collection). The earliest know hobby-horse print. Although dated simply "February 1819" it is featured as Plate 9 in Ackermann's *Repository of Arts* for 1st February 1819.

C

Match against Time or *Wood beats Blood and Bone*, 1819 (author's collection). Both riders are similarly attired as horse jockeys. The actual velocipede riders at the 1819 Ipswich races were to be "in jockey dresses".

D

diameter front wheel and a 27" rear wheel (the jacket illustration of *The Dandy Charger* shows the front wheel slightly larger but this should probably be interpreted as a perspective distortion). Most known examples have ten spokes per wheel (two have twelve). The extant Johnson machines detailed in Appendix 2. are of varying sizes, and were no doubt supplied in accordance with the requirements of individual purchasers. Some of the surviving examples are fitted with a simple metal rod stand for use when the machine is not being ridden. No known Johnson velocipede has or had a brake fitted, even though von Drais had allowed for one on his Laufmaschine.

Several of the existing Johnson hobby-horses have his brass oval name-plate on the front of the steering handle stating "JOHNSON'S PATENT" above the Royal Coat of Arms, with his address "75 LONG ACRE LONDON" underneath, as shown in the photo illustration of the Science Museum Wroughton machine. Likewise, in most examples, the short steering bar commonly employed (discussed below) is immediately above a brass dome, the inspiration for which has been said to be the nearby dome of St. Paul's cathedral, and there is sometimes a brass leafy ornament at the front and rear. Additionally, several of the known machines have a piece of ornamental metalwork bridging the dome. In contemporary literature the weight of the manufactured item was commonly given as about 50 lb.s but some of the surviving examples weigh considerably less than this.

It seems that, in addition to his two-wheelers, Denis Johnson also made a three-wheeler. This is shown in the colour illustrated print *Pedestrians travelling on the New Invented Hobby horse!* published by Sidebethem in 1819, the artist/engraver being Robert Cruikshank (as well as in another, unillustrated, Cruikshank print *Dandies on their Hobbies!*, the machines in this case also having a seat for a lady passenger).

As can be seen from the print, the two rear wheels are relatively close together, and the suggestion is that the machine was intended to provide simply an aid to balancing, rather than to create a tricycle as we would understand the word today. The fact that the steering bar is of the "indirect" type by a curved bar to the front wheel axle, also the print title words "New Invented", perhaps indicates that this was a "swift walker" dating from the early Spring of 1819 and later abandoned, though it is impossible to be categoric. What is fairly certain is that such machines were actually made, as the hobby-horse print artist is unlikely to have depicted this relatively small but important variation of the Johnson item if it had not in fact existed. Some imaginary three-wheeled hobby-horses are featured in the colour illustrated Robert Cruikshank print *Every Man on his Perch, or Going to Hobby Fair*, published by G. Humphrey dated 10th July, 1819.

A certain "E.B.", writing at some length in the *Monthly Magazine* for July 1819, describes the two-wheeler as "a very superior mode of exercise" and adds "I do not believe those of two wheels behind will answer, as they would require very great exertion". And it appears there was a German version of such a three-wheeler based on von Drais' invention. An article in the magazine *Miscellanies for Instruction and Entertainment*, Dresden, 28th November, 1817 (the translation by Prof. Lessing appears in *The Boneshaker* for Spring 1995) contains the same reservations as E.B. : "Those who believe to do better with two hind wheels side-by-side instead of one in order to

Child's hobby-horse (Worthing Museum). A unique machine, by or after Johnson.

be spared of balancing, err considerably, because of the arising threefold track instead of the single one and therefore increased friction, the machine goes of course much harder and the feet are prone to mingle with the hind wheels".

What may just possibly be a child's machine by Johnson (though there is no nameplate or visible number) is shown in the photo illustration. Both wheels have a diameter of 18.5". This item is in the custody of the Worthing Museum, who are unable to provide any provenance other than the fact that the machine came to them in the 1930s from a Mr. R.E. Aldard of Worthing. It is also illustrated in Henfrey Smail's *Coaching Times & After* (Worthing, 1948), above the title "The Hobby Horse of 1819, the Forerunner of the Bicycle". At the "nose" end of the main beam is a small silver crest of a cubit arm in armour holding a cutlass. According to Hubert Chesshyre, Norroy and Ulster King of Arms at the College of Arms in London, this is identifiable with the Seventeenth century Beadle family of Essex, and it may well be that the child's hobby-horse belonged to a descendant.

Denis Johnson used Roman numerals to number his machines, presumably on a consecutive chronological basis. The Account Book of the House Steward of the Third Duke of Northumberland contains a payment item for 26th May 1819 "Bill for new pedestrian machines 22 – –" (i.e. £22). This clearly relates to the Duke of Northumberland's two machines numbered 299 and 300. Sir John Leicester of Tabley House bought two machines, the receipts for which are dated 1st April and 12th May 1819 respectively. As far as we know, the only machine now extant is the one bearing the number 100. It seems most unlikely that a machine of this number would have been sold only a fortnight before ones bearing the numbers 299 and 300, which suggests that the existing Tabley hobby-horse was the one with the receipt dated 1st April, 1819. If we have roughly an eight week gap between items 100 and 300, this in turn suggests that Johnson was manufacturing about 25 machines a week, which seems a reasonable enough figure if we assume perhaps that he had a small team of workmen to assist him to meet the demand.

On this straight line basis the first machine would have been made at the beginning of March, but no doubt the manufacturing process was speeded up as both proficiency and demand increased, so that

35

the earliest items could perhaps date from nearer the beginning of the year. As we know of no machine with a higher number than 320, production may have largely ceased by about June or July, 1819. It must however be emphasised that for the moment these suggested dates are mainly uncorroborated and further evidence will need to be forthcoming before anything like a reliable chronology can be established. In particular it should be borne in mind that the quoted dates of payment/receipt may not be equally related to the respective dates of manufacture/delivery. A number of Johnson machines have come to light in recent years, and with renewed interest in the topic

Denis Johnson velocipede no. 316 (courtesy of "Velorama", National Bicycle Museum, Nijmegen, The Netherlands). The underside of the saddle displaying the number CCCXVI.

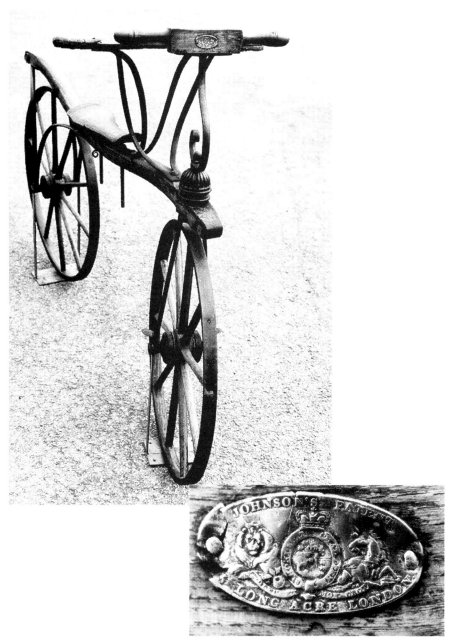

Denis Johnson velocipede no. 204 (courtesy of Science Museum Wroughton) - two views. Note straight handle, direct steering bar and arm rest with four supports. Johnson's name plate, despite being worn and cracked, is still an attractive item.

we can hope that more information will become available.

Johnson usually numbered his machines by scoring the Roman numerals on the top of the beam or backbone underneath the saddle, sometimes also on the underside of the wooden saddle itself, and on at least one occasion on the arm rest or balance-board. The illustrated Nijmegen example is of the underside of the restored saddle upholstery, with the all-important (and late) number CCCXVI (316) now framed in a leather window.

The patent specification contains one puzzle. The drawings show the steering of the machine to be by way of a handle and light curved bar to "the axis, or axis carriage of the front wheel" as Johnson describes it. In fact, this early arrangement had by the June 1819 date of the specification to some extent given way to the more direct steering shown in the colour illustrated drawing *Jack mounted on his Dandy Charger*, which is dated 1st March, 1819 (the joke is a play on the term "dandy charger", which the artist takes to mean a machine for

Denis Johnson velocipede no. 221 (courtesy of Copenhagen City Museum). This machine has apparently been at the Copenhagen City Museum since its inception in 1901.

charging dandies – instead of a machine on which dandies charge). According to John Fairburn, the author of the contemporary work in which this print appears as a frontispiece, it was "drawn by an eminent Artist, from one of the latest improvements of the Machine." One might have expected Johnson to have referred to the later arrangement in his patent specification, at least as an alternative. The fact that he did not do so perhaps suggests that, although he certainly incorporated direct steering in his machines, he did not claim to have originated this important improvement.

The wooden handle to which the metal steering bar was attached was again of two different types. The more common one (to judge from the surviving examples) was straight and comprised a square

Denis Johnson velocipede no. 100 (Tabley House). Johnson's machines were finished in a variety of colours. This item was canary yellow coachlined in black.

39

central section with rounded hand grips at either end (see e.g. the illustrated Science Museum machine). A less common version (see for example the illustrated Copenhagen and Tabley House machines) was attractively curved and lacked the bulbous hand grips.

Another minor modification of the Johnson velocipede involved the metal supports to the balance-board. The patent drawings show a machine with just three support bars, two at the front and one at the rear. The surviving Johnson machines are of two types. In one there is indeed only one rear support rising from the main beam, but this splits higher up to form a "V" and so provide two attachment points in addition to the two front supports. The illustrated Johnson item, discovered by Glynn Stockdale in a cellar at Tabley House, Cheshire, in 1989, has a single rear stay of this type (this is in fact a replacement as the original was missing). In the second type there are identical twin support bars at front and rear (the illustrated Science Museum machine is an example). The illustrated machine with two support bars at the rear and one at the front is obviously by a different maker

Hobby-horse (by courtesy of the National Museum of Science and Technology, Ottawa, Canada). Another of several machines that have found their way abroad. Although in the photo the rear wheel looks larger than the front one, they are in fact both said to be 27.5" diameter.

Denis Johnson velocipede no. 25 (Mark Hall Cycle Museum, Harlow) -
three views. Details from the earliest known machine, showing the brass
ornamentation on the "nose" and dome, also footrests. The general view
is by courtesy of the Mark Hall Cycle Museum.

Denis Johnson velocipede no. 31 (private owner) - two views. Whilst the "indirect" steering is the most significant feature, the machine also displays the single "V" rear support bar to the arm rest. The close-up of the front wheel hub and boss shows what may originally have been hinged foot-rests, now however fixed flush to the front fork.

but based on the Johnson item. It formerly belonged to the Duke of Argyll.

The earliest known Johnson machine is number 25 (XXV), which can be seen at the Mark Hall Cycle Museum in Harlow. As can be seen from the photo illustration, this already incorporates the "improved" i.e. direct steering. The next earliest example is number 31 (XXXI) (the number was prior to restoration on the arm rest – the original has been retained – as well as underneath the saddle and on the main beam). This is the only known Johnson machine with the original "indirect" steering, and hence an item of particular interest. As the photo illustration shows, it is very similar to the patent specification drawings – even to the extent of being painted green (a portion of the main beam had to be replaced during restoration – part of it has been retained with the machine and displays the same colour, as does the original saddle cover).

As the original steering arrangement is featured in a number of hobby-horse prints dating from March and April 1819 (the illustrated *Johnson's Pedestrian Hobbyhorse Riding School* dated 17th April, 1819 depicts only indirect steering machines), it would seem that for

Johnson's Pedestrian Hobbyhorse Riding School, 1819 (author's collection). Although all the machines have indirect steering, Johnson himself is depicted on a direct steerer just fourteen days later.

43

Hobby-horse (Ipswich Museum) - two views. An interesting machine by an unknown maker. The saddle spring (obviously the saddle itself) and chest rest and bar may be later modifications.

some while both types of machine were being made. One of only a few known surviving pedestrian hobby-horses with steering by a long curved bar to the front wheel hub is the one at the Ipswich Museum's store shown in the photo illustration. Unlike the Johnson original, the curved steering bar is supported and pivots at the top just in front of a relatively wide handlebar. This was a sensible modification as the curved bar of the Johnson machine of this type would fall forward onto the ground when not in use, to judge from the surviving example (hence the restraining modern "bunjee" seen in the photograph).

Another occasional modification not shown in Johnson's patent drawings appears to have been the addition of projections on either side at the base of the front forks, to serve as foot rests when a good speed had been achieved, no doubt particularly when going

Hobby-horse (© The Trustees of the National Museums of Scotland 1997). The suggestion has been made that the metal saddle bar might originally have been suspended within the spring, and that as there were both front and rear fork adjustments the original saddle would not itself need to have been height adjustable.

Hobby-horse copy (Snowshill Manor, near Broadway, Glos). An attractive item but probably a late Nineteenth century version of the original Johnson machine.

Hobby-horse (courtesy of British Cycling Museum, Camelford) - two views. An unusual machine by an unknown maker.

downhill. This small detail is of some importance in the history of the bicycle. Although von Drais must be given all credit for the invention of the two-wheeler, he did not in fact provide his machine with foot rests. Johnson's incorporation of this item underlines his confidence in the notion that it is entirely feasible to balance on two wheels without relying on the rider's feet as supplementary supports.

The early Mark Hall machine by Johnson has small rests attached to the front forks just above the axle, and as these are also a feature of the Science Museum's exhibit they were presumably a common if not a standard fitting (the two Alnwick Castle machines both have holes for foot rests but no such accessory). A fine machine possibly built in the 1820s for the young 13th Earl of Eglinton, now owned by the National Museums of Scotland, is also fitted with foot rests (see photo illus.) as is the item formerly at the National Cycle Museum, Lincoln.

Hobby-horse copy (courtesy of Ulster Folk & Transport Museum, Belfast). An excellent early replica of one of the two Johnson velocipedes still belonging to the Duke of Northumberland.

The only contemporary illustration of this useful accessory known to the author is in the colour illustrated print *Every Man on his Perch, or Going to Hobby Fair*, in which three of the twenty-four machines are shown apparently fitted with such a device. The small drawing of a dandy on his hobby clearly shows two long curved struts rising from the bottom of the front forks, with the actual foot rests somewhat above the level of the top of the front wheel. The individual riding a machine in the right foreground of the *Johnson's Pedestrian Hobbyhorse Riding School* print would appear to be using footrests.

There is an interesting hybrid hobby-horse at Snowshill Manor, Worcs. For the most part it is quite a close copy of a Denis Johnson machine, save that the front wheel (30.5") is larger than the rear wheel (26.5"), and the main beam has a much longer than usual "nose" attached to which are foot rests of the type commonly fitted to "boneshaker" bicycles of the c.1870 period. In the author's opinion the machine clearly shows the influence of "boneshaker" technology and probably dates from this later period. It was acquired by Charles Wade, the architect owner of Snowshill Manor, in August, 1935.

A fascinating non-Johnson machine with an unusual steering handle, combined arm rest and carrying box, a deeply curving frame with fixed saddle, and small foot rests, can be seen at the British Cycling Museum, Camelford, Cornwall, the owners of which have kindly supplied the modern photo illustration. What would appear to be the same item is also shown in the illustrated photo from *The Hub* for 20th February 1897, where it is described as "Dandy and Hobby Horse, about 1819". The photo (with three others) was taken for the magazine, but the machine itself may date from the hobby-horse era.

Another interesting early copy is the illustrated item at the Ulster Folk & Transport Museum, on long term loan from the Science Museum. We know a certain amount about the origins of this machine. A letter dated 20th May 1904 to the Estates Office at Alnwick Castle from the Victoria & Albert Museum refers to "the "Hobby Horse" which His Grace the Duke of Northumberland has been so good as to have prepared for this Museum." It is an accurate copy of the larger of the two machines still at Alnwick Castle, albeit that the wheels are slightly smaller (the photo also displays the steering column the wrong way around).

Denis Johnson's original name for the machine was the "Pedestrian Curricle". A curricle was – and is – a two-wheeled open carriage drawn by two side-by-side horses. It features in a short poem "The Whip Club", published in the *Sporting Magazine* for June 1809 :-

> *What can <u>Men of Fashion</u> do ?*
> *Why, drive a <u>Curricle and two</u>.*
> *Can Men of Fashion do no more ?*
> *Yes, drive a smart <u>Barouche and four</u>.*
> *Do Men of Fashion end with this ?*
> *May they not <u>drive too fast</u> ? – Oh yes !*

In fact, Johnson's "Pedestrian Curricle" name was seldom if ever used, and indeed by the beginning of April, 1819, he himself was referring to the invention as a "Pedestrian Machine" (receipt with Tabley papers, John Rylands Library, Manchester), though he did also describe it as a "Velocipede, or Patent Curricle" in a May 1819 advert (see below).

An early term employed was "Pedestrian Hobby-Horse" (or "Hobbyhorse", "Hobby Horse" or "Hobby") and hence the title of this book. It is not known who first applied the "hobby-horse" epithet, but it was an obvious enough term to describe a machine which could be seen as distantly related to the ancient stick-between-the-legs child's toy of the same name. Indeed, a certain "Square Toes" (in today's parlance "Senior Citizen"), whose letter is reproduced in *The Kaleidoscope* for 23rd March, 1819, ungenerously gives von Drais little credit for originality of thought, comparing the invention to the "cock-horse" (child's hobby-horse) of nursery rhyme fame. He points out that the child "sits, like the traveller, on the seat of this *original machine,* and the cock-horse, if one of the improved sort with which our toy-shops are supplied, has, like the *original machine*, a wheel behind, to promote the motion of the infant boy." Other writers have compared the hobby-horse to the "go-cart", which likewise "supported the body, and the feet of the child supplied the motive power" (*Velocipedes, Bicycles and Tricycles* by "Velox").

"Hobby-horse" was probably the most popular name used to describe the English version of the invention, but there was really no standard term, and there were a wide variety of other descriptions, including "Pedestrian Carriage", "Walking Accelerator", "Swift Walker",

"Wooden Horse", "German Horse", "French Hobby-horse" and "Irish Jaunting Car". Another popular name was "Dandy-charger" (or "Dandy-horse" or "Dandy Hobby"), referring as previously stated to the foppish individuals who often rode the machines. The fact that this came later than the "hobby-horse" epithet is confirmed in the *Bath Chronicle* for 9th April, 1819 : "The new hobby-horse machines have been nick-named *dandy chargers*." But in many instances newspapers and periodicals referred more respectfully to the hobby-horse by the French word apparently coined by von Drais i.e. "Velocipede".

It is perhaps worth highlighting the distinction between the term "Hobby-horse" (or its variations) and "Velocipede". Both words were used synonymously to describe Johnson's machine in England in 1819. However, the essence of the "hobby-horse" was that it was propelled by pushing with the feet on the ground (which usually meant that it only had two wheels). The word "velocipede" soon came to have a wider use in this country, covering all types of rider-propelled machines including those with three or four wheels often driven by some form of treadle mechanism. It continued to be used as the main generic term for some fifty years, when it was largely superseded by the words "bicycle", "tricycle" and related terms.

Having obtained his patent three days before Christmas, 1818, we can perhaps reasonably assume that Denis Johnson began manufacturing the new machine in earnest during January, 1819. The *Monthly Magazine* for 1st March, 1819, has a lengthy article on "Mr. Johnson's Velocipede, or Swift Walker", which concludes : "It is exhibited daily ; and, *although never made public*, [author's italics] has been already viewed by many thousands, many of whom have exercised, and all have approved, it." This appears to have been part of a clever marketing strategy, that is, to whet the public appetite before actually selling the machine on the open market (or perhaps Johnson was simply waiting until he had built up a sufficient stock to meet the anticipated demand). Fairburn's booklet on the *New Pedestrian Carriage* is undated but appears to have been written circa April, 1819. It contains the following passage :-

> *Mr. Johnson's Repository is daily thronged with visitors, and it is amusing to see his servant riding about a long room to show the Horse, threading the carriages, and wheeling and turning*

with great precision. They may also be seen in a large Exhibition-room, near Exeter-Change, Strand; and at another in Brewer-street, Golden-square; which have been engaged for that purpose.

Despite the statement in the *Monthly Magazine*, the likelihood is perhaps that the item was first publicly sold some time during February – both the *Gentleman's Magazine* and the *Sporting Magazine* for March, 1819, refer to is as being "already in general use."

It was probably at or about this time that a certain R. Childs devised "An economical plan for examining the merits of the Velocipede, or Swift Walker, and a chance of obtaining one for five shillings." He explained his scheme in his own handwriting on the left-hand side of a large piece of paper, (now in the custody of the Science Museum Library), at the head of which was an illustration of a man on a hobby-horse beneath the somewhat hackneyed Shakespearian quotation "A horse, a horse, my kingdom for a horse." This was the velocipede plan :-

Forty persons subscribing five shillings each, will raise a sum sufficient to purchase one and pay the expenses of carriage &c attending it. After the subscribers have investigated the principle of the machine it is proposed to dispose of it by lottery, and whoever shall be so fortunate as to draw the ticket, marked <u>prize,</u> will be owner of a horse that will eat neither hay nor corn, for the small sum above-named.
N.B. The Lottery to be drawn at the Fleece Inn.
Money to be paid at the time of Subscribing.
R. Childs.

The right-hand side of the sheet was left clear for the names of forty subscribers who wished to take part in the sweepstake. One can imagine the paper being perhaps left on the bar of the Fleece Inn (presumably a London tavern – the name was a popular one, no less than a dozen being listed in Foster's c.1900 *Inns, Taverns, Alehouses, Coffee Houses, etc. in and around London*). Forty punters duly subscribed their names, and no doubt paid their stakes to the organiser. Against each name are three numbers, 11-7-12, 7-4-5, 9-5-8 and so on. In the case of the first few names a total is also shown i.e. 30, 16, 23 (someone couldn't count) etc. What the author surmises must have happened is that someone suggested it would be more fun if, instead of simply drawing a ticket, each participant had three throws of a set of two dice, the player with the highest total score winning the sweepstake and acquiring the velocipede. And as if to prove that fortune favours the brave – and the enterprising – the winner with a total score of 32 turned out to be none other than – Mr. R. Childs ! One can imagine the comments of his friends and acquaintances.

It was probably in March, 1819, that Denis Johnson opened his riding schools at 377, Strand, and 40, Brewer Street. The *Literary Gazette* for 27th February, 1819, has an item on the "Pedestrian Carriage, or Walking Accelerator" stating that "a riding-school is about to be opened for them", and (as previously stated) the well-known print *Johnson's Pedestrian Hobbyhorse Riding School* is dated 17th April,1819, and makes reference to both addresses.

But Johnson did not confine his activities to London. At the end of April and beginning of May, 1819, the *Manchester Mercury* and *Cowdroy's Manchester Gazette* both on two occasions carry an advert for the "Velocipede ; or, Swift Walker", which was exhibiting at the Old Assembly Rooms in Brown Street, Manchester. There is an illustration of a rider on a Johnson hobby-horse with indirect steering. The admission charge was a shilling and the exhibition was open for a full fifteen hours a day from 6.00 a.m. to 9.00 p.m. Although perhaps surprisingly the advert does not specifically refer to Johnson, it must surely have been inserted by him and he may well personally have visited the city.

The story continues in *Aris's Birmingham Gazette* for 10th May 1819:-

VELOCIPEDE, OR PATENT CURRICLE. MR JOHNSON takes the Liberty of announcing to the Gentry and Inhabitants of Birmingham, that he will display before them the various Revolutions and Changes of Motion which are capable of being shown on this truly unique Vehicle, at the Stork Hotel, Square, Birmingham.
Admission, 1.s each – Youths, 6d. N.B. Six Lessons is sufficient to perfect any one –
Hours of Exhibition from Ten till Seven.

By the end of the month Denis was in Liverpool. *The Liverpool Mercury* for 28th May 1819 speaks of "the performance of Mr. JOHNSON, who exhibits at the Music-hall", referring to "the graceful movements of which [the velocipede] is capable in skilful hands ... as performed by the gentleman we have mentioned." The same issue of the newspaper tells us that elsewhere in the city a less graceful performance had taken place:-

On Tuesday evening, while a gentleman was exercising on one of the Velocipedes at the Assembly-room in Cook-street, he was thrown with such force from his seat that he had three of his teeth knocked out by the fall. – It is added that notwithstanding this unpleasant accident, the gentleman means to persevere "in spite of his teeth".

Johnson was again exhibiting the merits of the velocipede at the Music Hall, Bold Street, at the beginning of July. It seems that by later the same month he had arrived in America, an unidentified New York paper being quoted as saying that "the constructor himself" had "imported himself by the last arrival from London, in order to supply the market". Clearly our hero was no slouch when it came to promoting his product.

No business accounts are known to survive, but the suggestion has been made that Johnson must have done well financially from selling his machines (quite apart from his other related activities). *La Belle Assemblee ; being Bell's Court and Fashionable Magazine* for May 1819 states "The first cost of the machine to the patentee was not more than forty or fifty shillings; but the price to the public is from eight to ten pounds." There is no doubt that large numbers were seen at the height of the craze, but the only reliable guide we have is the actual numbering on extant Johnson machines, the highest currently known being as previously stated 320 (see also Appendix 2). If we take an average sale price of £9.0.0. and an average manufacturing cost of £2.5.0. (based on the *La Belle Assemblee* figures), and assume conservatively a sale of only 320 machines, the net profit would have been £2,160.0.0., a quite substantial sum in 1819.

There is no indication that Johnson reduced the price of his machines after they had been on the market for a few months. In February

1819 the poet John Keats wrote to relatives referring to the Velocipede as "the nothing of the day", adding that "a handsome gelding will come to eight guineas, however they will soon be cheaper, unless the army takes to them" (*Collected Letters*, as quoted by Jeanne Mackenzie in her 1981 *Cycling* anthology). Nevertheless, the Duke of Northumberland paid £22.0.0. for two machines as late as the end of May 1819.

But it is possible that Denis Johnson may not in fact have made quite the "killing" which these figures indicate. An item in *Aris's Birmingham Gazette* for Monday, 22nd March, 1819, refers to Johnson as the patentee, threatens legal proceedings if the patent is breached, and states that the machine is exhibiting at 377, Strand "where orders for the same will be taken and executed accordingly." Yet at the end of the same week we find a notice in substantially the same form, but with one vital difference, inserted in the *Norfolk Chronicle and* Norwich Gazette for Saturday, 27th March, 1819 (as well as in the S*alisbury and Winchester Gazette* and the *Hampshire Chronicle & Courier* two days later, and presumably also elsewhere). This reads:-

THE PEDESTRIAN CARRIAGE OR MACHINE

For promoting Health, diminishing the Labour of Persons in Walking, and enabling them to Travel with greater ease and celerity.
His Majesty, by Letters Patent of the last year (1818), having granted to Mr. DENNIS JOHNSON, (the Patentee of the invention), the sole licence and authority to make and vend the above Patent Machine, and Mr. Johnson having assigned all his right and interest therein to S. MERSEY, of Long Acre, London, Notice is hereby given to all persons that in case they shall in any way or manner infringe on the said letters patent, by making or selling such Carriage or Machine or any Machine in imitation thereof, they will, on discovery, be immediately proceeded against either at law or in equity, as shall be thought most adviseable. The public are respectfully informed, that the above machine is now exhibiting at No. 377, in the Strand, London, opposite to Mr. Ackerman's Repository, and that all orders for the same, directed to Mr. Mercey, No. 71, Long Acre, London, (the Assignee of the patent), will be duly attended to and executed accordingly. The price for the Machine Eight Guineas.

Where did all this leave the entrepreneurial Denis Johnson? Samuel Merscy (apparently the correct spelling) was a "laceman", not a coachmaker. He had obtained a patent (no. 4156 of 1817) for an improved method of weaving livery and coach lace. No doubt he had premises amongst the "great colony of coachmakers" of Long Acre in order to supply coach lace and livery lace for coachmen. Exactly how he fits into the hobby-horse story is not clear. On the face of it the notice suggests that Merscy had become the absolute owner of Johnson's patent and business. But despite the fact that, as assignee of the patent, he requested all orders be sent to him at 71, Long Acre, the evidence of the London trade directories is that throughout the period of manufacture of the machine Samuel Merscy remained a laceman and Denis Johnson remained a coachmaker. And of course we hear more of Johnson after March, 1819, but nothing of Merscy.

Possibly further research will throw more light on the business relationship of the two individuals. In the meantime the author's tentative conclusion is that Merscy may have acquired Johnson's patent for a sum which Johnson used as working capital to finance his expanding hobby-horse manufactory. Merscy may at the same time have granted Johnson a licence to continue to make and vend machines on payment of a royalty for each item sold. It may have been agreed that orders for machines would be directed to Number 71 but executed at Number 75 so that Merscy could keep a check on the position. However at the moment all this can only be a working hypothesis.

There is another reason to suppose that Denis Johnson may not have become a rich man as a result of his hobby-horse activities. The Paving Rate books for the parish of St. Martin-in-the-Fields tell an interesting story. They reveal that, after Johnson took over the premises at 75, Long Acre, on Lady Day, 1818 (25th March), he made no payments of paving rate whatsoever for the five years 1818 to 1822 inclusive, so that by Lady Day, 1823, he owed arrears of £20.8.4. The position was then regularised by writing off a deficiency Johnson had inherited and reducing his own carried-forward arrears to £14.10.0., which were cleared by payments over the next four years. Although Johnson did make regular poor rate payments of about £12.0.0. per annum, his non-payment of the paving rate during the very period when one might have expected him to be in funds suggests he may have been having financial problems of one sort or another. Unless perhaps for some reason he objected as a matter of principle to being required to pay paving rate!

But to return to the Merscy notice. The fact that it was thought necessary to issue a strongly-worded warning against infringement of the Johnson patent in a number of newspapers, suggests that there had already by March, 1819, been perhaps fairly widespread unauthorised copying. No doubt some of these copies were simplified versions produced by local craftsmen on a one-off basis. It may not be without significance that Appendix 2 lists about twice as many non-Johnson as Johnson machines (though a number of copies date from later in the Nineteenth century).

As early as the beginning of February, 1819, we learn that : "On Monday last, was exhibited at Swaffham, one of the new invented walking machines, or Accelerators, made of iron by Mr. Drake Youngs, an ingenious blacksmith, at Castleacre" (*Norwich Mercury*, 6th Feb 1819). Bearing in mind that Denis Johnson only obtained his patent on 22nd December, 1818 (and that the specification and drawings were only filed six months later), the Norfolk blacksmith can have lost no time in producing his version of the machine – presumably without applying to the patentee for permission to do so.

It is interesting to read that this early copy was "made of iron", as the Johnson patent specification does state : "The machine ... consists of a beam made of wood *or metal* [author's italics] of sufficient strength to bear the weight of the person who is to ride it." In an unpublished doctoral thesis *The Bicycle Era in American History* (Harvard University, 1957) Norman Dunham states : "Riders soon noted a defect in construction, however. The first British vehicles, like the French, had been built almost entirely of wood, but when the damp island climate caused this to warp or crack, makers changed many parts to iron or steel." Only a Twentieth century American source is quoted in support and the present author is sceptical. The notion that Britain's "damp island climate" should within a very short time cause machines "to warp or crack" seems somewhat improbable. The only significant known change in the Johnson velocipede was the early one from "indirect" to "direct" steering. And the only known all-iron machine is the possibly one-off Norfolk one referred to above.

Another Norfolk example is shown in the photo illustration and can be seen at the Strangers' Hall Museum in Norwich, being said to date from around 1820. Like a number of other copies, the design is more primitive than the Johnson hobby-horse and lacks the forearm rest. However, it has two interesting features. Although essentially a wooden machine, the wheel rims (but not the spokes) are metal. The seat (the height of which is adjustable) is attached to a rudimentary metal spring.

Nearer to London, a young Chelmsford man named Bacon travelled the twelve miles from Braintree to Chelmsford in an hour-and-a-half "on a velocipede, of his own construction" (*Belfast Newsletter*, 18th May 1819).

Johnson machines found their way to distant parts of the realm, but there is some evidence of commercial production by others makers. On 2nd April 1819 the Editor of *The Liverpool Mercury* recorded that a velocipede "has been manufactured in this town, from the description given in the *Mercury;* and that it has been found to answer beyond the expectation of the makers". The author suspects the following advert inserted in the *Salisbury and Winchester Journal*

Hobby-horse (courtesy of Strangers' Hall Museum, Norfolk Museums Service). A curious piece. The carved horse's head is reminiscent of the child's hobby-horse stick.

58

for 3rd May, 1819, by a Dorset maker is an unauthorised attempt to undercut the London manufacturer:-

> *VELOCIPEDES. THE Public are respectfully informed, they may be supplied with the newly invented Machine, called a VELOCIPEDE, at various prices, from four to seven guineas, (according to the make and decorations), by John Rutter, of Shaftesbury, who will feel obliged by any orders he may be favoured with. One at four guineas constantly kept for inspection; and with which any individual may be accommodated, for a short time, at a reasonable charge.*

Of course, it could be that John Rutter was simply a West Country agent for Johnson (or should we still be saying Mersey), but the low prices quoted – which would have had to include the agent's commission and transport from London – makes this seem unlikely. Another possibility is that Rutter obtained a licence from the patentee to make the machines himself, but again this seems unlikely as Johnson's own machines were being promoted on a nationwide basis.

Denis Johnson continued in business as a coachmaker at 75, Long Acre, for a number of years after the pedestrian hobby-horse had been largely forgotten, initially on his own account. He is still to be found under his own name in the *Post Office London Directory* for 1824, but the following year the same directory refers to Johnson & Allen, Coach-makers, 75 Long Acre (with no individual coachmaker of either name being listed). Denis Johnson's partner was another coachmaker, John Allen, who also became his son-in-law as a result of marrying Denis' daughter Mary. The partnership between the two men continued for about nine years, until Johnson's death aged 73 years on Christmas Day, 1833. He was buried at St. Martin's Chapel, Campden Town, on 2nd January, 1834. Denis Johnson's undated Will was proved in the Prerogative Court of Canterbury, London, on 24th March 1834. The Estate Duty Register (IR 26/1355 no.1101) records that he left personal estate (including leasehold) to the value of nearly a thousand pounds (£943.9.4.), a fair sum by early Nineteenth century standards.

Johnson's holograph Will (reproduced in Appendix 4) provides us with an insight into his character. He was clearly a methodical individual, giving precise instructions as to how his wishes were to be carried into effect, for example his executors (his two sons-in-law) are to have "the stock of all descriptions taken and minutely taken as if it were strangers coming in on purchase". He was careful with his money, and anxious to save "unnecessary expense" either in connection with his funeral or the administration of his estate. He was obviously proud of the business he had built up over the years "whatever I am possessed of has been gained by sheer Industry and Labour", and anxious that it should not be adversely affected by the sudden withdrawal of his capital – the payment of gifts and legacies was to be "at the time most convenient for the business, I mean that money should not be drawn out of the business to check its progress."

But he was not only a business man he was also a kindly man, making especially thoughtful provision for his sister (leaving her to the care of his two daughters "should she survive me and want that assistance that the aged require") and his daughter Ann ("in case that anything should happen that she my daughter Ann, which God forbid, should want a home, it is my will that she shall have a sitting room, a bedroom, a kitchen and servants room etc in this house").

Denis Johnson refers in his Will to his "dear wife" who predeceased him. Nevertheless, it appears he had a son born out of wedlock, John Johnson, to whom he left the sum of £100 by his Will (the reference to illegitimacy comes in a sworn statement to the probate court by John Allen). We should possibly link this with an entry in the Overseers of Poor Accounts, Long Acre Ward, 1821, which reads : "To cash received of Mr. Johnson *in lieu of Security* for Mary Hughes child ... £40.0.0." Let him who is without fault cast the first stone...

As Denis Johnson expressly requested in his Will, the firm name of Johnson & Allen remained unchanged for many years after Denis' demise, but by 1840 the address has altered to 72 Long Acre (the 1851 Census return shows John Allen, age 63, his wife Mary, age 56, his sons John and Francis aged 19 and 16 years respectively and two younger daughters Frances and Martha, as well as another family, living at the 72 Long Acre address). By 1853 John Allen (probably still the father but conceivably the elder son) was simply using his own name. The next change had occurred by 1867, in which year *Kelly's Post Office London Trades Directory* shows "Allen, John and Francis, coach and harness makers" at 71 & 72 Long Acre. The two brothers appear to have worked hard and prospered, as by 1880 *Kelly* is referring to them as being at "27, 28 & 29 & 117 Long Acre WC & 3 Davies Street Berkeley Square W". At this date both members of the firm were tricycle riders (and were it seems selling such machines as agents), according to a letter in *Bicycling News*. In 1887 we find a first reference to Frank Allen (possibly a grandson of the original John Allen and great-grandson of Denis Johnson) carrying on the coachmaking business now only at 27, 28 & 29 Long Acre. The last entry for Frank Allen is in the directory for 1908.

It would seem that the Long Acre coachmaking firm originally founded by the redoubtable Denis Johnson, pedestrian hobby-horse patentee, manufacturer and seller, was kept in existence by the Allen branch of his family for a further three generations spanning some 90 years, until the early years of the present century.

Chapter 4

THE HOBBY-HORSE ON THE ROAD

The invention soon became known in London, and many persons now present can, no doubt, remember, how quickly this novelty was adopted by the public. The equality and swiftness of the motion when compared with walking which it so much resembled, recommended velocipedes to many persons who disliked the trouble and expense of keeping a horse, and the rapidity which could be acquired bore some resemblance to skating. The novelty and ingenuity of the idea quickly brought this invention into common use : in the New Road they might be seen in great numbers running every fine evening especially near Finsbury Square, and the top of Portland Road, where they were let out for hire by the hour. Rooms for practice were opened in various parts of the town, and several expert riders made it their business to exhibit them in the principal cities of England. I am acquainted with individuals who went with their velocipedes from twenty to thirty miles in a day on excursions into the country, and many young men were in the habit of riding sixty miles or more in the course of a week. It is easy to see how beneficial this exercise must have been to the health of the riders, who were generally inhabitants of cities, and often occupied during the day in sedentary pursuits connected with their business.

Thomas Davies's lecture "On the Velocipede" (previously referred to at the end of Chapter 2), from which this quotation is taken, was delivered in May 1837, enabling him to speak both with first-hand knowledge of his topic and with the benefit of historical perspective. It encapsulates the scene in town and country during the heyday of the pedestrian hobby-horse. In view of the relatively primitive nature of the machine the distances regularly covered may seem surprising. But even more impressive is the account of a "very adroit velocipedean" who rode the 400-odd miles from London to Falkirk in

Scotland, and later made a long excursion in France, on a "wooden horse" (*Howitt's Visits to Remarkable Places*, vol.2, 1841). And it was from Pau in Southern France, that an English engineer made a 300-odd mile journey on a velocipede (probably the continental version) over the Pyrenees to Madrid, apparently during the early part of 1820, according to von Drais himself writing in a German fashion magazine (*Journal für Literatur, Kunst, Luxus und Mode*, Weimar, July 1820).

In his 1869 book *The Velocipede, its Past, its Present & its Future*, "J.F.B." (identified as J.F. Bottomley-Firth) tells us : "Clergymen used the new machine to visit their parishioners, and to travel between scattered parishes. Postmen with their letter bags sailing in the wind, rode the dandy-horse; young swells of the period used it, not only for exercise but for the purpose of making calls; and strangest if not saddest spectacle of all, old men who had hitherto borne blameless characters for sedateness and respectability, were to be seen careering along on the dandy horse."

Although these substantially later comments by J.F.B. must be treated with some reserve, according to von Drais (writing in the German fashion magazine), the velocipede was indeed used in Britain for the carrying of mail in 1820. The (unillustrated) Sidebethem print *Hobby-horses jockying the Mail !!* shows a "four-in-hand" team of riders pulling a Royal Mail coach in the open country, but in reality the machine would presumably have been employed by individual postmen around town. Contemporary records at Post Office Archives in London appear to contain no reference to the use of the hobby-horse for delivering mail, which perhaps suggests that this was on a brief trial basis only. A Post Office "Green Paper" *Post Office Cycles* by H.S. Shipway (1933-34) states that "before 1880 a few "velocipedes" had been bought or hired by the Post Office as an experiment", but the probability is that the writer was referring to pedalled bicycles or tricycles of the 1870s.

The legend below the colour illustrated print *Pedestrian Hobbyhorse* published by R. Ackermann in February, 1819, describes how to employ the new means of locomotion. "This Machine is of the most simple kind, supported by two light wheels running on the same line; the front wheel turning on a pivot, which, by means of a short lever, gives the direction in turning to one side or the other, the hind wheel always running in one direction. The rider mounts it, and seats himself in a saddle conveniently fixed on the back of the horse (if allowed to be called so), and placed in the middle between the wheels; the feet are placed flat on the ground, so that in the first step to give the Machine motion, the heel should be the part of the foot to touch the ground, and so on with the other foot alternately, as if walking on the heels, observing always to begin the movement very gently. In the front, before the rider, is placed a cushion to rest the arms on while the hands hold the lever which gives direction to the Machine, as also to balance it if inclining to either side when the opposite arm is pressed on the cushion."

According to James T. Lightwood in his 1928 book *The Romance of the Cyclists' Touring Club*, an enterprising London shoemaker "netted a pretty sum by manufacturing a shoe with iron sole which greatly aided the rider in his velocipeding exercise." In the first issue of *Bicycling* (later *Cycling*) in August, 1878, in an article "Riders I have known", Mark Mitton tells us : "The very first rider I knew was a solid, good-hearted, self-denying, tradesman in Shropshire, who rode nearly half a century ago a fearfully and wonderfully constructed "Dandy Horse". ... I heard of his former exploits – how he had steel caps to his boot toes, and that even then these soon wore thin with perpetually spurring mother earth." And a lengthy poem *Jonah Tink* by John Atkin (pub. Newark, 1823) contains the following lines:-

> *A dandy youth he was, whose mien,*
> *Could scarcely for shirt neck be seen;*
> *With copper soles, and spurs of steel,*
> *Each boot a plate upon the heel;*
> *That he might faster on proceed,*
> *He rode on a <u>velocipede</u>.*

Whilst there is ample evidence that the pedestrian hobby-horse became the plaything of the Regency dandies, to the extent that the machine even became known in some quarters as the "dandy-horse",its use was by no means confined to the London beaux. A check on a sample of regional newspapers suggests that the hobby-horse in its Johnsonian form was widely available throughout the country by about April 1819, confirming the statement of Thomas Davies on this point. We read for example in the *Norfolk Chronicle and Norwich*

Gazette for 17th April, 1819, under the heading *Velocipedes*, that "Several of these machines, denominated Pedestrian Hobby Horses, have been exhibiting here this week" i.e. presumably Norwich, where the paper was published. On the same day the *Norwich Mercury* contained an advert for the machine :-

PANTHEON, RANELAGH GARDENS. THE Nobility, Gentry, and Public are very respectfully informed, that FINCH has procured an ACCELERATOR, or WALKING PERAMBULATOR, which will be opened for inspection on Monday next. In order more fully to satisfy the minds of such Gentlemen as may choose to honour it with their approbation, he has engaged a young man to instruct them in its use, as it appears there is some difficulty in their first management, as well as a liability to damage. It will most necessarily require some regulation, for the convenience of all, which must of course be produced by a series of rules, which he will have the honour of submitting for the Public's approbation. To digress upon the qualities of this ingenious and portable machine, would carry more explanation with it than Finch is capable of performing towards it; but takes leave to observe, should the taste and inclination of Gentlemen be directed towards it, he will provide, for their comfort and entertainment, ANOTHER.

Just two days later we read in the Lewes column of the *Sussex Weekly Advertiser* that "The Dandy's Hobby was exercised here on Saturday, and underwent the discipline of many *rough riders*." The following week the same newspaper reported that "The Dandy Hobby, stated in our last to be under exercise here, soon broke down, so that there appears, in this species of horse-dealing even, to be *Jockeyship*; but quere, was this Hobby *warranted sound* to the purchaser?" The week after this the paper carried a short verse :-

On seeing the Dandy Hobbies at Lewes

Astride a <u>Broom</u> in days of old,
Wizards and Witches, as we're told,
Skim'd thro' the air so quick;
But <u>Dandies</u> in the present day
(No <u>Conjurors</u> in truth are they)
Bestride the simple <u>Stick</u> !

The extent of interest in the new machine is clear when we read that : "There was an attempted exhibition of three of the Velocipedes, on Sunday, in Hyde Park; but they were so much impeded in their operations by the curiosity of the promenaders, that after getting about half way along the King's private road, towards Kensington Gardens, they suddenly turned about, and retired by the gate at Hyde Park-corner, amidst the shouts of some two or three dozen lads, who seemed disposed to persecute them with still more serious annoyance" (*Birmingham Commercial Herald*, 3rd April, 1819). The previous week the same newspaper had reported: "A gentleman, mounted upon his wooden hobby-horse, on the Camberwell-road, on Monday, attracted a great crowd, from the pressure of which he was, at his earnest solicitation, extricated by a passing stage-coachman, who carried him and his horse off on the roof."

According to Mrs Alec Tweedie in *Hyde Park, its History and Romance* (London, 1908), "practically every surviving method of locomotion has heralded its earliest votaries within the precincts of the Park, where the foot-propelled "hobby-horse" proved the forerunner of the bicycle." Mrs Tweedie later states the machine "was almost a peculiarity of Hyde Park, where the young beaux of the middle-nineteenth century disported themselves on the bone-racking contrivance, for few ventured out into the streets or to the open country upon it." The reference should of course have been to the *early* nineteenth century, and their are numerous examples of much wider use of the machine than the authoress suggests. However, the contemporaneous author Fairburn does comment "If we are *literally* to shoot folly as it flies, Hyde-park, on a Sunday would be strewed with dead, and not a Dandy left to tell the tale." And one of the many 1819 prints depicting the hobby-horse in use is titled *Perambulators in Hyde Park !*

The novel item was such a newsworthy phenomenon that, like the modern "UFO", reports of its appearance were not always to be relied on. Under the heading *The Velocipede or Wooden Horse* in the *Sussex Weekly Advertiser* for 5th April, 1819, we read :-

This hobby having excited much public curiosity, it was, as we are informed, on Wednesday evening given out at Worthing, that it would, on the following morning, be exhibited in all its paces, at one of the Libraries; a great number of the amateurs of novelty,

and others, in consequence assembled in the South-street, to witness the movements of this mechanical <u>prodigy</u>; but after buzzing and bustling about for a considerable time without seeing any preparation made for the wonderful performance, they at length found out –
That 'twas <u>April Fool Day</u>! – So they all slipt away,
Abashed at their credulity, but not offended with the worthy Librarian, who had no hand in the <u>hoax</u>, and has intimated his intention of yet gratifying the curiosity of his friends, by getting a hobby from town for that purpose."

Coincidentally, on the same day a somewhat similar event took place further west. One cannot help thinking that it would make a fine silent movie clip:-

A HOAX. On Thursday morning last a placard was posted up in one of the principal shops in Blandford, stating that a bid of 50 guineas was depending between one of the new-invented <u>Hobby Horses</u> and the Mail Coach, which should arrive first at the Crown Inn. Accordingly, about half an hour before the arrival of the Mail, the road between Blandford and Pimperne was thronged with spectators to see this new-invented mode of travelling; but on the arrival of the Mail, it was discovered to be a hoax, – as a boy appeared with a pole, having a card affixed with the words "This is the first of April." (Salisbury and Winchester Journal, 5th April, 1819*).*

There must have been an impish essence in the English air on Thursday, 1st April, 1819. A poem "The Velocipede" (published in full in the *Birmingham Commercial Herald* for 10th April, 1819), somewhat reminiscent of Browning's "The Pied Piper of Hamelin", tells the metropolitan story so vividly that it seems worth quoting at length :-

By hand-bills it was publicly made known
That some high-mettled hobby would be shown,
On Thursday afternoon at half-past three,
By that fam'd jockey, call'd the patentee;
Who would display its most surprising power,
And ride on foot twelve hundred poles an hour.

68

The "fam'd jockey, call'd the patentee" was of course Denis Johnson. The old "rod, pole or perch" measurement was equivalent to 5.5 yards, so the claimed riding speed of 1,200 poles an hour was only 3.75 miles an hour. No doubt Johnson could in fact have done better than this. The poem continues :-

The bait was laid : – not sooner laid than taken;
Some shops were clos'd and many more forsaken;
Some took two hours to put themselves in state,
Some could not dine for fear of being late;
Some crept, some walk'd, some ran with all their speed,
To see this wonder, call'd Velocipede.
Soon from Wake Green to Smithfield market-place
The windows were replete with "magic grace";
The road was all confusion, life, and noise,
And evr'ry tree a rookery of boys.
Indeed, some time before the clock struck two
The streets were swarming with a motley crew,
Of ev'ry shape and colour, sex, and size,
Profession and description, save the wise :
Foot men in companies, and horse in troops,
And smirking belles in formidable groups;
Old men with crutches, and old maids with staves,
Monkeys and mountebanks, and other knaves;
Mechanics, farmers, and a specious show
Of dandies : – ten or twenty in a row;
Whose heads were blocks of most prodigious size,
And whisker'd from the ARM-PITS to the eyes.
These things were bound and bandag'd, neck and waist,
With steel and whalebone, buckram, starch, and paste;
So uniform their motions and their features,
They looked like wax-work more than living creatures.
These, with the rest, stood still or stalk'd about
In great suspense, though no one seem'd to doubt :
They waited long; the go-cart did not come;
Some few, at length reluctantly went home.
At five o'clock some one was heard to say -
"Why, – it's the First of April ! – All fools' day !"
It was enough. The final blow was struck,

It circulated like th' electric shock.
A shock it was to all the gaping crowd;
Though whisper'd low, their feelings spoke aloud :
They slunk away, as from a dirty action,
Fill'd with chagrin and sore dissatisfaction;
And evr'y one was ready, for a wonder,
To blame himself for making such a blunder.

In the late Eighteenth and early Nineteenth centuries wagers and "matches against time" were very much in vogue and provided great interest. One of the most famous involved the pedestrian feat of a certain Captain Barclay, who undertook in 1809 to walk a mile every hour for a thousand consecutive hours. He succeeded and won a bet of 1,000 guineas. It was to be expected therefore that when the hobby-horse appeared on the scene there would be similar challenges. As early as 17th March, 1819, we read in the *Bury and Norwich Post* that "A Military Gentleman has made a bet to go to London by the side of the coach", and the same month the *European Magazine* records that "the Accelerator has even beat the Brighton four horse coach by half an hour". Exactly a month after the *Bury and Norwich Post* report we hear in the *Norwich Mercury* of a "person from the country" who "exhibited, upon the Castle Hill, an Accelerator, or Wooden Horse, with which he appeared to travel at a considerable rate". This individual "offered to make a bet that he would travel to London in 14 hours by the help of the machine."

Much further South, we learn that "THURSDAY, April 15, a lad of the name of Wilds, of Canterbury, undertook for a considerable wager, to ride a *velocipede*, or dandy charger, from Upstreet to Canterbury, a distance of six miles, within an hour, which he accomplished with apparent ease, nine minutes and a half within time" (*Sporting Magazine*, April, 1819). Other reports tell us "he was accompanied by some persons in gigs and on horseback" (also giving the youth's name as Wild, not Wilds). But the previous month an even faster time had been achieved. "A curious wager was decided on Saturday at Chigwell-row, between 2 gentleman of Chinkford, [presumably Chingford, Essex] named Brown and Jones for 25 gs. which went the greatest distance in one hour, each mounted on his 2-wheel hobby, which was determined in favour of Mr. Brown, who did nearly eight miles, beating his antagonist a quarter of a mile" (*Simpson's Salisbury*

Gazette, 25th March 1819).

A surely even more impressive feat was performed later in the year. "AN extraordinary bet of 50 guineas has been decided by two gentleman of St. Columb, Cornwall, one of whom undertook to run a velocipede from that place to Liskeard, a distance of 26 miles, in four hours. Notwithstanding the badness of the road, which caused the machine to move very heavily, he won his wager, by performing the journey twenty-one minutes within the time, with perfect ease" (*Sporting Magazine*, September, 1819). An average speed of just over seven miles an hour.

Apart from these "matches against time", there seems to have been a limited amount of "official" racing involving the "wooden horse". One of the earliest prints the illustrated *Modern Olympics* (pub. 23 Feb

Modern Olympics, 1819 (courtesy of Museum of British Road Transport). The reference in the title is to the ancient Greek Olympian Games as the modern Olympic Games were only inaugurated in 1896.

1819) shows dandies racing on the new velocipede, and another *Modern Pegasus or Dandy Hobbies in Full Speed* (pub. 24 Mar 1819) depicts a dandy racing a John Bull figure along a country road. The idea also occurred to the Lewes correspondent of the *Sussex Weekly Advertiser*, who in the column for 31st May, 1819, commented:-

At our ensuing races, we understand, that the Members' Plate is to be restored; and we should like to see the Gold- cup subscription now in progress, extended sufficiently to afford a purse of twenty guineas for VELOCIPEDES, as it would introduce novelty – diversify the sport to the gratification of thousands – promote muscular exertion – give ample scope for betting amongst the black legs – bother the knowing ones – and furnish some dashing, athletic sprigs of fashion (after a due course of training for the purpose) with an opportunity of showing off, to the best advantage, before the ladies – and furthermore, it is <u>important</u>, that the character of the <u>Johnsonian Hobby</u> should be rescued from the

MODERN PEGASUS or *Dandy Hobbies in full Speed*

Modern Pegasus or Dandy Hobbies in Full Speed, 1819 (courtesy of Museum of British Road Transport). This print interestingly depicts both types of Johnson machine apparently available at this date i.e. with indirect and direct steering. The artist has decided to omit the arm rest or "balancer" which each machine would have had.

72

disgrace and odium of DANDYISM.

The subsequent report of the Lewes Races contains no reference to any velocipede contest. However, more positive steps were taken in Suffolk. "A subscription purse is to be run for on the first day of Ipswich races by *velocipedes,* five of which are already named and entered. The *riders* in jockey dresses, are to contend for the victory from what is called the Natton [this should be Nacton] corner of the race course to the winning post" (*Simpson's Salisbury Gazette,* 3rd June 1819). It seems the new machine had become established at an early stage in this particular town, as we read in *The Bury and Norwich Post* for 17th March, 1819, that "The road from Ipswich to Whitton is travelled every evening by several pedestrian hobby-horses; no less than six are seen at a time, and the distance, which is three miles, is performed in 15 minutes." Speedy stuff !? And the *Ipswich Journal* for Saturday, 10th July, 1819, tells us what happened at the races :-

A great number of pedestrians and others ventured to the course, very many of whom got completely drenched by the heavy rain which fell just as the horses started. The promised contest with Velocipedes, however, kept the company together after the race for the 100gs. Three persons started for this prize, but so great was the eagerness of the multitude to be near them, that the riders, for want of scope, had no opportunity for showing their skill either in speed or jockeyism. Several persons with no other advantage than a nimble step, took the lead of them and kept it to the winning post.

The situation at Ipswich is very reminiscent of the occasion in Hyde Park three months earlier (referred to above) when three velocipedists were "much impeded in their operations by the curiosity of the promenaders". Hopefully the same problem was not encountered in connection with the much longer race on the outskirts of London, referred to in *Simpson's Salisbury Gazette* for 6th May, 1819: "A grand velocipede match is spoken of between four amateurs. The distance to be 50 miles, and to be decided on Blackheath. It is to be for a sweepstake of 25 guineas; the first to pocket the whole. The parties are in training."

There is an interesting paragraph in *Cowdroy's Manchester Gazette* for 1st May 1819, which reads:-

Velocipedes. We are credibly informed that Mr. W____d, a Clerk in an eminent Solicitor's office in this town, is matched against Mr. C___ ___n, in the same office , for 20gs. Aside, to ride on a Velocipede twice round Kersall Moor, on Wednesday in the race week, after the heat for the Gold Cup, by permission of the Stewards. We understand considerable sums are depending on the above match.

The Manchester Meeting took place during the first week in June, but the newspaper does not report the result of the velocipede race.

And from Yorkshire we have a late record of yet another hobby-horse race, apparently from Hull to Beverley and back, a distance of perhaps fifteen miles or so. The illustrated engraving by J. Tupling is dated 1882 and carries the caption : "Returning to Hull, this mile was run in 4 minutes & a half, in 1835. J Tu/g. First, C. Leo/d. Second, Jos/h Jo/n. Third." This suggests a speed over a measured mile of 13.33 m.p.h., which with great respect to the late chronicler seems somewhat improbable.

The condition of the early Nineteenth century roads, coupled with the fact that (unlike the von Drais original) the English pedestrian

Returning to Hull, 1882 (courtesy of Hull Museum of Transport). This would appear to be Tupling's reminiscence of a triumph of his youth.

hobby-horse had no brake, inevitably gave rise to accidents –
particularly on downhill slopes. These are depicted in a number of
the hobby-horse prints. As Thomas Davies put it in his 1837 lecture:
"When the rider had acquired a certain velocity it became extremely
difficult to turn the machine to the right or to the left, or even to
touch the earth with either foot without instantly oversetting; and
this difficulty of checking or stopping the machine at full speed ended
in many accidents." He says later that other evils arose : "If
velocipedes ran on the foot pavements of the streets, which they
should not do, they got in the way of the children, or the children got
in the way of them, and alarmed the ladies maids. Rash and heedless
riders ran unluckily against fat people, and all fat men and old women
cried out that velocipedes took up too much room on the pavement,
especially if it was a narrow one."

The Sussex newspaper contains reports of two early velocipede
incidents. On 26th April, 1819, we read that : "A melancholy accident
has occurred from the use of these newly invented machines. Monday,
as two of these vehicles were descending the hill leading from
Durdham Down to the Black boy public house, with prodigious
velocity, one of them came in contact with a lad at the bottom of the
hill, who was thrown down by the force of the machine, which passed
over his leg and fractured it in a dreadful manner. – The rider had
not the humanity to take the least care of the unfortunate sufferer,
but again mounting his velocipede (which had been upset), pursued
his course with the greatest unconcern." In another report of the
same incident we are told that "the father of the child has been making
every effort to discover the author of his child's misfortune, but
hitherto without effect." The following week it was the turn of the
hobby-horseman himself to suffer injury : "A gentleman at Farnham
had the misfortune to have one of his arms broken by the fall of his
Dandy Hobby, which in going down a hill got the better of him, and
running in contact with a post, was thrown down with great violence."

The Times newspaper for 9th June, 1819, has an even sorrier tale to
tell. "Mrs. Bearham, wife of Mr. Bearham, maltster, of Hunsley, Hants,
returning home lately in her cart, the horse took fright at a velocipede,
and she was thrown out and killed on the spot." The local newspaper
gives the family name as Bareham and the place as Hursley (not
Hunsley), which is near Winchester, adding "her loss is sincerely felt
by her disconsolate husband and family, and by a large circle of

friends" (*Salisbury and Winchester Journal*, 31st May, 1819). This type of accident (hopefully not normally fatal) may not have been uncommon, and indeed throughout the Nineteenth century we read of the basic incompatibility on the road of the wooden or iron steed and its flesh and blood counterpart.

On a lighter note we have the following "Whimsical Anecdote" (possibly related to an actual event but if so obviously much elaborated) from the pen of John Fairburn in his circa April, 1819, booklet *The New Pedestrian Carriage* :-

A MOUNTED TAR CAPSIZING A HOST OF CORRUPTION

A naval officer mounted one of these <u>chargers</u> in Pall Mall, and, as sailor like, no great adept in riding, he swore he would steer a straight course and run down the devil if he came across his hawse. The black gentleman did not appear to obstruct his course; but running at the rate of <u>ten knots</u> an hour, he capsized a Dandy, a Member of Parliament, a Pig, an Apple-woman, a Cabinet Minister, a Prince, a Newfoundland Dog, and a Bishop. The rapidity with which all this was executed, proves that, under the guidance of <u>discretion,</u> these Hobby-Horses may be made very useful in <u>accelerating</u> every wise and nobler art of man.
The print *Jack mounted on his Dandy Charger* (referred to earlier) depicts the scene.

A more likely story is that recounted by the "very adroit velocipedean" referred to at the beginning of this chapter. He told how whilst riding his wooden horse he met a gentleman "on the highway by a river side, who, requesting to be allowed to try it, and being shewn how he must turn the handle to guide it, set off with great spirit, but turning the handle the wrong way, soon found himself hurrying to the edge of the river; where, in his flurry, instead of trying the effect of turning the handle the other way, he began lustily shouting "woh! woh!" and so crying plunged headlong into the stream" (*Howitt's Visits to Remarkable Places*). The account is reminiscent of a reported incident in which "A velocipede ran away with its master a few evenings ago, and actually threw him into the dock, at Hull" (*Salisbury and Winchester Journal*, 7th June, 1819).

In all probability accidents caused by hobby-horse riders gave rise to prosecution. Fairburn refers to one incident in which : "A Dandy mounted upon one of these chargers, *charged* a watchman in Catharine-street, who instantly knocked him down horse and all, and carried both to the watch-house, where the Dandy and his horse were released after a night's incarceration upon paying "fines and charges", which, with his doctor's bill, (for his head was well scarified), would amount to full £3:10:0, the price of *Aske's* best pair of Dandy stays." But accident or no, hobbyhorsemen were liable to prosecution if they rode upon the pavement. Again Fairburn's *New Pedestrian Carriage* contains an interesting and amusing item (the main details of which are corroborated in contemporary newspapers for March 1819) :-

Captain Hoy, a hero reeking from the field of Waterloo mounted one of Johnson's Chargers, (his own, I have no doubt, has his bones whitening in the summer's sun on the bed of honour), he dash'd up Long Acre, and had proceeded as far as Duncombe's, in Little Queen-street, where he curbed the impetuosity of his fiery charger, and stopped to read the bill of Matthews's budget.

Ah, me ! what perils doth environ
The man who meddles with cold iron.

The bridle of the charger was rudely seized, and, before he could draw his cold iron from its sheath, he was man-handled by some half-dozen men in buckram, and a fellow in a laced hat and shabby blue coat roared –

"Zounds, I'm the beadle of the parish."
To Marlborough-street, the Captain he drags,
And swore he would fine him because on the flags
He had caught him; for he had stuck close to his heels,
As he rumbled along them his charger's wheels.

It was in vain to attempt fighting a cock on his own dunghill, so the Captain bowed to superior force and attended the farce of

THE BEADLE OUTWITTED

John Kendrick, the beadle, who I am sure has had as many of

Mother Cummins's fair and frail disciples in tow, as he has drunk glasses of gin at their cost, laid his charge against the captain, who was convicted under the Paving-Act, (and a d----d hard-headed act it is for poor barrow-women and sellers of dogs-meat). He paid his fine of £2, and instanter laid an information against the "Jack in Office", who had imprudently mounted the captain's charger, and rode her through Queen's Court (a paved one) in triumph. The worthy Magistrate, Mr. Farrant, of Marlborough-street-office, convicted him also, and he paid the penalty of £2, amidst the laughter of a crowded office.

The Marlborough Street magistrate subsequently dealt with more cases. Under the heading "Velocipedes" in the *Birmingham Commercial Herald* for 3rd April, 1819, we read : "A young gentleman, of fashionable fame, was, on Monday, at Marlborough-street Office, charged with riding his hobby on the foot-pavement, and fined 40s. which he immediately paid." Later the *Sussex Weekly Advertiser* for 26th April, 1819, records that : "Saturday Wm. Harrison, Esq. was charged by several watchmen of the parish of St. Giles's with riding his hobby on the foot pavement from King street, Holborn, to Southampton row, Russell square. Mr. Harrison, in defence, said, that the hobby horse was not on the foot pavement, but in the road. Several witnesses deposed to the same effect. The Magistrate (Mr. Farrant) ordered Mr. Harrison to be discharged, and the horse to be given back to him." The case underlines the point that an offence was only committed under the Metropolis Paving Act if the machine was being ridden on the pavement, whatever over-zealous enforcers of the law might have wished to be the position. This seems to have been the position in other parts of the country as well, perhaps under local Acts or bye-laws, as we read : "The magistrates of Bristol last week fined a person in the penalty of 20s. and costs, for riding a velocipede on the pavement of that city" (*Salisbury and Winchester Journal*, 21st June 1819).

And it was not only the pavement from which the early velocipede was banned. At the end of May 1819 the Lord of the Manor of Berkhamsted, Herts, whilst agreeing that the playing of cricket should continue to be allowed on the common at the time of the Berkhamsted Sports, decreed that "women bruising for a prize, trap ball, quoits and Dandy Horses" were forbidden (quoted in *The*

Evolution of English Sport by Neil Wigglesworth, London, 1996).

Hobby-horse riders were allowed on the King's highway, but what happened when they came to a toll-gate? There is a satirical depiction of the scene in the illustrated print *The Female Race ! or Dandy Chargers Running into Maidenhead*. Later in the century there was to be considerable controversy as to whether cyclists should pay tolls, and if so of what amount. Perhaps it was a matter of serious dispute when the two-wheeler first appeared on the road, but the author is only aware of the following anecdote, told in the *Sporting Magazine* for March 1819:-

> A <u>Velocipeder</u> *presented himself at a turnpike, and demanded,* "What's to pay ?" – That (said the waggish gate-keeper) depends *upon whether you ride upon your hobby or pull it through; in the latter case, you know, a two-wheel carriage, drawn by any horse, mule or ass, is liable to the toll; and you will, I suspect, <u>come</u> <u>within the meaning of the Act</u>.*

We know quite a lot about "the hobby-horse on the road", but what about the hobby-horse on the road to war ? The received wisdom is that the bicycle was first seriously considered for military use in or about 1870, the earliest army cycling corps being established in England in 1888 and the first actual wartime deployment taking place during the Boer War 1899-1902. But the idea of a military role for the newly-invented velocipede had surfaced in England as early as the Spring of 1819. "The Velocipede is one of those machines which may probably alter the whole system of society; because it is applicable to the movement of armies, and will render rapidly practicable marches far more distant than have ever yet been undertaken" (*Monthly Magazine*, 1st May, 1819). The colour illustrated print *Military Hobbyhorse* published by John Hudson dated 2nd March, 1819, bears the legend "Particularly recommended to Cavalry Officers". And as we shall read in the next chapter, the idea of a corps of velocipedists was apparently at one stage under consideration. In the event, the era of the pedestrian hobby-horse was a relatively brief one, and there was no substantial military employment of the machine.

Just then how brief was the hobby-horse era, and what were the reasons for its decline ? Things seem to have been going well enough some four months after the machine was first introduced to the public at the beginning of the year. "Southampton, Saturday May 29. To such utility is the velocipede already advanced, that we frequently observe the arrival here of fanciful pedestrians from places 40 and 50 miles distant; their adoption is becoming very general in this town, and no inconsiderable degree of mechanical genius is evinced by the several juvenile persons who exhibit them" (*Salisbury and Winchester Journal*, 31st May 1819).

No doubt there were a variety of reasons why shortly after this date the invention began to fall into disuse. In the author's view the machine suffered considerably from its association with the much despised dandies (to whom we shall be referring again shortly), even though dandies were by no means the only riders. It will be recalled that the *Sussex Weekly Advertiser*'s correspondent shared this opinion ("it is important that the character of the Johnsonian Hobby should be rescued from the disgrace and odium of DANDYISM"). The legal restrictions on the use of the vehicle were not particularly severe, as they appear only to have prohibited pavement riding in the metropolis.

The principal reason why the machine fell out of favour was probably because it acquired a reputation for causing serious injury. That this would probably be the case had already been observed by the medical profession in the Spring. A delightfully sardonic report appears in the *Birmingham Commercial Herald* for 12th June, 1819 :-

ROYAL COLLEGE OF SURGEONS, LINCOLN'S INN FIELDS.
At a General Meeting of the Master, Governors, and Assistants of the Royal College, held at their Hall in Lincoln's Inn Fields, on Monday, May 10, 1819,
A motion was made, seconded, and carried unanimously - That the Thanks of the College be voted to the inventors and multipliers of the VELOCIPEDES and ACCELERATORS, for the able assistance they are likely to give to the profession.
Resolved also unanimously – That the said Vote of Thanks be written in the most beautiful manner on ASS SKIN, with the arms of the College emblazoned thereon.

Just three months later, the surgeons' prognostication had come true.

Not just through the occasional accident but more generally due to the strain the machine placed on certain parts of the anatomy. A note in the *Sussex Weekly Advertiser* for 16th August, 1819, says it all:-

IMPORTANT CAUTION. – The fatal efficacy of the Velocipede in producing ruptures has been formally announced by the London Surgeons. An alarming number of cases of Hernia have within the last two months, offered themselves at the Hospitals of the Metropolis; all occurring among poor mechanics, who had indulged themselves in the Sunday use of this vehicle. In consequence of this most mischievous property, the amusement is much on the decline.

If the use of the hobby-horse velocipede was for health reasons "much on the decline" in August, 1819, by the end of October of the same year it had "in consequence been laid aside" according to the *Monthly Magazine* published 1st November, 1819. The magazine refers to the fact that "the peculiar muscular action attending its frequent use causes ruptures and inflammations of certain muscles of the thighs and legs." The suggestion that on this account the use of the machine had entirely ceased would seem to be an over-pessimistic assessment of the position. It is nevertheless clear that the heyday of the pedestrian hobby-horse lasted for little more than six months during the year of its introduction.

By 1821 Lewis Gompertz of Kennington (of whom more anon) felt able to say in an article in *The Repertory of Arts* (vol.39, 2nd series) that "it is worthy of observation how much delighted the public were with the velocipede on its first appearance, and how soon it was thrown aside as a useless toy" – a description with which Gompertz himself does not agree. In his 1837 lecture *On the Velocipede*, already quoted at the head of this chapter, Thomas Davies states "as is usually the case with every remarkable invention, it was not long before an outcry was raised against velocipedes. The old ladies remarked "They are such foolish looking things"." In his *Slang Dictionary* of 1823, "John Bee" (John Badcock) having defined the Dandy Horse as a "Velocipede or instrument for journeying far and fast : two wheels, one behind the other supporting a bar of wood", says that "hundreds of such might be seen in a day : the rage ceased in about three years, and the word is becoming obsolete" (though in the same year John

Atkin published his epic poem *Jonah Tink* with its reference to a "dandy youth" who "rode on a velocipede", as referred to earlier in the chapter).

But having emphasised the relative briefness of the hobby-horse era, it is perhaps finally worth making the point that some machines continued in use, or were made and used, in a few corners of the realm right up until the late 1860s, when the pedalled "boneshaker" came on the scene. During this period of nearly fifty years there were a variety of foot-treadled, hand-lever propelled and other velocipedes, mostly "one-offs" or at any rate made only in small numbers, but these are really outside the scope of the present work. Our concern is with the hobby-horse (and its derivatives), in which the machine is propelled by pushing the feet on the ground.

There is an interesting passage on this in the 1869 "Velox" (Tom Burgess) book *Velocipedes, Bicycles and Tricycles*:-

Non-steerable hobby-horse (Velocipedes, Bicycles & Tricycles, "Velox", 1869). The implication from the milestone is that the rider has 10 miles to go to home - wherever that was.

This brings us to the regular historic period of the introduction of velocipedes. Amongst those which were then introduced was [this one], sketched more than thirty years ago. It was rude and primitive in construction.

A velocipede somewhat similar in construction was brought regularly into Northampton market from Yardley Hastings until a few years ago; but it was fancifully ornamented with gnarled pieces of wood in the form of serpents, snakes, and animals; and one yet remains in the little village of Harpole, near Weedon, in the same county. The use of this machine caused a tendency to rupture, and, as accidents were frequent, it became neglected, and has long since been disused. It comes nearer to the "Dandy-horse" – the well-known velocipede of fifty years since.

The suggestion is that the machines referred to by "Velox" may all have been of the non-steerable variety, though (unlike Leftwich and his "Patterson" hobby-horse) he avoids saying that they pre-dated von Drais and Denis Johnson. Indeed the specific machines to which

"Oliver", the author's replica non-steerable hobby-horse. The wooden stand is of course removable.

83

"Velox" refers appear to have been in use in the 1830s to 1860s period. The present author can vouch for the fact that a non-steerable hobby-horse does work (albeit as one would expect much less efficiently than the normal type), as he had the illustrated experimental model based on the "Velox" sketch specially made for him a few years ago. "Steering" is achieved by forcing the rear wheel to skid to one side or the other, using one's body weight, or if a more major turn is required by simply lifting and moving the front wheel in the required direction.

A recent exciting discovery was made by the author in the archive of the Cyclists' Touring Club at Godalming. This is the colour illustrated watercolour depicting two velocipedists titled "A meeting on the road from Layston Villa to Hormead Cottage." The painting is signed by James Wilcox and dated 1st November 1849. The four-wheeled machine appears to be hand-propelled, with the rider's feet off the ground, but the three-wheeler seems to be in the hobby-horse

A Sketching Party (watercolour by James Wilcox, 1850, Hertford Museum). With even less detail than the earlier painting by the same artist, we can only guess at the means of propulsion of the machine depicted.

tradition with the rider propelling his velocipede as envisaged by von Drais and Johnson.

James Wilcox (1778-1865) lived at Hormead Cottage, Great Hormead, near Buntingford, Herts, from 1827 for the rest of his life. He was a man of many talents and in particular was "an amateur artist of no mean ability", to quote his biographer Herbert Andrews. There is a collection of Wilcox's drawings and watercolours at the Hertford Museum. He travelled extensively around the country. According to his biographer, writing in 1921, "The mode of travelling was probably by postchaise : but for jaunts nearer home either in Herts, or extending over the border into Essex, Wilcox built and used one of the earliest tricycles, a cumbersome though useful vehicle as his sketch (Book 6.54b) shows it to have been, which required the auxiliary assistance of small boys to propel it uphill."

The illustrated sketch to which Andrews refers is titled "A Sketching Party" by Wilcox and is dated 16th August 1850. The three ladies in their poke bonnets and shawls are apparently James Wilcox's daughters, who inherited his artistic tastes. The machine around which they are grouped is in fact a quadricycle, not a tricycle, but it is clearly not the same four-wheeler as depicted in the earlier watercolour as this has all four wheels the same size. So the indications are that at this period there were a number of velocipedists riding a variety of machines, including at least one hobby-horse tricycle, around the lanes of Hertfordshire.

We also have some evidence with regard to later use of the ordinary hobby-horse in connection with the illustrated example in the Hull Transport Museum. This is one of the few hub-steering machines known to the author, and like the example at Ipswich it would appear to be an approximate copy of a Johnson velocipede. A museum pamphlet dated 1905 records that the hobby-horse was donated by one J.W. Mayfield, who stated that his father, in his younger days, "frequently traversed the Yorkshire Wolds upon it", and that it was ridden "for many hundreds of miles", apparently last being used around 1860. The machine had originally been purchased at Scarborough by J.W. Mayfield's great-uncle, presumably in the hobby-horse era. It is fascinating to read of a velocipede of this type owned by three generations of the same family (and ridden by two of the them) throughout the greater part of the Nineteenth century.

A further interesting report of occasional use throughout much of the Nineteenth century is to be found in *Bicycles and Tricycles Past and Present* by Charles Spencer (the book is undated but would appear to have been published in 1883). The author refers to an "ancient specimen of the Dandy horse, or original velocipede, at the establishment of Mr. Goy, 21 Leadenhall Street, London, to whose courtesy I am indebted for the following history of this very interesting machine." Goy's was a long-established, well-known and successful "Athletic Outfitter", who at this period was specialising in all cycling requirements. The photo illustration is believed to be of Goy's "dandy horse", which was apparently exhibited at the 1891 Stanley Cycle Show with other "ancient and historical machines which were lent for the occasion". Spencer's account (courtesy of Goy) with regard to this "original velocipede" is as follows :-

It was originally purchased by Mr. Frederick Roberts of Acre Lane, Brixton, at the sale of effects of a deceased gentleman, Mr.

Mayfield family hobby-horse (courtesy of Hull Museum of Transport). Although it proved to be a trusty steed, this item lacks the stylish quality of the Johnson velocipede.

86

Wilkinson, in the year 1851. Mr. Wilkinson lived at Clapham Common many years ago, and he used to ride his Dandy horse round his grounds every morning. When Mr. Roberts bought it, in 1851, he soon found that when he appeared upon it in the public streets it attracted too much attention to be agreeable, and he was consequently compelled to restrict his practice to moonlight nights, when there were but few observers. Mr. Roberts says that the great objection to its general use was "the tendency it had for rupturing, and the labour of propelling it", but, he adds, "I used it, more or less, for years."

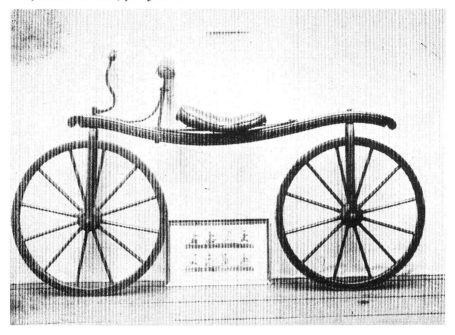

Goy's dandy-horse. Another non-Johnson machine which seems to have stood the test of time.

After the pedalled "boneshaker" was introduced into this country, half a century after the hobby-horse made its appearance, the earlier machine was no doubt regarded as little more than a curious relic. A report on the Barnes Common tricycle "meet" in *The Cyclist* for 17th May 1881 makes the point : "A gentleman, attired in the costume of a past age, amused the spectators with riding a hobby horse, built in 1819, about the Green."

Chapter 5

A PEDESTRIAN CARRIAGE FOR DANDIES, NOBILITY & ROYALTY

The price of Denis Johnson's patent pedestrian machine was normally between eight and ten pounds, a high price in 1819 for a beam on two wheels. Only the reasonably well off could afford such an extravagance, though many more took to the road on hired machines. But the Dandies and the Nobility – including Royalty – were it seems its principal purchasers.

According to *The Slang Dictionary* (1874 edition) the dandy was "a fop, or fashionable nondescript ... DANDIES wore stays, studied a feminine style, and tried to undo their manhood by all manner of affectations which were not actually immoral." *The Oxford English Dictionary* (1989 edition) says the term was in vogue in London from about 1813 to describe the "exquisite" or "swell" of the period.

Certainly the expression was well-established before the pedestrian hobby-horse arrived on the scene. A disconcerted lady wrote to the editor of the *Sporting Magazine* in March, 1817, telling of the visit of a smart young gentleman down from London. A party of youngsters was arranged to entertain him, when during a game of "innocent romps" he was observed to have a pair of stays on. The lady wrote : "On this circumstance being mentioned to one of my acquaintance, she said he was only – a *Dandy*. – Now Sir, I am quite ignorant what a Dandy is, or of what sex a Dandy may be, and should be glad if any of your correspondents could inform me : because – because (I am sure, I am quite ashamed when I think of it) if I was to marry something in a pair of stays – though they may call it a Dandy, it would be no consolation to me. – As I cannot subscribe my real name, I must sign myself, EMILY DOUBTFUL. Hempstead, Essex."

Lest there should be any doubt as to the extent to which a Dandy might go in his attempts to out-do the "fair sex" at their own game, we are told in the *Sporting Magazine* for August, 1818, that : "The lodgings of a *dandy* were lately robbed of a pair of *stays*, a *smelling bottle*, two pairs of artificial *eye-brows*, and a white *surtout*, in a pocket of which there were *three love-letters*, written to himself, in his own hand-writing !" During the following six months the magazine contains an amusing "Diary of a Fashionable Dandy", an article "Misfortunes of a Dandy", a poem "The Dandy" and an article on "A modern Narcissus". *Simpson's Salisbury Gazette* for 15th April, 1819, has an item "On the Fluctuations of Fashionable Phraseology" which is even more disparaging : "The modern *Dandy* has usurped the place of the *Beau*, the *Buck* of former years. Its external character – a pair of stays – high heeled boots – short waist – starched cravat – narrow brim'd hat – sans sense, sans brains, sans wit, sans everything that a man should possess. Its specific character – vast self importance – selfishness the ruling principle – affecting to despise all things not within the pale of the Dandy community, exactly as they are unaffectedly despised by all wise and respectable persons."

These, then, were the individuals who eagerly took to the hobby-horse on its arrival on the London scene in the Spring of 1819. There can be little doubt of the extent of their patronage, as the very name "dandy-horse" sometimes used to describe the new machine shows. In the light of the supposed effeminacy of these Regency beaux, it seems surprising that they were prepared in such numbers to undertake such energetic exercise as the velocipede required, and to take the risk of falling off and even of serious accident or injury. Perhaps we should revise our opinion of these young gentlemen, on the basis that you can't always judge the contents of a parcel by its wrapping. The *Birmingham Commercial Herald* for 5th June 1819 contains the following amusing account (though Mr. Lund may not have found it funny at the time) :

THE UNFORTUNATE DANDY. On Friday afternoon, about one o'clock, four gentlemen, mounted on their hobbies, undertook for a wager of one guinea to run a race from the Half-way-house, Lower-road, Deptford, to Chinahall, being a distance of half a mile. On coming facing Mr. L.'s, the Cottage of Content, which is about mid-way, and where there is an angle in the road, Mr. Lund, who was second, attempted by an act of dexterity to drive before his leader, when, going too near the bank, which sloped downwards, he was precipitated headforemost into the ditch, and was completely covered over with the mire, which stuck to him like pitch. He was taken into Mr. L.'s, where he was washed and cleaned, and accommodated with a change of clothes, until he sent home for others. His companions seeing the accident, did not proceed on their journey, but deferred it to another opportunity.

The important print *Johnson's Pedestrian Hobbyhorse Riding School* (referred to on several points in Chapter 2) appears to provide a portrait of one particular dandy. According to Dorothy George (in the British Museum *Catalogue of Political and Personal Satires*), "In the foreground on the extreme right a dandy walks forward; he resembles Lord Petersham." The individual in question has a moustache and small beard, is top-hatted and sports a cane. The fact that he is not actually riding may indicate that he was in sympathy with the new fad but not actually a participant – though an oblique reference in the play *Comedy of Honour* (see below) suggests otherwise. In any event, as late as 1874 (in *The Slang Dictionary*) it is still recalled that "Lord Petersham headed them" i.e. the dandies.

It is probably Lord Petersham who is the hero (or perhaps anti-hero) of *Hobbyhorsiana,* a light-hearted contemporaneous account of the dandy and his "charger" by "Joe Dobbin", who is referred to as "a biped blood horse of the true breed, and a member of the new rocking-horse university." His Lordship is described in the opening paragraph of the booklet as follows :

IN a small parlour, furnished in the first style of fashion, sat Lord P_____ over his breakfast. His red hair, to the oiling, curling and brushing of which he had devoted the best part of an hour, was surmounted with a green silk nightcap; his elegant form was obscured by a roomy surtout, his feet were enclosed in Turkish slippers, with toes turning up somewhat after the Chinese fashion; and his body filled out a large arm chair with some dignity.

A dandy was nothing unless he was showing off, and Johnson's new machine allowed him to do this in some style. The author of *Hobbyhorsiana* explains "How to make yourself conspicuous" :

91

Paint your charger all manner of queer colours, and spot your face with blacking. Instead of a hat, wear a red night-cap, to which, instead of a tassel, hang a few rush-lights; turn your coat inside out, and wear the seat of your breeches in front : then wheel along the street with a hymn book in your hand, and sing as loud and as merrily as though you had a whole nest of nightingales in your belly. This has such an imposing effect, that all those who are influenced by outward appearances, mark you down as a very spirited fellow, whose acquaintance deserves cultivation; and as for those lovely young creatures called females, let them be ever so pretty, their tender affections can never withstand the wink of so important a personage.

The dandy and his hobby-horse even featured in a nursery rhyme of the period, written by eleven-year-old Caroline Sheridan, the granddaughter of Richard Brinsley Sheridan. The illustration by

The Dandies' Rout, 1820 (reproduced from A Nursery Companion by Iona & Peter Opie by courtesy of Oxford University Press). The artist's simplistic representation of the machines seems appropriate for a nursery rhyme.

Robert Cruikshank of three individuals on their machines is from *The Dandies' Rout* (the word is used in the archaic sense of a social gathering), originally published by John Marshall in 1820. The verse accompanying the drawing reads :

> *A hobby-horse apiece, they all*
> *With speedy steps go to the ball.*
> *Their wives and daughters there they'll meet,*
> *The Dandizettes so mild and sweet,*
> *As you will soon have an example,*
> *In my Lady Fimple Fample.*

Amongst the relatively better off it was not only the dandies who were affected by the hobby-horse fever. According to a late source (the *English Mechanic* for 1868) : "Fox, Sheridan, Pitt and other notabilities of the period, patronized the velocipede in St. James' Park, taking the constitutional daily on the Dandy Horse, after a hard night spent in the House of Commons or around the gaming tables." However, little weight can be given to this statement as the dramatist and politician Sheridan, Caroline's grandfather, had died in 1816,

Enamelled hobby-horse pill box (author's collection). An appropriate accoutrement for the Regency dandy. Painted or transfer-printed scenes on small white-enamelled copper boxes became popular in England in the Eighteenth century,

some three years before the hobby-horse came into use. Charles James Fox, statesman and orator, had died ten years before this in 1806, the same year as the Tory prime minister William Pitt the Younger. Perhaps it was their ghosts seen riding in the park on spectral machines !

But we do know of one young hobby-horseman who went on to become a famous politician in later life, the Right Honourable Robert Lowe M.P., Chancellor of the Exchequer from 1868 to 1873 (and later Viscount Sherbrooke). The *Dictionary of National Biography* records him as being an "ardent advocate of bicycling". As President of the West Kent Bicycle Club he made a speech on 15th September 1877 (reported in *Bicycling News*) in which he stated, after referring to the introduction of the velocipede : "I had the honour in the reign of [George IV] of riding one of these machines, so that I may term myself

A fob seal for the dandy's chain - two views. The message "EVERY ONE HAS HIS" and the "hobby" image are of course in reverse in order to produce the correct impression on the wax. Courtesy of Lorne Shields.

an ante-bicyclist or anticipator of the bicycle. I was considered quite an adept at the exercise, and remember once riding a mile race on one of these dandy-horses with His Majesty's mail, and contriving to get in before it to my infinite delight." As Robert Lowe was born at the end of 1811, he would only have been seven years old in the Spring of 1819, and even at the end of the reign of George IV he was still only eighteen. Clearly therefore his velocipedic activities must have taken place some years after the pedestrian hobby-horse was largely out of fashion.

As quoted in the previous chapter "Clergymen used the new machine to visit their parishioners, and to travel between scattered parishes". There is indeed a satirical 1819 engraving published by Tegg, *The*

The Right Hon. Robert Lowe M.P. In his youth a master of the dandy charger, in later years Chancellor of the Exchequer in the first Gladstone administration.

Parsons Hobby – or – Comfort for a Welch Curate, on precisely this topic. The Reverend Joseph Coltman M.A., J.P., 1776-1837, Vicar of Beverley Minster, Yorkshire, for almost a quarter of a century, was a real life example. The earliest date the illustrated silhouette of this oversize gentleman astride his machine could have been produced is Spring 1819, when Coltman was already forty-two years old. Unlike the majority of riders, it would seem that he employed his velocipede regularly for many years, perhaps until his death at age sixty, as a note written thereafter states this was his "favourite mode of travelling".

The Reverend Coltman was a highly gifted individual, much loved

Silhouette of the Reverend Joseph Coltman on his velocipede (author's collection).

by his parishioners – an elaborate memorial inscription extolling his virtues can be seen in Beverley Minster. It is said that at one time he weighed as much as 43 stone, although 37.5 stone is the figure usually quoted. Apparently Joseph Coltman actually rode his machine into church, as it seems that it became the only way he could transport his enormous bulk (when not travelling in his carriage). As walking up the steps to the altar was impossible, a board was placed sloping from the pulpit floor down to the nave. Coltman rode to a convenient spot where three vergers were waiting to receive him. The head verger "took aim", and the three together rushed the priest up into the pulpit.

There are also accounts of Coltman travelling around his parish on his hobby-horse assisted by a boy who pulled on a rope attached to the machine (which on other occasions travelled with him in his carriage), and of his "old and trusty servant" helping him to mount

Dandy-horse playing card (author's collection). Grandfather on his early two-wheeler. One of six "Cycling" items from a card game probably dating from the mid-1890s.

and dismount and "keeping his inanimate charger in the highest possible condition". It is reported that on one occasion Joseph Coltman fell into a ditch whilst riding his velocipede. Further details of Coltman's life (and an early portrait) can be found in various publications at the Beverley Reference Library. There is also a brief biography in *John Markham's Colourful Characters* (Highgate Publications (Beverley) Ltd., 1992).

At the beginning of the hobby-horse craze the machine received considerable attention at the London theatres. Indeed, according to "Square Toes", whose comments on the invention were noticed earlier: "It made its first appearance on the English stage, in conjunction with an appropriate character, in the late Covent Garden Pantomime, and has since become generally known to the town, by our artizans who fabricate vehicles, and our artists who furnish the designs, which attract the gazers at the principal shop windows."

The Covent Garden Pantomime *Harlequin Munchausen, or, The Fountain of Love* ran from Boxing Day 1818 to mid-February 1819 (with a final performance on 1st March), which certainly suggests a very early public display of the item, even if it was not introduced into the script at the very beginning of the run. The probability is that the "appropriate character", who presumably rode a hobby-horse on stage, was the enormously versatile and popular English clown and pantomimist Joseph Grimaldi, who played "My lord Humpy-Dandy" in the scene entitled "The Chateau of Sir Hilario Frosticos".

In April, the Epilogue of *Comedy of Honour* at the Drury Lane Theatre concluded with twenty-odd lines on the new machine, referring to the author's hopes in appropriate terms : "Hobbies, he hears are now the mode accounted, So for nine nights, at least, he hopes he's mounted" (there may also be a reference to Lord Petersham – " Should one of you – perhaps his dandy lordship – be riding past "). The following month the Epilogue to *Carib Chiefs* by The Hon. W.R. Spencer was almost entirely given over to the hobby-horse, and concluded :-

> *Our Cocknies now shall fear no break-neck tumble*
> *On steeds that never start, and seldom stumble;*
> *And hunters only one small danger find,*
> *To break their horses wheels, and not their wind.*
> *Then for our letters – Oh the sweet invention !*

And Johnson well deserves a <u>Palmer's</u> pension !
Bus'ness or Love may travel by express,
With speed far greater, and expense far less,
On wood scarce thicker than a witch's broomstick.
Laden with news I see the Hobby <u>groom-stick</u>
Speed the soft intercourse from soul to soul,
And weft a sigh o'er England – on a pole !

Our "<u>wooden walls</u>" were long the Patriot toast –
Soon <u>wooden cavalry</u> shall be our toast;
And when some WELLINGTON to conquest leads
Our new-built squadrons of – Velocipedes,
What foe will dare our prowess to withstand,
Borne on our native oak o'er sea and land !

(*Simpson's Salisbury Gazette,* 27th May 1819*)*

The suggestion that Johnson "deserves a <u>Palmer's</u> pension" perhaps requires explanation. In 1784 John Palmer began operating a mail-coach service which was subsequently expanded and greatly expedited the delivery of the post. For this public service he was eventually granted a state pension and other benefits. The suggestion now made is that the Johnson velocipede could be employed to even greater effect, and so entitle our hero to a similar reward. A suggestion which appears to have been adopted – perhaps on a trial basis and with only limited benefit to Johnson – the following year.

Even as late as June 1819 the patrons of the Covent Garden Theatre's production of Sheridan's *The School for Scandal* were regaled with a speech by "Mr. Liston, riding on a Velocipede", playing the part of a dandy and favourably comparing the hobby-horse to the "living steed", concluding with the stirring words :

Methinks I see Newmarket's glories fade –
Egham and Ascot sink into the shade.
No more the mettled Courser's swift career
Shall fire the soul of Commoner or Peer :
Brittania's Horsemen, for a bit of wood,
Have barter'd their old boast – their <u>bits of blood</u>.
(*Sporting Magazine,* June 1819)

99

The only known engraving with a thespian theme is the illustrated *New Reading – or – Shakespeare Improved* (published by Thomas Tegg). One of Edmund Kean's principal roles was as Richard III in Shakespeare's play of the same name. The king is made to proclaim the immortal (?) words "A Hobby ! A Hobby my Kingdom for A Hobby !!!" The print is "Humbly Dedicated to the Keen Critic of Drury Lane, by a poor Author". This would appear to be a reference to the very public and acrimonious dispute between Kean and the playwright Bucke, whose tragedy *The Italians* the celebrated actor described as "the worst of the bad".

A number of the hobby-horse velocipedes still in existence belonged to the nobility – using the term in its wider sense to include knights. A reference to Appendix 2 reveals machines owned by Sir John Leicester of Tabley House, the Duke of Marlborough of Blenheim Palace, the Duke of Northumberland of Alnwick Castle, the Earl of Durham of Lambton Castle, the Earl of Eglinton of Eglinton Castle Scotland, the Duke of Argyll of Roseneath Castle, Scotland, and the

New Reading - or - Shakespeare Improved, 1819 (author's collection). Unlike the Military Hobbyhorse print, only <u>wooden</u> horses are to be seen on the field of battle.

Duke of Leinster of Carton House, Ireland. In the present century machines have been owned by Sir Philip Brocklehurst and Sir Edward Iliffe which may have been in their families for several generations.

But whilst the pedestrian hobby-horse clearly achieved a measure of popularity amongst the titled class, one must be careful in drawing a conclusion from the fact that they owned a not insubstantial proportion of the extant machines. This can to some extent be explained on the basis that such artefacts were more likely to survive within the confines of a stately home remaining in the ownership of the same family for many generations. It is nevertheless clear, on the basis of the evidence of the successors to Denis Johnson's firm (letter in *Bicycling News*, 17 Sept 1880) that "the *accelerator* was much used by the nobility in the early part of the present century and brought many patrons to their predecessors."

Appendix 2 reveals that two Johnson hobby-horses (consecutively numbered 299 and 300) are still to be seen at the Duke of Northumberland's country seat at Alnwick Castle. They were ancient relics more than 150 years ago, when Howitt wrote volume 2. of his *Visits to Remarkable Places* in 1841. He was told the story of how the "pranks" of the Duke's "horse" caused it to be "disused and stabled". "The Duke and his physician used to amuse themselves with careering on these steeds about the grounds; but one day, being somewhere on the terrace, His Grace's Trojan steed capsized, and rolled over and over with him down the green bank, much to the amusement of a troop of urchins who were mounted on a wall by the road to witness this novel kind of racing."

The Duke of Northumberland's machines may well have inspired what is by far the longest versification on the subject of the hobby-horse, which was printed at Alnwick in 1819 and sold for "Price Twopence". The poem is called simply "The Velocipede", and tells in no less than fifty six-line verses how Tom Stirabout, "a dandy of prime merit" (whose friend was a Marquis), had been forced to sell his horses to pay his debts and decided to acquire a more affordable wooden horse instead. He goes to a shop to inspect the machines, tries one and immediately falls off, much to the amusement of the shopkeeper and his staff. The shopkeeper offered tuition in a field nearby, where "the painted charger was upon the ground". The poem concludes :

Led by the shop-boy, firmly on his seat
Tom sat; and us'd, as precept taught, his feet.

Till, bolder grown, triumphantly he utter'd,
"Give him his head; – I see that I can do it:"
Though as he spoke, his very heart-strings flutter'd, –
There was a hill, and he had just come to it.
The instant it departed from the level
Down ran the dandy-charger like the devil.

Tom loudly roar'd, (whilst down ran lad and master)
Cursing Velocipedes with all his soul:
The pertinaceous frame work went the faster,
But near the bottom pitch'd into a hole;
It's headlong speed could then no further go,
And Tom perform'd a volti subito.

His head was proof; and Heaven most kindly granted
That part should first arrive upon the green;
So (as some castigating lash was wanted)
A broken leg was all that clos'd the scene:
And Tom was homeward carried from the hill,
With scarce one doit to pay the doctors bill.

Fairburn's *New Pedestrian Carriage* contains an amusing description of a race through London between two members of the aristocracy, under the heading "A Race from Alpha-Cottage to Tyburn". As with the "Mounted Tar capsizing a Host of Corruption" referred to in the previous chapter, it is not easy to decide whether the event being recounted is fact or fiction or a mixture of both, though further research might well provide the answer. In the meantime the reader can form his own view on the following account :

A noble Dandy-Race was run for the purpose of trying the bottom and mettle of these dumb animals. The bet was one hundred guineas a side, from the Alpha cottages, on the Edgware-road, to Tyburn-turnpike. At one o'clock Lord Y_____ mounted Whiskerandos, and the Earl of B____ mounted Smoothchops. They started at full speed and kept neck and neck until near the water-works, when Whiskerandos became restive and ran against *a cow : by the help of a chimney-sweep, the <u>noble rider</u> preserved his balance, tightened his reins and again dashed forward on the course. At the corner of Connaught-mews <u>Smoothchops</u> bolted, but the Earl brought him up in style, by the end of Lady Augusta Murray's Mansion, and pull baker, pull devil, on they drove, helter skelter, and at Tyburn-turnpike <u>Whiskerandos</u> gained the heat by half a neck; scarce a ragamuffin in London but had assembled to view the contest and pick pockets; the applauses which they bellowed upon the victory were loud and long, and extended from St. Giles's to Long-Acre, and from thence to Carlton-House, where a <u>carrier</u> pigeon conveyed the glorious tidings to Brighton under his wing.*

It is hard to tell which of these two nobles merited first to arrive at <u>Tyburn</u> and win <u>by the neck</u>, but as both did their best, their claims <u>to be exalted</u> might be considered as equal. [This would appear to be a satirical reference to the use of the old gallows at Tyburn which apparently stood near the North East corner of Hyde Park.]

It is again from Fairburn that we learn of the Prince Regent (later George IV) as a patron of the hobby-horse. His principal interest was in flesh-and-blood fillies – and not only the equine variety as we shall soon learn. But whilst the present author has so far been unable to come across any reference to the Prince Regent actually riding a machine, either in London or Brighton (where he spent much of his time at his Pavilion remodelled by John Nash) there seems no reason to doubt Fairburn's account of his involvement. We read that : "The fame of Johnson's Walking-Accelerator reached Brighton, and attracted the attention of one, from whose name we may hereafter have them called, JOHNSON'S ROYAL HOBBY-HORSE CHARGERS. Four of them have been sent down to the Kremlin, at Brighton; when it was whispered they were on the go, numbers assembled to view this new addition to the royal stud, and addition to the cares of Sir Benjamin Bloomfield and the Duke of Montrose. The Duke, as Master of the Horse, must be a judge of the *new built* animal. Sir Benjamin, as *Comptroller of the Stud-House*, must rub down Johnson's *Patent Charger* to a brilliancy fit to dazzle royal eyes."

Fairburn describes the departure of the machines from (presumably) London for Brighton. "Numbers attended to see the steeds go forth, no Arabians clad in gold coverings, no harnessing of Eastern splendour, no prancing heroic animals appeared. A military waggon received the *wooden carcasses* of four well-painted *Dandy Chargers,* and in all the waggon-train pomp of peaceful military parade, Colonel Jen__k__n trotted off with them as guide and guard on the road to his royal master's pavilion. If the creatures give satisfaction, it is understood to be the royal intention to mount upon them a regiment of Lancers, to be called THE DANDY PEDESTRIO EQUESTRIA CHARGERS. They are to be stationed on the Steyne, and assist in conveying the royal household to and from London. Young Chiffney, from the high estimation in which he is held, will probably command *this invulnerable* corps."

Contemporaneous corroboration of this proposal is quoted in *Cycling* for February 1880 :

> *Dandy Dragoons. – It has been whispered that a corps of velocipedists is about to be raised in this country, to be called the* <u>*Dandy Dragoons*</u>*; such a corps might be very useful for home service, particularly upon the occasion of public spectacles. If a proper selection of men were made, there would be no danger of either the horses or their riders doing any mischief. The corps would also possess an advantage over* <u>*four-legged*</u>*, or we should rather say* <u>*six-legged*</u>*, cavalry, in being admirably adapted for standing fire, without starting; to be sure, there would be some danger of their taking fire, they being formed of rather combustible materials. A* <u>*Dandy*</u> *regiment in a* <u>*blaze*</u> *would be an awful sight; but what an expense would be saved in feeding, littering, farriering and doctoring ! A glue pot, hammer, bag of nails, and a little oil would supply every want. If the* <u>*head*</u> *of the* <u>*Dandy charger*</u> *were shot off the rider would only have to dismount and nail it on again.*

As one might expect, the Prince Regent's seaside base became the terminus for journeys on the new machine. *The Times* for 9th June 1819 records that "Mr. T. Alford, and three others, travelled lately on a velocipede from London to Brighton (50 miles) in 9 hours." And we learn that : "It is now become quite common for persons to come down to Brighton from London on *Velocipedes*" (*Simpson's Salisbury Gazette*, 10th June 1819). But whilst it seems clear that for a time

Economy - or a Duke of Ten Thousand, 1819 (author's collection). The Duke of York on the Windsor road to visit his ailing father George III. A gold bag contains his annual salary for the task.

the Prince Regent (now in his mid-fifties) took a keen interest in the new machine, there is no reason to suppose that this in fact progressed beyond the acquisition of the four examples referred to by Fairburn. The author has been in touch with the Director of the Royal Pavilion at Brighton who has no knowledge of the present whereabouts of any of the machines.

It appears that the Prince Regent's younger brother, the Duke of York, also owned a hobby-horse. Fairburn tells us : "As £10,000 per annum is not sufficient to maintain a *prince's horse*, one of *Johnson's Chargers* has been bespoke to convey the royal duke *once a month* to Windsor, and as the animal cannot eat, the expense of *baiting* on the road will be saved. A penny sav'd is a penny got, To go to *Mother Carey's* pot" (Mrs Carey was a lady friend of the Duke). This requires a little explanation. In January, 1819, the Duke of York was nominated by his brother to the sinecure of *Custos Personae Regis* (guardian of the body of the King), which apparently involved little more than a regular trip to Windsor to visit his ailing father George III. For this

A P....e, Driving his Hobby, in HERDFORD !!!

*A P****e, Driving his Hobby, in HERDFORD !!!*, 1819 (courtesy of Museum of British Road Transport). The Prince Regent and his Lady friend both appear to be enjoying the ride ! But this hobby-horse is of course a fiction of the caricaturist's imagination.

106

the Duke received an indeed princely sum of £10,000 per annum. Perhaps not surprisingly the appointment met with much disapproval.

When the Duke of York acquired a pedestrian hobby-horse satirists were quick to portray this as a miserly attempt to save travelling expenses. In a print published by Thomas Tegg of Cheapside on 8th April, 1819, *More Economy or a Penny Saved a Penny Got*, the Duke is made to say "I gave Mr Johnston [sic] £8 for this Charger the Cheapest I could get." Another print *Making Most of £10,000 per ann. by saving Travelling Expences* refers, obviously sarcastically, to the fact that the Duke "has wisely procured a Pedestrian Hobby Horse". The illustrated *Economy – or a Duke of Ten Thousand, Taking a Monthly Journey* makes the same point. As the Duke's country residence at Oatlands Park (three miles South East of Chertsey) was only a dozen miles from Windsor Castle, it is entirely feasible that during 1819 he may have used his velocipede to visit his father, though one would suppose that his real reason for employing this form of transport was to participate in the current fad rather than to save the expenses of a coach and four.

The British Museum catalogue (see Chapter 7.) contains references to more than a dozen prints satirising the Prince Regent and the Duke of York, depicting them as velocipede riders. A number show the Prince with his supposed mistress Lady Hertford. The illustrated engraving *A P****e, Driving his Hobby, in Herdford !!!* [sic] is typical. According to Charles Carlton in his book *Royal Mistresses* (Routledge, 1990), "Wrinkles did not discourage the Prince, for, as one court gossip noted, older dames seemed to be his taste." In 1819 Lady Hertford was in her sixtieth year (the Prince was a couple of years younger). The print strongly suggests a sexual connection, but in fact although their relationship was a long-standing one, according to Dormer Creston in *The Regent and his Daughter* (Eyre & Spottiswoode, 1932) "It is thought that she never actually became his mistress, but, whether she did or not, she risked the appearance of being so."

Publication of the affairs of the royal brothers went beyond these prints. Another of the Prince's favoured ladies was the Duchess of Richmond. The illustrated Staffordshire pottery jug (sold at auction by Sotheby's, Sussex, in June 1991) depicts the Duke (presumably) and Duchess of Richmond on a long-backed hobby on "A Visit from

Richmond to Carlton House", the Prince's London residence (the other side of the jug has a picture of "The Lady's Accelerator"). Another copy of the same jug is illustrated (both sides) in *Printed English Pottery*, 1992. "A visit to Carlton House" employing the same illustration (but without background) is featured on a plate in the Brighton Museum collection (ref. HW 1177).

But it was not only English royalty who took to the English version of the Draisienne. The House of Orange-Nassau Historic Collections Trust at The Hague has a hobby-horse which belonged to the Dutch royal family – this being indicated by the frame mark "A" below a crown. According to Gertjan Moed, Director of the National Cycle

Staffs. pottery jug, c.1819 (courtesy of Sotheby's Sussex). The machine depicted is again likely to be an invention of the caricaturist, though we know that von Drais had the idea of a tandem machine.

The velocipede of Willem, Prince of Orange, later King Willem II, 1792-1849 (courtesy of the House of Orange-Nassau Historic Collections Trust and of the National Cycle Museum of the Netherlands) - two views. Clearly based on the Johnson machine, the most noticeable differences being the arm rest support and handlebar stem. The backbone close-up shows the mark of Queen Anna Paulowna, the wife of Willem II, who died in 1865.

109

Museum of the Netherlands, the presumably original owner of the machine was the Prince of Orange (later King Willem II), who used to ride it in the park of his hunting seat Soestdijk in Baarn. The Prince was born in 1792, so would still have been a young man at the date the hobby-horse was probably acquired around 1820. Although as can be seen from the illustration it is very similar to a direct-steering Johnson machine, the maker's name stamped in three places is T. Kerr. The only references to an individual of this initial and surname in the London Trade Directories between 1810 and 1830 are Thomas Kerr, a bootmaker, of various addresses in The Strand throughout virtually the whole of this period, and Thos. Kerr, a chairstuffer, of Blackfriars Road, only present in the 1823 Directory. Of course, T. Kerr the velocipede maker may not have been either of these individuals – if, for example, he was not based in London.

Chapter 6

VELOCIPEDES FOR LADIES

Whilst there is little direct evidence that ladies actually rode hobby-horses, the circumstantial evidence is overwhelming. The contemporaneous booklet *Hobbyhorsiana* contains several references to the riding of hobby-horses by ladies. Firstly, there is an illustration of a "Ladie's Dandy Hobby" straddled by a skirted female rider – the road sign points to "The New Way to Strechit". The machine is virtually identical to the normal "Gentlemen's Dandy Hobby" also illustrated in the booklet. Then, in a report of a supposed lecture on the velocipede which starts by categorising the new machines, we read of : "A Lady's Horse. This is a truly elegant machine, the back is in general formed of wood, and either plated, gilt, or painted with variegated and elegant devices. The saddle is made soft by a horse-hair stuffing and a covering of red velvet, whilst the saddle cloths are, for the most part, either made of silk or satin and richly embroidered."

Finally, at the end of the booklet we have : "Rules for the Fair Sex. If my fair countrywomen should feel ambitious of emulating the male sex, she must remember that the Velocipede will not admit of her sitting sideways. No, no, females are at length put to such an extremity that they must wear the breeches whether they be shrews or no; therefore, on with a pair of yellow leathers and top-boots – on with them, I say, and mount your charger strideways, like the gentlemen. Then roll away like a billiard bowl, throwing you legs elegantly to the right and left, captivating the heart of every gentleman who passes you, by the grace of your motions and attitudes."

One of Denis Johnson's two pedestrian hobby-horse riding schools may have been given over in whole or part to teaching the "fair sex" the art of velocipede management. The illustrated print *FASHIONABLE EXERCISE or The Ladies Hobby School* published by J. Johnstone in 1819 may be both satirical and salacious, unlike the straightforward engraving *Johnson's Pedestrian Hobbyhorse Riding School* illustrated earlier. But as we have seen in the previous chapter, the satire may sometimes have a basis in reality, and the author suspects this may well be the case here.

We know that Johnson had riding schools both at 377 The Strand and at 40 Brewer Street. The colour illustrated print *Views of the Lady's Pedestrian Hobbyhorse* states the machine depicted "is now exhibiting at 40 Brewer Street" (the gentleman's version was on show at 377 Strand). It seems reasonable to surmise that the Brewer Street premises were also used as a ladies riding school. The older lady to the left of the *Fashionable Exercise* print comments "if he dont give me a shove forwards I wont contribute to keep up the concern !!", perhaps indicating actual use of the premises for the purpose depicted. If this is so, the engraving is likely to date from around April 1819, as we know that the gentlemen's school probably started in March and the ladies' one is unlikely to pre-date it. The gentleman's machine

FASHIONABLE EXERCISE, or The Ladies Hobby School, 1819 (cliché Bibliothèque Nationale de France). Clearly the long skirts of Regency times were a problem when riding the machine designed for gentlemen.

illustrated would presumably have been replaced in the ladies' school by the one specially designed for them when this became available in May 1819.

The lady's machine was also made by Denis Johnson. An advertisement in the *Liverpool Mercury* for 2nd July 1819 states :-

LADIES' VELOCIPEDE. MR. JOHNSON, the original Constructor and Patentee of the Velocipede, having completed one for the use of the Ladies upon entirely new principles is exhibiting its merits at the MUSIC HALL, Bold-street, from ten till six. – Admittance, One Shilling.

The new velocipede was not the subject of a separate patent, but this expensive exercise may have been considered unnecessary in view of the protection supposedly afforded by patent no. 4321 of 1818. The machine's main feature was a dropped frame to allow for the long skirts worn by the ladies of the period (a modification re-introduced at the end of the Nineteenth century when women took to riding safety bicycles). A commentator in the issue of the *Liverpool Mercury* quoted above states : "examining its merits we find that it may be conducted or rode by either gentlemen or ladies, or by a gentleman and lady at the same time." How this latter alternative could be achieved must be a matter for speculation.

John Fairburn tells of the new machine's imminent arrival on the scene in his *New Pedestrian Carriage* booklet of circa April 1819. The title page refers (inter alia) to "the ANTI-STRADDLING CHARGERS for the use of THE DANDIZETTES". A dandizette was a female dandy. At the very end of the booklet Fairburn states : "There is now constructing a Charger for females of the same nature – wood and paint – for the use of the ladies, it is to be named the ANTI-STRADDLING CHARGER. *Fairburn*, with his usual attention to the public, will, in a few days, present an exact print of it, drawn from the thing itself, by the same artist who has so admirably designed the plate to this little work" (i.e. Charles Hayten). No copy of this print is known to survive, but we do have the previously referred to Ackermann lithograph of 12th May, 1819, *Views of the Lady's Pedestrian Hobbyhorse*. The print legend explains the item as follows:

THIS MACHINE is an ingenious apology for the Ladies : it

possesses equal power with the Gentlemen's, will turn as short, and is not so liable to upset, having the perch below instead of above. It is of the most simple kind; two light wheels running on the same line, the front wheel turning on a pivot, which, by means of a short lever, A, fig.1. gives the direction in turning to one side or the other, the hind wheel always running in one direction. The Rider being conveniently seated on the small square board B, leans forward against a well-padded cushion C, which terminates with a cross balance-board D, on which the arms rest, to balance the Machine if inclining too much either way : in this position the drapery flows loosely and elegantly to the ground, whereupon the feet are placed as in walking; so that in the first step to give the Machine motion, the heel should be the part of the foot to touch the ground, and so on with the other foot alternately, as if walking on the heel, observing always to begin the movement very gently.

How many of these machines were made is not known. The only surviving one of which the author is aware is the illustrated Science Museum exhibit, which has been on loan for many years to the Shuttleworth Collection at Biggleswade, Bedfordshire. The item appears to be in substantially original condition. It has 30" wheels and is said to weigh a relatively heavy 66lbs. Both the seat and the arm and body rest are adjustable, an improvement on the gentlemen's machine (where only the height of the saddle can be altered). Recent conservation work carried out at the Science Museum reveals that the original colour was dark brown with white coach lining.

We know that the Science Museum's other Johnson hobby-horse belonged to the Duke of Marlborough (this would be George Spencer-Churchill, the Fifth Duke, who inherited the title and Blenheim Palace on the death of his father at the beginning of 1817). This has the inventory number 1924-70, the lady's machine having the consecutive number 1924-71. The Science Museum's records indicate that both machines were obtained in 1924 from Oxford Motors. They also reveal that the gentleman's machine was bought by the same firm (then the Oxford Cycle Company) at a sale at the Combe Works on the Blenheim Estate on 27th June 1884.

One might have expected the lady's hobby-horse also acquired by the Oxford firm to have come from the same source, but this was not in

Lady's hobby-horse (Shuttleworth Collection, Biggleswade, Herts) - three views. The general aspect shows that the actual item was very much as illustrated in the contemporaneous print. The finial and curly steering rod are typical Johnson, though the "St. Paul's dome" has become a beehive. The arm and body rest (see underside detail) are fully adjustable.

fact the case. A letter from the proprietor of Oxford Motors Ltd. to the Science Museum dated 1st February 1924 states : "The Lady's Hobby Horse I bought some 25 years ago from an old Coachbuilder at Hastings, he was an old man and he informed me that his Father had told him that the Lady's Hobbyhorse had been in their Family for some generations, I have not the least doubt about its being genuine."

There were several other machines designed specially for the use of ladies in 1819. None seem to date from earlier than May, some three months after the gentleman's version first became known. All these machines were three-wheelers and as such would presumably not have infringed the Johnson patent. The best known today is probably the Pilentum (the word is from a carriage of this name apparently used by the Roman ladies and referred to in the *Aeneid*), otherwise known as as the Lady's Accelerator or Ladies Hobby. The illustrated print *The Ladies Hobby* (dated 22nd May 1819, published by Tegg) is one of several depicting the machine. The method of propulsion is explained at the base of another print with virtually the same title in the following terms :

The Ladies Hobby, 1819 (cliché Bibliothèque Nationale de France). If the print is to be believed, half-a-dozen such machines could be seen together at one time. The author suspects this may be wishful thinking.

116

The principle of this Machine consists in two boards acting on cranks, on the axle of the fore-wheel, in a similar manner to those used for the purpose of turnery, and is accelerated by the use of the handles, as represented in the plate; the direction is managed by the centre handle, which may be fixed so as to perform any given circle.

Although this three-wheeled velocipede was mechanically inefficient to the modern eye, at the time it must have appeared to be a real advance on the ordinary hobby-horse driven forward by placing the rider's feet on the ground. Indeed it came tantalisingly close to the much later pedalled machine of the 1860s – in essence only requiring foot pedals to be added to the "cranks on the axle of the fore-wheel" in substitution for the complicated arrangement depicted. Another print (*A Pilentum* published by S. & J. Fuller) refers to the machine as having been invented by Hancock & Co. of St. James's Street and exhibited at 97 Pall Mall. The caption reads : "This elegant little Vehicle is peculiarly adapted for the use of the Ladies, as well as Gentlemen. It is impelled, by the slightest touch of either the hands or feet, at a rate truly astonishing; and it is so completely secured from upsetting, that the most timid person might use it with the greatest confidence."

Another three-wheeler is described in *The Gentleman's Magazine* for June 1819 in the following terms : "Lady's Velocipede. A model of a velocipede, invented for the use of ladies, is now exhibiting at Ackermann's, in London. It resembles Johnstone's [sic] machine, but has two wheels behind, which are wrought by two levers, like weavers' treadles, on which the person impelling the machine presses alternately with a walking motion. These move the axle by means of leather straps round the cramps; and the wheels being fixed revolve with it. The lady sits on a seat before, and directs the velocipede as in the original invention." Unfortunately there appears to be no extant print or drawing of this item, but the notion of propelling a tricycle by means of rods or levers turning a cranked axle between two rear wheels was employed on a number of occasions during the early and middle years of the Nineteenth century. Indeed a similar idea occurred to Dr. Edmund Cartwright (the inventor of the power loom), who wrote in May 1819 to *The Philosophical Magazine and Journal* with details of a four-wheeled carriage he had had made "having two cranks upon the axis to be moved, standing perpendicularly to each other and the operator shifting his weight alternately from the treadle of one crank to the other."

We have seen in the last chapter that the Royal mistresses were dealt with by the hobby-horse artists in a less than sympathetic manner. There are a number of other prints depicting attractive young ladies riding (or preparing to ride) ordinary hobby-horses which were obviously produced to titillate the male libido. One blatant example is *FASHIONABLE EXERCISE or The Ladies Hobby School* referred to at the beginning of the chapter. The groom peeping round the curtain at the two half-dressed young women, whilst holding the front of a hobby-horse in a suggestive manner, says : "Now Ladies ! if either of you is ready I have got hold of the primest thing in the school. Its christened the Favorite."

The illustrated print *The Female Race ! or Dandy Chargers running into Maidenhead* is not much better. The figureheads of dandies on the front of the machines ridden by the ladies make it clear that we

The Female Race ! or Dandy Chargers running into Maidenhead, 1819 (cliché Bibliothèque Nationale de France). The young ladies are clearly enjoying the ride - but why are they not wearing their riding breeches ?

are looking at a variation of the *equus eroticus* theme. The foremost rider says : "We have 'em in Maiden head at last ! Who would have thought that we should have been able to drive them so far into the Country on the first trial ?" There are several more engravings of a broadly similar (if not quite so scurrilous) nature, involving sailors, undergraduates – and even Quakers ! As it happens, we know of a Mr William Pollard, a "gentleman of great respectability, one of the Society of Friends", who after being fined only five shillings for riding his dandy charger on the foot-pavement, "mounted and rode off at top speed, leaving a crowd of people much astonished at his expertness in the management of his steed". But the item in *The Liverpool Mercury* for 21st May 1819 does not indicate that Mr Pollard was chasing a female !

There is one print which in the author's opinion does provide further corroborative evidence of actual hobby-horse riding by ladies. This is the illustrated George Cruikshank engraving *The Hobby Horse Dealer*. The lady rider in the background is incidental to the main subject of

The Hobby Horse Dealer, 1819 (courtesy of Museum of British Road Transport). The Johnson hobby-horse is critically examined as if flesh and blood. A respectable lady leads the background riders.

the illustration and is drawn in a perfectly straightforward manner. It seems reasonable to assume that the artist was depicting a known and perhaps not uncommon situation. It is of interest to note that, although skirted, the lady appears to be riding an ordinary Johnson machine and not the distaff version which by the 25th July 1819 date of the print had been available for some months.

Some three-wheel velocipedes were designed to have women as passengers and not riders. Possibly the most successful was the "Velocimanipede, or Lady's Hobby" invented by a London coachmaker Charles Lucas Birch and marketed by him in May 1819. This is shown in the colour illustrated Hudson print *More Hobbies, or the Veloci Manipede*. The machine was described in *The Times* for 13th May, 1819, in the following terms :

> *It is calculated to accommodate three persons : the front compartment is constructed in the same manner as the common velocipede; the centre consists of a convenient seat, fitted up like the seat of a jig; and the third portion is behind the centre, in the shape of a dicky. It is worked by the person in front and the person behind, the person in the middle sitting perfectly easy. The man in front has work of the same kind to do as the rider of the common velocipede; the one behind sits in the dicky, with his foot supported by a foot-board, and the exertion he has to make is to turn with each hand the wheels beside him : for this purpose a handle is fixed to the axis of each wheel, and which is turned round in the same manner as a common hand-mill. The machine combines ingenuity with use, and must produce admiration. It is particularly available in private roads and gentlemen's parks.*

The Velocimanipede (i.e. a velocipede to be worked by hands and feet) was exhibited by Birch to the Duke and Duchess of Kent in the grounds of Kensington Palace on the afternoon of 11th May, 1819 : their Royal Highnesses were duly impressed. The following month the inventor was to be found displaying his machine in the grounds of Marlborough House when the Duchess of York was visiting Prince Leopold. Clearly Charles Lucas Birch knew the right people (a few years earlier, at the beginning of 1814, he – or possibly his father – had built "a fine carriage" for the Prince Regent's daughter the ill-fated Princess Charlotte, according to Dormer Creston in *The Regent and his Daughter*). The newspaper report on this later occasion (*Sussex Weekly Advertiser* 28 June 1819) confirms that "the centre, or chaise-seat" was "intended for a lady". The vehicle was claimed to do eight miles an hour with ease.

Another three-wheeler with a seat for a fair companion is shown in the colour illustrated April 1819 print *The New Invented Sociable, or The Lover and his Hobby.* It is a matter of speculation whether this machine was ever in fact seen in England. The engraving is an Anglicised version of an 1818 French print entitled *Vélocipède Sentimental !! ou Draisienne Francaise.* Karl von Drais had the original concept. His October 1817 leaflet had referred to four types of machine, including ones with three or four wheels with an ordinary, comfortable seat between the two front wheels and another seat behind for the individual propelling the carriage. A velocipede of this type can be seen at the Fürstenburg-Sammlungen, Donauschingen, Germany. It may have been made by one Diemer of Mannheim, whose three-wheeler is illustrated in an 1820 article by von Drais (*Histoire du velocipede*, Kobayashi, p.33 & illus.)

It is impossible to estimate the extent of actual female participation in the hobby-horse craze, either as riders or passengers. The fact that a number of machines were produced exclusively or primarily for ladies does not of course of itself indicate that they achieved any degree of popularity. It would however be somewhat surprising to find at least three makers, including the astute businessman Denis Johnson, all attempting to sell velocipedes for which there was absolutely no market. It seems reasonable to conclude that there must have been some use of the new machine by the fair sex, but that for the most part the riding of velocipedes was regarded as a male prerogative.

Chapter 7

THE ENGLISH HOBBY-HORSE PRINTS

The story of the pedestrian hobby-horse is brought vividly to life by more than eighty prints published in London (and a few also in Dublin), largely during the first half of the year 1819. The author knows of no English depictions of the machine before February, 1819, and only three after September of the same year (published c.Nov 1819, c.Nov 1820 and Aug 1821). Oddly enough, one of the best collections is to be found in the Département des Estampes of the Bibliothèque Nationale, Paris, where there are more than 60 English prints, ignoring duplicates (in addition to a number of Continental ones). These are part of the substantial collection of "engravings, drawings, water colours, etchings or other pictures" depicting various types of early transport bequeathed by the pioneer motoring enthusiast Sir David Salomons of Tunbridge Wells to the French library "in memory of the kindness and courtesy I always received in that country". The Museum of British Road Transport, Coventry, has a similar number of items, closely followed by the British Museum, which has about 50 prints in the Department of Prints and Drawings, and the National Museum of Science and Technology, Ottawa. Examples may also be seen in the John Johnson collection at the Bodleian Library, Oxford, at the the Science Museum, South Kensington, the Cyclists' Touring Club headquarters at Godalming, and elsewhere. The author himself has some 25 original items.

Appendix 3 contains details of the hobby-horse prints in the major public collections known to the author. Most of these prints measure about 8" (20cm) x 12" (30cm), but there is no absolutely standard size and a few items e.g. those from magazines are considerably smaller. The great majority are hand-coloured engravings, but there are a few lithographs and aquatints. Impressions of the same print can be found with completely different colourings. It is believed to be a reasonably comprehensive list, though obviously there may be a

The Dandy Charger, 1819 (by courtesy of the National Museum of Science and Technology, Ottawa, Canada). The association of the pedestrian hobby-horse with the dandies came at a very early stage. This print is dated 23rd February 1819.

few more surviving items of which the author is unaware. The known prints are for convenience grouped together under five headings. This categorisation is more practical than scientific and certain prints could have been listed under more than one heading (for example, the item *Views of the Lady's Pedestrian Hobbyhorse* in the "Ladies" section could obviously also have been placed in the "Machines" section). A detailed explanation of many of the prints can be found in the British Museum's *Catalogue of Political and Personal Satires* (Vol.s IX and X) compiled by Dorothy George.

An article *Hobby Horse Prints* by the noted French cycling historian Jacques Seray (author of *Deux Roues*) appeared in issue No. 132 of the Veteran-Cycle Club magazine *The Boneshaker,* published in Summer 1993. The writer then claimed to be aware of only about forty prints (i.e. roughly half the known total) and there are several unfortunate errors and omissions. Nevertheless, some interesting points are made and the article is a welcome contribution to a previously neglected topic.

It has often been said that a major reason for the demise of the hobby-horse was the scorn poured on it in the many prints published and sold in London in the Spring of 1819. This is an over-simplification of the position. The illustrations can be divided into three broad types. Firstly, those in which the velocipede is depicted simply as a phenomenon of current interest without any hint of ridicule or satire. Secondly, those in which the prime intention is indeed to ridicule the new machine and the dandies and others who rode it. And thirdly, those in which the satire is really political (including attacks on royalty), the hobby-horse being merely a convenient and topical means by which the message could be portrayed.

Some of the most attractive prints fall within the first category. The well-known Rudolph Ackermann – whose premises in the Strand were opposite Johnson's riding school – was the publisher of a number of items depicting the pedestrian hobby-horse in a sympathetic manner. The *Pedestrian Hobbyhorse, Johnson's Pedestrian Hobbyhorse Riding School,* (drawn by Henry Alken, a noted exhibitor at the Royal Academy), *Johnson, the First Rider on the Pedestrian Hobbyhorse,* and *Views of the Lady's Pedestrian Hobbyhorse,* have all been referred to previously and are illustrated. The author's illustrated version of the *Riding School* print is uncoloured, having been printed in sepia, but there are also a number of differently coloured versions known. It is interesting to speculate whether Ackermann was simply taking an independent and encouraging interest in the hobby-horse velocipede, or whether there was a direct financial link between him and Denis Johnson i.e. with the object of providing favourable publicity. The author suspects the latter, and this view appears to be shared by Jacques Seray.

John Hudson of 85, Cheapside, was the publisher of half-a-dozen well-drawn prints, all but one of which appear to be by the same artist, identified only by his initials " W C " in one of the drawings (*Military Hobbyhorse* dated 4th March 1819). Hudson was active throughout the early part of 1819 when most of the engravings and

"Dandy Charger" plate (courtesy of Brighton Museum). The rhyme's claim "many a crowd is gaping seen" is no doubt correct : the claim to "gaining ten miles an hour" is unsubstantiated.

other items were being produced, his *Modern Olympics* print dated 23rd February being the earliest in the British Museum collection, with the illustrated print *The Dandy Charger* (also reproduced on the jacket) bearing the same date. *The Ladies Hobbye* dates from 21st May 1819, *More Hobbies, or the Veloci Manipede* from 18th June 1819, and *An Unexpected Occurence* has the relatively late date of 17th August 1819 (and is probably not by "WC"). *The Dandy Charger* drawing was copied on the illustrated plate (Brighton Museum ref.HW 1179) which carries the following rhyme :

> *I scud along on this machine*
> *While many a crowd is gaping seen*
> *Accelerating power*
> *Gaining ten miles an hour.*

There is an interesting link between the well-known Ackermann print *Pedestrian Hobbyhorse* and Hudson's *The Dandy Charger*, both dating from February,1819. The Bibliothèque Nationale has a copy of an untitled, unascribed and undated print based on the Ackermann one,

GOING to the RACES.

Going to the Races, 1819 (author's collection). Note that again the team of five hobby-horsemen are all dressed in jockey uniform.

apparently by Hudson's enigmatic artist "W C". We have the same woodland scene, but this time the rider is depicted coming down a slope at some speed. The dandy figure astride the machine is identical to the one in *The Dandy Charger,* but in reverse. Presumably this untitled print also dates from about February 1819.

Another attractive first category print is the colour illustrated *Match against Time or Wood beats Blood and Bone* published 17th April, 1819, by Thomas Tegg of 111 Cheapside (the artist's name is not shown). The legend below the drawing provides a potted history of the pedestrian hobby-horse in a single sentence : "This famous *Hobby* was bred in Germany after winning every thing there was Shiped [sic] for Long Acre Patronized by the Dandies and is now Expected to out run all the First Blood on the Turf". Thomas Tegg was probably the most prolific publisher of hobby-horse prints (twenty are noted in Appendix 3), most falling into the second category i.e. taking a humorous view of the machine and its riders, varying from scenes of

Anti-Dandy Infantry Triumphant, 1819 (author's collection). According to a contemporary New York newspaper "Horses, it is said, in England, have fallen in price 10 per cent, in consequence of the sudden appearance of these velocipedes". The author would require more evidence to support this assertion.

Pedestrians Travelling on the New Invented Hobby-Horse!, 1819 (courtesy of Walter Branche). An important print depicting a presumably Johnson three-wheeler. Note the foreground rider's travelling box and back-pack.

Jack mounted on his Dandy Charger, 1819 (author's collection). The sailor's claim to be doing "ten knots an hour" (about 11.5 m.p.h.) seems somewhat excessive - eight m.p.h. was probably about the maximum on level ground.

Military Hobbyhorse, 1819 (author's collection). Horses and hobby-horses charge together on the battlefield. Even at this early date - 2nd March 1819 - one of the machines has direct steering.

A meeting on the road from Layston Villa to Hormead Cottage (watercolour by James Wilcox, 1849, Cyclists' Touring Club, Godalming). The road configuration and windmill in the background, coupled with the artist's title, allow the exact location on the B 1038 one mile East of Buntingford to be established. The scene is little changed today, though the windmill has long since disappeared.

F

Views of the Lady's Pedestrian Hobbyhorse, 1819 (author's collection).
The only known surviving print of the ladies' version of the Johnson
machine. Why the ladies should need such an extended rest is a matter for conjecture.

More Hobbies, or the Veloci Manipede (author's collection). One of four
known prints illustrating Birch's invention, which was exhibited to royalty. An amusing contemporaneous comment was that "The
Velocimanipede is not likely to take with either male or female dandies,
as being anagrammatized, it says, I can impede love."

The New Invented Sociable, or The Lover and his Hobby (author's collection). Von Drais recommended such machines be used on wide, level promenades in good condition. The family man at the foot of the hill stands no chance. And the chances of survival of the apparently wooden-legged hobby-horse rider on the way down must be regarded as slim !

The Pedestrian Carriage, or Walking Accelerator, 1819 (by courtesy of the National Museum of Science and Technology, Ottawa, Canada). The illustration on the proposed Denis Johnson commemorative wall plaque at 75 Long Acre is based on this print.

H

mild amusement (the illustrated *Going to the Races*), to those of outright opposition or ridicule (the illustrated *Anti-Dandy Infantry Triumphant or the Velocipede Cavalry Unhobby'd*). About half of the prints in the author's own collection are published by Tegg.

The opportunities for wit provided by the advent of the hobby-horse were many and various. Several prints show a variety of imaginary machines based on the hobby-horse idea. The illustrated *Every One His Hobby* Plates 1 & 2 (pub. Tegg 24 Apr 1819) are good examples. The parson rides his bible, the lawyer his brief, the doctor his pestle and mortar, the sailor his anchor, and so on. A cheery John Bull sits astride his "rump of beef" with a tankard of "porter" in his hand. This particular drawing was copied onto a two-handled pottery jug (see illus.). This is rather a puzzle piece since the item bears the date

Pottery jug, c.1819 (author's collection). The author will be pleased to hear from anyone who is able to supply further information on Sgt. J. Wilson of the West Riding Constabulary.

129

Every One His Hobby, plates 1 & 2, 1819 (author's collection). The Duke of Wellington's cannon hobby also features in the print The Master of the Ordnance exercising his Hobby ! A young lady onlooker remarks " Bless us ! what a Spanker ! - I hope he won't fire it at me - I would never support such a thing !"

130

1872 and is inscribed *J. Wilson. Police Sergeant. W.R.C. Normanton.*
The puzzle lies in the correct dating of the item. In view of the motif
(there is a "Farmer's Velocipede" based on Tegg's "Irishman's Hobby"
on the reverse), the item is likely to date from 1819 and not the later
date. The jug was apparently over-painted (and reglazed) in 1872, in
order perhaps to be presented to Sgt. Wilson of the West Riding
Constabulary on the occasion of his promotion, transfer or retirement.

There were in fact a variety of plates, jugs, snuffboxes and other
items with velocipede motifs produced during the hobby-horse era.
They are now very collectable. Three pottery examples can be seen
in the Willett Collection at the Brighton Museum.

But Tegg was certainly not the only publisher to pour scorn on the
velocipede. The illustrated print *Enough to make a Horse Laugh ! or
The World upon Wheels* is by J. Sidebethem, who like Ackermann
was based in The Strand. Seventeen Sidebethem prints are listed in
Appendix 3, which makes him the next most prolific publisher after
Tegg. But whereas Ackermann's early print *Pedestrian Hobbyhorse*
shows the principal rider smartly dressed propelling his machine

Enough to make a Horse Laugh ! or The World upon Wheels !!

Enough to make a Horse Laugh ! 1819 (author's collection). More
horse than hobby-horse in the picture, but the satirist's point is well
made.

purposefully through an Arcadian countryside, Sidebethem is far less respectful. Both the horse in the foreground and his liveried groom view the hillside scene with great amusement. A dandy is kicked off his mount by a braying donkey. A lady and gentleman have apparently been involved in a collision and lie on the ground on top of their machine, the gentleman losing his hat and wig. A rider careers downhill seemingly out of control of his hobby. And in the background we see more riders speeding downhill (one falling off), whilst others are climbing back up with their machines on their shoulders.

The engraver of Sidebethem's *Enough to make a <u>Horse</u> Laugh !* print was (according to Dorothy George) possibly Robert Cruikshank, of whom more anon. An interesting tale is told by Charles Spencer in his c.1883 book *Bicycles and Tricycles Past and Present* with regard to Sidebethem's relationship with Cruikshank (no Christian name is given but probably the reference is to Robert's more famous brother George). It purports to explain why both James Sidebethem and Cruikshank were distinctly unsympathetic to the new walking machine. The story goes as follows :

> *Cruikshank was on very friendly and intimate terms with his publisher, James Sidebethem, and on one occasion, in the winter of 1819, the two cronies, dressed in the extreme of the preposterous fashion of the day, set forth on an excursion, mounted each on his hobby-horse. All went well for a considerable distance, but when coming down Highgate Hill at full speed – at a rate of nearly ten miles an hour – the riders "cannoned", or "collided", to use the expressive Americanism, and away they went, each falling with considerable violence on an opposite side of the road, the result being that the machines sustained serious injuries, while they themselves were severely shaken. Mr. Cruikshank (who it is to be presumed was not then a teetotaller) was led by his friend, who was the less injured of the two, into the Archway Tavern, where they obtained as much consolation as was possible under the circumstances, finally returning to London on one of Wiber's coaches.*

Spencer concludes that Cruikshank's subsequent "droll sketches of mournful-looking individuals" were "exhibited in Mr. Sidebethem's window in the Strand, and promptly excited the risibility of passers-by to such an extent that it became positively unsafe to appear in public on a Hobby-horse, so loud and universal was the laughter at the resemblance between the rider in the street and his caricature in the shop window." The present author suspects this may be something of an exaggeration of the true position, though there is plenty of evidence to suggest that, particularly when the machine made its first appearance, it engendered much idle curiosity. The colour illustrated print *The Pedestrian Carriage, or Walking Accelerator,* with its descriptive narrative, published by Sidebethem, is in no way derogatory, but would presumably be early and perhaps pre-dating the Highgate Hill episode.

The most numerous prints in the third category – political satire – are those relating to the Prince Regent and his brother the Duke of York, which have been referred to already in Chapter 5. Apart from these, there are relatively few relating to political issues of the day. One example is *The Chancellors' Hobby, or More Taxes for John Bull,* again published by Tegg and dated 19th June, 1819. The illustrated

The Chancellors' Hobby, or More Taxes for John Bull, 1819 (courtesy Museum of British Road Transport). The signposts point "To Ruin", "To Starvation" - and "To America" !

133

The Devil alias Simon Pure, 1821 (courtesy of the Trustees of the British Museum). The queen to whom reference is made is presumably Queen Caroline, estranged wife of George IV, who was forcibly prevented from attending his coronation in July 1821 and died the following month.

engraving depicts Vansittart, Chancellor of the Exchequer, astride a large green bag representing the budget, running down the archetypal citizen John Bull. The reference is apparently to the additional taxes to reduce the national debt proposed in Vansittart's Budget.

Another illustrated attractive third category print is *The Devil alias Simon Pure*, subtitled *Say's the King of the Radicals "Hurt not the soldiers"*. This item is of particular interest as it is dated August, 1821, and is accordingly the latest known hobby-horse velocipede engraving. The Johnsonian hobby-horse is equipped with a stand (which can also be seen on some of the surviving examples). According to Dorothy George (Item 14234 of *Catalogue of Political and Personal Satires*), : "On 11th Sept. the subject of this print, one Charles Wheatfield Squires, presented a paper containing this caricature to the Lord Mayor, saying that a copy had been sent to Lord Bathurst (Secretary for War). He was dressed as a Quaker, with a beaver hat and tricolour cockade, as in the print. For some days he had been conspicuous in London, having come to town on a velocipede with a plan which "it was given out, will astonish and benefit the nation when it is divulged"." Dorothy George adds that "Accounts of his eccentricities appeared in the papers and he was identified by his brother as insane." Whether the riding of a pedestrian hobby-horse was by 1821 regarded as a sign of insanity is not stated ! Simon Pure was a Quaker character in Susannah Centlivre's 1718 play *A bold stroke for a wife.*

As Appendix 3 confirms, there were quite a number of different publishers issuing hobby-horse prints in London in the year 1819. It is useful to understand the relationship between the artist, the engraver (or lithographer), the printer and the publisher. In many (but by no means all) cases these four roles were filled by just two individuals. According to John Wardroper in his introduction to *Cruikshank 200,* (the 1992 catalogue of the travelling exhibition to celebrate the bicentenary of George Cruikshank's birth) : "The prints were etched on copperplate, generally by the artist himself, and printed on a small press behind the shop."

In some instances (J.L.Marks of Bishopsgate is a good example) the print shop owner not only printed and as publisher sold the items, he was on at least some occasions also the artist and engraver. Even where this is not expressly stated, it may have been the case that one individual effectively filled all four roles. This could be so in respect of the unsigned engravings of the print shop owner Thomas Tegg. Indeed in his book *Bicycle People* (Washington D.C. 1978), Roland Geist states categorically (in his chapter entitled "The Art Gallery") "Most of the hobby horse print caricatures illustrated in this book were drawn by Thomas Tegg of London." However the more authoritative Dorothy George (in her *Catalogue of Political and Personal Satires*) attributes a number of the Tegg prints to the artist William Heath, and it is probably unwise to jump to the conclusion that the publisher was also the anonymous artist and engraver unless there is a good reason to do so.

Appendix 3 shows that, in addition to the many London publishers (apparently for the most part print shop owners), McCleary of Dublin produced quite a number of prints, other Dublin publishers being T.Le Potit and Clayton. These items seem to have been copies – pirated or otherwise – of items first published in London. The *London Chronicle* for 10th May 1819 records that "A velocipede recently imported from England was exhibited in the Assembly Rooms, Cork, on the 26th ult. for the joint benefit of the North Infirmary and the

Hobby-horse (courtesy of the Museum of Irish Transport, Killarney). The sprung saddle is adjustable for both height and position.

Fever Hospital." According to R.J. Mecredy, editor for many years of *The Irish Cyclist*, writing in 1893, "The mania seems to have spread to Ireland; and Mr. James Talbot Power, of Leopardstown, Stillorgan, has in his possession one of these machines" (*The Art and Pastime of Cycling*, 3rd edn., p.29).

The Irish connection is confirmed by the fact that there are two known original machines remaining to this day in the Republic of Ireland. The illustrated item with attractive ornamental iron supports to the balance-board belonged it is said to the Duke of Leinster of Carton House, County Kildare. It was apparently acquired from the Estate of the then Duke of Leinster in 1942, having it seems for many years been stored in a dry loft over the coach house in the stable yard. The other (unillustrated) machine would appear originally to have been owned by John Talbot Power of the Dublin distilling house of John Power and Son, which started business in 1791. The design of the front and rear forks and saddle spring suggests that this is a less ornate version of the Duke of Leinster's velocipede. This is presumably the machine referred to by Mecredy as belonging to James Talbot Power at the end of the Nineteenth century.

Most of the hobby-horse prints were unsigned and unattributed, making the naming of the artist largely a matter of speculation. Credit must be given to Dorothy George for most of the identifications shown within square brackets in Appendix 3, which cannot necessarily be regarded as conclusively proved. Of the known hobby-horse artists the most famous was undoubtedly George Cruikshank (1792-1878) who "left an everlasting hoard for all ages to delight in" (John Wardroper in *Cruikshank 200*). However his input in terms of hobby-horse prints would appear to have been rather less than that of his much less well-known elder brother Isaac Robert Cruikshank (known as Robert). The illustrated *Stop him who can !!* lithographic print of Denis Johnson referred to in Chapter 3 is, according to Dorothy George, possibly "by or after G. Cruikshank".

A collaboration between Robert Cruikshank and the London publisher G. Humphrey gave rise to no less than five late prints with "Hobby-Horse Fair" or "Hobby Fair" in the title – see Appendix 3. for details. As with the two Tegg prints *Every one his Hobby* referred to above, these amusingly depict a large number of imaginary machines. Two are of particular interest – both slightly confusingly entitled *Hobby-*

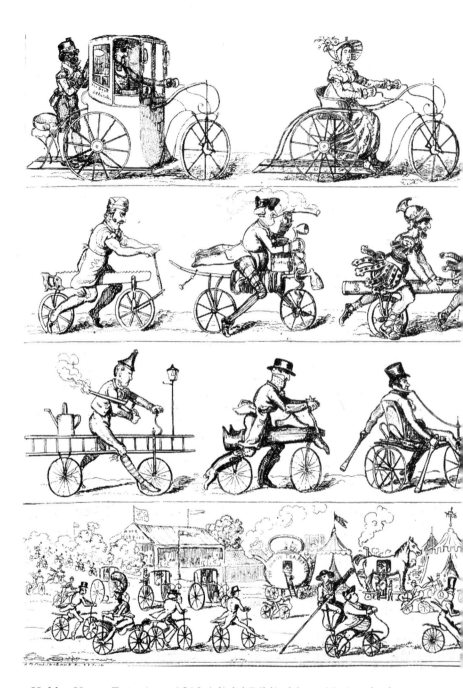

Hobby-Horse Fair, Aug. 1819 (cliché Bibliothèque Nationale de France). Robert Cruikshank presents a fascinating "world upon wheels". Was there indeed a Pilentum coach (with "the door behind"), as depicted top left and bottom right (plus three more bottom left)?

138

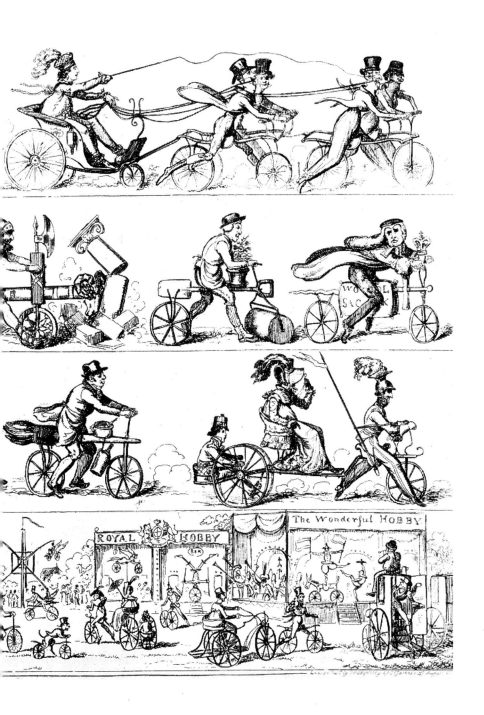

Horse Fair – one being dated 12th August and the other 10th September 1819. Both prints contain a mixture of real and imaginary items, the earlier one (see illustration) depicting a Pilentum and a Velocimanipede (the second machine in the first line and the fifth in the third line), as well as showing (in the fourth line) what a "Hobby-Horse Fair" was supposed to look like. *Horse* fairs had of course been held for centuries and it seems reasonable to assume that the notion of a *hobby-horse* fair was a Cruikshank invention never in fact actualised – although we cannot of course be categoric, and no doubt had the velocipede in its various forms continued to be popular beyond the year 1819 such an event could well have taken place. In the late Nineteenth century annual bicycle shows (notably the Stanley Show) were very popular.

There are no known hobby-horse illustrations by that other famous artist of the period Thomas Rowlandson, 1756-1827 (though a number of modern cycle histories refer to him as one of the hobby-horse artists). A book *The Amorous Illustrations of Thomas Rowlandson,* U.S.A. 1969, contains an undated illustration with the modern title *Love on a Bicycle* depicting a couple making love whilst the woman is seated on a padded chair with two parallel legs, each having a small wheel at its base. This can hardly be described as a hobby-horse print. Henry Alken (1785-1851), was "one of the most prolific sporting painters and illustrators of his time" (per *The Oxford Companion to Art*), but only *Johnson's Pedestrian Hobbyhorse Riding School* has been ascribed to him. William Heath (1795-1840) may (according to Dorothy George) have been responsible for the largest number of prints, although so far as the author is aware none actually bear his name as artist. The only other individuals known to have produced any significant output of hobby-horse drawings are J.L. Marks, C. Williams and Yedis. The mysterious " W C " has already been noticed in connection with the Cheapside publisher John Hudson, and it seems likely that he also worked for Sidebethem.

Chapter 8

AN EXPLOSION OF INVENTION

If we discount the Patterson story, the author knows of no rider-propelled machines being produced in England during the early years of the Nineteenth century. George Medhurst took out a patent for "Driving Carriages without the Use of Horses" at the turn of the century (no. 2431 of 1800), but the power to be applied was compressed air and the invention is therefore of more interest to the motor vehicle historian than the cycle historian.

A lengthy article in the April and June issues of the *Sporting Magazine* for 1802 titled "Entertaining Remarks upon the Origin and Use of Wheel Carriages" by Joseph Moser contains no reference to any velocipede-type item. Just six years later the same periodical carries an extract from a letter from "a very ingenious gentleman, a Fellow of the Royal Society", which states : "When you do me the favour of coming to this part of Middlesex, and are inclined to sail on dry land, I can indulge your disposition, having built a sailing chariot, which, with a moderate wind, and four persons on board, will run fifteen knots an hour, close hauled." But again this was a wind-driven not a rider-propelled vehicle. At this period "hobby-horses" were "only the passions which impel men through the career of life" ("On Hobby-Horses", *Sporting Magazine*, December, 1811).

All this was to change in the year 1819. Denis Johnson acknowledged his debt to "a certain Foreigner residing abroad" and a contemporary newspaper commented that "the rage for inventions of this sort appears to be travelling from one end of Europe to the other". In England the Johnson velocipede acted as a catalyst to inventors up and down the country, who produced a wide variety of machines. We have already noticed a few made specifically or primarily for ladies. The majority of machines may have been little more than prototypes (some may never have been made at all), but a few were certainly produced commercially.

Probably the earliest English machine at this period was the illustrated "British Facilitator, or Travelling Car", which according to an article in the *Imperial Magazine* for 31st May, 1819, was "Invented by B. Smythe, Surveyor, Liverpool, January 25th, 1819." If the January date is correct, it seems unlikely that Johnson's much simpler machine patented only a month before was the inspiration for the Smythe vehicle. Could it be that he named it the British Facilitator to distinguish it from the von Drais inventions, or from some other carriage without horses which had appeared abroad?

Whatever the reason for its name, Smythe's brain-child was a

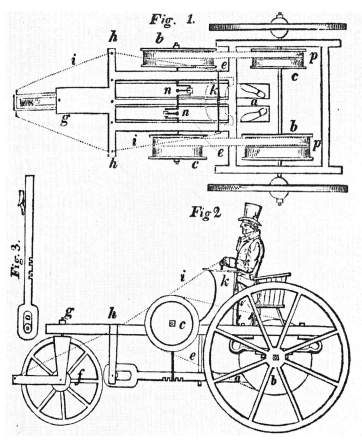

British Facilitator, or Travelling Car, (Imperial Magazine, May 1819, by permission of The British Library, shelfmark PP5483). It appears that if both the rear drum wheels were thrown out of gear the rider could free-wheel when going downhill - possibly a dangerous manoeuvre !

142

remarkable machine. It was operated by "treaders, upon which the whole weight of the body and the strength of the knees are exerted." The action of the "treaders" caused cranks to revolve and turn the two forward drum wheels. These were connected to the two rear drum wheels by straps, so turning the rear axle and driving the back wheels. What is most surprising however is that, in the early morning of cycle technology in this country, Smythe's "Travelling Car (to use its alternative name) had a gear-changing device incorporated. The rider could choose to drive either of the rear wheels, one being geared high and the other low for hill work. "The two drum wheels upon the axle of the two hindmost wheels are each in two parts; the one part fixed and the other loose in the centre, for the purpose of being thrown in and out of gear, by the means commonly used in ascending and descending the hills, the wheels having different diameters." The reference to "the means commonly used" is a little odd : the earliest reference to a change-speed gear of which the author is aware is that used by W.H. James in his steam carriage patented in August, 1832 (referred to in *The World on Wheels* by H.O. Duncan, Paris, 1926).

Another intriguing early machine was apparently made by "a very ingenious person" of Yarmouth. A report appears in the *Norwich Mercury and Yarmouth, Lynn and Ipswich Herald* for 20th March, 1819, under the Yarmouth column, in the following terms :

The Accelerator, or Walking Machine, is the general topic of conversation in this town. Two have been manufactured here, differing slightly from Johnson's machine, and used every morning during the week ..... but if we are rightly informed, it will soon be superseded by one which is now making [sic] by a very ingenious person here, after the manner of the razor-grinding wheel – to be worked by a treadle for both feet. If it succeeds it is expected it will move at the rapid rate of 12 miles an hour.

The puzzling words are those which tell us that the new machine is made "after the manner of the razor-grinding wheel – to be worked by a treadle for both feet." The razor-grinding wheel at this time was operated by a hand-crank, as shown in the illustrated 1802 print "Grinders" (although another print in the same series depicts an itinerant knife-grinder operating his machine by means of a single foot treadle). This suggests that the Yarmouth machine was driven

Grinders, 1802 (author's collection). Both one and two crank-handle machines are depicted.

by cranks attached to the hub of the front wheel, worked by foot pedals (in the Nineteenth Century the word "treadle" was sometimes used where we would now refer to a "pedal"). If this is correct we have the prototype of a machine which was not to reappear in this country (imported from France) for something like half-a-century, when it was known as the "boneshaker". We can only surmise why nothing more was heard of the Yarmouth machine, but perhaps its inventor was inhibited by the breach of patent warning in respect of the Johnson velocipede referred to earlier. The whole topic was discussed at greater length in a paper entitled *A "Boneshaker" Hobby-Horse* delivered by the author to the Third International Conference of Cycling History at Neckarsulm, Germany, in June, 1992 (subsequently printed in the Veteran-Cycle Club magazine *The Boneshaker*, no. 139, Autumn 1995).

For the sake of completeness a brief reference should perhaps be made to one of cycling history's many myths. This is that one of the 1819 prints (*R***L HOBBY's !!!* – not illustrated) shows the Prince Regent recumbent on an elongated hobby-horse and being "ridden" by his supposed mistress Lady Hertford. The Prince supports himself by hand rests attached to the front wheel hub which several commentators have suggested are cranks and pedals. Whatever the status of the Yarmouth machine, this theory is clearly untenable, as has been demonstrated by the noted cycle historian Derek Roberts on more than one occasion and again quite recently by Jacques Seray in an article in the Spring 1997 issue of *The Boneshaker.*

Another active manufacturer (though not patentee) of velocipedes in 1819 was Charles Lucas Birch, to whom reference has already been made in Chapter 6. Like Denis Johnson he was a coachmaker working in the Long Acre area (his actual address being 71, Great Queen Street, a road which was virtually a continuation of Long Acre on the other side of Drury Lane). Charles was the son of William Birch, who was elected Master of the Worshipful Company of Coachmakers and Coach Harness Makers in both 1801 and 1802 (Charles himself later being elected to the same post in 1827). As has already been noted there were medical objections to the use of the hobby-horse. According to the *Monthly Magazine* for November, 1819, these objections "led Mr. Birch to apply a simple arrangement of machinery with which to turn the wheels by the action of the hands or feet." This was presumably his well-publicised "Velocimanipede or Lady's Hobby" described in the chapter on Velocipedes for Ladies.

But Charles Lucas Birch did not rest on his laurels. After his Velocimanipede had been launched he worked on three further machines. An advert in the *Morning Post* for 15th September, 1819, proclaims :

> *C.L. Birch has the honour to inform the Nobility, Gentry and Public, that he has invented a Machine, called the Trivector, which travels without horses : it has been to Brighton in seven hours. To be seen with his Velocimanipede, Manivelociter, and Bivector, at Spring Gardens, from Ten in the Morning till Dusk in the Evening. Admittance One Shilling. Orders received at 71 Great Queen Street, Lincolns Inn Fields.*

All three new inventions abandon entirely the use of the feet pushing on the ground (retained in the Velocimanipede) in favour of a hand-propelled lever action, as shown in the illustration from the *Monthly Magazine* for November, 1819. In the simplest version (the

145

Manivelociter, Bivector & Trivector (Monthly Magazine, Nov 1819, by permission of The British Library, shelfmark 260d14). Mr. Birch's range of manumotive "Carriages for Conveyance without Horses". "The muscular and bodily action is like that of rowing, but far more easy."

Manivelociter) it must surely have been difficult to obtain any real speed, particularly with a passenger on board, but the tandem and triplet varieties would have been more efficient. The Trivector's voyage to Brighton was reported in the *Monthly Magazine* as follows : "This *Trivector* went from London to Brighton, on Saturday, Sept. 11, worked by three men, as represented in the engraving, in seven hours, where they dined; after which they proceeded thirteen miles further; making together a distance of sixty-seven miles within the day. It would, however, be possible to run this machine 120 miles in the day, without distressing the men."

A writer in the October, 1819, issue of the *Monthly Magazine*, after referring with approval to the manumotive principle, adds : "Mr. Birch, who has succeeded in this new application, may soon be expected to work his levers, not only by the hand, but by STEAM ! Indeed, there can be little doubt but this triumph of mechanics will be effected within the ensuing winter, as we have heard of a patent for securing a new French invention, by which fuel may be economised after the rate of one to ten." Perhaps a slightly later example of such a machine would be the Londoner Walter Hancock's "Phaeton" steam three-wheeler of 1829, which it seems travelled hundreds of miles on experimental trips (according to Duncan in *The World on Wheels*.)

With the wisdom of hindsight it is easy enough to see that Mr. Birch's three September 1819 machines relied too heavily on manumotive action, and as such were bound to remain outside the main stream of velocipede development (in the strict etymological sense they were not "velocipedes" at all). They were nevertheless viewed as in some respects superior to the Johnson hobby-horse, the author of the *Monthly Magazine* article describing them as having "elegance safety and power" and concluding "we view them as the germs of great social improvements; and amongst other results, we anticipate in them a means of realising the important design lately proposed by Mr. Burgess, for accelerating the circulation of letters by post."

It was not only Mr. Birch who realised that something had to be done to ease the jarring and even rupturing effect of the Johnson velocipede. A letter from "E.B." in the July 1819 issue of the *Monthly Magazine* (referred to earlier on another point) suggests a simple solution : "I think we have, in a great degree, got rid of jolting, by means of a spring of lance-wood lying along the whole length of the perch, which promises to answer well, with very little increase of weight" (lancewood is known for its tough but elastic quality). As previously noted, the illustrated Strangers Hall, Norwich, hobby-horse has the seat attached to a metal spring above the backbone, as does the illustrated machine in the Ipswich Museum store. And the hobby-horses originally belonging to the Earl of Eglinton in Scotland and the Duke of Leinster and John Talbot Power in Ireland have impressive seat springs.

The illustrated machine (with a wooden balance-board support, which may not be original), now in the Hufstetler collection, was for most of this century at the Wells Museum in Somerset. Its most interesting feature is the suspension spring above the front wheel − another attempt to improve the hobby-horse rider's comfort.

In August 1819 the *Literary Panorama* reports : "A *velocipede*, on a new construction, is said to be building [sic] by an artist at Hereford. It is said to have beams or bodies on springs, and four wheels, which will ensure its safety. It is to quarter on the roads like other carriages, and, with four impellers, it is supposed that it will proceed with

Hobby-horse with suspension spring (photo courtesy of Wells Museum). Reputedly made and ridden by William Plenty, a carpenter of North Wootton, near Wells.

148

astonishing rapidity; but its peculiar recommendation is to be, the conveyance of two ladies and two propellers, at the rate of six miles the hour." The "impellers" or "propellers" were the gentlemen who were to provided the motive power for the machine, though how they were to achieve this is not explained.

Another multi-wheeled machine, this time a three-wheeler, had already been devised further South. It is described equally enigmatically in the *Salisbury and Winchester Journal* for 5th April, 1819 : "The *hobby-horse* has at length made its appearance in Exeter, and is now exhibiting in the playground of the Exeter Grammar School. A gentleman of that city has succeeded in forming a machine with three wheels, with which he travelled on Friday evening, upon the first attempt, upwards of four miles in half an hour."

We know that Johnson was active in promoting his "Velocipede, or Patent Curricle" in Birmingham in the Spring of 1819. No doubt this was a source of inspiration for William Field, whose trade card (Birmingham City Library) describes him as a "Manufacturer of Plated Bridle Bitts & Stirrups, Coach & Harness Furniture etc." The following advertisement appears in *Aris's Birmingham Gazette* for 27th September, 1819 :

VELOCIPEDES

W FIELD respectfully informs the Gentlemen of Birmingham and its Vicinity, that he has now on sale a Variety of Velocipedes or Walking Machines, upon an improved Principle, which he can recommend for Swiftness and Durability, and on Trial will be found very amusing Exercise and conducive to Health. May be viewed at his Manufactory, Mary Ann Street, St. Paul's, Birmingham.
N.B. Price five Guineas. – Gentlemen at a Distance, by inclosing the Amount, may depend upon having their Orders punctually delivered to any Carrier they will please to name.
Admittance to practise, 6d. each.

Jim McGurn suggests (*On your Bicycle* p.22) that these machines were "presumably made under licence from Johnson". This is unlikely to have been the case, as Field's velocipedes were being advertised after the Johnson hobby-horse craze was largely over, and the Birmingham manufacturer refers to his machines as being "upon an improved Principle". Quite what this was we can now only guess, but the reference to them as "Walking Machines" suggests that, unlike the Birch velocipedes, they did not have manumotive drive.

Rather more detail is supplied in respect of another machine, apparently made in some numbers. A reference to propulsion by "two foot-boards moved up and down alternately ... with the assistance of the hand bars in going up steep hills", suggests that like the patented "Rantoone" of the 1860s ("a gymnasium in miniature") all four limbs could be employed to propel the vehicle. The source is *Norfolk Annals* (1901) by Charles Mackie, a work compiled from the files of the *Norfolk Chronicle*. An entry for 5th June, 1819, reads :

> *"Flying Actaeons were exhibited at the Prussia Gardens, Norwich, by Messrs. Brously and Stratford. "The machine consists of a chair fixed on to a four-wheeled carriage, in which the rider sits and guides the four wheels, turning corners in a similar manner to the velocipedes. One hand only, however, is necessary, the other being at liberty to hold an umbrella. The hind wheels, which force the machine along, are put in motion with the feet of the rider by means of two foot-boards moved up and down alternately. With the assistance of the hand bars in going up steep hills this carriage will travel at the rate of eight miles an hour, and may easily be made for two persons to sit abreast. It is equally convenient for both males and females."*

Apart from Johnson's "pedestrian curricle", the only other velocipede to be patented in 1819 was the "land punt" (as it has since been called) of John Baynes, a "Working Cutler" of Leeds (pat. no. 4389, 27th September, 1819). The way in which this machine worked is reasonably clear from the illustrated patent drawing. The seated rider steered by means of a "Bath chair" type handle to the front wheel, propelling his carriage forward by long foot treadles, which by means of connecting rods drove "legs or crutches, which bear against the ground as fulcrums, by which the carriage is moved forward", the treadles operating alternately. It is not known whether such a machine was ever actually produced, certainly there is no evidence of it coming into widespread use. Interestingly, one of the sketches in the illustrated print *Hobby-Horse Fair* (12th August 1819) is of a dandy supposedly propelling a three-wheeled hobby-horse with the aid of

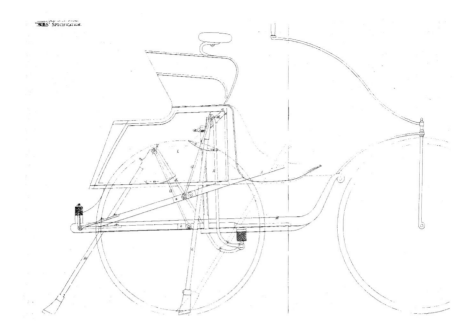

John Baynes' "land punt" (from pat. no. 4389 of 1819). "Machinery to be attached to carriages for giving them motion by manual labour or other suitable power." The idea of replacing human by mechanical feet on the ground was ingenious but probably impractical.

hand-held crutches pushing on the ground. As can be seen, steering is intended to be by means of a Bath chair type lever operated by the rider's head !

An equally strange machine was Sievier's "Patent Pedestrian Carriage", shown in the illustrated print engraved by Williams. This is undated but seems to be a product of the hobby-horse era. It is somewhat reminiscent of a two-wheeler of the 1880s known popularly (if not officially) then and now as the "Otto dicycle" – the important distinction being that the later item was driven by pedals. The author has come across no other reference to Sievier's machine apart from this print from the archives of the Bibliothèque Nationale (to which it was apparently given by Sir David Salomons in 1935). However the article was obviously made in London in some numbers as the print legend states "Manufactured and Sold by LEES COTTAM & HALLEN at their Repository Winsley Str opposite the Pantheon Oxford Str Steel Yard Wharf, Upper Thames Str and at their

Sievier's Patent Pedestrian Carriage c.1820 (cliché Bibliothèque Nationale de France). The progenitor of the two-track two-wheel velocipede which was to reach its apotheosis some sixty years later.

Manufactory, Cornwall Road, Surrey side of Waterloo Bridge." A presumably contemporaneous handwritten comment on this particular copy of the print states "Exhibiting at the Great Rooms Spring Gardens". Lees, Cottam and Hallen were advertising a wide range of items (though not at this stage the Sievier machine) in the *Salisbury and Winchester Journal* in the early months of 1819.

The carriage is said to be "for Ladies & Gentlemen". There would appear to be an important difference between the types provided for each sex. The lady has a seat seemingly suspended from the axle, the use of which would no doubt considerably reduce the efficacy of foot propulsion. As in the case of the much later "Otto dicycle", a "tip-tail" is provided to prevent the lady from falling over backwards. The gentleman's version would seem to be rather different in that he is shown apparently standing, not sitting, between the two large wheels. It may be that there was some sort of saddle or sling suspended from the axle, enabling the rider to take the weight of his body off the ground, leaving his feet free to propel the wheels by pushing forward along the path in hobby-horse fashion, but this is far from clear. It is also not apparent how the vehicle was steered. No doubt we shall have a much better idea of exactly how it operated if and when the patent is discovered. Searches of the British, French and American patent records over a large period of years has so far produced no result.

The Sievier pedestrian carriage print legend claims : "The superiority and safety of this machine above all those before invented is immediately discovered upon the least attention to its mechanic properties. A mile has been performed in less than 3 minutes and 12 miles within the hour. It is particularly well adapted for Gentlemen's pleasure grounds, or persons whose occupation in the Country requires a large quantity of ground to be gone over." The claim that the machine could travel at more than 20 m.p.h. over a measured mile is certainly an astonishing one.

Remarkably similar to the Sievier machine is one described in the *Gentleman's Magazine* for June, 1819 (and elsewhere) as follows :

PEDESTRIAN CHARIOT. Mr. Howell, of Bristol, has invented a machine, of infinitely greater power and utility than the Velocipede. Its chief attractions are its simplicity and perfect safety, being eligible for the conveyance of ladies, and even children. The wheels, which are upwards of six feet in diameter, run parallel to each other; and as the seat is below the centre of gravity, the rider can neither be thrown, nor easily lose his equilibrium. From the increased circumference of the wheel, and the consequently decreased friction of the axle, a greater degree of velocity may be given, with a considerably diminished impetus; and this renders it of much greater facility of management, either on the level road or the most rapid descent. The machine may be constructed to carry two or three persons, with a portmanteau or other luggage.

It would appear from an item in the Liverpool Mercury of 28th May 1819 that Mr Howell's machine was known as a Gymnasidromist (the Regency inventors seemed to have had a penchant for long and supposedly impressive names for their brainchildren). In another newspaper item briefly referring to the machine we are told that "it is at present exhibiting in London".

A brief reference was made at the end of Chapter 4 to Lewis Gompertz of Kennington, who emphasised how short was the heyday of the ordinary hobby-horse velocipede. He himself made a valiant effort to revive its fortunes by an invention which provided an additional method of propulsion to the simple expedient of pushing with the feet on the ground. The illustration from *The Repertory of Arts* (vol.39, 2nd Series, 1821) shows how Gompertz modified the velocipede by the addition of a rack-and-pinion mechanism. Strangely, although Gompertz's illustration is clearly of a modified Johnson machine, he gives no credit to the London coachmaker, referring only to "that ingenious and well-known invention, the velocipede, of Baron von Dray".

Gompertz describes the use of his machine as follows : "The chief object is to bring the arms of the rider into action, in assistance to his

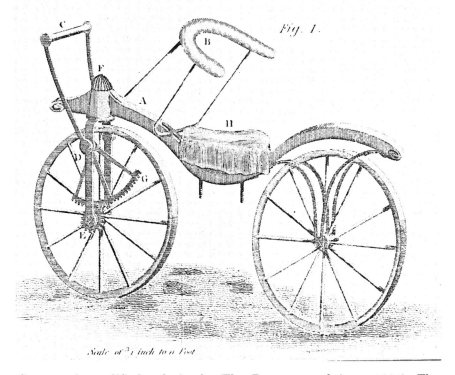

Gompertz's modified velocipede (The Repertory of Arts, 1821). The first two-wheeler which envisaged the possibility of the rider's feet being kept off the ground for an extended period - though unlike the Johnson machine no foot rests appear to have been provided.

154

legs, and consists in the application of a handle C, which is to be worked backwards and forwards, to which is attached a circular rack DG, which works in a pinion E, with a ratch-wheel on the front wheel of the velocipede, and which, on being *pulled* by the rider with both hands, propels the machine forwards, and when thrust from him (in order to repeat the stroke) does not send it back again, on account of the ratch which allows the pinion to turn in that direction free of the wheel". Gompertz envisages the possibility of his two-wheeler being driven by the arms alone with the rider's feet off the ground "if the ground be good, and if he can balance himself." (It has been said that the Gompertz machine had the first "free wheel" to be fitted to a cycle, but Smythe's "British Facilitator" of 1819 referred to above may be an earlier candidate for this honour i.e. if both rear drive wheels could be thrown out of gear at the same time.)

Gompertz was it seems closely involved in 1824 with the foundation of the Society for the Prevention of Cruelty to Animals (now the RSPCA). The suggestion has been made by Les Bowerman in a paper read at the Third International Cycle History Conference that Gompertz's interest in the velocipede would have stemmed from the fact that he was anxious to encourage a substitute for the horse-drawn vehicle of his day. However, it is likely that at most only a few of his machines were made. It appears one was displayed as a historical item at the Stanley Show (the late-Nineteenth century equivalent of today's Motor Show) as late as 1881, possibly loaned by the Polytechnic Institution.

THE MARINE VELOCIPEDE.

Kent's Marine Velocipede. It "excited a degree of interest scarcely warranted by any practical utility likely to arise from its adoption."

What is probably the earliest of a number of Nineteenth century water cycles was the illustrated "Marine Velocipede" of a Mr Kent, described in *The Kaleidoscope* of 24th July 1821. The invention had been widely criticised as being of clumsy construction, as a result of which Mr Kent was "engaged in simplifying and reducing the bulk of his apparatus". It was claimed that "Walking on the Water" the inventor was "enabled to advance at the rate of five miles an hour". The journal's Editor comments that "if Mr Kent can, as he informs us, manoeuvre his Marine Velocipede, when the sea runs very high, perhaps the contrivance may be turned to good account, by enabling a person to take out a rope to a vessel in danger near a lee shore".

The Times for 23rd September, 1822, has an interesting item :

Last week a man upon a new sort of Velocipede attracted a number of people together at the Elephant and Castle, to witness his activity and the swiftness with which he travels. He is a shoemaker by trade, and finding the trade bad at Newark-on-Trent, Nottinghamshire, of which place he is a native, he built this mechanical horse, as he terms it. It is on a different plan from the others; it is worked by two handles, which set two wheels in motion, and causes two levers in front to be put in action, which set the machine going at the rate of at least six miles an hour. It is the completest machine of the kind that has as yet been invented. He has travelled in fine weather 60 miles a day. He has two iron stirrups, in which he places his feet – they keep him steady on the saddle.

It is tempting to think that we have here a very early, if manumotive, two-wheeler – "it is worked by two handles, which set two wheels in motion..." But these particular wheels would seem to be no more than part of the drive mechanism, which "causes two levers in front to be put in action." At this stage – apart perhaps from the Yarmouth velocipede, and as modified by Gompertz – the probability is that Johnson's two-wheeler remains in a class of its own.

POSTSCRIPT

The unanswered questions

It is perhaps inevitable that in a work of this nature there will be a number of unanswered questions. Indeed the author's own research has given rise to a crop of new queries. It may be useful to end with a summary of what the author considers to be the more important points, on which further research may hopefully shed fresh light.

Chapter 1 *The quest for the medieval hobby-horse velocipede.* The pre-history – if any – of the hobby-horse is highly speculative. It would be marvellous to find further details of the Marquis of Worcester's Seventeenth Century "artificial horse", but at this late stage this seems unlikely. A more fruitful line of enquiry might be into Patterson's alleged Hyde Park hobby-horses of the 1796-1804 period, if only to explain away what may well be a Leftwich myth. If, contrary to the author's expectation, evidence of a pre-1817 pedestrian hobby-horse should be forthcoming, this might justify a re-appraisal of the 1787 Enigma poem.

Chapter 2 *Karl von Drais and his Running Machine.* Of particular relevance to the English hobby-horse story is the suggestion that "Karl von Drais paid a visit to London around 1818 and had a machine made for him by a mechanic called Knight." Nothing more seems to be known about this individual, assuming he existed, or indeed about von Drais' supposed visit, but a detailed search in the London newspapers and periodicals for the year in question might be productive.

Chapter 3 *Denis Johnson and his Pedestrian Curricle.* Though the author has managed to establish some basic facts, we still know very little about Johnson's life before he achieved a certain success and fame in his late fifties. We also have the mystery surrounding the assignment of the "pedestrian curricle" patent to Samuel Merscy. Even if there is no record of the actual document at the Public Record Office or elsewhere, there could be accounts or other evidence in existence supplying further information and clarifying the exact nature of their business relationship. Related to this is the more general question of the extent of the Johnson enterprise, which the author suspects may not have been quite as successful as has been assumed by some writers. There are a number of subsidiary points relating to modifications of the Johnson machine, who first named it the "hobby-horse", when manufacture of the item ceased, and so on, which hopefully further research will elucidate.

Chapter 4 *The hobby-horse on the road.* We know a lot about the hobby-horse craze during the Spring and Summer of 1819. But is there further evidence of organised racing, as took place in 1819 at Ipswich and apparently also at Blackheath (and later in Yorkshire) ? And were there any velocipede clubs proposed or formed at this early date ? The extent to which hobby-horses were still used during the period (say) 1820-1870 is largely unknown and certainly deserves further study.

Chapter 5 *A pedestrian carriage for Dandies, Nobility & Royalty.* The principal query under this head concerns the extent of the Prince Regent's flirtation with the hobby-horse. The suggestion is that this involved no more than the acquisition and transport to Brighton of the four machines referred to by Fairburn. According to the Deputy Registrar of the Royal Archives, there are no personal papers at Windsor Castle which might throw any further light on the matter (and the Prince Regent's Accounts Ledger for Carlton House and Brighton and the Lord Chamberlain's Account Book for the early part of 1819, both held at the Public Record Office, contain no relevant entry). The Prince was an active equestrian and must surely have tried out the substitute "horse", if only for a few yards and in private, but at present we have absolutely no evidence to support even this hypothesis.

Chapter 6 *Velocipedes for ladies.* The author has suggested that the circumstantial evidence for the riding of hobby-horses by ladies is overwhelming, in view of the fact that a dropped-frame

158

machine was made specifically for their use. However despite this, and the "evidence" of the prints, the author has somewhat surprisingly come across not a single reference to any sort of velocipede actually being ridden by a named female. Likewise the author's surmise that Johnson's premises at 40, Brewer Street, may have been used wholly or partly as a ladies riding school (as depicted in the J. Johnston print) is entirely uncorroborated. This would seem to be a promising field for further research.

Chapter 7 *The English hobby-horse prints.* Probably the most difficult area is the identification of the artist, expressly stated on only about a quarter of the prints and then often only by initials. Tentative identifications need to be confirmed and additional attributions made. Further prints may also of course come to light.

Chapter 8 *An explosion of invention.* So far as the author is concerned, there are two important velocipedes which have been entirely overlooked by other modern writers. The first is the machine invented by the "very ingenious" Yarmouth individual "after the manner of the razor-grinding wheel – to be worked by a treadle for both feet." The addition of cranks and pedals to the front wheel hub of a two-wheeler is supposed to have taken place in France in the early 1860s. Did this important development really occur in England more than forty years earlier, who was the anonymous inventor – and why was nothing more heard of the machine ? Then we have Sievier's astonishingly speedy Patent Pedestrian Carriage. But who was Sievier, exactly how did his machine work, and when and where did he obtain his patent ? Answers on a postcard please to the author !

APPENDIX 1

[Royal Coat of Arms]

A.D.1818 .... No. 4321.

Pedestrian Curricle or Velocipede

JOHNSON'S SPECIFICATION

TO ALL TO WHOM THESE PRESENTS SHALL COME, I, DENIS JOHNSON, of 75, Long Acre, in the County of Middlesex, Coach Maker, send greeting.

WHEREAS His most Excellent Majesty King George the Third did, by His Letters Patent under the Great Seal of the United Kingdom of Great Britain and Ireland, bearing date at Westminster, the Twenty-second day of December, in the fifty-ninth year of His reign, give and grant unto me, the said Denis Johnson, my exors, admors, and assigns, His especial licence, full power, sole privilege and authority, that I, the said Denis Johnson, my exors, admors and assigns, during the term of years therein mentioned, should and lawfully might make, use, exercise, and vend, within England, Wales, and the Town of Berwick-upon-Tweed, my Invention of "A MACHINE FOR THE PURPOSE OF DIMINISHING THE LABOUR AND FATIGUE OF PERSONS IN WALKING, AND ENABLING THEM AT THE SAME TIME TO USE GREATER SPEED, AND WHICH HE INTENDS TO DENOMINATE THE PEDESTRIAN CURRICLE;" in which said Letters Patent there is contained a proviso, that if I, the said Denis Johnson, shall not particularly describe and ascertain the nature of my said Invention, and in what manner the same is to be performed, by an instrument in writing under my hand and seal, and cause the same to be inrolled in His Majesty's High Court of Chancery within six calendar months next and immediately after the date of the said Letters Patent, that then the said Letters Patent, and all liberties and advantages whatsoever thereby granted, shall utterly cease, determine, and become void, as in and by the same, relation being thereunto had, will more fully and at large appear.

NOW KNOW YE, that in compliance with the said proviso, I, the said Denis Johnson, do hereby declare that the machine herein-before mentioned, and for which the said herein-before recited Patent has been granted and obtained, is fully and faithfully described, as well as the manner of constructing and using the same, in the following description, and the Drawing thereunto annexed (that is to say):-

Fig. 1 in that Drawing represents the machine as it appears without its furniture or trimmings, and when not in use; and Fig. 2 shews the same machine with its furniture or trimmings, and with a person upon it, and in the act of using it, by which such manner of using will be sufficiently obvious.

The machine, in its naked state, as shewn at Fig. 1, consists of a beam A, B, made of wood or metal of sufficient strength to bear the weight of the person who is to ride or use it.

This beam is supported upon two light wheels, C, D, by means of the light iron work $e,e,$ and $f,g,$ the hinder wheel D being so fixed as only to revolve on its axle or centre pin in the direction of the beam, while the front wheel C not only turns in like manner upon its center, but has a motion for turning the carriage by a pivot or axle passing through the beam, and secured by a key or screw at g; h is a saddletree or seat, supported by the two long screws $i,i,$ passing through the beam and fixed by two nuts upon each screw, one above and the other below the beam, and by these the seat may be raised or lowered, and fixed at a convenient height to the person using the machine, who, for this purpose, must stride the same, as if on horseback, the height of the seat having been previously adjusted to the length of his legs, so as to allow convenient foothold upon the ground, which will best be determined by trial.

The person thus seated leans his body forward, as in Fig,. 2, resting his elbows upon the cushion k, so as to support himself with the full muscular use of his legs, and with one or both hands he holds the handle *l*, which communicates by the light bar *m* with the axis, or axis carriage of the front wheel C; and thus he will be able to guide himself and the machine, and to turn the same when going at the greatest speed.

The dimensions of this machine must depend upon the height and weight of the person who is to use it, as well as the materials of which it may be formed, consequently no specific directions can be given about them, further than saying that the lighter and more free from friction the whole can be made, and the larger the diameter of the wheels, the better and more expeditious the machine will be. The more effectually to obtain these ends the beam, A, B, may be considerably curved or bent downwards at the part where the saddle or seat is placed, and thus it will still pass over the tops of the wheels, though their diameter may be considerably increased.

The wheels, C, D, may be placed nearer or further asunder, but must not be so close as to interfere with the legs of the person using the machine while turning it out of its straight direction.

In witness whereof, I, the said Denis Johnson, party hereto, have hereunto set my hand and seal, this Twenty-first day of June, in the year of our Lord One thousand eight hundred and nineteen.

DENIS (L.S.) JOHNSON.

And be it remembered, that on the Twenty-first day of June, in the year of our Lord 1819, the aforesaid Denis Johnson came before our said Lord the King in His Chancery, and acknowledged the Specification aforesaid, and all and every thing therein contained and specified, in form above written. And also the Specification aforesaid was stamped according to the tenor of the Statute made for that purpose.

Inrolled the Twenty-first day of June, in the year of our Lord One thousand eight hundred and nineteen.

[Inrolled drawing – Fig. 1. & Fig. 2. – see Frontispiece]

APPENDIX 2

Surviving early Hobby-Horses in U.K. and elsewhere

Custodian	Original/early owner	DJ no.	Comments/literature ref.s
			(see Note (2) at end for abbreviations used)

Denis Johnson machines

Mark Hall Cycle Museum Harlow, Essex		**25** (XXV)	Earliest known DJ machine HVDM pp.61-62 & illus. Pl.s 60 & 61 DR illus. p.60 also T Bic illus. p.17 (in each case badge only)
Private owner	Sir Philip Brocklehurst (20th Century)	**31** (XXXI)	Only known DJ machine with indirect steering Sold Christie's auction Swythamley Hall 17/5/76
Tabley House, Cheshire	Sir John Leicester	**100** (C)	Restored c.1990 TB 129/4 illus. TW Nov 1992 illus. T Bic illus. pp. 15 and 16/17
Science Museum, Wroughton	Duke of Marlborough	**204** (CICV)	HDC p.4 & illus. Pl.1 HC pp.1-2 HVDM pp.61-62 & Pl.s 26 & 30
Copenhagen City Museum, Denmark		**221** (CCXXI)	Small illus. in LVH p.253

Alnwick Castle, Northumberland	Duke of N.umberland	**299** (CCXCIX)	Howitt *Visits to Remarkable Places* 1841 HVDM pp.61-64 & illus. Pl.s 27,28,58,&
Alnwick Castle	Duke of N.umberland	**300** (CCC)	Howitt *Visits to Remarkable Places* 1841 HVDM pp.61-64 & illus. Pl.29 DR illus. Pp.59/60
Velorama Museum, Nijmegen, Holland	Earl of Durham	**316** (CCCXVI)	Sold Sotheby's auction W. Marden Hall 17/9/1991 (cat. illus.) NV 226/45 NV 227/34-35 illus. NV 228/45 NV 229/34
Monkwearmouth Museum, Sunderland	Earl of Durham	**320** (CCCXX)	Latest known DJ machine Restored c.1988 NV 228/45 illus.
Private owner	International Horseless Carriage Corporation (Nash Collection) (Early/mid 20th Century) **No number visible**		Foreshortened machine DJ badge on steering handle
Shuttleworth Collection Biggleswade, Beds.	**No number visible**		Only known surviving DJ lady's machine (SM loan) HDC p.4 & illus. Pl.1 HC p.2

Other makers (inc. early DJ copies)

Anonymous owner			Illus. in *Cycles in Colour* 1978 plate 2 - indirect steering
Brighton Museum	Rev. S.W. Thomas		Primitive machine (late 19th Century)

British Cycling Museum, Camelford, Cornwall		C19 machine, illus. *The Hub* 20.2.1897
House of Orange-Nassau Historic Collections Trust, The Hague, Holland	Queen Anna Paulowna	Johnson-type HH marked "T.Kerr" LVH pp.252 & 254, small illus. P.253
Hull Transport Museum	Mayfield family	Still in use mid-C19 – indirect steering Described & illus. in Hull Museum 1905 pamphlet
Ipswich Museum		Indirect steering
Lancaster City Museum		Johnson-type machine (but without arm rest)
Loren Hufstetler, Tranent, E. Lothian		Reputedly made by Wm. Plenty of Wells Sold Veteran-Cycle Auctions Kidderminster 20/4/1991 NV 223/21
Museum of British Road Transport, Coventry	Sir Edward Iliffe (early 20th Century)	*Bartleet's Bicycle Book* 1931 pp.26-27, illus.Pl.4
Museum of British Road Transport, Coventry		DR illus. p.62 (detail only)
Museum of Irish Transport, Killarney	Duke of Leinster	High quality machine by unknown maker
Museum of Transport, Glasgow		Believed locally made
National Museum of Science and Technology, Ottawa	Duke of Argyll	Early C19 DJ-type machine (ex. coll. Lorne Shields)

Ned Passey, Benson, Oxford		Illus. in *Cycles in Colour* 1978 plate 1 (child's machine)
Ned Passey, Benson, Oxford		Illus. in *Cycles in Colour* 1978 plate 3
Private collector, America	T. Sisson (1852)	Apparently a later copy of a DJ machine Illus. in CRAB Fig.2-6.
Raleigh Collection, Nottingham		Serena Beeley *A History of Bicycles* 1992 p.15 illus.
Royal Museum of Scotland, Edinburgh	Earl of Eglinton	TB 130/13-18 illus.(2) TB 31/29-30
Snowshill Manor, Worcs.		Probably late C19 copy DJ showing "boneshaker" influence TB 117/14
Strangers Hall Museum, Norwich		Primitive machine with horse's head
The Old Jameson Distillery, Dublin	John Talbot Power	Less ornate version of Duke of Leinster's machine
Ulster Folk & Transport Museum, Northern Ireland		Late C19/early C20 copy of DJ 299/ 300 (SM loan) TW Nov 1992
Worthing Museum		Child's machine, possibly by DJ

NOTES :-

(1) The numbering of Johnson machines is by way of Roman numerals both on the frame below the saddle and (sometimes) on the underside of the saddle and on the arm rest. The Science Museum's machine is numbered CICV i.e. 204, although one would perhaps expect CCIV. Likewise CCXCIX for the Duke of Northumberland's earlier machine seems unnecessarily complicated for 299 – why not CCIC ?

(2) References to e.g. TB 31/29-30 are to the volume and page numbers of articles or letters in *The Boneshaker*, the four-monthly publication of the Veteran-Cycle Club. References to e.g. NV 223/21 are to the volume and page numbers of items in *News and Views*, the bi-monthly publication of the Veteran-Cycle Club. The references to HDC and HC (with page numbers) are to the Science Museum booklets by Caunter detailed in the Select Bibliography. The TW references are to *The Wheelmen*, the bi-annual magazine of the American veteran-cycle club also known as "The Wheelmen". CRAB refers to Adams' *Collecting & Restoring Antique Bicycles* (see Select Bibliography). HVDM refers to Kobayashi's *Histoire du Velocipede de Drais a Michaux 1817-1870* (see Select Bibliography). DR refers to Seray's *Deux Roues* (see Select Bibliography). T Bic refers to Dodge's *The Bicycle* (see Select Bibliography). And LVH refers to Plath's *Laufrad – Velocipede - Hobbyhorse* (again see Select Bibliography).

(3) The Denis Johnson machines are listed in numerical order. The former Nash Collection item has at some stage had a section of its beam or backbone replaced, resulting in the loss of its number. The only known surviving lady's machine has no visible number (it is just possible a number may be obscured by the arm rest or seat upholstery). The machines by other makers are listed alphabetically by reference to the present custodian.

(4) All machines are direct steering except where indicated.

(5) Although a few Denis Johnson type hobby-horses known to be in foreign countries have been noted, the above list is primarily concerned with machines in the United Kingdom. Helmut Plath's 1978 monograph *Laufrad – Velocipede – Hobbyhorse* (see above) includes illustrations of a large number of mainly Continental machines.

(6) Various museums and private individuals in the United Kingdom have modern copies of hobby-horses in their possession. No attempt has been made to list them.

APPENDIX 3

The Hobby-Horse prints
(including other velocipedes of the hobby-horse era)

Caricatures

Short title	Date
A FAMILY PARTY TAKEING AN AIRING	24.3.1819
A LAND CRUISE ON ONE OF THE PATENT HOBBY HORSES	1819
A LAND CRUISE ON ONE OF THE PATENT HOBBY HORSES	1819
A NEW IRISH JAUNTING CAR, THE DANDY'S HOBBY etc.	[1819]
ANTI-DANDY INFANTRY TRIUMPHANT	1819
AN UNEXPECTED OCCURENCE	17.8.1819
CLERICAL SHOWFOLK AND WONDERFUL LAYFOLK	[1819]
COLLEGIANS AT THEIR EXERCISE ! etc.	1819
DANDIES ON THEIR HOBBIES !	1819
ENOUGH TO MAKE A HORSE LAUGH ! etc.	1819
EVERY MAN ON HIS PERCH, OR GOING TO HOBBY FAIR	10.7.1819
EVERY ONE HIS HOBBY plate 1	24.4.1819
EVERY ONE HIS HOBBY plate 1	24.4.1819
EVERY ONE HIS HOBBY plate 2	24.4.1819
FAVOURITE HOBBIES. FASHIONABLE WALTZING	[1819]
FOUR & TWENTY HOBBY-HORSES ALL OF A ROW	1.5.1819
GOING TO THE RACES	19.5.1819
HOBBIES OR ATTITUDE IS EVERYTHING	17.4.1819
HOBBY-HORSES JOCKYING THE MAIL !!	1819
JACK MOUNTED ON HIS DANDY CHARGER	1.3.1819
MATCH AGAINST TIME OR WOOD BEATS BLOOD AND BONE	17.4.1819
MILITARY HOBBYHORSE	4.3.1819
MILITARY HOBBYHORSE	[1819]
MILITARY ACCELERATOR [poss. copy *MILITARY HOBBYHORSE*]	[1819]
MODERN OLYMPICS	23.2.1819
MODERN PEGASUS OR DANDY HOBBIES IN FULL SPEED	24.3.1819
NEW READING – OR – SHAKSPEARE IMPROVED	[1819]

Publisher	Artist/engr./lith.	Print type	Collections
T.Tegg	[W.Heath]	Engr.	BM BN MBRT
J.Johnston	[C.Williams]	Engr.	NMST BM BN
McCleary *		Engr.	NMST MBRT
S.W.Fores	I.R.Cruikshank	Engr.	BM BN MBRT
T.Tegg	[Williams]	Engr.	NMST BM BN MBRT
J.Hudson		Lith.	NMST BN MBRT
W.Hone	F.Moore /G.Cruikshank	Aquatint	BM
J.Sidebethem	[I.R.] Cruikshank	Engr.	BM
J.Sidebethem	Yedis /I.R.Cruikshank	Engr.	BM
J.Sidebethem	Yedis /[I.R.Cruikshank]	Engr.	NMST BM MBRT
G.Humphrey	I.R. Cruikshank		NMST BN
T.Tegg	[W.Heath]	Engr.	NMST BM BN MBRT
McCleary*	[W.Heath]	Engr.	NMST
T.Tegg	[W.Heath]	Engr.	BM BN MBRT
McCleary *			Nick Clayton
R.Ackermann		Aquatint	NMST BM BN MBRT
T.Tegg	[W.Heath]	Engr.	NMST BM BN MBRT
T.Tegg	[W.Heath]	Engr.	BM BN MBRT
Sidebethem		Engr.	NMST MBRT
I.Fairburn	Chas.Hayten	Engr.	NMST BM MBRT
T.Tegg		Engr.	BN MBRT
J.Hudson	"W C"		NMST BN MBRT
T.le Potit *		Engr.	NMST MBRT
McCleary *	Jacques Seray		
J.Hudson	["W C"]	Engr.	NMST BM MBRT
T.Tegg	[W.Heath]	Engr.	BM BN MBRT
T.Tegg	[Williams]	Engr.	NMST BM MBRT

PATENT PUFFS TO RAISE THE WIND etc.	1819
PEDESTRIANS TRAVELLING ON THE NEW INVENTED etc.	1819
PERAMBULATORS IN HYDE PARK !	1819
STOP HIM WHO CAN !! AN ENGLISH PATENTEE etc.	[1819]
THE DANDY AND HIS POSTILION etc.	1819
THE DANDY CHARGER	23.2.1819
THE EPPING HUNT OR HOBBIES IN AN UPROAR	4.4.1819
THE HOBBY HORSE, 1819	16.7.1894
THE HOBBY HORSE DEALER	25.7.1819
THE PEDESTRIAN HOBBIES etc.	8.4.1819
[*Two hobby-horse riders – one fat, trailing tortoise, one black*]	[1819]
[*Two hobby-horse riders – poss. a priest and a butcher*]	[1819]
[*Hobby-horses & their fashionable riders*]	[Late 19C]

Ladies

A PILENTUM OR LADY'S ACCELERATOR	[May 1819]
BOARDING SCHOOL HOBBIES ! OR FEMALE AMUSEMENT !	1819
BOARDING SCHOOL HOBBIES ! OR FEMALE AMUSEMENT !	1819
FASHIONABLE EXERCISE OR THE LADIES HOBBY SCHOOL	1819
LES MACHINES D'AUTREFOIS [French copy of English print]	[19th Cent.]
THE FEMALE RACE ! OR DANDY CHARGERS etc.	1819
THE LADIES ACCELERATOR	1819
THE LADIES HOBBYE	21.5.1819
THE LADIES HOBBY	22.5.1819
VIEWS OF THE LADY'S PEDESTRIAN HOBBYHORSE	12.5.1819
VIEWS OF THE LADY'S PEDESTRIAN HOBBYHORSE	[May 1819]

Machines

CRUISING ON LAND OR, GOING TO HOBBY-HORSE FAIR –	10.9.1819
GOING TO HOBBY FAIR	19.7.1819/1.8.1835
HOBBY-HORSE FAIR etc	12.8.1819
HOBBY HORSE FAIR etc	10.9.1819
JOHNSON'S PEDESTRIAN HOBBYHORSE RIDING SCHOOL etc.	17.4.1819
JOHNSON, THE FIRST RIDER etc.	1.5.1819
MORE HOBBIES, OR THE VELOCI MANIPEDE	18.6.1819

J.Sidebethem			BN
J.Sidebethem	I.R.Cruikshank		NMST BN
J.Sidebethem	["W C"]	Engr.	BN MBRT
	[G.Cruikshank]	Lith.	BM BN
T.Tegg		Engr.	BN MBRT
J.Hudson	["W C"]	Engr.	NMST BN MBRT
T.Tegg	[W.Heath]	Engr.	NMST BM BN MBRT
The Leadenhall Press Ltd.		Engr.	NMST BN MBRT
G.Humphrey	"J.S." /G.Cruikshank	Engr.	NMST BM MBRT
T.Tegg	[W.Heath]	Engr.	NMST BM BN MBRT
			BN
			BN
			See end of note (5) below

S.& J.Fuller		Lith.	BN MBRT
J.Sidebethem	Yedis /[I.R.Cruikshank]	Engr.	BM
McCleary *	Yedis /[I.R.Cruikshank]	Engr.	NMST
J.Johnston			BN
			BN
Sidebethem Y	edis /[I.R.Cruikshank]	Engr.	BM BN
S.W.Fores	I.R.Cruikshank	Engr.	NMST BM BN
J.Hudson	["W C"]	Engr.	BN MBRT
T.Tegg		Engr.	NMST BN MBRT
R.Ackermann		Lith.	NMST BN
McCleary *		[Engr.]	MBRT

G.Humphrey	I.R.Cruikshank	Engr.	BM
G.Humphrey	I.R.Cruikshank/T.McLean	Engr.	NMST BM BN MBRT
G.Humphrey	I.R.Cruikshank		BN
G.Humphrey	I.R.Cruikshank		NMST BN
[Ackermann]	Henry Alken	Aquatint	NMST BM BN MBRT
R.Ackermann		Lith.	NMST BN MBRT
J.Hudson	["W C"]	Engr.	NMST MBRT

PEDESTRIAN HOBBYHORSE	Feb 1819
PEDESTRIAN HOBBYHORSE	[Feb 1819]
[PEDESTRIAN HOBBYHORSE]	[Feb 1819]
[PEDESTRIAN HOBBYHORSE]	[Feb 1819]
PEDESTRIAN HOBBY-HORSE, 1819	[Late 19C]
PICCADILLY IN 1800	[Late 19C]
SIEVIER'S PATENT PEDESTRIAN CARRIAGE etc.	[1819/20]
THE DRAISENE OR DANDY HORSE ... THE ANCESTOR etc.	[Late 19C]
THE NEW INVENTED SOCIABLE etc.	9.4.1819
THE NEW LONG BACK'D HOBBY etc.	19.6.1819
THE PEDESTRIAN CARRIAGE, OR WALKING ACCELERATOR	[Early 1819]
THE VELOCIMANIPEDE	[Mid 1819]
WIGLEY'S SPRING-GARDENS	[1819]

Political

BONEY'S CAVALRY – A RUSE DE GUERRE etc.	4.3.1813
BUM BAILIFF OUTDONEs etc.	1.4.1819
THE CHANCELLORS' HOBBY, OR MORE TAXES etc.	19.6.1819
THE DEVIL ALIAS SIMON PURE etc.	Aug 1821
THE FUNERAL PROCESSION OF THE RUMP	22.3.1819
THE "GREEN BAG" HOBBY TO FRIGHTEN THE INNOCENT etc.	[Nov 1820]
THE MASTER OF THE ORDNANCE EXERCISING HIS HOBBY!	Apr 1819
THE MASTER OF THE ORDNANCE EXERCISING HIS HOBBY!	Apr 1819
THE PARSONS HOBBY – OR – COMFORT FOR A WELCH CURATE	[1819]
THE SPIRIT MOVING THE QUAKERS UPON WORLDLY VANITIES!!	1819

Royalty

ACCIDENTS IN HIGH LIFE ...	14.4.1819
A MAD BULL ! OR UPSETTING THE ROYAL HOBBIES!	[May 1819]
*A P****E, DRIVING HIS HOBBY,IN HERDFORD!!!*	9.4.1819
A R___L HOBBY	[Jun 1819]
A VISIT TO RICHMOND – TO – ALLEVIATE THE GOUT	[May 1819]
DUTIFUL CHILDREN ON A VISIT TO THEIR FATHER -! etc.	[Nov 1819]
ECONOMY – OR A DUKE OF TEN THOUSAND ...	[May 1819]
EXERCISING A HOBBY FROM WALES TO HERTFORD!!	30.3.1819

174

Ackermann		Lith.	NMST BN MBRT
Clayton *		[Engr.]	MBRT
[J.Hudson]	["W C"]		BN
			BN
	"W.B."		BN
	Gordon Brown	from Painting	NMST
Williams			BN
		Ink drawing	MBRT
J.Jenkins		Engr.	BN MBRT
T.Tegg	G.Harris	Engr.	NMST BM BN MBRT
J.Sidebethem	Marks	Engr.	NMST BN MBRT
T.Griffiths		Lith.	BN MBRT
			BN

T.Tegg		[Engr.]	David Baldock
J.Johnston	Marks	Engr.	NMST BM BN MBRT
T.Tegg	[W.Heath]	Engr.	NMST BM BN MBRT
"Simon Pure"	Simon Pure /[R.Dighton]	Engr.	BM BN MBRT
G.Humphrey	G.Cruikshank	Engr.	BM
Langham		Lith.	BM MBRT
J.Sidebethem	Yedis /I.R.Cruikshank	Engr.	BM BN
McCleary *			NMST
T.Tegg	Williams	Engr.	NMST BM BN MBRT
J.Sidebethem	Yedis /[G.Cruikshank]	Engr.	BM BN

E.King	[G.Cruikshank]	Engr.	BM BN
Sidebethem	[I.R.Cruikshank]	Engr.	NMST BM
E.Brooks	[Marks]	Engr.	BM BN MBRT
Bon Ton Mag.		Engr.	BM BN MBRT
Sidebethem	[Williams]	Engr.	BM BN
Sidebethem	[Williams]	Engr.	BM BN
Bon Ton Mag.	[Williams]	Engr.	NMST BM BN MBRT
J.Sidebethem	[Marks]	Engr.	BM

MAKING MOST OF £10,000 PER. ANN. etc.	[Apr 1819]
MAKING MOST OF £10,000 PER. ANN. etc.	1819
MAKING MOST OF £10,000 PER. ANN. etc.	[1819]
MORE ECONOMY OR A PENNY SAVED A PENNY GOT	8.4.1819
*R***L HOBBYS !!!*	1819
ROYAL HOBBYS	9.4.1819
R__L HOBBYS !!!	27.4.1819
ROYAL HOBBYS, OR THE HERTFORDSHIRE COCK-HORSE!	20.4.1819
ROYAL HOBBYS, OR THE HERTFORDSHIRE COCK-HORSE!	[1819]
THE HERTFORD HOBBY (also titled *THE PERAMBULATOR* etc.)	15.3.1819

****

NOTES :-

(1) Square brackets indicate an assumption as to the print title, date or name of the publisher or artist/engraver/lithographer, or that the information is from an external source

(2)* indicates a Dublin publisher (otherwise London)

(3) Extracts from the print *Hobby-Horse Fair* dated 12.8.1819 by Robert Cruikshank were apparently produced in a larger format as individual items. The Bibliothèque Nationale has nine of them, bearing the titles *The Roman's Hobby, The Brewer's Hobby, the Dustman's Hobby, the Joiner's Hobby, The Shoemaker's Hobby, The Dandy's Hobby, The Lamp-lighter's Hobby, The Gardener's Hobby* and an untitled print which might on the same basis be labelled *The Lord Chancellor's Hobby.* The precise status of these derivative items is unclear.

(4) Where a single name is shown under the heading "artist/eng./lith." this indicates the artist (or assumed artist), who may also have been the engraver/lithographer. Where two names are given the artist and engraver/lithographer are shown in that order e.g. Yedis/I.R.C. shows that the drawing was by Yedis and that Isaac Robert Cruikshank was the engraver.

(5) Terms commonly used on the print to refer to the artist are "drawn by", "delt." or "del." (i.e. delineated by) or "invt." (i.e. invented by). The engraver/etcher/lithographer is normally identified by "sculpt." or simply "f.", "fect." or "fecit" (i.e. Latin "he made it"). If no artist's name is given, "fecit" probably indicates that the individual is both artist and engraver/etcher/lithographer. The publisher is more simply identified by the term "published" or "pubd." or "pub.", and in most cases the publisher can also be assumed to be the printer of the engraving, etching or lithograph.

J.L.Marks	Marks	Engr.	BM MBRT
Sidebethem	[Marks]	Engr.	NMST BM
McCleary *	[Marks]	Engr.	BN
T.Tegg	[W.Heath]	Engr.	NMST BM MBRT
J.L.Marks	Marks	Engr.	BM
T.Tegg	[G.Cruikshank]	Engr.	BM BN MBRT
T.F.Flook		Engr.	BM BN
M.Clinch	[Cruikshank]	Engr.	BM BN
McCleary *	[Cruikshank]	[Engr.]	BN
S.W.Fores		Engr.	BN NMST MBRT

****

(6) Details are given in respect of prints in the four known major public collections i.e. British Museum, London, (BM), Bibliothèque Nationale, Paris, (BN), the Museum of British Road Transport, Coventry, (MBRT), and National Museum of Science & Technology, Ottawa, (NMST). Where there is no impression of a particular print in any of these places, the name of the individual having an impression is shown. The untitled and undated print described as "Hobby-horses & their fashionable riders" is illustrated in *A History of Bicycles* by Serena Beeley (1992).

APPENDIX 4

WILL of Denis Johnson

[P.R.O. ref. PROB 10/5457 28681]

In the Name of God Amen

I Denis Johnson of Long Acre in the parish of Saint Martins in the fields in the city of Westminster Coach Maker Being in perfect health and of sound mind and Memory But Considering the Uncertainty of Life do make this my last Will and Testament give and Bequeath my Worldly property in the following manner, First I Desire to buried in the above parish and that my funeral be Conducted without unnecessary Expences

I Leave in Trust the Whole of my property to Mr John Allen of Long Acre <u>Now</u> my partner in Business, and my Son in law, And Mr Henery Bandrett of St James Street in St James parish my other Son in law to Arrange and pay my Funeral Expenses and Debts, And also to see my Will Carried into Efect, with as little Expence as possible I also beg their Acceptance of Fifteen pounds for each of them hoping they will not think it too small a Gift as their own families are Chiefly Concerned and will have the Benefit of their trouble & atention

My Next is that the Book Account & House Acct be settled so as to ascertain minutely the part that belongs to me, I mean after the trade Accounts are all Setled & paid, It will not be amiss to observe here that Whatever I subsequently may give as Gifts or Legacies that the payment of such shall be at the time most convenent for the Business, I mean that money should not be drawn out of the Business to Check its progress, for Whatever I am poss'd of has been gained by Sheer Industry and Labour therefore I do not feel Bound to give away from my own immediate Family that which they might consider their right Saving and Except a deserving object or of long Memorance or Kin to me or my Late Wife, therefore they must wait that convenient time

The next thing to be done and my Sincere Wish that it may done to the Satisfaction of those Concerned that is to have the Stock of all descriptions taken and minutely taken as if it were Strangers coming in on purchase

And when my Half of this stock is ascertained to be Clear of all Claims the disposal of it of Course is in my power, And that Leads me Direct to the Arangement I have Contempl'ed

I Will to my sister Mrs. Gwyne the Sum of Ten pounds for Mourning, And in Case she should survive me and she should want that assistance that the aged require I leave her to the Care of my two daughters Mary A and Ann B.

I Will to my son John Johnson of Bow Street the Sum of One Hundred pounds

I Will to Mary Ann House the Elder the Sum of Thirty pounds She being a favorite of My Dear Wife

I Will to Richard Steventon Walker Forty pounds for his long and faithful service

In Case the funds are inadequate to the Amount of these legacies /which I hope will not be the case/ then each to have a reduced proportion

The Residue of my property all and every thing I Will to my two Daughters Mary Allen & Ann Banderett under these restrictions which I shall state by and by

That they Keep it in their own possession or their Childrens and I Will that it Continue so, Either of them offering to dispose of their part shall forfeit the Whole and in that Case it shall go to the other sister

To Explain the Residue of the property it is necessary here to Mention what I mean it is the Leases of this House and premises, my Share of the Lease in Charles Street, and my Share of the Lease in Drury Lane And my Half of the Stock and my Half of the business share and share alike With this Restriction on the part of my Daughter Mary that out of the profits of her Share of the Business that she for the first Seven years must Allow five pr Cent to my daughter Ann

And Also that in Case that any thing should hapen that she my daughter Ann / which God forbid/ should want a Home it is my Will that she shall have a Siting Room, a Bed Room, a Kitchen and Servants Room etc in this House

What have Willd to my daughters is in their own Right and the above Restriction and that their Husbands shall have no Controul over it to dispose it away from ther Children

I Also Will that name of Johnson be kept up with the Length of the Lease, After that at their pleasure

SELECT BIBLIOGRAPHY

Adams, G.Donald *Collecting & Restoring Antique Bicycles*, Tab Books Inc., Pennsylvania, 1981 (chapter on "The Hobby Horse 1817-21" with section on establishing authenticity and condition), 2nd edn. 1996, Pedaling History Bicycle Museum, New York

Beeley, Serena *A History of Bicycles,* Studio Editions, London, 1992 (well produced book with reasonable short section on the hobby-horse – however there are contradictory statements on the date of origin of the Draisienne, wrongly stated to be non-steerable, and the book contains many other errors)

Caunter, C.F. *The History and Development of Cycles*, Science Museum, London, 1955, and *Handbook of the Collection illustrating Cycles*, Science Museum, London, 1958 (includes illustrations and descriptions of SM exhibits, historical narrative has some inaccuracies)

Davies, Thomas *On the Velocipede*, May 1837, reproduced in Veteran-Cycle Club magazine *The Boneshaker*, no.108, Autumn 1985 (early lecture on hobby-horse possibly delivered to Royal Institution)

Dobbin, Joe *Hobbyhorsiana; or Every Ass his Own Horse*, Duncombe, London, [1819] (one of only two known contemporary booklets on the hobby-horse, copy at National Museum of Science & Technology, Ottawa)

Dodge, Pryor *The Bicycle*, Flammarion, Paris & New York, 1996 (superbly produced and largely accurate general history with short illustrated section on the hobby-horse)

Duncan, H.O. *The World on Wheels*, Paris, [1927] (lengthy section on pre-history and early velocipedes, many illustrations, narrative contains some inaccuracies)

Fairburn, J. *An Accurate, Whimsical, and Satirical, Description of the new Pedestrian Carriage, or Walking Accelerator!!,* John Fairburn, London, [1819] (one of only two known contemporary booklets on the hobby-horse, copy ex libris Sir David Salomons in author's possession)

Geist, Roland C. *Bicycle People*, Acropolis Books, Washington D.C, 1978 (chapter "The Art Gallery" has illustrations of hobby-horse prints with details of artists etc., some inaccuracies)

George, Mary Dorothy *Catalogue of Political and Personal Satires in the British Museum*, British Museum, London, 1935-1949 (contains detailed historical explanations of prints in BM collection)

Kobayashi, Keizo *Histoire du Vélocipède de Drais a Michaux 1817-1870, Mythes et Realities*, 1993 (first part comprises five illus. chapters on "Le baron de Drais et la draisienne", ch.4 has section on Denis Johnson)

Lessing, Prof. Dr. Hans-Erhard *Karl von Drais' two-wheeler – what we know* (paper read at First International Conference on Cycling History, Glasgow, May 1990)

Lessing, Prof. Dr. Hans-Erhard *Karl von Drais : Der Empire-Technologe wird rehabiliert* – monograph in *Mannheimer Geschichtsblätter Neue Folge*, Sigmaringen, 1996 (detailed account of von Drais' inventions)

Lightwood, James T. *The Romance of the Cyclists' Touring Club*, London, 1928 (chapter "The Coming of the Velocipede" quotes original source material but references to 1815 dandy-horse and to Royal hobby-horse with cranks attached to front wheel hub should be discounted)

McGurn, James *On your Bicycle*, John Murray, London, 1987 (chapter "The Prehistory of Cycling" has illustrated sections on "Ancestral Vehicles", and "The Running-Machine" with details of the development of the early velocipede in England and abroad)

Perry, David *Bike Cult*, Four Walls Eight Windows, New York/London, 1995 (contains some interesting material on the pre-history of the

FAIRBURN'S

WHIMSICAL DESCIRPTION

OF THE NEW

PEDESTRIAN CARRIAGE,

OR,

Dandy Hobby-Horse.

INCLUDING

A SATIRICAL ACCOUNT

OF

A RACE FROM ALPHA COTTAGE TO TYBURN,

BETWEEN THE TWO NOBLE LORDS

Whiskerandos and Smoothchops.

WITH SOME ACCOUNT OF A NEW MILITARY CORPS ABOUT TO BE RAISED,

CALLED,

The Regent's Pedestrio Equestria Chargers,

TO BE COMMANDED BY

TOM CHIFFNEY, JUN.

AND STATIONED ON THE STEYNE.

AND OF THE

Anti-Straddling Chargers,

FOR THE USE OF

THE DANDIZETTES.

Mount, Dandies, mount, and roll along,
Subjects of satire, mirth, and song;
Grease as you like the Hobby's wheels,
Fairburn will still stick to your heels,
And wield his lash of playful satire,
O'er all who over-step Dame Nature.

Embellished with a Caricature Frontispiece.

LONDON :

PRINTED AND PUBLISHED BY JOHN FAIRBURN, 2, BROADWAY,
LUDGATE-HILL.

The title page of *Fairburn's Whimsical Descirption* [sic] *of the new PEDESTRIAN CARRIAGE, or Dandy Hobby-Horse.* An extremely rare item, even the British Museum no longer has a copy. The author's copy is ex libris Sir David Salomans, the pioneer motoring enthusiast.

machine, but gives unnecessary emphasis to some now discarded myths)

Plath, Helmut *Laufrad – Velocipede – Hobbyhorse – eine typologische Untersuchung* – monograph in *Festschrift for William Hansen*, Munster, 1978 (many illustrations of principally Continental machines)

Ritchie, Andrew *King of the Road*, Wildwood House, London, 1975 (chapter "Bicycle Archaeology" is illustrated and has details of the development of the early velocipede in England and abroad but the de Sivrac myth and Niepce claim should be discounted)

Roberts, Derek *Cycling History – Myths and Queries*, John Pinkerton, 1991 (Items 10.-23. deal with the hobby-horse)

The Repository of Arts, Literature, Fashions, Manufactures etc., R. Ackermann, London (issue of periodical for 1 Feb 1819 contains what is probably the earliest detailed English description of "The Pedestrian's Hobby-Horse")

Seray, Jacques *Deux Roues : la véritable histoire du vélo,* Rouergue, 1988 (beautifully produced, well-illustrated book with lengthy chapter on "La Draisienne" and section "La draisienne en Grande-Bretagne")

The Sporting Magazine or Monthly Calendar, of the Transactions of The Turf, The Chase, And every other Diversion Interesting to the Man of Pleasure, Enterprize & Spirit, London, 1792 onwards (dandy and hobby-horse references)

"Velox" (Tom Burgess) *Velocipedes, Bicycles, and Tricycles*, George Routledge and Sons, 1869, facsimile edition S.R. Publishers Ltd. & A.G. Jackson, 1971 (chapter "The Velocipede of the Past" contains early, largely accurate, summary of position up to 1860s)

INDEX

Alexander, medieval illustration of horse on wheels 1, 2

Allen family :

    Continuation of business started by Johnson 60, 61

    Family relationship with Johnson 59-61

    Johnson & Allen partnership 59

"Artificial horse", Marquis of Worcester's description 3-5, 157

Barclay, Captain, famous pedestrian wager 70

Bath, early use of Laufmaschine 23-25

Baynes, John, patentee of "land punt" 150

Berkhampstead Sports, banning of dandy horses 78

Beverley :

    activities of Rev. Coltman at 96-98

    race from Hull and back 74

Birch, Charles Lucas, velocipede maker 120, 121, 145, 146 (illus.), 147

Birmingham :

    Field, William, velocipede maker 149, 150

    Johnson exhibiting at 53, 149

Bivector, manumotive machine 145, 146 (illus.), 147

Blackheath, proposed racing at 73

Blandford, hobby-horse hoax 68

Boots, metal strengthening for riding 65

Braintree, velocipede ride from 58

Brighton, hobby-horse journeys from London 104

Bristol, invention of machine by Howell 153

British Facilitator, or Travelling Car 142, 143

Canterbury, "match against time" ride to 70

"Cantering Propeller" velocipede horse 4, 5

Cartwright, Edmund, inventor 117, 118

Chelmsford, velocipede ride to 58

Child's early horse on wheels 2, 3

Chingford, hobby-horse race between two riders 70

Coltman, Rev. J., weighty hobby-horse rider 96-98

Commemorative plaque to Denis Johnson 30 (illus.), 31

Comte de Sivrac célérifère myth   vi
Dandies :
   conspicuous display proposed   91, 92
   character of   89, 90
   Lord Petersham   91, 98
   nursery rhyme about   92, 93
   racing incident involving   90, 91
Dandy-horse – *see* Hobby-horse
Deptford, dandies race at   90, 91
Draisienne – *see* Laufmaschine
Draisine – *see* Laufmaschine
Drais, Karl von :
   birth and early life   15-17
   death and erection of monument   22
   English visits   23
   first use of Laufmaschine   13
   inventor of Fahrmaschine   17
   inventor of Laufmaschine   13, 17, 18
   making of Laufmaschine   20
   other inventions   17
   portrayed in Mannheim Castle gardens   15, 16
   promotion of Laufmaschine   18-22
Duke of York :
   acquisition of Johnson machine   106, 107
   depiction as hobby-horse rider   105 (illus.), 106, 107, 133
   monthly journey to Windsor   105 (illus.), 106, 107
Durdham Down, hit-and-run rider at   75
Exeter :
   the hobby-horse at   149
   three-wheel machine made   149
Fahrmaschine :
   invention by von Drais   17
   reasons for relinquishment   17
Falkirk, tour from London to   63, 64
Farnham, accident to rider at   75
Flying Actaeons, at Norwich   150
Field, William, velocipede maker   149, 150
Finch, advert for instruction in use of hobby-horse   66
Fob seal depicting hobby-horse rider   94 (illus)
Frankfurt, demonstration of Laufmaschine   21

Free wheel, who first invented 155

Gompertz, Lewis, inventor of modified hobby-horse 81, 154, 155

Goy, "Athletic Outfitter", ownership of dandy horse 86, 87 (illus.)

Grimaldi, Joseph, probable pantomime hobby-horse rider 98

Gymnasidromist, term employed for Howell's machine 153

Hereford velocipede (four-wheeler with "impellers") 148, 149

Hobby-horse :

  Johnson machines :

      arm rest (or balance board), metal supports for 40, 43

      brake, absence of 33, 74, 75

      child's (possible) 34 (illus.), 35

      colours 39 (illus. caption), 43

      cost 54, 55, 89

      details of surviving machines 32-43, 45, 48, Appendix 2

      earliest known 43

      foot rests 42 (illus.), 45, 48, 49

      handle (handlebar) 39, 40

      lady's, with dropped frame 113-116

      latest known 36

      manufacture and marketing 51-54

      materials employed 57

      name plate 33, 37 (illus.)

      numbering and dating 35, 36, 38

      ornamentation 33, 41 (illus.)

      patent frontispiece, 31, 32

      Royal ownership 89

      seat (adjustable) 32

      stand for 33

      steering, "direct" and "indirect" 38, 39, 43, 45

      three-wheeler 33-35

      weight 33

      wheels and spokes 32, 33

  Miscellaneous :

      alternative names 50, 51

      archetypal bicycle viii

      child's cock-horse, comparison made with 50

      child's go-cart, comparison made with 50

      commercial production of non-Johnson machines 58, 59

      details of surviving non-Johnson machines 40 (illus.), 44 (illus.), 45-49,
           Appendix 2

Enigma verse (*County Magazine*) 9, 10, 157

frame spring, addition of 148

German origin of machine ix, 31, 32

hoaxes 67-70

"hobby-horse" word contrasted with "velocipede" 51

Ireland, hobby-horse in 136, 137

iron machine 57

medieval origin of horse on wheels 1

non-steerable machines 82-84

Patterson machines (supposed) 5, 6, 11

poem on "The Velocipede" 101, 102

public interest 67

seat spring, addition of (illus.), 45 (illus. caption), 58, 137, 147, 148

Scotland, hobby-horse in 43, 48, 100

sweepstake 52, 53

theatrical interest 98-100

various meanings of word 7-10, 141, 158

velocipede clubs (whether any) 158

Use :

accidents 74-76

carrying of mail 64

dandies, by 89

decline in, reasons for 79-81

distances ridden 63, 64

early use in London 63

Grimaldi, by, in pantomime 98

hiring 59, 63, 89

Hyde Park 5, 6, 11, 67, 157

instructions for riding 64, 65

ladies, by 111, 119-121, 158, 159

medical implications 80, 81

military (envisaged) 55, 79, 104

Nineteenth century generally 82-87, 141, 158

nobility, acquisition and use by 89, 100-103

pantomime, first appearance on stage in 98

prosecutions for pavement riding 77, 78

Quakers, by 119

speed achievable 56, 69-71, E (colour illus. caption)

racing 71-74, 102, 103, 158

tolls, liability to pay 79

      tour from London to Falkirk 63, 64

      tours on continent 64

      wagers and "matches against time" 70, 71

      widespread use 65, 66

Hobby-horse prints :

  Ackermann, Rudolph, publisher 125, 126

  Alken, Henry, artist 125, 140

  Anti-Dandy Infantry Triumphant 128 (illus.), 129

  An Unexpected Occurence 127

  A Pilentum 117

  *A P****e, Driving his Hobby, in HERDFORD !!!* 106 (illus.), 107

  artist identification 137, 159

  Boney's Cavalry etc. (retreat from Moscow) 8 (illus.), 9

  categorisation of 125

  Cruikshank, George, artist 132, 135, 137

  Cruikshank, Robert, artist 132, 137-140

  Dandies on their Hobbies ! 33

  detailed list 123, 125, Appendix 3

  Draisiennes dites Velocipedes 21, 22

  Dublin, prints published in 136

  earliest and latest 123

  Economy – or a Duke of Ten Thousand 105 (illus.), 107

  Enough to make a Horse Laugh ! 131, 132

  Every Man on his Perch B, 34

  Every One His Hobby (two prints) 129, 130 (illus.), 137

  FASHIONABLE EXERCISE etc. 111 (illus.), 118

  Going to the Races 127 (illus.), 129

  Heath, William, artist 140

  Hobby-Horse Fair 137, 138/9 (illus.),140

  Hobby-horses jockying the Mail !! 64

  Hudson, John, publisher 126-128

  Humphrey, G., publisher 137

  Jack mounted on his Dandy Charger 38, 39, 76, E (colour illus.)

  Johnson's Pedestrian Hobbyhorse Riding School 43, 49, 91, 125, 126, 140

  Johnson, the First Rider etc. – Johnson portrait 27 (illus.), 28, 125

  Making Most of £10,000 etc. 107

  Marks, J.L., print shop publisher/artist 135, 140

  Match against Time etc. D, 128

  Military Hobbyhorse 79, F, 126

  Modern Olympics 71, 72, 127

189

Modern Pegasus etc.   72

More Economy etc.   107

More Hobbies, or the Veloci Manipede   120, G, 127

New Reading – or – Shakespeare Improved   100

Pedestrian Hobbyhorse   C (colour illus.), 64, 65, 125, 127, 131, 132

Pedestrians Travelling on the New Invented Hobby-Horse !   33, 34, E

Perambulators in Hyde Park !   67

political satire   125, 133, 134 (illus.), 135

public collections   123

relationship between artist, engraver, printer, publisher   135, 136

Rowlandson, Thomas – hobby-horse artist myth   140

R***L HOBBY's !!! – pedals myth   144, 145

Sidebethem, James, publisher   131-133

Sievier's Patent Pedestrian Carriage   151-153

Stop him who can !! etc. – Johnson portrait   A (colour illus.), 28, 137

Tegg, Thomas, publisher   128, 129, 131, 136

The Chancellors' Hobby etc.   133, 134 (illus.), 135

The Dandy Charger   jacket, 33, 124 (illus.), 127, 128

The Devil alias Simon Pure   134 (illus.), 135

The Female Race etc.   79, 118, 119

The Hobby Horse Dealer   119, 120

The New Invented Sociable etc.   121, H

The Ladies Hobby   116

The Ladies Hobbye   127

The Parsons Hobby   95, 96

The Pedestrian Carriage, or Walking Accelerator   H, 133

types of print   123

Vélocipède Sentimental !! etc.   121

Views of the Lady's Pedestrian Hobbyhorse   F (colour illus.), 112-114, 125

"W C", artist   126-128, 140

Williams, C., artist   140, 151

Yedis, artist   140

Howell's "dicycle"-type machine   153

Hull :

    incident at   76

    race to Beverley and back   74

Hursley, fatal accident at   75, 76

Hyde Park :

    attempted exhibition of hobby-horses   67

    extent of use in   67

190

supposed Patterson machines 5, 6, 11, 157

Ipswich :

    daily riding from, to Whitton 73

    racing at 73

Ireland, the hobby-horse in 136, 137

Johnson, Denis :

    assignment of patent 55, 56, 157, 158

    birth date and early life 25, 27, 28, 157

    business premises in Long Acre 30, 31

    character as revealed by Will 59, 60

    children of 27

    commemorative plaque 30 (illus.), 31

    continuation as coachmaker 59

    death and burial 59

    financial success, extent of 54-57, 59, 158

    firm, continuation of by Allen family 60, 61

    handwriting and signature 28-30, 59

    improvements to Laufmaschine 31

    machines – *see* Hobby-horse : Johnson machines

    manufacture and marketing by 51-54, 158

    marriage to Mary Newman 25, 26 (illus.), 27

    partnership with John Allen 59

    patent frontispiece, 31, 32, Appendix 1

    portraits A (colour illus.), 27 (illus.), 28

    relationship with Samuel Merscy 56, 157, 158

    riding schools 53, 111, 112

    suspected unauthorised copying of his machines 57-59

    Will 59, 60, Appendix 4

Jug depicting "John Bull's Velocipede" 129, 131

Jug depicting supposed tandem hobby-horse 107, 108

Karlsruhe :

    birthplace of von Drais 16

    monument erected to von Drais 22

Kean, Edmund, actor, depicted with hobby-horse 100

Keats, John, poet, comments on velocipede 54, 55

Kent, Mr, inventor of Marine Velocipede 155 (illus.), 156

Kerr, T., hobby-horse maker 110

Knight, supposed English mechanic 23, 157

Ladies' hobby-horse riding :

    evidence for 111, 119-121, 158, 159

191

instructions for   111

riding school theory   111-113, 159

suggestive depiction in prints   118, 119

Lady's Velocipede, treadled three-wheeler   117

Lady's version of Johnson hobby-horse   113-116

"Land punt", patented by Baynes   150

Laufmaschine :

advantages described   18, 19

Badenian privilege   21

early use in Bath   23, 24

exhibition in Nancy   22

exhibition in Paris   21, 22

first use   13

French patent   21

invention by von Drais   13, 17, 18

journey over Pyrenees   64

"Loda", first name given   13

making of, by von Drais   20

plagiarism   20

promotion by von Drais   18-23

three & four-wheeled machines   20, 21

Lees, Cottam & Hallen, makers of Sievier machine   151, 152

Leftwich, F.S., claim for Patterson hobby-horse   5, 6, 157

Leonardo da Vinci bicycle myth   vi

Lewes :

proposed racing at   72, 73

the hobby-horse at   66

Liskeard, "match against time" ride to   71

Liverpool :

accident at   54

early invention of machine by B. Smythe   142

Johnson exhibiting at   54

velocipede manufacture in   58

London :

early use of hobby-horse in   63

hobby-horse hoax poem   68-70

hobby-horse journeys to Brighton   104

tour to Falkirk in Scotland   63, 64

Long Acre:

Denis Johnson commemorative plaque   30 (illus.), 31

Johnson's premises at 75 Long Acre   29 (illus.), 30, 31

Lowe, Robert, M.P., youthful hobby-horse rider   94, 95

Machines – *see* Hobby-horse and Laufmaschine

Mackenzie's "Cantering Propeller"   4, 5

Manchester :

   Johnson exhibiting at   53

   racing at   74

Manivelociter, manumotive machine   145, 146 (illus.), 147

Mannheim :

   first use of laufmaschine   13

   von Drais family move to   17

Mannheim Castle gardens, von Drais portrayed in   16

Manumotive machines of Charles Lucas Birch   145, 146 (illus.), 147

Marine Velocipede, invention of Mr Kent   155 (illus.), 156

Marlborough, Duke of, hobby-horse owner   100, 114

Mechanical horse (manumotive machine)   156

Merscy, Samuel :

   assignee of Johnson patent   55

   relationship with Denis Johnson   56

Metropolis Paving Act, prosecutions under   77, 78

Nancy, exhibition of Laufmaschine   22

New York, Johnson promoting machine   54

Nobility, acquisition and use of hobby-horses   100, 101

Northumberland, Duke of, hobby-horse incident   101

Norwich :

   Finch advert for hobby-horse instruction   66

   Flying Actaeons at   150

   the hobby-horse at   70

Palmer, John, mail coach service of   99

Paris, exhibition of Laufmaschine   21, 22

Patent Pedestrian Carriage, Sievier's   151-153, 159

Patterson family (supposed early hobby-horses)   5, 6, 11, 141, 157

Pedestrian curricle – *see* Hobby-horse

Pedestrian hobby-horse – *see* Hobby-horse

Petersham, Lord, leading dandy   91, 98

Pilentum, lady's three-wheel velocipede   116, 117, 140

Pilentum coach, whether actually existed   138, 139 (illus.)

Pill box depicting hobby-horse riders   93 (illus.)

Playing card depicting hobby-horse rider   97 (illus.)

Plate depicting dandy riding machine   126 (illus.), 127

193

Prince Regent (later George IV) :
    acquisition of Johnson machines 103, 104, 106, 158
    depiction as hobby-horse rider in prints 107, 133
    military use apparently considered by 104
    relationships with titled ladies 107, 108
Pyrenees, journey over from Pau to Madrid 64
Queen Anna Paulowna, owner of hobby-horse 108, 109 (illus.)
Riding schools 53, 111, 112
Royal College of Surgeons, interest in the velocipede 80, 81
Rutter, John, velocipede supplier 59
Sachsenspiegel, medieval illustration of horse on wheels 2
Salomons, Sir David, bequest to Bibliothèque Nationale 123
Scotland, the hobby-horse in 43, 48, 100
Seine, Bernhard, early user of Laufmaschine in Bath 23-25
Shaftesbury, velocipedes supplied at 59
Sheridan, Richard Brinsley, grandfather, politician, playwright 92-94, 99
Sievier, inventor of Patent Pedestrian Carriage 151-153, 159
Smythe, B., inventor of British Facilitator 142, 143
Sociable, lady passenger machine, Continental origin of 121
Southampton, the hobby-horse at 80
Southern Veteran-Cycle Club, commemorative horse-brass 23 (illus.)
St. Columb, "match against time" ride from 71
Steam, anticipated use of 147
Theatrical interest in hobby-horse 98-100
Tolls, hobby-horse riders' liability to pay 79
Trivector, manumotive machine 145, 146 (illus.), 147
Upstreet, "match against time" from 70
Velocimanipede, lady passenger machine 120, 121, 140, 145
Velocipede – *see* Hobby-horse and Laufmaschine
"Velocipede" :
    contrasted with "hobby-horse" 51
    French origin of term 13, 14
"Velocipedi", supposed early use of word in Italy 14, 15
Whitton, daily riding to, from Ipswich 73
Wilcox, James, Hertfordshire velocipedist and artist 84, 85, G (colour illus.)
Willem, Prince of Orange, owner of hobby-horse 108, 109 (illus.), 110
Worcester, Marquis of, "artificial horse" 3-5, 157
Worthing, hobby-horse hoax 67, 68
Yarmouth machine, pedals hypothesis 143, 144, 156, 159

ABOUT THE AUTHOR

Roger Street was until his recent retirement the senior partner in an old-established South Coast legal practice, but for more than a quarter of a century his principal spare-time interest has been veteran cycles. He bought his first "Ordinary" ("penny-farthing") bicycle in 1970 and soon became an avid collector of old bikes. In 1975 he formed the eccentric Christchurch Ramshackle Antique Bicycle Society – the CRABS – which is still going strong twenty-three years later. In 1979 his book *Victorian High-Wheelers* was published – the story of an "Ordinary" bicycle club which existed in Christchurch in the late Nineteenth century. In April, 1985, Roger launched the world's first museum devoted solely to multi-wheeled cycles, the Christchurch Tricycle Museum, which had over 100,000 visitors but sadly had to close in 1995. Over the past dozen years or so Roger has researched and written a number of articles for the national Veteran-Cycle Club magazine *The Boneshaker,* as well as preparing papers for the annual International Cycle History Conference. Whilst he retains an affection for the tricycle his main research interest in recent times has been the pedestrian hobby-horse, the forerunner of today's pedal bicycle.

Young Roger Street on his wooden horse: a Devon idyll.

195